RECOGNITION

SUNY Series in Hegelian Studies
William Desmond, Editor

RECOGNITION
Fichte and Hegel on the Other

ROBERT R. WILLIAMS

STATE UNIVERSITY OF NEW YORK PRESS

Published by
State University of New York Press, Albany

For information, address State University of New York
Press, State University Plaza, Albany, NY 12246

Production by Ruth East
Marketing by Dana E. Yanulavich

Library of Congress Cataloging-in-Publication Data

Williams, Robert R.
    Recognition : Fichte and Hegel on the other / Robert R. Williams.
        p.   cm. — (SUNY series in Hegelian studies)
    Includes bibliographical references and index.
    ISBN 0–7914-0857–4 (alk. paper). — ISBN 0–7914-0858–2 (pbk. :
alk. paper)
    1. Hegel, Georg Wilhelm Friedrich. 1770–1831. 2. Fichte. Johann
Gottlieb, 1762–1814. 3. Philosophy, German—19th century.
4. Consciousness. 5. Interaction (Philosophy) 6. Other minds
(Theory of knowledge)   I. Title. II. Series.
B2949.C6W54   1992
126—dc20

                                                90–27203
                                                CIP

10 9 8 7 6 5 4 3 2 1

For Diana and Daniel

CONTENTS

PART THREE: HEGEL

PREFACE

Hegel often delighted in the speculative multidimensionality of the German language. His discussion of the term *'aufheben'*, which means both to cancel and to preserve in transformation, is a well known example. He thought German was a language particularly well suited and adapted for philosophy. But precisely because Hegel's thought is embedded in such multidimensional German expressions, it is extremely difficult to translate. This is one obstacle to the successful exportation of Hegel's thought to other linguistic cultures. Kant's thought has enjoyed much greater success in translation than has Hegel's. It is extremely difficult to make Hegel speak English, or at least "intelligible English."

This judgment in no way is meant as a disparagement of the recent new English translations of Hegel's thought—the Jena Manuscripts, *Lectures on the Philosophy of Religion,* and *Lectures on the History of Philosophy.* I am not asserting that translation is impossible. However, I fear that those who read Hegel only in translation will almost surely receive a distorted and truncated picture of his thought. This has been my own experience: neither English translation of the *Phenomenology* is intelligible without constant reference to the German original. Moreover, the Hegel of the older English translations is a "metaphysical Hegel," for it is the metaphysical language of the "House of Being" that provided the basis of translation. No wonder the English speaking world has tended to regard Hegel simply as an idealist, a metaphysician, a representative of onto-theology.

My understanding and appreciation of Hegel changed dramatically as a result of a year's leave in Germany on a Fulbright grant. Confronted by Hegel in his own language, hearing Hegel expounded *auf Deutsch* in German universities, opened my eyes and ears. I realized that although I had previously read Hegel in translation (and worked much too hard doing so) I scarcely understood his thought. It was not paragraph length complex German sentences, but rather the little terms, *an sich, für sich, Geist,* that express the fundamental tendency and deep structure, that had not 'come through,' at least to me, in translation.

Moreover, I discovered that recognition (*Anerkennen*) has recently become a topic of considerable interest in German scholarship. *Anerkennen* is the rubric under which German Idealism discussed the topic of the Other, intersubjectivity, the interhuman. The discovery of this story—all but unknown in English—provided additional reasons to believe that Hegel's thought had not penetrated very far beyond the borders of his homeland.

If, as Hegel claims, spirit (*Geist*) has its existential-phenomenological genesis in intersubjective recognition (*Anerkennung*), then is not spirit a fundamentally intersubjective and social concept? And if spirit is fundamentally social, how should the standard textbook picture of Hegel as a so-called 'idealist' be regarded? For it is a contemporary dogma that idealism excludes intersubjectivity, and conversely, the 'problem of the other' amounts to a postmodern attack on metaphysical idealism, a 'deconstructionist litmus test' that 'everyone knows' idealism could never pass. In my view, it is the label of idealism—always dogmatically pinned on Hegel—that is the problem. It has blinded us to Hegel, who was the first to raise all the standard objections—including the problem of the other—against idealism as it is usually understood.

But if Hegel is not an idealist in the textbook sense, and if he not only treats the topic of intersubjectivity, but considers it to be the phenomenological genesis of his central concept of spirit, this means that we have yet to grasp, much less understand or appreciate, the vital center of his thought. Moreover, deprived of the label of idealism, we have lost any fixed or secure point from which to orient ourselves towards his thought. Does he belong to the discredited past of metaphysics? Or is he the first thinker of difference, and so still in the vanguard of philosophical reconstruction and postmodern alternatives? Obviously everything turns on how the terms of such questions are to be precisely refined and understood. But the analytical task of clarification will be short-circuited if Hegel's concept of spirit is erroneously assumed to be merely a terminological variant of Kant's transcendental ego. Such an interpretation fails to take the measure of Hegel's thought. It fails to recognize, much less appreciate, the significance of the concept of recognition. When the latter is appreciated, it becomes apparent that Hegel is still an important voice in the contemporary discussions.

But how to make Hegel speak English? The difficulties lie deeper than translation problems. For the latter are relatively susceptible to solution. The deeper problems lie in the different social, political and historical developments of German-speaking and English-speaking countries in the past two centuries. The latter have appropriated Enlightenment formal instrumental rationalism and individualist modes of thought. It is no accident that formal rationalism and its indigeneous abstract individualism and privatism are deeply entrenched here. But Hegel is a critic of Enlightenment formal rationalism, as well as its individualism, and represents a major post-Enlightenment (or to use the term fashionable today, "post-modern") mode of thought. Unfortunately, the linguistic culture of instrumental rationalism and individualism has no adequate vocabulary or conceptuality into which key Hegelian concepts such as *Anerkennen, Geist, Sittlichkeit,* can be readily translated.

To make Hegel speak English at a deeper, more fundamental level, it is necessary to confront and review major issues and developments in continental philosophy. These include such issues as the crisis of Enlightenment rationalism, also known as anti-foundationalism. For the post-Kantian German Idealists all struggled with the problem of how to philosophize in the aftermath of the collapse of rationalistic foundationalism, including Kant's transcendental program. It is this crisis that leads to the turn to the life-world, to existential themes such as the other, alienation, the struggle for recognition, and the search for liberation from oppression. Such is the soil from which Hegel's thought springs. These themes have long been suppressed in Anglo American thought. For how can one speak of struggles for recognition, liberation from oppression within the ideological blinders of "free enterprise" and the so-called "Free World"? It is only with the recent ending of the Cold War and the rise of multiple centers of power seeking liberation from the stultifying Cold War polarization that Hegel's thought may finally gain a wider, receptive audience.

I should like to express my gratitude to the Fulbright commission for a leave at the University of Tübingen, Germany, during which this project was begun, to the National Endowment for the Humanities for research support, and to Hiram College for a sabbatical leave during which this book was written. In addition, several people helped to make this study a better one. I have profited from conversations with Ludwig Siep, Walter Jaeschke, Josef Simon, Joseph C. Flay, Otto Pöggeler, Hans-Christian Lucas, Edith and Klaus Düsing, and Eberhard Braun. I am indebted to Klaus Hartman, who expressed disagreement with this project while generously encouraging the author. The Hegel Society of America has been a source of friendly critics and scholarly support. Robert F. Brown, editor and co-translator of Hegel's *Lectures on the History of Philosophy,* went through an earlier version of the manuscript and helped the author purge his Germanisms and rehabilitate his English style. Edward Farley made suggestions for the chapters on Hegel and Husserl. Peter C. Hodgson, co-editor and translator of Hegel's *Lectures on the Philosophy of Religion,* helped to clarify the interpretation of chapter 10. William Desmond made helpful suggestions for the final revisions. None of these are responsible for the defects that remain despite their suggestions. Finally I should acknowledge my gratitude to my family who endured my 'absent presence,' surely a case of unequal recognition passed over in Hegel's account.

Robert R. Williams
Shaker Heights, Ohio

ABBREVIATIONS

TWA   *Hegel Werke, Theorie Werkausgabe,* Suhrkamp

VPR   Hegel, *Vorlesungen über die Philosophie der Religion (Meiner Verlag, 1985)*

VR   *Walter Jaeschke,* Vernunft in der Religion

WL   Hegel, *Wissenschaft der Logik*

PART ONE
INTRODUCTION

ONE

INTRODUCTION

THE HIDDEN THEME OF INTERSUBJECTIVITY IN GERMAN IDEALISM

The following monograph explores the topic of the other within German Idealism, in particular, the thought of Fichte and Hegel. Few studies recognize that German Idealism deals with intersubjectivity. The philosophies of Fichte and Hegel supposedly represent the culmination of idealistic metaphysics, and it is far from clear whether it is possible for idealism to raise, much less give an adequate account of, intersubjectivity. That is because the general principle of idealism, whether ontological or methodological, is said to be "no object without a subject," or that objectivity is dependent on and relative to subjectivity. If the interpersonal other were an object, he/she would be dependent on, and in some sense derivative from, primal transcendental subjectivity. Thus the other would not be genuinely other. If the other is genuine, it must be transcendent to consciousness, and cannot be reduced to primordial self-identity or immanence.

Owing to its Cartesian heritage, idealism seems haunted by solipsism.[1] Since "everyone knows" that Fichte and Hegel are idealists, intersubjectivity seems excluded a priori—at least that is how the story usually goes. On the other hand, if they do raise and deal with intersubjectivity, that is an anomaly in tension with or in violation of their fundamental philosophical position. If so, this is an anomaly that calls for inquiry and explanation. What is intersubjectivity doing in a supposedly idealist philosophical program? How and with what justification does it arise there?

The theme of intersubjectivity in German idealism is all but unnoticed, not only in the English speaking world, but even in meticulous German scholarship as well. To be sure, Fichte and Hegel do not speak of intersubjectivity per se, but instead speak of recognition (*Anerkennung*). The recognition of the significance of "recognition" is so recent that the term *Anerkennung* is not indexed or even mentioned in Glockner's *Hegel Lexicon*. Only in the last ten years has the topic of recognition surfaced in the German Hegel discussion, and appropriate studies have appeared.[2] There are only a few articles on it in English.[3]

This recent interest in *Anerkennung* is due in part to the emergence of the problem of the other, not simply as a problem of intersubjectivity, but as

1

a problem which threatens to undermine philosophy itself as traditionally conceived. Yet few have done more to raise the problem of the other in this global sense than have Fichte and Hegel. It is no exaggeration to say that the problem of the other and the related problem of otherness, first becomes explicit in these philosophies. Recent interest in the problem of the other and the related problem of difference, stands in the long shadows cast by Fichte and Hegel, and its relation to them is at best ambiguous. On the one hand, current philosophical consensus repudiates their thought as "metaphysics," and on the other, it continues to borrow substantially from them, often without acknowledgment.

Another reason to study recognition is to clarify one of Hegel's central concepts—that of *Geist*. In the *Phänomenologie des Geistes,* the central concept of *Geist* first emerges as the result of reciprocal recognition. The concept of recognition provides the existential phenomenological genesis of Hegel's concept of *Geist,* an I that is a We, and a We that is an I.[4] It is significant that *Geist* originates in recognition, for this suggests that *Geist* is a fundamentally social concept. But the heretofore dominant interpretations treat *Geist* as simply another term for a transcendental or absolute ego,[5] and thus suppress its intersubjective dimension. In the *Phenomenology* at least, the intersubjective-social dimension of *Geist* is the bearer of the transcendental dimension, and the latter is an abstraction from the former.[6] For this reason interpretations which see Hegel's philosophy as simply transcendental philosophy must be called into question. If *Geist* has its genesis in intersubjective recognition, then *Geist* is not an example of transcendental philosophy, but instead its transformation.

Existing English translations of Hegel obscure this departure from, or transformation of, transcendentalism. There is no single English term that is equivalent to *Geist,* which gets translated sometimes as mind *(mens)* and sometimes as spirit. The two English translations of the *Phänomenologie* reflect this ambiguity in their respective renderings of the title: the *Phenomenology of Mind* and the *Phenomenology of Spirit*. The translation of *Geist* as "mind," although correct in conveying the Latin lineage, suffers the drawback that it calls up the very Cartesian foundationalist metaphysical connotations that Hegel seeks to overcome—namely abstract, formal, disembodied, worldless subjectivity. Moreover it utterly fails to convey the intersubjective-social meaning that Hegel also intends. The attempt to correct this omission by translating *Geist* as "spirit" suffers the drawback of being either too narrowly theological (e.g., Holy Spirit) or conveying far too weak a sense of the social (e.g., team spirit, which is not a normative or ethical concept), and it suppresses the first person sense which is also an element of Hegel's concept.

Given the absence of an equivalent synthetic concept for *Geist,* English translations vacillate between "mind" and "spirit," as in the following translation of the *Encyclopedia* by William Wallace:

The absolute Mind (*Geist*) while it is a self-centered identity, is always also identity returning and ever returned into itself. If it is the one and universal substance, it is so as a spirit (*geistige*), discerning itself into a self and consciousness. Religion, as this supreme sphere may in general be designated, if it has, on the one hand, to be studied as issuing from the subject and having its home in the subject, must no less be regarded as objectively issuing from the absolute spirit (*Geist*) which as spirit (*Geist*) is in its community.[7]

In the first sentence *Geist* is rendered by mind, a translation that suggests a Cartesian metaphysical-transcendental reading. Yet in the last sentence *Geist*, rendered as spirit, is an intersubjective conception, namely, *Geist in seiner Gemeinde*. The English reader, deprived of the interpretive work of the translator, fails to appreciate that *Geist* is being translated in two different ways, as mind and as spirit. The passage, obscure in itself, is given a misleading clarification by the translation.

These translation difficulties point to deeper philosophical problems. H. G. Gadamer observes that translations of Hegel into foreign languages have been only partially successful: "There is good reason for the fact that translations of him [Hegel] into the major cultural languages first appeared in this century—translations which, without recourse to the original German text, are only half successful in communicating Hegel's thought. The linguistic potentialities of these other languages do not permit a direct duplication of the multiple meanings contained in such concepts as *Sein, Dasein, Wesen, Wirklichkeit, Begriff*, and *Bestimmung*. Thinking in the possible translation of these thus inevitably leads one astray into the conceptual horizons of the Scholastic metaphysics and the more modern developments of their concepts."[8] In Gadamer's view, the conceptual horizons of metaphysics, enshrined in Latin and its linguistic offspring "provides the linguistic foundation for the translation of Hegel into Italian, Spanish, French or English."[9] Consequently it is no accident that Hegel tends to be regarded in English speaking circles as the culmination of the metaphysical tradition. Those who rely exclusively on translations tend to pick up only the associations with classical metaphysics—i.e., the common elements of the House of Being or metaphysics present in Western languages—and miss the countervailing nuances of the German language which signal Hegel's breaking up and departure from the metaphysical tradition. Hegel's speculative dialectical critique of metaphysics gets lost in the translation. This concealment of Hegel's concrete meaning in metaphysically-determined translation, lies behind the dominant interpretation of *Geist* as mind and the suppression of its social-intersubjective sense.

Even German scholarship is unclear concerning the meaning and significance of Hegel's concept of *Geist*. For example, H. F. Fulda's article on Hegel's concept of *Geist* in the *Historisches Wörterbuch der Philosophie*, exhibits two different senses, the logical and the intersubjective, without mentioning, much less dealing with, the problem of their relation. Fulda identifies the logical sense of *Geist* as an identity that divides itself and opposes itself to itself, and then overcomes this disunity by restoration of identity and self-sameness. The following text exhibits this pattern:

> This substance is, as subject, pure simple negativity. For this reason it is the division of what is simple, or the doubling which sets up opposition and then again negates this indifferent diversity and its opposite. Only this self-restoring self-sameness, or the reflection in otherness in itself—and not an original unity as such or a pure immediacy as such—is the true. It is the process of its own becoming, the circle that presupposes its end as its goal, having its end also at its beginning. And only by being worked out to its end is it actual.[10]

In this passage the other has no independent status. It is the result of the logical operation of negation which divides the primal simple unity. Since negation is determination, the other is a determination (= negation) of the original substantial unity, or self-othering. The other is logically derivative from and subordinate to unity and self-identity. But the other is also an instrument or means to the restoration of identity. For by cancelling or eliminating the other (as negation of identity), negation of negation restores the original identity.

The following passage from the *Encyclopedia* likewise exhibits the logical concept of *Geist* as self-mediating: "The appearance that *Geist* is mediated by an other is overcome by *Geist* itself, since *Geist* has as it were the sovereign ingratitude to sublate and mediate that through which it appears to be mediated. It reduces such instrumentalities to elements which have existence only through *Geist* itself, and in this way *Geist* makes itself completely independent."[11] Thus mediation turns out to be self-mediation and apparent determination by other is really *self*-determination. The other of *Geist* turns out to be posited and mediated by *Geist*. "What appears to be external to it or an activity opposed to it, is its own doing..."[12] On this reading the other is a self-othering (negation) of *Geist,* to be overcome by a further negation of negation. The negation of negation reinstates self-sameness by eliminating otherness. In this reading *Geist* is a logical-metaphysical principle.

However Fulda notes that for Hegel *Geist* has a second intersubjective sense. "The paradigmatic phenomenon of *Geist*...is for Hegel therefore not the ego or self-consciousness. Rather it is the relation of self-conscious individuals which are crucial to each other, since they give of themselves without reserve and at the same time know that the others on which they depend are nothing alien. Where Fichte posited the ego as absolute, Hegel posits this process of self-abandonment and finding of self in other."[13] Clearly this passage employs the concepts of other and mediation in a different sense from the first. The other here is an interpersonal other, another self-consciousness. This other is not simply a negation, or derivative from negation. And self-recognition in other is not simply a matter of determinate or double negation. Rather, determinate negation is an element in self-recognition in other. Self-knowledge here does not involve simple self-sameness or self-identity, but rather mediation by other. Thus Fulda observes, "It ceases to be simple self-knowledge and becomes instead, self-knowledge in self-externalization... [*Entäußerung*]"[14] This self-externalization presupposes and requires an intersubjective other.

Fulda does not recognize or call attention to any problem here, but the question is how these two senses of *Geist* are related, and whether they are compatible. Are all cases of reference to other, mediation by other, ultimately cases of self-reference and self-mediation? Such a claim conceals the theme of intersubjectivity and appears to reduce the other to a mere illusion or semblance. This is the conclusion drawn not by an existentialist critic such as Kierkegaard, but rather by Hegel's champion and defender, J. N. Findlay.

Findlay claims that Fichte's concept of the absolute ego is the background for Hegel's concept of *Geist*. In view of the self-positing of the ego, the chief question, says Findlay, is why the ego should posit anything other than itself, particularly an other that confines, bounds, vexes and bewilders it.[15] The answer lies in what Findlay calls an elaborate "myth of a barrier," or non-ego. "The Ego posits a resistant environment precisely because it *requires* such an environment to elicit its own activities, and to bring them to consciousness."[16] However, having completed this strange story, Fichte proceeds to retract it. "He drops the myth of a barrier: the existence of the Ego's object-positing activity cannot be explained by an impact or resistance, but must be a consequence of the Ego's own absolute activity."[17] The other turns out to be a myth, an illusion. "Since our rationality makes us look in the data of experience for what is universal, unifying and intersubjective, we must proceed *as if* such universality, unity and intersubjectivity were there to be found..."[18]

Although Findlay was an important interpreter and defender of Hegel, his interpretation of the other as a qualified illusion goes too far in the direction of metaphysical idealism and confirms the existentialist criticism that idealism is unable to take the other or otherness seriously.[19] The other is at best only ambiguous, never receiving consistent expression or treatment. It is not a central theme, but only a muted sub-theme in the system of identity. The other is not regarded as posing any problems in principle for idealism, because the other is a category, a part of the system. And so it is in the final analysis *not* other, but rather an expression of identity and self-sameness.

Thus several questions arise from the foregoing discussion. If Fichte and Hegel raise and treat intersubjectivity, how is this understood? If they raise the issue of the other, how does it accord with the putative idealist tendency of their thought? Does not their alleged metaphysical idealism override the other and reduce it to self-sameness and identity? Such is the received opinion. On the other hand, if no such reduction occurs, then with what justification is label of idealism pinned on these thinkers? Has the fundamental tendency of their thought yet been identified? On such an apparently elementary question there is scarcely any consensus.

Moreover, the recognition that Fichte and Hegel raise and treat intersubjectivity within a supposedly idealist framework does not make the interpretive task any easier, but serves to intensify the perplexity. My thesis is that Fichte and Hegel do raise and treat the topic of intersubjectivity, and begin a massive transformation of philosophy into social and historical modes of thought. The implications of this transformation are still being worked out and are controversial. This story, obscure and only recently surfacing in German scholarship, has been almost completely neglected and passed over in English. Uncovering this story and exploring some of its ramifications is the task of this study.

PHENOMENOLOGY AND GERMAN IDEALISM

The careers of German Idealism and phenomenology are intertwined and interrelated. On the one hand, German Idealism requires and anticipates aspects of the phenomenological method. In order to overcome Kant's a-historical formal transcendentalism, German idealism finds it necessary to introduce a phenomenological or descriptive moment into philosophical method. This is due in part to a crisis in foundations,[20] the recognition of the absence of unproblematic first principles and criteria. Both Fichte and Hegel confront the question, how to philosophize in the absence of a criterion? Such a situation compels philosophy to delve beneath the traditional theories of epistemology and ontology to concrete human existence and interests. This move discloses that reason itself is historical and social. The phenomenological description of ordinary consciousness (the natural attitude) begins with Fichte's *Wissenschaftslehre,* continues in his practical philosophy and popular writings, and culminates in Hegel's *Phenomenology of Spirit.*

On the other hand, Husserlian phenomenology, as it pursues the question of the ontological interpretation of its method, raises the issue of the relation between thought and being, or the ontological significance of phenomenological descriptions. Husserl was accused by his followers of either being naive about, or indefinitely postponing, the ontological question. When that question is faced, phenomenology is transformed into existential phenomenology. Husserl's late discovery of the life-world as the concrete a priori foundation of theoretical sciences, constitutes an anti-foundationalist departure from Cartesianism.[21] Husserl's call for an ontology of the life-world articulates the need for a new phenomenological ontology that deals, among other things, with the problem of the other. The discovery of the life-world as the a priori condition of science and the world of science, reopens and confronts fundamental questions of reason, as Husserl acknowledged.[22]

Those problems were also the concern of German Idealism. For, from Fichte on, the historical and social character of philosophical reason was recognized. This called forth efforts to treat the basic problems of reason within a genetic history. In that transcendental-genetic history, reason develops as the unifying subject of the various standpoints and categories, a process Hegel describes as the development of substance into subject. This raises the possibility that Hegel's *Phenomenology* may anticipate, if not actually provide, an ontology of the life-world that Husserl called for, but did not live to complete.

The last claim would be disputed by many, but by no means all, in the phenomenological tradition.[23] Although Hegel may have published a book with phenomenology both in the title and as the subject, it is a "different sort of phenomenology" from the Husserlian. For example, Heidegger denied that Hegel's *Phenomenology* is phenomenology. Rather it is metaphysics, the *parousia* of the absolute. This recalls the existential critique of Hegel, which can be traced to Kierkegaard.[24] Heidegger's denial that Hegel is 'doing phenomenology' is an oversimplification.[25] Moreover, Heidegger's relation to Hegel is complex and underwent a change from earlier rejection to later appreciation, even though their projects are different. These topics lie beyond the scope of this study.[26]

Nevertheless, Hegel's considerable influence on the phenomenological movement should not be overlooked. The appropriation of Hegel was itself a major event in the so-called 'existential turn' of phenomenology during its French phase. Kojève's lectures on Hegel are an important bridge between, and synthesis of, Hegel and existential phenomenology. These lectures were extremely influential on Sartre and others. Kojève identified master and slave, lordship and bondage, and death as central themes of Hegel's *Phenomenology*.[27] Sartre appropriated Hegel as filtered through this discussion and claimed that Hegel was far more significant for the topic of intersubjectivity than Husserl.

Ricoeur speaks of this Hegelian influence on phenomenology as due to the "implicit phenomenology" of Hegel's philosophy of existence.[28] Sartre goes further: he credits Hegel with making the real breakthrough to intersubjectivity as an internal relation. Hegel, says Sartre, shows that the self depends on the other to mediate its own "internal" self-relation. The autonomous self is nevertheless shaped by and must deal with the pervasive presence and influence of the other. Thus for Sartre, Hegel's *Phenomenology* and his account of the other are not merely important resources for phenomenological philosophy; Hegel's account of intersubjectivity is superior to Husserl's. To be sure, Sartre's Hegel is a 'left-Hegelian,' i.e., Sartre's appropriation of Hegel is piecemeal, embracing the *Phenomenology* but not the *Logic*.

Phenomenology in German Idealism

German idealism requires a phenomenological moment for several reasons. Perhaps the most important is to overcome the abstract formalism of Kant's transcendental philosophy. Kant's appeal to transcendental subjectivity—the ultimate condition of possibility of knowledge—is problematic and unstable, and called forth skeptical criticism.[29] The central problem is that Kant cannot, within the boundaries of knowledge set forth in the first Critique, explain how it is possible to draw those very boundaries.[30] This is due in part to his restriction of experience to sensible intuition and his denial of intellectual intuition. This restriction raises difficulties for Kant's conception of transcendental freedom. The problem is that transcendental freedom is only a possibility left open by the First Critique. It can be *thought,* but not *known,* and it is far from clear how the self-consciousness of freedom is possible. The official Kantian doctrine seems to be that freedom must be postulated, because it cannot, strictly speaking, be known (i.e., be an object).

Kant's transcendental philosophy is a restricted, mundane transcendental philosophy, carried out on the presupposition of the life-world.[31] But Kant never got beyond transcendental justification of the categories of Newtonian science, and so never reached, much less developed, an ontology of the life-world. Although Kant justifies science, he begs the question concerning the scope of experience by rendering alternative forms of experience (e.g., the aesthetic, the moral and religious) non-cognitive. For this reason, Hegel observes that Kant's restriction of experience to scientific knowledge is too narrow.

The 'phenomenological moment' of German idealism refers to the suspension of metaphysical debates as well as Kant's restriction of cognition to scientific experience.[32] It includes the expansion of experience in post-Kantian thinkers to include, in addition to theoretical-scientific experience, aesthetic, moral, social-intersubjective, and religious experience as well as the 'philosophical experience' required to do critical philosophy itself.[33] The phenomenological principle of evidence, or act-object correlation, is broader than Kant officially acknowledges. Moreover, Fichte claimed that Kant tacitly presupposes this broader sense of experience and evidence as a condition of possibility of his own critical philosophy.

Fichte developed further Kant's suggestions about the interests of reason. He moved the concept of interest from a topic buried in Kant's discussion of the antinomies to center stage, and thereby inaugurated an existential-pragmatic turn within German Idealism. Fichte's *First Introduction to the Science of Knowledge*[34] shows that there are two types of philosophical explanation that have mutually exclusive first principles, namely, idealism (Kant) and materialism (Spinoza). A first principle can neither be demonstrated nor derived from anything prior. However, since there are two possible, equally immediate or self-evident first principles, the impasse between them is theoretically undecidable. The foundationalist project shipwrecks on the irreducible plurality and opposition between first principles.

Fichte's critique of foundationalism raises the problem of the beginning or starting point. Foundationalist Cartesian transcendentalism separates the transcendental consciousness from the empirical and identifies the former as the starting point. Skepticism about the transcendental subject undermined this sort of transcendentalism. However, when the life-world lying beneath Kant's transcendental constructions is uncovered, not only is the scope of experience enlarged, the transcendental itself undergoes modification. It becomes embodied in the life-world. But this very embodiment of the transcendental calls into question its ability to serve as foundation or starting point, i.e., *episteme* is founded upon *doxa*. The transcendental subject is displaced from an a priori starting point, and becomes instead a subject which emerges and develops in history. Thereby it ceases to be a purely transcendental subject and becomes social, and socially mediated. Thus the starting point of philosophy shifts from a regressive transcendental inquiry into a-historical a priori conditions, to a phenomenological investigation of the natural attitude.[35]

Fichte claims the impasse concerning first principles cannot be settled on theoretical grounds. It can be settled, if at all, only by appeal to interests: what sort of philosophy one chooses depends upon the sort of human being one is. This turn to human interest is one example of a phenomenological moment in German Idealism. But when philosophical attention is directed to human interests, the problem of the other is not far behind, as Fichte shows:

> There are a few questions which philosophy must answer before it can become *Wissenschaft* and *Wissenschaftslehre*.... Among these questions are the following: ...How does the human being come to assume and recognize that there are rational beings similar to it outside of it, since such beings are not at all immediately or directly given to or present in its pure self-consciousness?... The relation of rational beings to each other I term *Gesellschaft*. But the concept of *Gesellschaft* is not possible except on the presupposition that there actually exist rational beings outside of us.... How do we come to such a presupposition...?[36]

We shall consider Fichte's answer to this question below. For the present it is sufficient to note that talk of transcendental constitution, and imposition of order on the world, reflects a subjective idealism that ill accords with ordinary interpersonal experience, the moral imperative, or religion. Taking the life-world context of the transcendental subject into account means removing the abstraction which makes that subject appear disembodied, a-historical and solipsistic, and finding it situated within and shaped by the social and the historical. Given such concrete re-contextualization, it is inevitable that the problem of the other becomes an explicit topic and calls for fundamental changes in the concepts of subjectivity and experience. This happens in the philosophies of Fichte and Hegel. Fichte's pragmatic history of spirit implicitly, and Hegel's *Phenomenology of Spirit* explicitly, are social phenomenologies, or archeologies, of so-called "pure reason." Reason is herein conceived as social. Intersubjectivity, ethics and religion figure prominently in the de-centering and transformation of the transcendental subject.

THE PROBLEM OF THE OTHER IN CONTEMPORARY PHILOSOPHY

The "problem of the other" has dominated the philosophical landscape for the last twenty years. Michael Theunissen characterizes the history of this development thus:

> ...the problem of the other has been thought through in former times and has at times been accorded a prominent place in ethics and anthropology, in legal and political philosophy. But the problem of the other has certainly never penetrated as deeply as today into the foundations of philosophical thought. It is no longer the simple object of a specific discipline but has already become the topic of first philosophy. The question of the other cannot be separated from the most primordial questions raised by modern thought.[37]

There is sharp disagreement concerning the exact nature of the problem and its significance. For example the choice of specific terminology such as "alien" or "alter ego," on the one hand, or "Thou" on the other, already implies a decision concerning what the other is. From the standpoint of transcendental philosophy and existential philosophy, the other has negative significance, i.e., it is the alien ego, the inaccessible subject of the look, etc. To be sure, there are radical differences concerning the sense of this negation. Some maintain that the other is simply another instance of general epistemological worries about knowledge, objectivity, transcendence, and presents no special problems.[38]

Others, like Emmanuel Levinas, challenge transcendentalism's claims concerning the primacy of cogito, methodological or ontological. The original being of the other is the Thou who summons the self to responsible dialogue. This sense of other is neglected and passed over by traditional and by existential ontologies. The intersubjective other presents a new issue which calls into question traditional epistemology and ontology. To be sure, ontology has not been a failure on its own terms: it has comprehended the other, but at the price of reducing the other to the same, the particular to the universal. Levinas writes that "Western philosophy has most often been an ontology: a reduction of the other to the same by the interposition of a middle and neutral term that ensures the comprehension of being."[39] The universality at which ontology aims, strips the other of its alterity and reduces it to the same (i.e., the universal).

For Levinas, Hegel is the arch-offender, because he allegedly subordinates infinity to totality. Levinas believes that Hegel falls under his criticism that philosophy is essentially egology, and that ontology dominates the other by reducing it to the same. "Hegelian phenomenology, where self-consciousness is the distinguishing of what is not distinct, expresses the universality of the same identifying itself in the alterity of objects thought and despite the opposition of the self to self.... The difference is not a difference; the I, as other, is not an other."[40] Levinas finds Heidegger even less satisfactory, since Heidegger's pursuit of the *Seinsfrage* through *Dasein* analysis affirms the priority of Being over existents. "In subordinating every relation with existents to the relation with Being, the Heideggerian ontology affirms the priority of freedom over ethics."[41]

These examples are not accidental or merely contingent. Levinas' thesis is that "the relation with Being that is enacted as ontology consists in neutralizing the existent in order to comprehend or grasp it. It is hence not a relation with the other as such, but the reduction of the other to the same.... Thematization and conceptualization, which moreover are inseparable, are not peace with the other but suppression or possession of the other.... Ontology as first philosophy is a philosophy of power."[42] From this critique it seems to follow that there can be no social ontology, because ontology subverts the very conception of the social that is its object.

Levinas' philosophy enters a protest on behalf of the other, and seeks to reverse the situation presented by ontology: infinity must be distinguished from totality, and ethics must take priority over ontology. The primacy of the ethical comes out in Levinas' concept of the face, an infinity which is irreducible to totality. "The way in which the other presents himself, *exceeding the idea of the other in me,* we here name face."[43] Because the other exceeds my idea of him, he can put my freedom in question and make the fundamental demand, "You shall not kill." Levinas explains "The notion of the face...brings us to a notion of a meaning prior to my *Sinngebung* and thus independent of my initiative and power."[44]

Amid such divergent estimates concerning the nature and significance of the problem of the other, two points need stressing: First, this controversy shows that the other has emerged as a fundamental problem of contemporary philosophy, but there is little consensus concerning its significance. To the extent that we identify first philosophy with traditional metaphysics, or with its successor transcendental philosophy, first philosophy appears to exclude the other, and vice-versa. For if the other is neither a percept nor a concept, neither an object, nor reducible to the immanence of pure transcendental constitution, how can there be social ontology or an ontology of intersubjectivity? On the other hand, isn't Levinas' attack on the ontologies of the other *itself an ontology*? Steven Smith observes that Levinas' phenomenological ontology of the other is in fact anti-phenomenological and anti-ontological.[45] But this makes it appear that Levinas must appropriate what he rejects in order to make his case. Thus he seems to be playing Hegel's game of dialectical opposition.[46]

Second, whenever the problem of the other is taken seriously, Hegel sooner or later becomes a topic of discussion. Classical ontology may not have done justice to alterity, but Hegel claims to have developed an ontology which gives difference its due. Thus Hegel not only shares Levinas' critique of classical ontology, but his concept of *Geist* may also represent an alternative social ontology. Levinas' charges that philosophy is an egology, that ontology reduces the other to the same, were anticipated and brought forth as a critique of idealism in Hegel's day by F. H. Jacobi.[47] According to Jacobi, idealism is the doctrine that the self can know only the products of its own activity. This makes self-knowledge the constitutive principle of all knowledge, and leads to a speculative egology that dissolves all reality into the self's representations. We do not know any reality that exists apart from the self's activity, be it nature, other minds, or God.

Hegel's response was to develop an account of intersubjectivity and to formulate an alternative to traditional ontology. Hegel's *Phenomenology* is a pre-categorial ontology of the *Gestalten des Bewusstseins,* that serves as the phenomenological introduction to the concrete identity that requires difference, and receives categorical articulation in the logic.[48] Hegel would probably regard Levinas as a latter-day Jacobi. Levinas' claim that ontology is an egology that reduces the other to the same, may turn out to be not so much a criticism of Hegel, as a restatement of Hegel's criticism of the traditional concept of abstract identity, the identity that excludes or suppresses difference. Levinas' opposition to Hegel may turn out to be a restatement of both Hegel's critique of traditional metaphysics and Hegel's existential phenomenological ontology.[49]

These comments are not intended to settle the issue, but rather to illustrate how the problem of the other—and Hegel—are at the center of contemporary discussions. For whether we think him successful or not, we cannot deny that Hegel remains an important party to the current discussion. Who better than Hegel has shown that first philosophy, as traditionally conceived, is committed to abstract identity that excludes difference? The problem of the other has no basis in the categories of traditional ontology. However, the other may not simply subvert philosophy, provided a way can be found to give difference its due. Such is Hegel's project from his early *Difference* essay on. Since Hegel's thought presents an important treatment of the other, an examination of the topic of recognition is long overdue in English scholarship.

PLAN AND OVERVIEW

This study takes the following form. Part One deals with Fichte, who first raised the problem of intersubjectivity within German Idealism. One reason why such a development may strike us as strange is the absence of attention to or knowledge of German philosophy in the period between Kant and Hegel, one of the most fertile periods in the history of philosophy. Although German Idealism has been traditionally and unfairly considered to represent a retrograde step from Kant to dogmatic metaphysics, it is now recognized that, in response to Kant, post-Kantian German idealism develops its own critique of traditional metaphysics and its inversion in transcendental idealism.[50] Moreover, once the fundamental problems are more clearly recognized, the commonly accepted picture of a development from Kant to Hegel must be set aside in favor of a divergent threefold response to Kant by Fichte, Schelling, and Hegel.[51] The Other is an element in this critique, and, for Fichte and Hegel, it requires the transformation of transcendental philosophy from an a-historical a priori philosophy to a concrete social philosophy of spirit.

Chapter 2 places the problem of the Other within the context of German Idealism's genetic history of consciousness. Fichte's *Wissenschaftslehre* began the transformation of Kant's critical philosophy into a transcendental-pragmatic system that includes a pragmatic history of spirit. In his *Naturrecht*, Fichte introduced the concept of recognition *(Anerkennung)* as a transcendental condition of natural law. This is not a formal categorical structure a priori, but a concrete life-world a priori that involves praxis and action. The traditional concept of subjectivity is transformed into a social intersubjective concept.

A study of Fichte's thought is long overdue in English, but lies beyond the scope of this monograph. The anomaly of Fichte's thought is its development from an early *(Wissenschaftslehre* 1794) methodological idealism that asserts the primacy of subjectivity, or the ego, to the later ontological turn (after the *Wissenschaftslehre* 1804) that asserts the priority of being over the ego. This ontological turn in Fichte's later thought is not extensively recognized, much less understood. The concept of recognition, and the problem of the Other, is an important first step down this path of ontological reversal. The focus of the present monograph is on the concept of recognition, and not on the *Wissenschaftslehre* 1794, much less the development of Fichte's thought in subsequent versions of the *Wissenschaftslehre*. Since the focus is on recognition, I shall consider Fichte from this perspective, and then turn to Hegel's appropriation and development of this concept, following the practice of two German studies.[52]

Part Three deals with Hegel, focusing on his early social philosophy and the development of his phenomenological project. Chapter 4 treats Hegel's early social theory in his theological writings. Prior to his appropriation of Fichte's concept of recognition, Hegel had already worked out analyses of domination, alienation and reconciliation in his treatment of the positivity of the Christian religion. His later accounts of master and slave, domination and servitude, continue his early themes, and transpose them into the framework of recognition. Hegel appropriates Fichte's concept of recognition (*Anerkennung*) and transforms it by integration with the themes of domination, alienation and reconciliation. He thus deepens and clarifies the intersubjective significance of his earlier social and religious themes.

Part Three is chiefly a study of Hegel's *Phenomenology of Spirit*, from the vantage point of recognition. I hasten to point out that this is not intended as a commentary on or study of the *Phenomenology* as a whole. The focus is on the concept of recognition and its significance. Although my concerns are more modest than a full commentary on the *Phenomenology*, the importance of recognition in its overall argument has not been widely appreciated.[53] When Hegel introduces the crucial concept of spirit (*Geist*) he shows that spirit originates in and results from a process of recognition that involves struggle, domination and reconciliation. Spirit has its existential genesis in interpersonal recognition. It is an I that is a We and a We that is an I. This suggests an hypothesis to be explored, namely, that just as the I is *aufgehoben* or sublated in the We, so recognition is *aufgehoben* in *Geist*. This implies that *Geist* is a fundamentally interpersonal and social conception. This hypothesis will be explored in the following examination of the *Phenomenology*. In support of this hypothesis is the fact that when Hegel introduces the concept of absolute Spirit, it is not as a transcendent metaphysical entity, but rather as the very accomplishment of mutual-reciprocal recognition. Absolute spirit is a divine-human, theo-anthropic community (*Geist in seiner Gemeinde*). Not only is religion thereby transformed into social and historical modalities, the social-historical nature of absolute Spirit is maintained even in the concluding chapter on Absolute Knowledge. Absolute Knowledge has the structure of and involves divine-human recognition. Thus the treatment of the *Phenomenology* from the perspective of recognition is at the same time an exploration of the social, religious and historical significance of recognition as *aufgehoben* in *Geist*.

Chapters 5 and 6 deal with Hegel's phenomenological project, and relate it to Husserlian phenomenology. I shall show that phenomenology is not an utterly equivocal term when used in reference to the Husserlian movement on the one hand, and Hegel on the other. There is common ground between the two, extending to the problem of the other as a life-world concern, and the need for philosophy to respond to the crisis in first principles raised by the antifoundationalist critique of traditional metaphysics.

Hegel is unique among his contemporaries, and certainly among 'typical Hegelians', in making perhaps the most serious study of skepticism of any modern philosopher. Skepticism is the self-styled "other" of philosophy, which it accuses of being dogmatic.[54] Hegel prefers ancient skepticism to modern skepticism of the Cartesian-Humean variety; he claims the former is far more radical than the latter.[55] Modern skepticism attacks reason and its claims, but uncritically accepts immediate perception as true, and relies upon immediate certainties. In contrast, ancient skepticism turned its attack on precisely such immediate certainties, the claim of immediacy to be true, and expressed utter hopelessness about all that is taken as stable, or typical.[56] This fact—that Hegel sides with ancient skepticism against Cartesianism and its alleged immediate facts of consciousness—shows that it is a mistake to regard Hegel as a Cartesian foundationalist, or metaphysician of subjectivity.

Hegel's *Phenomenology* is a self-accomplishing skepticism. Hegel's phenomenology begins at the abyss where Husserl's ends, namely the discovery of the groundlessness of the philosophical enterprise.[57] Hegel's *Phenomenology* begins with the recognition of the absence of any assured criterion, or rather that all philosophical criteria are mere assurances, to which other, equally plausible assurances can be opposed. The classical skeptical problem of equipollence—that to every argument there is an opposing argument of equal force and validity—sets the agenda of Hegel's *Phenomenology*. It is supposed to demonstrate by its traversal of all the shapes of consciousness (*Gestalten des Bewusstseins*) that all merely immediate certainties collapse and self-destruct, leaving no alternative to mediation and holism. The truth is the whole. That is why Hegel characterizes *Phenomenology* as a self-accomplishing skepticism, that serves as the critical introduction to philosophical science. Of course Hegel is not a skeptic, but he does maintain that skepticism raises rational demands, and, as a critical moment, belongs to every genuine philosophy.

The skeptical problem of equipollence shapes Hegel's phenomenological method, and underlies his characterization of experience as the highway of despair. Each shape of consciousness is self-subverting and undergoes a reversal or transition into its opposite. The truth of each turns out to be the opposite of what was originally intended, giving rise to a new shape. Hegel's analysis of recognition, including the famous example of master and slave, illustrates this general skeptical-phenomenological method of tropic reversal. The truth of Mastery is servitude. Self recognition by other and freedom turn out not to exclude, but to require each other. For these reasons an examination of Hegel and skepticism is an important part of the study.

Chapters 7 and 8 deal with Hegel's treatment of recognition (*Anerkennung*). This may appear to be a traversal of familiar territory. After all, the passages in question are among the most famous and well known in Hegelian literature. Nevertheless they have not been well translated or subjected to sufficiently detailed scrutiny, especially from a Husserlian perspective. I will show that Hegel makes an important distinction between two perspectives on the concept of recognition. The first is an eidetics, which sets forth the general concept of recognition from the perspective of the phenomenological "We" or "for us," the phenomenological onlookers. The second is an empirics, which treats particular forms and determinate modes of recognition from the perspective of ordinary consciousness in the natural attitude. It is important not to identify or confuse the concept of recognition with one of its possible instances or examples, e.g., master and slave. Such confusion leads many to the erroneous conclusion that master/slave exhausts Hegel's theory of intersubjectivity. This overlooks the point that the eidetic concept supports alternative modes of realization, and that master/slave is a deficient mode of recognition. The other possibilities include friendship, love, the devotion between brother and sister, and reconciliation.

Chapters 9 and 10 deal with further discussions of recognition in the *Phenomenology of Spirit,* including its social and religious dimensions. Here the hypotheses that recognition is sublated in *Geist* and that *Geist* is fundamentally social are explored and tested. Although Hegel maintains that alienation is not the final word and can be overcome, he nevertheless conceives recognition tragically, as is evident in his discussion of Greek *Sittlichkeit* as expressed in *Antigone,* and in the Christian motif of the death of God.

Chapter 11 treats Hegel's account of absolute knowing. There are at least two divergent readings of absolute knowledge. One is the idealist reading, in which all being is reduced to a metaphysical posit of subjectivity. The other, which I shall defend, is that absolute knowledge is inherently social and exhibits an intersubjective-social structure. This is not to claim that the two models are mutually exclusive; it is to claim that Hegel does not abandon the intersubjective-social conception of reason he develops in the course of the *Phenomenology,* and that while there is no way from the idealist model to the social, the latter model nevertheless can incorporate the former. The *Phenomenology* does not conclude with an absolute idealism of pure self-reflective transparency, but with an historical recollection of the realms of spirit without which the absolute spirit would be life-less, solitary, and alone.

The study concludes with an exploration of the significance of Hegel's recognition for the views of the interhuman in Husserl, Sartre and Levinas. It challenges Sartre's strange appropriation of Hegel and shows how the later Sartre drew closer to Hegel in his attempt to graft Marxist social philosophy onto the existentialist individualism of *Being and Nothingness.* It also compares the social ontological conception of reason that Hegel develops with the anti-phenomenological and anti-ontological deliverances of Levinas. I argue that Levinas' critique of ontology is already present in Hegel's critique of classical metaphysics, and that the position Levinas urges against Hegel in *Totality and Infinity* is in fact Hegel's own. The latter does not reduce the other to the same, but rather grants otherness its due and allows the other to be.

NOTES

1. Edmund Husserl, *Cartesian Meditations,* tr. Dorion Cairns (The Hague: Martinus Nijhoff, 1960).

2. Ludwig Siep, *Anerkennung als Prinzip der praktische Philosophie,* (Freiburg: Alber Verlag, 1979) [Hereafter cited as APP]; Andreas Wildt, *Autonomie und Anerkennung* (Stuttgart: Klett-Cotta, 1982); Edith Düsing, *Intersubjektivität und Selbstbewusstsein,* (Köln: Dinter Verlag, 1986); Vittorio Hösle, *Hegels System,* 2 vols. (Hamburg: Meiner Verlag, 1987). Although Hösle believes that Hegel deals with the problem of intersubjectivity, he does not mention or discuss Hegel's concept of recognition. Instead, Hösle seems to deal with every topic in Hegel except recognition, a remarkable omission from a book whose thesis is that Hegel raises but fails to resolve the problem of intersubjectivity. Hösle owes his readers some account of intersubjectivity to clarify his central thesis. It should be noted that Nicolai Hartmann identified intersubjective or objective *Geist* as Hegel's most original philosophical discovery without, however, calling attention to Hegel's concept of recognition as the specific contribution (*Philosophie des deutschen Idealismus,* 2 vols. (Berlin: Walter de Gruyter 1923–1929).

3. H. S. Harris, "The Concept of Recognition in Hegel's Jena Manuscripts," *Hegel-Studien Beiheft 20,* (Bonn: Bouvier Verlag, 1979), 229–248 [Hereafter cited as CR]; Robert R. Williams, "The Concept of Recognition in Hegel's Jena Philosophy," *Philosophy and Social Criticism* (Fall 1982); "Hegel's Concept of Geist" in *Hegel's Philosophy of Spirit,* ed. Peter Stillman (Albany, N.Y.: SUNY Press, 1986). In addition there is a Ph. D. dissertation "Hegel's Concept of Recognition," by Eliot Jurist, (New York: Columbia University, 1983).

4. G. W. F. Hegel, *Phänomenologie des Geistes,* Hrsg. Hoffmeister (Hamburg: Felix Meiner Verlag, 1952). [Hereafter cited as PhG.] There are two English translations: *Phenomenology of Mind* (J. B. Baillie, Macmillan, 1910), and *Phenomenology of Spirit* (A. V. Miller, Oxford or New York: Oxford University Press, 1977). [Hereafter cited as PhM and PhS respectively. All translations are my own.]

5. Two interpreters who find *Geist* to be a terminological variant of Kant's transcendental ego or transcendental unity of apperception are J. N. Findlay, *Hegel: A Re-Examination* (New York: Collier MacMillan, 1962); Robert C. Solomon, "Hegel's Concept of *Geist,*" in *Hegel: A Collection of Critical Essays,* ed. A. MacIntyre (New York: Doubleday Anchor, 1972), 125–149.

6. This means that for Hegel, *Geist* is not an a priori timeless structure everywhere the same; it is also social and historical. This acknowledgement of historicity underlies Hegel's analysis of cultural alienation in his *Differenzschrift,* and his elevation of the history of philosophy to the rank of a special philosophical discipline. The distinction between an essential structure and different degrees of its realization is clearly expressed in Hegel's *Vorlesungen über die Philosophie der Weltgeschichte,* Band 1, *Die Vernunft in der Geschichte,* Hrsg. J. Hoffmeister (Hamburg: Meiner Verlag, 1955): "...what *Geist* in itself is, it has always been, the difference is only in the development of this 'in itself'" (182).

7. Hegel, *Enzyklopädie* (*Werke,* Theorie Werkausgabe, Band 10, Frankfurt: Suhrkamp Verlag, 1970) § 554. [Hereafter cited as Enz. TWA Sk 10: 554]. ET *Hegel's Logic, Hegel's Philosophy of Nature, Hegel's Philosophy of Mind,* tr. W. Wallace together with the Zusätze in Boumann's text (1845), tr. A. V. Miller (Oxford: Clarendon Press, 1971), §554.

8. "Hegel and Heidegger" in *Hegel's Dialectic: Five Hermeneutical Studies,* tr. P. Christopher Smith (New Haven: Yale University Press, 1976), 112.

9. Ibid. 113.

10. PhG 20. ET 10, §18.

11. H. F. Fulda, "Der Begriff des Geistes bei Hegel und seine Wirkungsgeschichte," in *Historisches Wörterbuch der Philosophie,* Hrsg. Joachim Ritter, Band III (Stuttgart: Schwabe and Co, 1971), 191ff. Fulda's reference is to Hegel, *Enzyklopädie,* §381 Zusatz, TWA 10:25. Cf. also §442 Zusatz: "That the content or object is something that comes to knowing from without as a given, is therefore only an appearance, through the sublation of which *Geist* shows itself to be what it really is—namely the absolutely self-determining, the infinite negativity of what is external...the ideal [existence] which produces all reality out of itself."

12. PhG 32.

13. Fulda, *"Geist"* op. cit. 192. It is odd, if not astonishing, that Fulda calls the intersubjective sense of *Geist* "paradigmatic." The tendency of his article seems rather to point to the logical sense of *Geist* as the basic one.

14. Fulda, op. cit. 192.

15. J. N. Findlay, *Hegel: A Re-Examination* (New York: Collier Macmillan, 1962), 47.

16. Ibid. 48.

17. Ibid.

18. Ibid. [Italics in the original.]

19. Hegel criticizes such an idealism in the preface of the *Phänomenologie:* "The life of God and divine knowledge may well be spoken of as a play of love with itself. But this idea sinks into mere edification, even insipidity if it lacks the seriousness, the suffering, the patience and the labor of the negative. In itself (*an sich*), that life is indeed one of untroubled equality and unity with itself, which is not serious about otherness [*Anderssein*], alienation, and the overcoming of alienation. But this in itself is *abstract universality,* in which the nature of divine life to be for itself...is left altogether out of account. " PhG 20; ET §19, 10.

20. Kant's attack on metaphysics as science, shows that he sides with Hume's skepticism against transcendent metaphysics. Although Kant's critical solution is that only a metaphysics of experience is possible, Kant assumed that reason has an a-historical a priori structure which transcendental reflection can uncover. However, once

it is recognized that Kant's pure reason itself is historical and social, the result is an altered philosophical situation, which we now characterize anti-foundationalist.

21. See Ludwig Landgrebe, "Husserl's Departure from Cartesianism," in *The Phenomenology of Husserl,* ed. R. O. Elveton (Chicago: Quadrangle Books, 1970), 259–306; for the opposite view, that Husserl never abandoned his foundationalist project of phenomenologically grounding philosophy as a rigorous science, cf. H. G. Gadamer, "The Phenomenological Movement," in *Philosophical Hermeneutics,* ed. D. Linge (Berkeley: University of California Press, 1977), 151–181.

22. Husserl, *The Crisis of European Science and Transcendental Phenomenology,* tr. D. Carr (Evanston, Ill.: Northwestern University Press, 1970), 9. Husserl is thinking of positivism which, by reducing all questions to questions of fact, decapitates philosophy and suppresses the fundamental problems of reason, which Husserl identifies as freedom, the scope of knowledge, value, history, God and immortality. Such fundamental concerns mean that, despite significant differences, Husserl is located within the Neo-Kantian school.

23. For a sympathetic account of the interrelations between Hegelian and Husserlian Phenomenologies, see J. N. Mohanty, *The Possibility of Transcendental Philosophy,* [*Phaenomenologica Volume 98*] (Dordrecht, The Netherlands: Martinus Nijhoff, 1985).

24. Existentialism is notorious for neglecting the intersubjective and social dimensions of existence. As a philosophical movement it reinforced and rendered canonical the atomic individualism and privatism that are the targets of Hegel's critique.

25. Cf. Dennis J. Schmidt, *The Ubiquity of the Finite: Hegel, Heidegger and the Entitlements of Philosophy* (Cambridge, Mass: MIT Press, 1988). Schmidt shows that Hegel cannot be portrayed without caricature as the culmination of the metaphysical tradition, for Hegel has his own criticisms of the tradition. The tradition is no less problematic for Hegel than for Heidegger, which is why Hegel seeks to reconstruct it. Moreover, despite Heidegger's oft reiterated claims to have undermined Hegel qua metaphysics, Schmidt shows that Heidegger's attitude towards Hegel underwent a change from early rejection to later appreciation (92). The puzzle is, if, as Schmidt contends, Heidegger does not succeed in disentangling his thought from Hegel, what is the final import of his so-called destruction or overcoming of metaphysics? It would seem that it is a programmatic statement left unfulfilled, or a project more modest than it sounds since it does not include Hegel.

26. Two recent studies of Heidegger and Hegel, reach drastically different assessments of their relation. Dennis Schmidt, (op. cit.) contends that they are not mutually exclusive, and that talk of one refuting the other is out of place. On the other hand, in David Kolb, *The Critique of Pure Modernity: Hegel, Heidegger and After,* (Chicago: The University of Chicago Press, 1986) develops a reading that has each refuting or undermining the other's claims. For my own modest assessment that is somewhere between these extremes, see "Hegel and Heidegger," in *Hegel and His Critics,* ed. W. Desmond (Albany, N.Y.: SUNY Press, 1989), 135–157.

27. Alexander Kojève, *Introduction to the Reading of Hegel*, ed. Allan Bloom, tr. J. H. Nichols, Jr. (New York: Basic Books, 1969). However, Kojève's reading of Hegel is left-Hegelian, and presupposes the reduction of ontology to philosophical anthropology. Kojève thus presents a truncated account of the *Phenomenology*.

28. Paul Ricoeur, "Existential Phenomenology" in *Husserl: An Analysis of His Phenomenology*, (Evanston, Ill.: Northwestern University Press, 1967).

29. Until the past two years, there were scarcely any treatments of the period between Kant and Hegel in English. Now some primary sources are available in translation such as *Between Kant and Hegel: Texts in the Development of Post-Kantian Idealism*, ed. George di Giovanni and H. S. Harris (Albany, N.Y.: SUNY Press, 1985) which reveal the skeptical attack on Kant. There is also a useful historical monograph on the period, Robert Beiser's *The Fate of Reason* (Cambridge, Mass.: Harvard University Press, 1987).

30. Kant held that actual knowledge is the surmounting of the dualism between reason and sense, or between thought and being. But Kant allows for such surmounting only in 12 cases—the 12 categories. But on such a restriction of thought-being identity to experience, Kant cannot answer the question how critical philosophy itself is possible. Cf. Hegel, *Differenz des Fichte'sche und Schelling'sche System der Philosophie, Hegel Werke:* Theorie Ausgabe, Band 2, (Frankfurt: Suhrkamp Verlag, 1970); ET *The Difference between Fichte's and Schelling's System of Philosophy,* tr. H. S. Harris and W. Cerf (Albany, N.Y.: SUNY Press, 1977), 80.

31. See Edmund Husserl, *The Crisis of European Science,* op. cit. §§28–30.

32. J. N. Mohanty notes that Kant's transcendental philosophy is intended to be a defense of the truth and validity of Newtonian science. (op. cit. xxv.) He follows Husserl in interpreting Kant's transcendental philosophy as a mundane transcendental. On the other hand, Hegel uncovers a phenomenological moment in Kant's transcendental philosophy. Hegel criticizes metaphysics as a pre-critical mode of thought, and follows Kant's view that metaphysics falls within transcendental logic. Hegel writes: "According to my view, metaphysics in any case falls entirely within logic. Here I can cite Kant as my precedent and authority. His critique reduces metaphysics as it has existed until now to a consideration of the understanding and reason. Logic can thus in the Kantian sense be understood so that, beyond the usual content of so-called general logic, what he calls transcendental logic is bound up with it and set out prior to it. In point of content I mean the doctrine of the categories, or reflective concepts, and then of the concepts of reason: analytic and dialectic. These objective thought forms constitute an independent content [corresponding to] the role of the Aristotelian Categories [*organon de categoriis*] or the former ontology. Further, they are independent of one's metaphysical system. They occur in transcendental idealism as much as in dogmatism. The latter calls them determinations of being, while the former calls them determinations of the understanding." (Hegel, "Letter to Niethammer," 23 October 1812, in *Hegel: The Letters,* tr. C. Butler (Bloomington, Ind.: Indiana University Press, 1984), 277.

33. Jean Hyppolite calls attention to this enlargement in the conception of experience in Hegel's *Phenomenology;* it is the point of contact and basis of any compari-

son between Hegelian and Husserlian phenomenologies. See Hyppolite, *Genesis and Structure of Hegel's Phenomenology of Spirit*, tr. S. Cherniak and J. Heckman (Evanston, Ill.: Northwestern University Press, 1974), 8ff.

34. Fichte, J. G., *Erste Einleitung in die Wissenschaftslehre (1797)*, *Fichtes Werke*, I, Hrsg. I. H. Fichte (Berlin: Walter de Gruyter, 1971). ET *Science of Knowledge*, tr. and ed. Peter Heath and John Lachs (New York: Appleton Century Crofts, 1970).

35. The absolute knowledge which is the telos of Hegelian phenomenology is not other than, but implicit within, the natural attitude. See Joseph C. Flay, *Hegel's Quest for Certainty* (Albany, N.Y.: SUNY Press, 1984), Chaps 1–2.

36. Fichte, *Über die Bestimmung des Gelehrten* (1794), FW, VI, Hrsg. I. H. Fichte (Berlin: Walter de Gruyter, 1971), 302.

37. Michael Theunissen, *The Other: Studies in the Social Ontology of Husserl, Heidegger, Sartre and Buber*, tr. Christopher Macann (Cambridge, Mass.: MIT Press, 1984), 1.

38. See David Carr, *Interpreting Husserl* (Boston: Martinus Nijhoff, 1987), 68n. 23. Carr represents Husserl as holding a methodological idealism which finds no problems in speaking of the constitution of the sense of the other by the primordial ego. Intentional analysis brackets ontology, and phenomenology is the self-explication of the ego; in Ricoeur's extreme formulation, phenomenology is egology without ontology. But the question is whether such a sharp and neat separation between epistemology and ontology is possible. Hegel, who encountered and was sharply critical of such subjective idealism, thinks it problematic.

39. Emmanuel Levinas, *Totality and Infinity*, tr. A. Lingis (Pittsburgh: Duquesne University Press, 1969), 43 [hereafter cited as TI].

40. Ibid. 36–7.

41. Ibid. 45.

42. Ibid. 46.

43. TI 50. Italics mine.

44. Ibid. 51.

45. Steven Smith interprets the phenomenological descriptions of *Totality and Infinity* as negations of phenomenology and ontology. He writes "The idea of the infinite is presented in such a way that as to make clear that its overflowing, far from fitting into the grammar of ontology or phenomenology, disrupts and subverts the system of disclosures to which the grammar is keyed. The other is a phenomenological nonobject, absolutely nonevident and independent of any intentional correlation.... Levinas uses the language of ontology to express an anti-ontology.... Speaking within a theoretical vocabulary, Levinas registers a nontheoretical exigency, the claim of moral life; and the paradoxical antiphenomenology and anti-ontology of *Totality and Infinity* are to be taken, not as phenomenological and ontological theses, but as point-

ers from phenomenology and ontology to that which they fail to express." Steven G. Smith, "Reason as One for Another: Moral and Theoretical Argument in the Philosophy of Levinas," in *Face to Face with Levinas,* ed. Richard Cohen (Albany, N.Y.: SUNY Press, 1986), 55–56.

46. See Jacques Derrida, "Violence and Metaphysics," in *Writing and Difference,* tr. A. Bass (Chicago: University of Chicago Press, 1978), 99, 126.

47. See Frederick C. Beiser, *The Fate of Reason: German Philosophy from Kant to Fichte* (Cambridge, Mass.: Harvard University Press, 1987), 122ff. Jacobi stated his position in his *Brief an Fichte* (1799); English Translation "Open Letter to Fichte, 1799," tr. Diana I. Behler, in *Philosophy of German Idealism,* ed. Ernst Behler, [*The German Library: Volume 23*] (New York: Continuum, 1987), 119–142.

48. See Reinhold Aschenberg, "Der Wahrheitsbegriff in Hegels 'Phänomenologie des Geistes'" in *Die ontologische Option,* hrsg. Klaus Hartmann (Berlin: Walter de Gruyter, 1976), 230. Johannes Heinrichs maintains that the *Phenomenology* is a hermeneutical presentation of the Hegelian system which is co-original or equiprimordial with the logic. See Johannes Heinrichs, *Die Logik der Phänomenologie des Geistes* (Bonn: Bouvier Verlag, 1974), 515ff.

49. The irony is not lost on Derrida, who claims that Levinas' opposition to Hegel conceals his own proximity to Hegel's position: "Levinas is very close to Hegel, much closer than he admits, and at the very moment when he is apparently opposed to Hegel in the most radical fashion. " Jacques Derrida, op. cit. 99.

50. This is evident from Fichte's First Introduction to *Wissenschaftslehre,* and from the introduction to Hegel's *Phenomenology of Spirit.* For contemporary discussions, cf. Walter Jaeschke, *Die Vernunft in der Religion* (Stuttgart: Fromman-Holzboog 1986); English Translation: *Reason in Religion: The Foundations of Hegel's Philosophy of Religion,* tr. J. M. Stewart and P. C. Hodgson (Berkeley: University of California Press, 1990). William Maker, "Hegel's Phenomenology as Introduction to Science," *CLIO* 10:4 (1981): 381–397; see also Maker, "Reason and the Problem of Modernity," *The Philosophical Forum,* vol. 18, no. 4 (Summer 1987): 275–303; Maker, "Beginning" in *Essays on Hegel's Logic,* ed. G. di Giovanni (Albany, N.Y.: SUNY Press, 1990); Stanley Rosen, *The Ancients and the Moderns: Rethinking Modernity* (New Haven: Yale University Press, 1989), Chaps. 3, 7, 9; Tom Rockmore, "Foundationalism and Hegelian Logic," *OWL of Minerva,* vol. 21, no. 1 (Fall 1989); see also Richard D. Winfield, *Reason and Justice* (Albany, N.Y.: SUNY Press, 1988).

51. The standard view of a necessary development from Kant to Hegel that presents Hegel as the culmination of German Idealism, is classically expressed by Richard Kroner, *Von Kant bis Hegel,* (Tübingen: J. C. B. Mohr, 1921/24). A different reading of this "development" is set forth by Walter Schulz, *Die Vollendung des Deutschen Idealismus in der Spätphilosophie Schellings* (Pfullingen, Germany: Neske, 1955). On the other hand, the standard developmental hypothesis slights Fichte, and completely overlooks his later development that responds to Schelling and Hegel. For this story, cf. Wolfgang Janke, "Fichte," article in *Theologische*

Realenzyklopädie Band XI, 169ff. Janke thinks that it is more accurate to speak of a threefold completion of German idealism, in Hegel, as well as in the neglected later writings of Schelling and Fichte. Attempts to portray post-Kantian German Idealism in terms of a linear development, are unnecessarily reductionistic.

52. Both Ludwig Siep (op. cit.) and Edith Düsing (op. cit.) bracket the question of Fichte's later development, and treat recognition in the earlier writings of Fichte, and then its appropriation and transformation by Hegel.

53. H. S. Harris signals its importance when he writes: "The importance of the concept of 'recognition' in the *Phänomenologie des Geistes* can scarcely be overestimated since it is the root element of the concept of *Geist* itself." CR 229.

54. Hegel first uses the concept of recognition in reference to the recognition of one philosophy by another. Skepticism is a denial of philosophy, an unphilosophy in which philosophy supposedly cannot find recognition. But Hegel denies this, for the demands which skepticism brings forth are rational demands. That is why genuine philosophy can and must incorporate skepticism as a critical principle. See the Introduction to the Critical Journal of Philosophy in *Between Kant and Hegel*, tr. George di Giovanni and H. S. Harris (Albany, N.Y.: SUNY Press, 1985), 276. [Hereafter cited as BTKH.]

55. Descartes himself is no skeptic. Nevertheless the *cogito ergo sum* is defended as a rational intuition, which implies immediacy is one of Descartes' criteria of truth. When Descartes's arguments for God are set aside, immediacy alone remains. Such immediate intuition becomes the sole criterion of truth in British empiricism, e. g., Locke and Hume are both skeptical Cartesians who presuppose immediacy. Hegel's preference for ancient skepticism over the modern rests upon the fact that ancient skepticism attacked such presentational immediacy. To every immediate thesis there is an antithesis of equal weight and validity. Equipollence undermines immediacy and shows the necessity of either utter skepticism or acceptance of the claims of rational mediation.

56. Hegel, *Enzyklopädie*, §§39, 81 Zusatz. ET 119.

57. Husserl, *Crisis*, op. cit. 131–132. When the theoretical world of science is shown to presuppose the intersubjective communication of the life-world, the so-called objective world of science seems drawn into the subjective-relative sphere. This withdrawal shows the groundlessness of philosophy, the dependence of *episteme* upon *doxa*.

PART TWO
FICHTE

TWO

BETWEEN KANT AND FICHTE

Since Kant did not mention, much less raise the problem of the other, why begin a study of this topic with Kant? The answer is twofold: on the one hand, Kant's critical philosophy brings to fulfillment the Enlightenment critique of the metaphysical tradition, by raising the question of the scope and possibility of metaphysical knowledge. On the other hand, Kant's critical solution is only partially successful, and leads to an impasse between the ancients and the moderns. Unless this impasse is appreciated, the post-Kantian German Idealists such as Fichte and Hegel are usually regarded as relapsing into pre-critical metaphysics. For example, Hegel's defense of the ontological argument, and his rejection of Kant's demand for a prior verification of the possibility of knowledge, make him appear as a return to pre-critical epistemology and (dogmatic) metaphysics.

However, this widespread impression is a false one that fails to appreciate, much less engage, the concerns of post-Kantian German Philosophy. Hegel regards the search for foundations of knowledge from Descartes through Kant as a misguided attempt to impose on philosophy a pre-scientific, extra-conceptual method of proof borrowed from mathematics. The demand for the prior demonstration of the possibility of knowledge ends in the cul-de-sac of 'having to know before you know'. Hegel rejects Kant's transcendental and prolegomatic pretensions to neutrality vis a vis metaphysical disputes, and Kant's belief that such disputes can be settled without making any epistemological or ontological claims. On the contrary, the Critical philosophy, while pretending to be a second-order enterprise dealing with conditions of possibility, in fact is an interested party to the first-order metaphysical disputes concerning knowledge, freedom, world and God. Kant's critical philosophy is shot through with unexamined assumptions concerning the nature, scope and conditions of knowledge.

Kant's putative second-order neutrality is exposed as a first-order partisanship concerning metaphysics by the question concerning the status of the *Critique*: Is the critique of knowledge itself knowledge? If so, it is knowledge in some sense other than it purports to establish. This self-contradictory "uncritical criticism" signifies that the foundational problems of philosophy cannot be settled by a priori foundational treatment. Such an analysis points in the direction taken by Hegel, namely, that philosophical proof and demonstration must be immanent within philosophy itself. Philosophical knowledge cannot be determined in advance or rest upon external supports; it must be self-justifying. Therefore the transcendental-critical posture of searching for conditions a priori, or knowing before one knows, must be rejected in favor of the actual execution of a philosophical project. It is only by the execution—or the failure of such—that the question of possibility can be fairly and undogmatically decided.

Thus, rather than remaining ignorant of or unaffected by Kant's challenge, Hegel must be viewed as attempting to respond to it. This does not make his response *ipso facto* successful. But there are perhaps only two types of criticism that are possible: (1) To show that Hegel's project of demonstration residing immanent in the execution of his project is unacceptable because it may involve basic difficulties that give rise to critical reservations,[1] and (2) To accept Hegel's systematic project as reasonable in itself, but to show that Hegel fails to carry it out consistently and thus fails to conform to his own criteria.[2] The point I wish to stress here is that, whether successful or not, Hegel has not lost sight of the critical Enlightenment demands concerning knowledge, philosophy, and religion, and does not return to pre-critical modes of thought. Since he accepts these demands—but not necessarily Kant's way of meeting them—it is not Hegel's intention to repeat the traditional views or merely incorporate them into his philosophy. The quarrel between the ancients and the moderns must be mediated, and such mediation requires going beyond both, and breaking new ground.

The new ground is prepared in the discussion that went on in German philosophy between Kant and Hegel. Fichte's analysis of the quarrel between the ancients and the moderns shows it to be more than a quarrel; it is an impasse. The dispute between dogmatism and idealism over first principles is, he claims, theoretically undecidable, and for this reason it must be shifted to the practical and existential terrain of human interests. This break with the abstract intellectualism underlying both rationalism and empiricism, opens the world of everyday life to philosophy. The opening of this door is the reason why historical consciousness and the problem of the other became issues in the discussion after Kant. Fichte and Hegel make major contributions to both issues.

The fact that the other emerges as a distinct topic, indicates a dissatisfaction with and distancing from Kant's transcendental program. The emergence of the other points to the need to overcome Kant's formalism and abstract transcendentalism.[3] Kant's transcendental subjectivity and freedom must be historicized, contextualized, and these qualifications require that it be loosened up, be capable of receiving influence as well as shaping and influencing. This loosening up has several facets.

The historicity and social-intersubjectivity of pure reason must be acknowledged. First, the transcendental must be conceived as having an other, namely the empirical, to which it stands in some sort of reciprocal relation. The language of transcendental *constitution* of the empirical is one-sided, and must be given up in favor of a correlation between the transcendental and empirical. Second, Kantian formal-transcendental subjectivity must be expanded and deepened to an intersubjective conception. The formalism of Kant's concept of freedom and categorical imperative must be overcome by grounding these in concrete social-historical situations and praxis. Thus the theoretical and practical correctives of transcendentalism converge and result in a transformation of the transcendental subject into a social and historical intersubjectivity.

Philosophy is not simply a view from nowhere, but is rather embedded in a concrete social-historical context and is expressive of human interests. Since reason is embodied, it is historical, but it does not know itself until it understands its historical development. Thus its history must be reconstructed; the genetic history (*Sinngenesis*) of reason is a reconstruction and clarification of the 'deep structure' of actual history. The question of intersubjectivity, or the problem of the other, emerges as a result of this contextualizing of reason and transcendental philosophy. The concept of recognition (*Anerkennung*) points towards a life-world ontology implicit in and presupposed by Kant's second and third forms of the categorical imperative, namely, respect for humanity and the social kingdom of ends. Kant's transcendentalism is restricted to justifying and grounding scientific knowledge. However, its justification presupposes, rather than explains the life-world. The social is not a consequence, but rather a prior concrete condition of Kant's practical philosophy.

The following analysis proceeds in four stages: (1) The Kantian transcendental is theoretically problematic in that Kant's account of the conditions of possibility of knowledge does not reveal how such a transcendental account itself is possible. Kant may tacitly assume the very intellectual intuition that he denies. The self-consciousness of freedom is problematic for Kant, since transcendental freedom is sharply distinguished from everything phenomenal. (2) The Post-Kantian discussion focuses on the possibility of critical transcendental philosophy itself, the elimination of Kant's dualism between reason and sensibility, noumena and phenomena, and the reformulation of Kant's three critiques as a coherent system of philosophy deriving from a single first principle. Philosophy cannot rely upon external transcendental grounding, but must be self-grounding (Reinhold). (3) Reinhold's foundationalist project collapses under skeptical attack which forces him to abandon it, giving rise to a crisis in first principles. Fichte seeks to resolve this crisis on the non-theoretical grounds of human interests. Fichte regards the transcendental ego merely as an hypothesis that admits only a pragmatic justification. Fichte propounds a critical idealism, rather than a dogmatic metaphysical idealism. (4) But a critical idealism requires phenomenological grounding and introduction. Philosophy requires a phenomenological introduction to avoid lapsing into dogmatism and metaphysics. Transcendental 'deduction' requires a pragmatic history of spirit as its concrete correlate. The "other" to the transcendental must be phenomenologically described, in order to give otherness its due. Fichte turns to ordinary consciousness and thematizes the problem of intersubjectivity (*Anerkennung*). Although Fichte follows Kant in maintaining the primacy of freedom, he denies that the consciousness of freedom is immediate. Rather, the consciousness of freedom requires intersubjective mediation, i.e., mediation by other. For this reason Fichte identifies recognition as a transcendental condition of natural law.

THE PROBLEMATIC TRANSCENDENTAL IN KANT

Kant provided a metaphysics of experience that is a third alternative to the skepticism of Hume and the dogmatism of continental rationalism. Against Humean skepticism, Kant sought to secure the universality and necessity of judgements by grounding these in the a priori formal structures of transcendental subjectivity, i.e., space-time as pure forms of intuition, and the categories of the understanding. Against Wolffian dogmatism, Kant restricted the application of the categories to the limits of possible experience, and held that the attempt to make determinations beyond experience produced only the transcendental illusion of knowledge. Consequently he maintained that the grand themes of traditional metaphysics—the self, world, and God—are beyond the bounds of possible knowledge. Such special metaphysics (*metaphysica specialis*) is no longer possible as science. Instead Kant admits only a critical metaphysics of experience.

Kant characterized his alternative as a denial of knowledge in order to make room for practical faith. This denial he subsequently elaborated into the theory of the primacy of practical reason over theoretical reason. Kant reintroduced on practical grounds certain metaphysical questions concerning God, freedom, and immortality. He sought to make his treatment of such themes consistent with his rejection of special metaphysics by interpreting them as non-cognitive, i.e., as constitutive of praxis. However, such principles can be only regulative, or limit principles of theoretical knowledge.

Kant's critical solution to the problem of metaphysics raises several questions. I shall focus on two. First, the question of the status of the critical philosophy and its explanatory apparatus. Kant's discussion of the antinomies indicates that he held it possible to show the pointlessness of certain metaphysical debates, without making any cognitive or metaphysical claims of his own. Kant's critical solutions to the cosmological antinomies are not supposed to be metaphysics, i.e, a party to the metaphysical dispute, but rather 'neutral' second-order inquiry into its conditions. Kant is not 'doing' metaphysics but merely critique.

Such claims provoke several questions: Is not the critique of knowledge itself knowledge? It does not appear to be knowledge in the restricted and qualified sense that it purports to establish. But if critique is not knowledge, how can Kant pretend to adjudicate opposing cognitive and metaphysical claims? On the other hand, if critique is knowledge, then the examination of knowledge turns out to be itself knowledge, i.e., an act which is supposedly under 'neutral' critical investigation. But since the examination of knowledge is itself knowledge, it can no longer be neutral but is itself a party to the dispute concerning the nature and limits of knowledge. Kant is in the position of (uncritically) knowing before he (critically) knows.

But even if we assume that critique is successful on its own terms, Kant fails to show how such critical knowledge of the conditions of possible knowledge is itself possible. Moreover, his denial of intellectual intuition seems to undercut the possibility of any critical-cognitive justification of critique itself. Fichte held that Kant tacitly relies upon intellectual intuition in order to do critique at all.[4] If, as Kant thinks, there is no intellectual intuition, there would be no access to the transcendental grounding region, and the very possibility of critical philosophy itself is left hanging in the air.[5] Kant would then be vulnerable to the charge that pure reason, the transcendental ego, etc., are abstract hypostases, or mythic conceptions.[6]

Second, Kant's critical solution to metaphysics also creates problems for his practical philosophy.[7] For example, it seems impossible to have knowledge of freedom, for to know means to objectify and impose conditions, including phenomenal necessity. The knowledge of freedom—were such possible—would seem to transform it into its opposite. The consciousness of freedom is problematic given Kant's denial of rational self-knowledge in his paralogisms, and his salvaging of transcendental freedom from phenomenal necessity by assigning freedom to the noumenal realm. According to the first *Critique,* we can *conceive* freedom as the possibility of self-originated causality, but we cannot *know* that there is such freedom. Yet, according to Kant's practical philosophy, such freedom exists, and practical reason is held to be primary in relation to theoretical reason. Kant may not be consistent—in the *Grundlegung* he holds that there is a non-moral consciousness of intellectual spontaneity,[8] which appears to be a cognitive claim—but his official doctrine in the second *Critique* is that the consciousness of freedom is mediated exclusively and non-cognitively by the moral law. The moral law is the *ratio cognoscendi* of freedom, and freedom is the *ratio essendi* of the moral law.[9]

What is at issue is the possibility of the transcendental knowledge of freedom (or noumenal realm). The question is whether the existence of freedom presupposed and exhibited in the practical philosophy is consistent with the non-cognitive position Kant staked out in the first *Critique.* In the second *Critique* freedom is a postulate of practical reason which implies additional postulates, namely, God and immortality.[10] However, Kant contends that these postulates have no cognitive status because they do not amount to or extend knowledge to a supersensible realm. This claim is controversial, since it is inconsistent to deny access to the transcendent—e.g., freedom and God—on theoretical grounds, and to affirm it on practical grounds.[11] After all, there are not two reasons, but one reason with different interests and employments.

REACTION TO KANT: REINHOLD'S QUEST FOR CERTAINTY

The story of the development of German Idealism between Kant and Hegel has only recently begun to receive attention, and some of the texts of the German discussion have been translated into English.[12] Many of the issues debated during this period are still with us. The discussion focused on difficulties in Kant's philosophy, the problematic distinction between phenomena and noumena, the related conception of the *Ding an sich,* and the Kantian doctrine of the twofold origins and/or bases of knowledge, namely understanding and sense. Such dualisms threatened to undermine the Kantian idea of knowledge as a synthesis, which transcendental philosophy must justify.

The distinction between phenomena and noumena, originally formulated methodologically rather than ontologically, tends to turn into an ontological dualism and end in a subjectivism. Kant is then interpreted as dogmatically claiming that there are things in themselves, but inconsistently denying these are knowable. Moreover, the phenomena/noumena distinction, interpreted ontologically, has unfortunate implications for the relation between reason and sensibility. If reason and sense are utterly different, it is difficult to see how they can form a synthesis or unity. But without such a synthesis, knowledge is impossible, for knowledge is precisely this synthesis.[13] In view of such problems Kant's reply to Hume was only a beginning, and by itself, insufficient. Kant's transcendental strategy requires the reduction of knowledge to a single source. Kant however retains a transcendental idealism or critical realism that requires a distinction between phenomena and things in themselves.[14]

K. L. Reinhold began as a critic of Kant who subsequently became one of Kant's leading supporters and popularizers. While championing Kant, Reinhold thought that the Critical philosophy was incomplete because it lacked systematic form and rested upon certain unexamined presuppositions. Kant was insufficiently critical with respect to the possibility of transcendental knowledge, i.e., the kind of knowledge which makes the critique of reason possible. Reinhold demanded that transcendental philosophy explain not only the conditions of possible knowledge, but also that it explain itself. Philosophy must not only justify knowledge by inquiry into the conditions of its possibility, it must also justify itself. For Reinhold such justification can only occur in a system, which is unified by reference to and derivation from a single ultimate principle. By deriving everything from a single first principle or

Grundsatz, the alleged incompleteness of Kant's system, as well as the dualisms between reason and sensibility, and between phenomena and noumena, are to be overcome. And critical philosophy would be transformed into a system—a task which Kant hinted at but failed to deliver.

Reinhold was searching for a foundation of some sort. However his entire effort remains at the level of prolegomena, and Reinhold characterizes his enterprise as a propadeutic.[15] Thereby he condemns it to incomplete, prolegomatic externality. Even so, Reinhold wants a foundation for philosophy: "...philosophical reason can only find rest in a ground which is ultimate in an absolute sense..."[16] However it is not clear how Reinhold understands this foundation; it is not meant in a metaphysical sense. Nor is it a logical principle such as identity and/or contradiction, for that would amount to an empty formalism. Thus, to avoid formalism, the foundation must be real or material.[17] According to Reinhold, the foundation that Kant's philosophy presupposes, but does not make explicit, is representation (*Vorstellung*).[18] Representation distinguishes subject and object while relating them in a fundamental unity. In Reinhold's view, representation is the transcendental concept that overcomes the Kantian dualism between reason and sense.

However, the representation does not yet 'represent' the bedrock foundational stratum. Reinhold's ultimate foundation is the *Urfactum* of consciousness itself. Reinhold isolates consciousness as such as the representation of representation. As the representation of representation, consciousness grasps itself with immediate self-certainty, without any mediation, postulation or inference. It is this representation of representation that is the ultimate "*Tatsache des Bewusstseins,*" the ultimate condition of possibility of critical transcendental philosophy:

> My foundation is consciousness; and while consciousness itself is certainly not all that I offer as a scientific foundation, what I do offer rests on nothing else but consciousness.[19]

Reinhold's proposal is both complex and without detailed execution. Nevertheless, if consciousness is the *Urfactum,* the representation of representation, the formal transcendental subject is transformed into a concrete subject, and thus, despite his foundationalism, Reinhold prepares the way for a turn to consciousness and history.

Reinhold observes that first principles cannot be proven or derived from other anterior principles. Thus he appears to rest his case upon the self-evidence of consciousness as his first principle, and this appears to be Cartesian. However while Reinhold claims that first principles are autonomous and self-evident, he is also critical of the identification of epistemology as first philosophy in the continental tradition from Descartes through Kant. It is a blunder to take up the problem of knowledge before doing a phenomenological investigation of the representation.[20] Reinhold's inquiry into the representation "has nothing to do with with a metaphysical or psychological inquiry into the subject or causes of a representation."[21] The questions of knowledge (modern first philosophy) and metaphysics (classical first philosophy) must be bracketed in order to avoid dogmatic metaphysical prejudices. Transcendental philosophy requires phenomenology in order to complete its project, by explaining not only knowledge of objects, but its own conditions of possibility. Phenomenology is to ground transcendental philosophy, not only by preventing its lapse into pre-critical or dogmatic modes of thought, but by making it possible to give an account of the possibility of transcendental knowledge itself.

Reinhold's actual execution of his programmatic statements left much to be desired. In an essay called Anesidemus,[22] Schulze attacked Reinhold's concept of consciousness as the representation of representation, or the Urtatsache. Schulze singled out the strange concept of a "transcendental fact" or transcendental experience. It was not difficult to show that any fact (Tatsache) includes contingency, and for this reason is subject to doubt. But what is contingent and doubtful cannot serve as a foundation. Second, Schulze wondered whether Reinhold's bracketing of metaphysics, in order to describe the representation, did not amount to a forfeiture of the question of truth.[23] Moreover, Reinhold frequently changed his program; the result was a series of quite different prolegomena. Hegel poured scorn on Reinhold's multiple and varied prolegomatic attempts at founding and grounding, as a seemingly endless series of prolegomena that postpone, rather than provide justification for, philosophy as science (Wissenschaft).

Despite such devastating criticism, Reinhold was influential in shaping the post-Kantian development of German idealism. His project of overcoming the Kantian dualism between reason and sensibility by developing philosophy out of a single first principle or Grundsatz, and his attempt to provide phenomenological grounding for his transcendental program, were taken seriously by Fichte, Schelling and Hegel, and framed their common project. Moreover, these thinkers acknowledged historical consciousness, which resulted in a further transformation of transcendental philosophy, with implications at once pervasive and elusive.

FICHTE AND THE CRISIS IN FIRST PRINCIPLES

First Introduction to Wissenschaftslehre

According to Maimon, Kant's dualism between reason and sense both creates the need for the transcendental turn (to escape Hume's skepticism) and makes it impossible. What would a transcendental program of philosophy look like if, following Reinhold, one abandons Kant's dualisms between reason and sense, noumena and phenomena? The point is that the concept of 'transcendental' seems to be inherently dualistic in that something transcends and something else is transcended. If these dualisms are abandoned, the very meaning of "transcendental" seems to undergo a transformation. One possibility is that when transcendental idealism eliminates the thing in itself, it is transformed into absolute idealism. The intellectual intuition defended by Fichte provides access to and supports the unqualified primacy of subjectivity. Being is derivative from subjectivity, or being simply is subjectivity, which is the foundational principle of metaphysical idealism, the new substratum or *hypokeimenon*.[24] It is a question of carrying out Descartes' program without lapsing into Cartesian solipsism. This is the way Fichte is usually interpreted. But this interpretation is misleading.

Fichte remains faithful to the program, but not the terminology, of Kant's critical-transcendental idealism. This means that Fichte offers not a metaphysical, but a critical philosophy, which does not eliminate, but rather reinterprets the thing in itself. Moreover, in his earliest formulations, Fichte does not conceive the transcendental ego as a metaphysical entity. Fichte's critical idealism is to be distinguished from dogmatic metaphysical idealism that posits a 'self in itself'. Fichte's critical idealism leaves open questions of ontological or metaphysical interpretation, including the interpretation of the ego and the controversial 'thing in itself'.[25] This idealism has a more modest relation to empirical phenomena than the unilateral formal determination implied in Kant's concept of constitution. Although Fichte continues something like Kant's transcendental deduction, the transcendental subject, its categories, rules and principles, are treated in a non-foundational, hypothetical mode.

Fichte's Antifoundationalism

Like Reinhold, Fichte observes that first principles or *Grundsätze* do not allow of being proven or defined,[26] for if they could be proven, the proof would have to proceed in terms of premises already known. Consequently, to prove a first principle would amount to deriving it from something else. But what is thus derivative cannot serve as a first principle, because a first principle must not itself require a ground, but rather founds all the rest. Hence mediation does not apply to first principles. A first principle must therefore be immediate, i.e., self-evident.

But a simple appeal to immediate self evidence fails to establish a first principle. In his introduction to *Wissenschaftslehre*[27] Fichte shows that immediate self-evidence is problematic because there is a plurality of possible first principles, each claiming to be self-evident. For example, Fichte observes that there is a conflict of first principles between dogmatic materialism and idealism.[28] These rival and opposing metaphysics can account for and refute the other, provided that its first principle be granted. But that is precisely the point at issue. Although each may lay claim to self-evidence for its first principle, such immediate self-evidence provides no basis for deciding which is true, or which should be adopted. Any reasoning or arguments adduced for either side are circular, because reasoning proceeds from and in the light of a first principle. But what is at stake is precisely the determination of the first principle itself:

> There is no rational basis to decide this question, for we are not speaking here of the addition of a link to a chain of reasoning...rather we are here concerned with the beginning of the whole chain itself, which, as an absolute first act, depends simply on the freedom of thought...[29]

Fichte claims that the conflict between first principles is theoretically undecidable. The choice is decidable only on practical and existential grounds, i.e., by reference and appeal to interest. The difference between the systems of philosophical explanation reflects a difference of interest; as Fichte says, what sort of philosophy one chooses depends on what sort of human being one is, i.e., it depends on interests.[30] This determination of philosophy by reference to interest is Fichte's version of the primacy of the practical. Fichte not only continues Kant's theme of the interests of reason, but radicalizes it. "The controversy between the idealist and the dogmatist is whether the independence of the ego is to be sacrificed to the independence of things, or whether the independence of things is to be sacrificed to the independence of the ego."[31] In a passage which foreshadows Heidegger's distinction between inauthentic and authentic existence, Fichte writes:

> There are...two types of human being. Some who have not yet raised themselves to the full consciousness of their freedom and unqualified independence, find themselves only in the representation of things; they have only that dispersed consciousness which attaches to objects.... Their self-image is reflected back to them only by things, like a mirror; if these were taken from them, their 'self' would be lost as well. For the sake of their self they cannot give up belief in the independence of things, for they themselves exist only if things do.[32]

The point I wish to stress however, is not Fichte's anticipation of Heidegger, but rather his anti-Cartesianism and anti-Kantianism. The reference to human interests in determining the choice of philosophical first principle shows that the so-called 'transcendental turn' does *not* disclose a single apodictic foundation for knowledge or provide certain access to a foundational transcendental subject or substratum (*hypokeimenon*).[33] Fichte explicitly rejects such an interpretation of the so-called absolute ego:

> There is nothing in the ego but its actions, and the ego itself is nothing other than action [*Handeln*] reverting upon itself. I would not even say that the ego is something acting [*ein Handelndes*], in order to avoid the appearance

of a *substratum*.... It has been a frequent misinterpretation of the *Wissenschaftslehre* that it posits as the foundation of philosophy, an ego as a substratum which exists without the doing of an ego, an ego which is a mere thing in itself.[34]

Whatever transcendental consciousness may be, it is not an ultimate metaphysical foundation to be attained at a single stroke. Since there is no absolute ego qua substance, but only an act, Reinhold's dream of a deductive system derived from a single real first principle is excluded.

Although the *Wissenschaftslehre* is a system, it is not a deductive system in a mathematical sense which proceeds from general to specific.[35] For the second and third hypotheses (the non-ego and the opposition between ego and non-ego) are not so much derived from the first (the ego), as conditions of it. The third, which is supposed to be a synthesis, articulates the opposition of the first two. Yet the first and second, taken by themselves, are abstractions from the third. Thus Fichte's inquiry is not so much deductive as it is regressive, namely to conditions of possibility. True, it moves from the more abstract and indeterminate principles towards the concrete and determinate, but the latter include and ground the former, which are abstractions. Hence, it is misleading to speak of the *Wissenschaftslehre* as 'proceeding from a single first principle'. That makes it appear formal and deductive, when in fact Fichte's concern is to overcome just such formalism.

Fichte's discussion therefore is antifoundational in the following senses: (1) There is no unproblematic foundational first principle. Instead there is a plurality of contenders, and this very pluralism tends to discredit the idea of a single foundational principle. (2) First principles can neither be proven nor demonstrated. (3) Although such principles appear to be immediately certain and self-evident, such immediacy is refuted as a guarantee of truth by the existence of an opposite, mutually exclusive first principle. Immediacy, certainty and coherence are insufficient criteria of truth. (4) The selection or choice of first principles cannot be settled on theoretical grounds, but only on practical-existential grounds. Knowledge is reflective of human interests. (5) Fichte does not interpret the transcendental ego ontologically, but rather as a hypothesis. Such considerations undermine the traditional conception of first philosophy as pure theoretical epistemology. They prepare the way for a post-transcendental, or rather, pre-transcendental step.

FROM TRANSCENDENTAL PHILOSOPHY TO
THE PRAGMATIC HISTORY OF SPIRIT

Although the starting point of the *Wissenschaftslehre* is the formal principles of thought, namely identity, contradiction, and sufficient reason, Fichte moves quickly to introduce the doctrine of the ego as their basis. For the principles do not simply float in air, they must have a basis, namely the ego. This takes them out of any pure logical realm and identifies them as acts performed by the ego.[36] The ego is required to unify the three ultimate logical principles, identity, difference and sufficient reason. The ego is thus constructed or deduced as the unifying ground of the logical principles, which prevents these principles from being construed merely formally. Rather they are the elementary acts of thesis, antithesis, and synthesis.[37] Fichte's constantly reiterated theme is that knowledge is not a given but rather a synthesis, i.e., an accomplishment. Synthesis in turn requires opposing and contrasting elements. Therefore the ego must be opposed by a second element or a non-ego. Hence the synthetic unity Fichte is after is the unity of ego and non-ego. This is not an ego in an anthropological-psychological sense, but rather a speculative totality constituted by the clash of principles.[38]

However, Fichte does not develop an ontological interpretation of the ego and the deductions following from it. His transcendental ego has no existential ontological status, not even that of a substratum.[39] Instead it is hypothetical.[40] The first part of the first *Wissenschaftslehre* remains a statement of method, or a set of heuristic principles. Unlike Kant, the transcendental is not ontologically constitutive of its objects, even with respect to their formal structure.[41] Instead Fichte conceives the relation between transcendental and empirical differently, not as a radically legislative a priori, but a 'soft' a priori. If the transcendental 'apparatus' is an hypothesis, then questions of truth and validity cannot be settled simply at the level of transcendental deduction and argument. A post-transcendental move is required.

This step occurs in what Fichte calls "the pragmatic history of *Geist.*"[42] The pragmatic history is a prototype for Hegel's immanent description of ordinary consciousness in his *Phenomenology of Spirit.*[43] In order to understand this, the double series of the *Wissenschaftslehre* must be appreciated. Fichte explains, "In the *Wissenschaftslehre* there are two different series of spiritual action [des geistigen Handelns], that of the ego, which the philosopher observes, and the observations made by the philosopher."[44] To be sure, the distinction between the ordinary consciousness and the phenomenological observer is not very clearly formulated, and we may doubt whether Fichte allows ordinary consciousness to 'speak for itself'. The meaning of ordinary consciousness may be pre-determined by the philosopher observing and interpreting it. Nevertheless, Fichte at least signals a phenomenological intent, and prepares for Hegel's distinction between the experience of ordinary consciousness and the phenomenological observer(s) (or We) of ordinary consciousness.[45] Fichte elaborates:

> The philosopher says in *his* name: everything which is for the ego, is through the ego. The ego itself says...as truly as I exist and live, there exists something outside of me which is not the result of my own doing.... The first standpoint is that of speculation, the latter is that of life...[46]

The problem is to determine the relation of the two series, especially since Fichte's so-called idealism is supposed to reduce everything to immanence in consciousness, and thus reduce the two series to one. Were such a reduction to occur, Fichte would have failed by his own conception of the philosophical task, and would lapse into an a-historical dogmatism. For the essence of dogmatism is that there is but one series, one kind of explanation. In contrast, Fichte's position is that of a critical phenomenological idealism:

> In the *Wissenschaftslehre* there are two distinct series of spiritual action: that of the ego which the philosopher observes, and that of the observations of the philosopher. In opposing philosophies...there is only one line of thinking, namely that of the philosopher, and the content of his thought is not itself understood to be thinking and reflective, but rather as mere *Stoff*.[47]

Thus there are two levels of analysis, the natural consciousness and the philosophical consciousness; the latter reflecting on and interpreting the former. The ordinary consciousness is described and explained by the philosophical, and the philosophical consciousness depends on and is rooted in the experience of ordinary consciousness.

In asserting the 'dependence' of the philosophical consciousness on ordinary consciousness, Fichte does not claim that philosophy and its explanations are reducible to ordinary language. However, he implies that, rather than displacing or eliminating, ordinary consciousness and its experience, philosophy presupposes it. Hence Fichte construes the phenomenological and descriptive pragmatic history of Spirit as part of the task of philosophy:

> Therefore it describes the entire way which the former [viz., ordinary consciousness] has taken, but in reverse order. And the philosophical reflection, which can merely follow its subject, but prescribe to it no law, necessarily takes the same same direction.[48]

Philosophical reflection is a reconstruction in thought of the experience of ordinary or natural consciousness. Philosophical reflection cannot render the natural consciousness wholly transparent nor can it ultimately displace the latter.[49] Both standpoints are necessary, and irreducible to a higher unity. Thus the *Wissenschaftslehre* is a critical-phenomenological, not a dogmatic, or metaphysical, idealism:

> ...the critical idealism prevailing in our theory...runs...counter to dogmatic idealism and realism, in that it shows how neither does the mere activity of the self provide the ground of the reality of the not-self, nor the mere activity of the not-self [provide] the ground of passivity in the self; but when confronted with the question it is called upon to answer, namely what then may be the ground of the interplay assumed between the two, it is resigned to its own ignorance, and shows us that investigation of this point lies beyond the bounds of theory. In its account of presentation [*Vorstellung*], it

proceeds neither from an absolute activity of the self, nor of the not-self, but rather from a determinacy which is at the same time a determining.... As to what this determining may determine, the theory offers no decision at all; and in virtue of this incompleteness, we are driven on beyond theory to a practical part of the *Wissenschaftslehre*.[50]

Given the theoretical undecidability between putative first principles, the *Wissenschaftslehre* divides into two series, an ideal and a real, or a theoretical and a practical series. Its unity is not given a priori or at the outset, but rather is a task, a *Sollen*. The ideal ground and the real ground of the system cannot be finally identified or unified. There is only *striving* after unity, which, Fichte explains, is the meaning of the Kantian claim that reason is practical: "In the pure ego reason is not practical; neither is it practical in the ego as intelligence; it is practical only insofar as it strives to unite the two...a practical philosophy emerges by going through in descending order the stages which one must ascend in theoretical philosophy."[51] This suggests that the two series are related as theoretical and practical, or philosophical and ordinary consciousness. But the primacy of the practical means that the two series cannot be reduced to a final unity. This anomaly poses the question of the meaning and significance of Fichte's pragmatic history.

The *Wissenschaftslehre* provides a genetic or ideal history of consciousness. Kant's a-historical categories must be reconsidered, for the categories themselves have a genesis of sense, i.e., follow a logical order and sequence in their development and elaboration. The history of consciousness sets forth the self-constitution of reason in and through its categories. Once the categories have been reconstructed as modes of action of the subject, and the transcendental subject historicized, the way is prepared for the project of deriving the whole categorical system of reason from its first principle. The first or theoretical part of the *Wissenschaftslehre* is the reconstruction of the order of the categories as they logically imply one another. This is the hypothesis to be pragmatically verified in the phenomenological pragmatic history. Verification raises the problem of the relation between historical order and the transcendental logical order.

American pragmatism's conception of truth as what 'works', what gears into the world and situation, is present in Fichte's concept of the primacy of action and in his use of 'pragmatic'. The last term also suggests a practical verification of the transcendental hypothesis. For Fichte, the coherence sense of truth (namely the full coherent explication of a first principle) remains abstract and hypothetical. Hence, the transcendental is not directly or simply constitutive with respect to experience; it is rather set alongside empirical ordinary consciousness and stands in correlation with it. Thus, Fichte requires two series, ordinary consciousness and the observing-transcendental philosophy. The strictly theoretical transcendental deductions require further post-transcendental, or transcendental-pragmatic verification in experience.

But Fichte may also intend another sense of pragmatic. A pragmatic history teaches a moral lesson. A pragmatic study of history is to learn 'the lesson' which history teaches. Instead of the forward looking anticipation of confirmation of hypotheses based on experimental procedure that inspired American pragmatism, Fichte's pragmatic history is retrospective. Philosophical reflection can only follow experience, and can prescribe no laws to it.

The ordering problem is complex. The main idea is that of a critical correlation between transcendentally constructed order and the actual order of pragmatic history. The point to be stressed is that, whatever the order between transcendental and empirical turns out to be, the net effect is to loosen up the concept of transcendental constitution. Fichte's correlation between the transcendental and the empirical means that the transcendental cannot be a closed system of thought-determinations measured simply by the criterion of coherence. The irreducibility of the real to the ideal means that it is possible in principle that the transcendental order be subject to modification, if not correction, by the historical order. The ideal and real grounds can neither be identified nor separated. Their approximation is only partial; the final unity remains a *Sollen,* an infinite task, rather than an actual accomplishment.[52]

However, Fichte also conceives the relation of the two series of the *Wissenschaftslehre* as circular. The image of the circle points to some sort of unity between the two series. In the *Review of Aenesidemus* Fichte characterized the two series—the practical and the theoretical—as an ascending and descending order. In the *Wissenschaftslehre,* the two series stand in inverse relationship to each other. The consciousness of the two series, the *Rückkehr* of reflection, is the point of connection of the two. The circle metaphor spells out this suggestion: the end of one series is the beginning of the other. However, this image must not be taken too seriously for it implies, against Fichte's explicit statement, that the real and ideal grounds, the historical and the logical order can be identified, or completely coincide. Such coincidence would undercut the whole concept of the pragmatic history.

Although many perplexities about details remain, Fichte transforms transcendental philosophy from a pure a-historical system, into a pragmatic history of spirit. The necessity of a historical-pragmatic verification of transcendental philosophy shows the need to take seriously the claim of the non-ego, the other, or finitude. What prevents the *Wissenschaftslehre* from being a-historical transcendental philosophy is precisely the *Anstoß,* the non-ego, the other, which ordinary consciousness interprets realistically as a given, and which philosophical reflection interprets idealistically as a result of the self-restriction of the absolute ego. These two standpoints can neither be reduced to the other nor reduced to a superior unity. They cannot be finally unified or identified. Since the ideal and real ground cannot be identified, the transcendental that emerges in the *Wissenschaftslehre* is one which requires history.

FICHTE'S FOUNDATIONALISM?

There is a fundamental tension in the *Wissenschaftslehre*. On the one hand the system of transcendental philosophy is supposed to be complete, in that the transcendental philosopher has supposedly run through all the possible consequences and implications of the *Grundsatz* in advance of and independent of the pragmatic history. On the other hand, the insistence that the transcendental program is abstract and requires pragmatic verification, a 'descent into history' implies that the system is open, in principle at least, to historical modification. But Fichte does not provide concrete phenomenological descriptions of ordinary consciousness. His discussion remains abstract and formal. Moreover, Fichte's actual procedure seems to deny and exclude this openness to experience and history. The dominant impression is that Fichte thinks that history will 'of course' only serve to confirm the a priori transcendental categorical order and thus serve to illustrate and confirm the reflection of the philosopher. This confidence seems to arise out of a philosophical *hubris* that the philosopher is not subject to the constraints of finitude and history and is capable of providing a god-like survey of history. On the other hand, Fichte explicitly calls attention to and affirms that the philosopher's experience is finite like everyone else's. Nevertheless, Fichte's argument tends to become a closed circle, and with the closing of the circle, a reading of history a priori.

Should the circle close, ideal and real ground would be identified. If this actually occurs, then all otherness—the otherness of the *Anstoß*, the otherness of the non-ego—would be interpreted as self-othering, or self-otherness, and the foundationalist concern to ground everything in an underlying unity would not have been abandoned. As Hegel noted, however, this kind of foundationalism cannot fulfill its purpose because it ends by swallowing all the differences it is supposed to ground and explain.

But the pragmatic verification signifies only a correspondence, and not an identity, between the transcendental or ideal order and the empirical order. While the goal is that the two series meet or fully correspond, the correspondence is never full or perfect but only approximate. Fichte formulates the point thus:

> The finite *Geist* must necessarily posit something absolute outside of itself (*ein Ding an sich*), and nevertheless it must from the other side recognize that this absolute exists only for it [*Geist*] (*ein notwendiges Noumenon sei*)—this is the circle which it is able to expand to infinity but never escape.[53]

While pragmatic justification is circular, the circle is such that it is impossible for a finite intellect to *escape* it on the one hand, but equally impossible to *close* it on the other. Closure is limited, approximate, never completed or final.

For this reason, Fichte identifies his position as critical idealism, as a third alternative to dogmatism and skepticism. Pragmatic verification does not amount to a rigorous proof of Fichte's transcendental first principles, for he has already denied such was possible. But this point can equally well be reversed. The kind of verification of which Fichte believes his revised transcendental program capable is a pragmatic one. The system is *both* transcendental and pragmatic. The 'first principles' of the *Wissenschaftslehre* are hypothetical and admit only a pragmatic justification.

NOTES

1. One such critique is found in Tom Rockmore's *Hegel's Circular Epistemology* (Bloomington, Ind.: Indiana University Press, 1986).

2. Walter Jaeschke notes that "A critique not directed along these lines fails to do justice to the strategy employed by Hegel's philosophy in regard to proof and does not rise to its level of reflection." *Reason in Religion: The Foundations of Hegel's Philosophy of Religion*, tr. J. M. Stewart and P. C. Hodgson (Berkeley: University of California Press, 1990), 12.

3. Kant pursues his transcendental program that claims to justify scientific knowledge by uncovering the a-historical structures (categories) of the understanding, alongside of a philosophy of history, according to which reason undergoes historical development. These two concerns stand in tension with each other, and it is the surpassing of the former in the latter that led to Fichte and Hegel. For a valuable study, cf. Yirmiahu Yovel, *Kant and the Philosophy of History* (Princeton, N.J.: Princeton University Press, 1980).

4. See his *Zweite Einleitung in die Wissenschaftslehre, Fichtes Werke*, Band I, Hrsg. I. H. Fichte (Berlin: Walter de Gruyter 1971), 458ff. [Hereafter cited as FW I.] English Translation: *Science of Knowledge*, edited and translated by Peter Heath and John Lachs (New York: Appleton Century Crofts, 1970).

5. These issues are very much alive in the development of post-Kantian transcendental philosophy. See J. N. Mohanty, *The Possibility of Transcendental Philosophy*, [*Phaenomenologica Volume 98*] (Dordrecht, The Netherlands: Martinus Nijhoff, 1985). Mohanty shows that Hegel and Husserl are both concerned with the question of access to the transcendental region. "Hegel, more than any other philosopher, realized the force of this problem of access, and wrote his *Phenomenology* of 1807 as a response" (xx).

6. These charges have been levelled against Kant by Hamann and Husserl. For an account of Hamann's Kantkritik, see Frederick C. Beiser, *The Fate of Reason: German Philosophy from Kant to Fichte* (Cambridge, Mass.: Harvard University Press, 1987). For Husserl's discussion of Kant's 'mythic conceptions', see Edmund

Husserl, *The Crisis of European Sciences,* tr. D. Carr (Evanston, Ill.: Northwestern University Press, 1970). This does not mean that Kant's critical philosophy and phenomenology are necessarily incompatible. See Paul Ricoeur, "Kant and Husserl," in *Husserl: An Analysis of His Phenomenology* (Evanston, Ill.: Northwestern University Press, 1967).

7. These problems are not simply practical problems however. It is a question of access to the transcendental region, and whether such access is cognitive. This issue underlies Kant's discussion of freedom, the claim that practical reason is primary, and the question concerning the possibility of transcendental reflection and philosophy.

8. Immanuel Kant, *Foundations of the Metaphysics of Morals,* tr. Lewis White Beck (New York: Library of Liberal Arts, 1959), 71[451]; cf. Kant, *Critique of Pure Reason,* B157–158n, tr. N. K. Smith (New York: St. Martins, 1965). The former passage creates problems for those who interpret Kant's transcendental subject as a set of logical rules. Stanley Rosen writes "In Kant there is no absolute ego. The transcendental ego possesses neither self-consciousness nor life, but is a set of logical rules. In Fichte the transcendental ego is brought to life..." (Rosen, *The Ancients and the Moderns: Rethinking Modernity* [New Haven, Conn.: Yale University Press, 1989], 69). This interpretation slights Kant's practical philosophy and his philosophy of history, which point towards an identification of the transcendental ego with the historical human ego.

9. Kant, *Critique of Practical Reason,* tr. Lewis White Beck (New York: Library of Liberal Arts, 1956), 4n, [5]. For a discussion of the issues, see Lewis White Beck, *A Commentary on Kant's Critique of Practical Reason* (Chicago: University of Chicago Press, 1960), Chapters 4 and 11.

10. For a critique of Kant's doctrine of the postulates, see Hegel, *Glauben und Wissen,* ET *Faith and Knowledge,* tr. W. Cerf and H. S. Harris (Albany, N.Y.: SUNY Press, 1977); see also Yirmiahu Yovel, *Kant and the Problem of History,* op. cit.

11. G. E. Schulz attacked Kant on this issue. Cf. Beiser, op. cit. 282.

12. See BTKH. For an historical study of this period and its issues see Frederick Beiser, *The Fate of Reason,* op. cit.

13. This criticism was developed most fully by Solomon Maimon; see Beiser, op. cit. Chapter 10. Maimon claims that it is the dualism between reason and sensibility which makes transcendental deduction both necessary and impossible (292).

14. See Klaus Hartmann, "On Taking the Transcendental Turn," *Review of Metaphysics,* 20, 2:78 (December 1966): 223–249.

15. K. L. Reinhold, *The Foundation of Philosophical Knowledge (1794),* BTKH, op. cit. 67.

16. K. L. Reinhold, op. cit. 96.

17. Reinhold, op. cit. 55–56, 74. For Kant, possibility is superior to and explanatory of actuality. For this reason it is sufficient to construe the transcendental

subject as a system of logical principles or rules. However, the empty, purely formal character of Kant's position becomes apparent in his practical philosophy. Reinhold reacts to Kant's formalism.

18. Reinhold, op. cit. 67.

19. Reinhold, op. cit. 71.

20. Beiser, op. cit. 248.

21. Beiser, op. cit. 251.

22. For the text, see BTKH. For a discussion, see Beiser, op. cit.

23. See Beiser, op. cit. 278. These issues are familiar to students of Husserl's later development. For a similar problem in Husserl's phenomenological reduction, see Paul Ricoeur, op. cit. 177f; 202. It was just such problems which led Husserl to abandon the Cartesian type of phenomenological reduction: cf. Iso Kern, "The Three Ways to the Transcendental Phenomenological Reduction," *Husserl: Expositions and Appraisals* (Notre Dame: University of Notre Dame Press,1977).

24. Cf. Heidegger, *Age of the World as Picture, Holzwege* (Frankfurt: Vittorio Klostermann, 1950).

25. Fichte, *Wissenschaftslehre 1794*, FW I 178.

26. Fichte, op. cit. 91. ET 93.

27. Fichte, *Erste Einleitung in die Wissenschaftslehre*, 1797, FW I.

28. Fichte and Schelling both wrote on the opposition between dogmatism and idealism at about the same time. See Schelling's *Philosophical Letters On Dogmatism and Criticism*, tr. Fritz Marti, in *The Unconditional in Human Knowledge* (Lewisburg, Pa.: Bucknell University Press, 1980).

29. Fichte, *Erste Einleitung in die Wissenschaftslehre*, FW I, 432–433.

30. Ibid. 434. This is probably the best known passage from Fichte, and for this reason he is widely regarded as having debunked the illusion of 'purely objective knowledge'. However, although Fichte's quotable formulation has attracted notice, it should be pointed out that Kant introduced the concept of interest in the *Critique of Pure Reason*, A462, B490. Fichte develops the concept of interest further by concretizing it and by displacing traditional first philosophy.

31. Fichte, *Erste Einleitung in die Wissenschaftslehre*, FW I 432.

32. Ibid. 433. ET 15. Heidegger and Sartre elaborate further Husserl's concept of the natural attitude and the 'immersion' in the natural attitude. Husserl regards such immersion and naivete as the mundanization of consciousness. In Heidegger, Fichte's dogmatic self becomes inauthentic existence, or Being-in-the-world in the mode of the anonymous "they" self. In Sartre, dogmatist self-hood becomes bad faith, an attempt to construct a rigid self-identity like a stone.

33. This of course is Heidegger's claim. Cf. *"Die Zeit des Weltbildes,"* *Holzwege* (Frankfurt: Klostermann, 1950), 86, 104f. Heidegger charges the modern tradition from Descartes through Hegel with substituting the concept of subjectivity, understood as *hypokeimenon,* for the classical conception of being or substance (*ousia*). This does not overcome metaphysics, but merely shifts the metaphysical foundation from the world to subjectivity.

34. Fichte, *Grundlage des Naturrechts* (1796), FW III 1–2n. This passage calls into question Heidegger's reading of German Idealism, and Hegel in particular, as Cartesian foundationalism, as an inversion of metaphysics that shifts the *hypokeimenon* from world to subjectivity.

35. Stanley Rosen obviously appreciates, but exaggerates, Fichte's radicalism when he writes, "There can...be no correct or coherent analysis of the 'structure' of self-consciousness.... Not merely is there no deduction of the categories from a single principle; there is no formulatable principle." "Freedom and Spontaneity in Fichte," *The Philosophical Forum,* vol. 19, no. 2–3, (Winter-Spring 1988): 153.

36. Fichte, "Review of Aenesidemus," BTKH 150; FW I 21; see also W. L. FW I, 93. Moreover, the *Wissenschaftslehre* grounds logic, rather than the reverse. See *"Über den Begriff der Wissenschaftslehre,"* FW I 69.

37. It is Fichte, not Hegel, who introduces the familiar terminology of thesis, antithesis, and synthesis. See Fichte, *Wissenschaftslehre,* FW I 205–6. See *"Grundriss des Eigentümliche der Wissenschaftslehre,"* FW I 337.

38. Fichte, *Wissenschaftslehre.* FW I 194–200.

39. See n. 34 above.

40. *Wissenschaftslehre,* FW I 222. Cf. also *Zweite Einleitung in die Wissenschaftslehre,* FW I 515f.

41. See Kant's second Preface to the *Critique of Pure Reason.*

42. *Wissenschaftslehre,* FW I 222.

43. See Jean Hyppolite, *Genesis and Structure of Hegel's Phenomenology of Spirit,* tr. Cherniak and Johnson (Evanston, Ill.: Northwestern University Press, 1974), 9.

44. Fichte, *Zweite Einleitung in die Wissenschaftslehre,* FW I 454.

45. Hegel, *Phänomenologie des Geistes* (Hamburg: Meiner Verlag, 1952), Hegel adds yet another distinction which transforms Fichte's twofold distinction into a three-fold distinction between ordinary consciousness, phenomenological observers, and speculative philosopher. This allows Hegel to highlight in a way that Fichte does not, the phenomenological aspect and element of this general framework and problematic.

46. Fichte, *Zweite Einleitung,* op. cit. 455n. [Emphasis mine.]

47. Fichte, *Zweite Einleitung,* FW I 454.

48. *Wissenschaftslehre,* FW I 223. ET 199. Cf. Edmund Husserl, "...phenomenological explication does nothing but explicate the sense this world has for us all, prior to any philosophizing, and obviously gets solely from our experience—a sense which philosophy can uncover but never alter..." *Cartesian Meditations,* tr. Dorion Cairns (The Hague: Martinus Nijhoff, 1960), 151. This phenomenological principle calls into question George Armstrong Kelley's claim that the relation between philosophy and ordinary consciousness is one of leadership and discipleship. ([*Idealism, Politics and History: Sources of Hegelian Thought* (Cambridge: Cambridge University Press, 1969), 215]) Were that the case, Fichte would have failed in his phenomenological task of following and prescribing no laws to his subject. This is not to deny that the pragmatic history includes education, but to insist that the education must be conceived differently from leadership and discipleship. This point did not escape Hegel, who elaborates phenomenology as an immanent criticism of ordinary consciousness, and criticizes Master and Slave.

49. Fichte *Wissenschaftslehre,* FW I 234; ET 208: "We shall see that in natural reflection, as opposed to the artificial reflection of transcendental philosophy, we are able, in virtue of its laws, to go back only so far as the understanding, and then always encounter in this something given to reflection...but we do not become conscious of the manner in which it arrived there. Hence our firm conviction of the reality of things outside us, and this without any contribution on our part, since we are unaware of the power that produces them."

50. Fichte, *Wissenschaftslehre,* FW I 178; ET 164.

51. Fichte, *Aenesidemus Review,* BTKH 152.

52. Cf. *Zweite Einleitung,* op. cit. Fichte distinguishes between the ego as intellectual intuition as the starting point of the *Wissenschaftslehre,* and the ego as Idea or the final goal of the *Wissenschaftslehre.* The theoretical part of the *Wissenschaftslehre* begins with the ego as indeterminate formal structure. The full explication of this requires a surpassing of the theoretical in the practical, and the practical culminates not in a vision of the whole but rather in a striving for totality. (FW I 515f.) Fichte's later position is implicit here, because the totality towards which reason strives is the idea of deity. Cf. *Review of Aenesidemus,* BTKH 152.

53. *Wissenschaftslehre* FW I 281; ET 247.

THREE

FICHTE ON RECOGNITION

There are a few questions which philosophy must answer before it can become *Wissenschaft* and *Wissenschaftslehre*....Among these questions are the following: ...How does the human being come to assume and recognize that there are rational beings similar to it outside of it, since such beings are not at all immediately or directly given to or present in its pure self-consciousness?... The relation of rational beings to each other I term *Gesellschaft*. But the concept of *Gesellschaft* is not possible except on the presupposition that there actually exist rational beings outside of us.... How do we come to such a presupposition...?[1]

I have shown that Fichte broadens transcendental philosophy beyond a mere egology or explication of the cogito, and concretizes the transcendental in the framework of a history of consciousness. Hence it is not only not surprising, but virtually inevitable that he should identify and take up the problem of the other. The other is an essential dimension of and aspect in the genetic history of consciousness that is supposed to cover all aspects of experience. Nevertheless it is not generally recognized that Fichte explicitly formulated the problem of the other and pursues it within the context of a project of systematic philosophy.[2] The above quotation dates from the same year as the *Wissenschaftslehre*, which shows that the issue was alive for Fichte at the very origins of his systematic philosophy, and was by no means an afterthought. Moreover, Fichte clearly thinks that the problem of the other is not a derivative question. Rather he identifies the problem of the other as a prior question for first philosophy.

The problem of the other arises as a vital question within Fichte's program of transcendental-critical idealism. As Husserl was later to observe, transcendental idealism, even of a methodological type, is haunted by the problem of solipsism. If, following Descartes, reflective self-certainty is taken as the paradigm case of apodictic certainty, not only the other but also the body and world become epistemologically problematic. The other is a special puzzle, for the other is not immediately present, or reducible to immediate presence. Fichte agrees: "I cannot be immediately conscious at all of a freedom outside of me."[3] But Fichte hastens to add: "Moreover, I cannot be immediately conscious of a freedom in me, or of my own freedom, because freedom is, in and for itself, not the first but rather the final ground of clarification of all consciousness, and cannot therefore belong within the sphere of [immediate] consciousness."[4] Thus, Fichte both implies a critique of immediate knowledge and makes a fundamental determination of the problematics of freedom and the other: both are connected and both involve a complex mutual mediation. Freedom as ontological, is a universal feature of human being; however there are differences in the realization or consciousness of freedom. The consciousness of freedom is a result of mediation in and through an historical career. As immediate, the consciousness of freedom is not explicit, but merely implicit. Freedom becomes explicit only as the result of intersubjective mediation.

First, I shall take up the general question of the significance of the problem of the other for philosophy, the relation of intersubjectivity to first philosophy—not the issue in and for itself, but only in relation to Fichte's thought as a whole. The problem compels a further transformation and clarification of Fichte's supposed idealism, and of the doctrine of the *Anstoß* in particular. There are several interpretive issues that must be sorted out, and since Fichte's thought is virtually unknown in English, I shall review some of the continental interpretations and disputes. Then I shall take up Fichte's theory of intersubjectivity, his account of *Aufforderung* and *Anerkennung*. These concepts concretize Kant's moral philosophy—the consciousness of freedom, the categorical imperative, kingdom of ends—and transform it into a social philosophy.

THE STATUS AND 'LOCATION' OF THE PROBLEM OF THE OTHER

Fichte raises the fundamental question concerning the location of the problem of the other on the philosophical map. He identifies the issue of intersubjectivity as the issue of recognition (*Anerkennung*). Recognition is the transcendental condition of natural law and right (*Naturrecht*). Although Fichte distinguishes the question of right from ethics, the theme of recognition emerges in both his *Grundlage des Naturrecht*[5] and *System der Sittlichkeit*[6] as a transcendental condition of rights and ethics. This assignment of transcendental status to intersubjectivity, specifically, as a transcendental condition of possibility of ethics and law, not only breaks new ground, but is directed against Kant's ethical formalism. As we will see, Fichte brings to light the existential-intersubjective presuppositions of Kant's categorical imperative and the concept of the 'community of ends'. Intersubjectivity is not only a condition of morality in Kant's sense, but also a condition of law and rights. The latter institutions are determinate forms and modes of intersubjective recognition.

How does intersubjectivity, as a transcendental condition of right, relate to the transcendental program of the *Wissenschaftslehre*? Some scholars interpret Fichte's social philosophy as a determinate instance of the general categorical ontology sketched in his *Wissenschaftslehre* of 1794. This view, if correct, would imply that the other is not genuinely other, but rather posited by and metaphysically derivative from the ego. According to the fundamental principle of the *Wissenschaftslehre,* all determinations in the ego, including that of the non-ego, must be posited by the ego: "...the interaction between the ego and the non-ego is at the same time an interaction of the ego with itself.... In such interaction nothing new or alien is introduced into the ego; everything that develops in the ego to infinity, is developed simply out of the ego in accordance with its own laws...."[7] If everything in the ego must be posited by the ego, it *may* follow that the other or non-ego is reducible to the ego itself.[8]

We have already noted J. N. Findlay's claim that Fichte reduces the other to a mere myth or illusion.[9] According to Findlay, what appears to be other turns out to be the result of the ego's own action. The other, which at first appeared to be necessary, turns out to be a myth, an illusion, because it can be collapsed into the ego's self-positing.

Findlay's account is a half-truth: close enough to be plausible, but ultimately misleading. Not only does Fichte not abandon the so-called myth of the other, he claims it is impossible to do so.

> This fact—that the finite *Geist* necessarily must posit something absolute outside of itself (a thing in itself) and nevertheless on the other hand must recognize that this something exists only for the Ego (a necessary noumenon), is that circle which it can expand to infinity, but never escape. A system which has no regard for this circle is a dogmatic idealism, for it is only this circle which limits us and constitutes our finitude.[10]

Findlay's "Fichte" is the dogmatic metaphysical idealist which Fichte criticizes.

Fichte does not assert the absoluteness of the ego in all respects. The ego is absolute in its self-determinations, but it is not self-creating. The absolute ego is a contingent absolute. In respect to its existence it is dependent on something other than itself:

> The final ground of all actuality [*Wirklichkeit*] for the ego is, according to the *Wissenschaftslehre,* an original interaction between the ego and something beyond the ego, of which nothing more can be said except that it must be absolutely opposed to the ego.... Through this opposite, the ego is simply set in motion in order to act, and without such a first mover outside of the ego, the ego would never have acted. Since the existence of the ego consists simply in being an act, [without this Other] the ego would never have existed.... The ego is dependent in respect to its existence; but independent in respect to the determinations of its existence.[11]

Fichte stops short of the absolute monism that is usually ascribed to him. The Ego is not self-creating: it is dependent in respect to its existence. The Ego is absolute and autonomous only with respect to its determinations of sense.

Findlay's account reduces critical idealism to metaphysical idealism in which all interaction between Ego and other is an interaction of the ego with itself. But Fichte himself explicitly rejects such a reduction: "The final ground of all consciousness is an interaction of the ego with itself which is mediated by a non-Ego to be considered from different points of view. This is the circle from which finite spirit cannot escape, nor can it wish to escape without denying reason and willing its own destruction."[12] Although the ego interacts with itself, this interaction is mediated by an other which is not simply reducible to the ego. The other is more than a myth. If this seems paradoxical, the paradox is unavoidable and must be embraced.[13] If the paradox is embraced, then the position undergoes a transformation from its initial apparent idealism towards dialectical holism.

The Naturrecht *in the Development of Fichte's Thought*

The difficulty may also be expressed in the following way: How are the *Grundlage des Naturrechts* and the *Wissenschaftslehre* related? The former is a concrete discipline constructed according to the principles of *Wissenschaftslehre,* but what does this mean? On this question there are a variety of conflicting interpretations, and the debate is relevant to our topic. According to Ludwig Siep, the *Wissenschaftslehre* is the foundational discipline which grounds the *Naturrecht,* and the latter is an application and/or extension of the former. The transcendental ego of the *Wissenschaftslehre* must be distinguished from *Anerkennen* as a transcendental condition of right.[14] In other words, there are levels within Fichte's transcendental program, and the ultimate level is the absolute ego, metaphysically interpreted. Fichte's theory of intersubjectivity or *Anerkennung* refers to a *Bewusstseinshandlung,* a lower level than that of the transcendental ego.[15] Since *Bewusstsein* is transcendentally constituted, this implies that intersubjectivity must also be a transcendentally constituted phenomenon, i.e., subordinate to and derivative from the absolute ego.

Wilhelm Weischedel offers an account of the ontological implications of such an interpretation. The *Naturrecht* is related to the *Wissenschaftslehre* as a regional ontology to a universal or general ontology. Consequently, the concept of the other in *Naturrecht* is a particular instance of the more general ontological concept of the *Anstoß* or the non-ego.[16] This assumes that the direction of Fichte's analysis moves from the universal to the particular, and that the other is a particular instance of the *Anstoß*. However, neither Siep nor Weischedel take up the formidable problems implicit in this interpretation: the apparent ontological separation between the transcendental and the empirical human ego, and the problem of the pluralization of the transcendental in a multiplicity of subjects. Nor do they show how the transcendental ego of the *Wissenschaftslehre* is capable of supporting or accounting for intersubjectivity.

Alexis Philolenko holds that Fichte does not move from the *Wissenschaftslehre* to the *Naturrecht* as an application; rather, the problem of intersubjectivity is already present in the *Wissenschaftslehre* as Fichte's first philosophy.[17] Basing this claim in part on Fichte's assertion, *"Kein Du, Kein Ich,"*[18] Philolenko contends that the problem of the other is already an element of Fichte's project in the *Wissenschaftslehre*. The problem with Philolenko's interpretation is that the *Wissenschaftslehre* (1794) does not explicitly formulate the issue of intersubjectivity, much less develop a concept or theory.[19]

On the other hand, Peter Baumanns contends that the *Wissenschaftslehre* (1794) cannot and does not serve as foundation for the *Naturrecht* because it neglects the deduction of the social.[20] Hence, it cannot serve as the foundational discipline. Consequently, *Naturrecht* is not a particular instance of the *Wissenschaftslehre*. It is an independent but complementary statement of the position. In *Naturrecht* the introduction of the social is accomplished with the aid and extension of principles which go beyond but are congruent with the *Wissenschaftslehre*. The crucial step is taken in the introduction of the concept of right itself. "The concept of right is supposed to be an original concept of pure reason."[21] Thus the concept of right is part of the original structure of reason. It must be noted that reason, its theoretical categories, as well as the concept of right, are, phenomenologically considered, modes of action (*Handlungsweisen*). The concept of right is immanent in reason's practical activity; reason is practical and thus social.

Consequently, intersubjectivity is not an afterthought tacked on later to an already complete concept of reason. Reinhard Lauth points out that contemporaneously with the composition of the *Wissenschaftslehre* 1794, Fichte formulated the problem of intersubjectivity in his lectures on the *Vocation of the Scholar*.[22] Moreover, the issue of intersubjectivity is explicitly identified as a prior question for philosophy, specifically the *Wissenschaftslehre*. If this is correct, then the *Wissenschaftslehre* 1794 must be regarded as a tentative statement which brackets this prior question. It need not be construed as a complete transcendental foundation for intersubjectivity.[23] This explains in part Fichte's abstention from ontological interpretation in *Wissenschaftslehre*. The absolute ego is both distinguished from the empirical human ego and identified with it. The nature of the distinction and the identity remains a problem, particularly in view of the claim that intersubjectivity (*Anerkennung*) is a transcendental condition of *Naturrecht*.[24] Nevertheless, any claim that the *Wissenschaftslehre* 1794 is foundational for the rest of the system ignores the sweeping changes which Fichte subsequently made in his system.

In Fichte's multiple reformulations of the *Wissenschaftslehre*, an inversion of his original argument occurs—from the assertion of the priority of transcendental subjectivity over being, to the assertion of the priority of being over transcendental subjectivity.[25] Wolfgang Janke shows that the concept of being undergoes modification, from a negative conception of a mere object constituted by and relative to transcendental subjectivity, to a more positive conception of being as life and medium (*Durch*). This implies that subjectivity ceases (if in fact it ever was intended) to be a metaphysical foundation of being, and instead becomes a transparent medium of access to being and others. Fichte's interpretation of the *Anstoß* likewise undergoes a change. One consideration in the interpretation of the *Anstoß* is the issue of intersubjectivity. The intersubjective other plays a part in the inversion whereby the *Anstoß* acquires ontological heft and becomes equiprimordial with subjectivity, without thereby relapsing into pre-critical metaphysics.

THE CONCEPT OF RIGHT

The introduction to the *Naturrecht* both reformulates some of the major themes of the *Wissenschaftslehre* 1794, and breaks new ground by explicating the concept of right as "an original concept of pure reason."[26] Fichte begins by reiterating that the ego is no substrate, no substance, but rather an act. Further, being is a determinate modification of consciousness or action, such that without active consciousness there would be no being.[27] According to this doctrine, the self is not a being or an object, and cannot make itself into an object. Thus, Fichte conceives being as a negative concept, an object, or mundane entity. Whatever freedom actually is or may be, it cannot be a mundane object, and therefore cannot be grasped or known as a thing. The problem of the self-consciousness of freedom is the starting point for Fichte's account of intersubjectivity.

Fichte expounds the concept of right by noting that the self and others are equiprimordial, mutually delimiting:

> I posit myself as rational, that is, as free.... I posit another free being at the same time in the same undivided action. I describe through my imagination a sphere for freedom which is shared by a plurality of free beings. I do not ascribe to myself all the freedom which I have imagined, because I posit still other free beings and must ascribe to them a share in the same freedom. I restrict myself in my appropriation of freedom through the fact that I leave 'space' for other freedom. The concept of right is accordingly the concept of a necessary relation of free beings to each other.[28]

It is of no little interest that Fichte describes right phenomenologically, as leaving space for the other's freedom. However, this is still not yet the full unfolding of the basic concept of right. For what is the above-mentioned "necessary relation of free beings to each other"? The relation is a morally necessary one, i.e., the idea of a rational-moral community, not unlike Kant's kingdom of ends.[29] In his concept of community (*Gemeinschaft*), Fichte reflects the concept of a universal law made by freedom that places restrictions upon the freedom of all, a freely imposed self-restraint:

> The whole object of the concept of right is that of a community between free beings as such.... We find that every member of such a community freely allows his/her external freedom to be restricted so that all others next to him may be also externally free. This is the concept of right.[30]

The concept of right is a social concept arising out of mutual restriction and correspondence of freedoms. Such mutual restriction Fichte identifies as a "condition of self-consciousness."[31]

Fichte makes explicit the intersubjective social presuppositions and conditions of Kantian ethics. Kant sharply separated transcendental from empirical subjectivity, and spoke rather abstractly of a kingdom of ends following universal self-legislated laws. Fichte systematizes Kant's thought by means of the history of consciousness concept. The systematization of Kant's thought from the perspective of the history of consciousness overcomes the transcendental subject's abstract separation from the empirical subject by embedding it within a history. This involves a shift of attention that brings intersubjectivity into focus. The concretizing of the transcendental is immediately evident in Fichte's claim that the concept of right is an original or a priori concept of pure reason. Kant did not make this claim, and his formal concept of transcendental philosophy might preclude it. Nevertheless, the claim is not incompatible with Kant's practical philosophy and seems implied by it. Can it be seriously maintained that Kant's kingdom of ends is a solipsistic rather than a social concept?[32] Rather it seems that Kant's ethics presupposes an ontology of interpersonal relations.

FREEDOM AS INTERSUBJECTIVE

Fichte's so-called deduction of the concept of right is an account of how the self comes to be conscious of its own freedom. Fichte denies a substantial self or self as substratum. Rather the 'being' of the self consists in action, and freedom is inherent in action. As the First Introduction to Wissenschaftslehre makes clear, although freedom is fundamental to human beings, the consciousness of freedom is not given but must be developed. Moreover, until it is developed the human being remains in a diminished state or condition.

There are several reasons why the consciousness of freedom is problematic. The first is theoretical, grounded in Kant's first and second Critiques. Kant's critical program denies knowledge in order to make room for moral faith. Consequently, Kant denies cognitive access to transcendental freedom or self-originating causality. The first Critique neither affirms nor denies such causality through freedom, but merely establishes that it is not incompatible with phenomenal-natural causality. The subsequent development of practical philosophy, however, culminating in the second *Critique*, affirms that there is transcendental freedom, apprehended through the moral law. Despite this assertion of the existence and reality of freedom, Kant denies that the primacy of practical reason involves a theoretical cognitive claim; it only involves an apprehension of freedom for practical purposes. Thus, the self-*knowledge* of freedom is problematic.

A second reason freedom is problematic is that ordinary consciousness is naive. Its naivete is due in part to the fact that consciousness is a transparent medium that is unaware of its own activity. Owing to such transparency, the natural attitude focuses on its objects, and does not bend its attention back upon itself or its own contributions to perception, i.e., it is not reflective. Thus Fichte writes:

> For the ordinary consciousness...there are only objects, and no concepts [*Begriffe*]; the concept disappears in the object and coincides with it. The philosophical genius or talent, that finds in and during the act itself, not only what originates through the act, but also *the act as such,* and that unites these opposite tendencies in a single concept...discovers the concept in the object, and the field of consciousness obtains a new sphere.[33]

The transcendental turn overcomes the naivete, but not the general thesis, of the natural attitude. "The transcendental philosopher must assume that everything for the ego, or supposed to be for the ego, can only be through the ego's own doing. The ordinary consciousness on the contrary gives both elements a separate existence, and asserts that the world would always exist even if it [consciousness] did not."[34] From the transcendental standpoint "the concept and its object are not separated, nor could they be separated."[35] The problem is how it is possible for consciousness to overcome its naive immersion in the world, and become conscious of itself as free. Fichte's account of ordinary consciousness assumes the transcendental phenomenological standpoint, but it does not exhibit the transition from consciousness to the self-consciousness constitutive of freedom.

Fichte poses the crucial question, How does the subject find itself as object?[36] It is necessary to overcome the tendency of the natural attitude to construe everything, including the self, as a mere object, or thing. Thus, this question is equivalent to: How does the self discover that it is not a mere thing, or mundane object? How does it discover its freedom? How does the self discover its "determination to self-determination"?[37] Despite the so-called 'idealist' primacy of freedom, Fichte revisits the *Anstoß*. Although freedom is a capacity for self-originated action, it is not a capacity for self-origination. According to the *Wissenschaftslehre*, the self depends upon an *Anstoß*, a shock or repulse from something external, as a stimulus to free action. But in the *Naturrecht* the *Anstoß* is reinterpreted as a summons (*Auf-*

forderung) to free and responsible action: "It could not find itself as determining itself to self-activity [*Selbsttätigkeit*] but only as determined thereto by an external *Anstoß*, which nevertheless must grant its full freedom to self-determination...."[38] In referring once again to the *Anstoß*, Fichte reiterates the doctrine of the original *Wissenschaftslehre*, but also goes beyond it. Concretely or phenomenologically viewed, the *Anstoß* to freedom is not a metaphysical force, but an interpersonal summons (*Aufforderung*).

THE OTHER AS A SUMMONS (*AUFFORDERUNG*) TO FREEDOM

Fichte's theory of intersubjectivity finds expression in the twin concepts of Summons (*Aufforderung*)[39] and Recognition (*Anerkennung*). Its basic idea is that freedom and responsibility must be mediated through an objectification of the self which the self both requires in order to become conscious of its freedom, and yet cannot accomplish by itself. The ego is so far from being absolutely autonomous that it is dependent on the recognition of others to become conscious of its freedom. Summons and recognition refer to the mediation of the self to itself by the other, through which freedom becomes explicit. We are thus confronted with the following paradox: *autonomous* self-consciousness is not a given; it is a mediated result of interpersonal interaction.

Aufforderung *and the* Anstoß

Fichte's analysis of *Aufforderung* or summons in *Naturrecht* is parallel and related to his concept of the *Anstoß* in the *Wissenschaftslehre*. First, let us note the similarities. The common assumption is the finitude of the subject, which requires some sort of external stimulus to action. In the *Wissenschaftslehre* of 1794, Fichte refers to the *Anstoß* as a "first mover"[40] which simply sets the ego in motion in order to act. Moreover, "without such a first mover outside of it, the ego would never have acted, and, since its existence consists entirely in action, it would also not have existed."[41] The relation between the *Anstoß* and the ego appears to be causal, although the *Anstoß* is supposed not to undermine freedom, but rather to summon the self to freedom and responsibility. But how it can do so and remain a mere '*Anstoß*' remains a mystery. The main point however is that the *Anstoß* is not simply invoked as a transcendental condition of possibility. Rather it is a fact, a *transcendental* fact. That is, if freedom as transcendental depends on a fact, this fact must likewise be transcendental in some sense. Without this fact, the ego, whose being consists in action, would never have acted or existed. This puzzling factual conditioning of the transcendental subject finds expression in Fichte's repeated assertion that the *Wissenschaftslehre* is realistic, as well as idealistic. The self and the *Anstoß* can neither be separated nor identified.

In *Naturrecht,* Fichte takes up the *Anstoß,* but in a slightly different context, namely, in regard to the question, how may the self find itself as object, and so become conscious of its freedom.[42] The *Anstoß* is described as a determination of the self to free self-determination. To give a further account of the influence (*Einwirkung*) of the *Anstoß,* Fichte identifies this influence as a summons or call (*Aufforderung*).[43] Human freedom becomes object for itself through and by means of the summons (*Aufforderung*) of the other.[44] Fichte's thesis is that self-consciousness and freedom are intersubjectively mediated. The explicit self-consciousness of freedom is not something that the self can give to itself. Rather my consciousness of freedom arises out of the claims of the other upon me.

Does this analysis mean that the summons (*Aufforderung*) must be sharply distinguished from the *Anstoß?*[45] Düsing thinks so, and bases her view on the ontological separation of the pure ego of the *Wissenschaftslehre* from the empirical human ego which she claims is the subject of the *Naturrecht.* "In clear distinction to the transcendental mode of explanation [of the *Wissenschaftslehre*] the *Anstoß* in *Naturrecht* signifies an empirical event in space and time. Through this *Anstoß* the concrete subject finds itself determined by a reality outside of itself."[46] This assumes that the *Wissenschaftslehre* (1794) is foundational for the *Naturrecht.* I believe however that the *Wissenschaftslehre* is incomplete, and that the *Naturrecht* is a further development of Fichte's thought.

Yet, Fichte himself makes no clear distinction between *Anstoß* and *Aufforderung;* he slides easily from the former to the latter in the *Naturrecht.* Fichte does not, at least in the *Wissenschaftslehre* 1794, make an ontological separation between the transcendental ego and the empirical ego, but leaves open virtually all ontological issues except for one: the ego—whether transcendental or empirical—is finite. Moreover, both the *Wissenschaftslehre* and the *Naturrecht* are realistic, although in different senses. The realism finds expression in the portrayal of the *Anstoß/Aufforderung* as a fact, as a given, limiting the ego and establishing its finitude and dependence. This limitation of transcendental freedom by a conditioning fact or *Anstoß* shows that Fichte's is a transcendental which does not simply exclude, but rather requires an opposing other.

However, in the case of the *Anstoß,* the other is not a given object, but rather is non-objective; it is merely felt and not known. It is not evident that there is or could be a relation of reciprocity between ego and the *Anstoß.* In contrast, the other who summons me to freedom and responsibility, also evokes my recognition (*Anerkennung*) of him. Thus, reciprocity seems to be both necessary and possible. The intersubjective human other is an essential element in the problem of the other in Fichte's thought, even if it does not exhaust that problem. Openness to the other led Fichte to modify his *Wis-*

senschaftslehre and abandon (if he ever held it) the idealist thesis of the reduction of being to thought.[47]

The call of the other is not a physical force or compulsion, nor a command that must be obeyed. The one receiving the summons "is in no way compelled or necessitated to action, like an effect is rendered necessary by its cause."[48] Rather, the summons is an occasion for decision: the self can accede to the summons, deny it, or ignore it. The summons of the other presupposes the capacity for, and mediates the consciousness of, freedom in the one to whom it is directed. It should be noted that what is externally mediated by the other is not freedom per se, but only the *consciousness* of freedom. Freedom belongs ontologically to human nature even though it remains a mere potentiality and/or possibility until the self is summoned to freedom. It is the *consciousness* of freedom, and not the *ontological capacity* or potentiality of freedom, that requires intersubjective mediation, "a determination to self-determination" as Fichte puts it.

Although Fichte does not provide a phenomenology of the summons, he does hint at its teleological nature. Neither a push nor a shove (i.e., a mere *Anstoß*), the summons involves an intelligible communication, not simply conveying information but rather directed to some purpose.[49] It comes from an intelligent being: "The cause [of the summons] must therefore, necessarily have the concept of reason and freedom; it must itself be a being capable of entertaining concepts, an intelligence, and since this is not possible without freedom, it must also be free...."[50] In short, the call is an intelligible communication directed by one rational being towards another. What is distinctive is that the summoner restricts his/her freedom for the sake of the one summoned.[51] For this reason Fichte identifies summons (*Aufforderung*) with education (*Erziehung*).[52]

The summons has ethical significance.[53] Its telos is an acknowledgement of the claim of the other, a summons to responsible freedom. "The human being becomes genuinely human only among human beings; and since he neither can nor would be anything else, a human being should be humanity, and exists only in the plural."[54] Human existence, as distinct from bare existence, is possible only as an intersubjectively mediated social reality. And it is the accomplishment of ethical culture, brought about by intersubjective summons to responsible freedom, which makes existence distinctively human.

It is also crucial that the summons be recognized by the one to whom it is directed. That is, the summons must be received and understood by the one to whom it is addressed.[55] On the one hand, this means that the summoner presupposes that the one summoned is capable of understanding the summons, and is free to accept or reject it. On the other hand, the one receiving the summons must recognize that it comes from another intelligent being, an ego. Fichte writes: "I cannot comprehend this summons to self-activity without ascribing it to a real being outside of me, that wishes to communicate to me the concept of the summoned action, and consequently is capable of a concept of a concept. Such a being is rational, a self-positing being, therefore an ego."[56] Again, it is the moral education metaphor which lies in the background: "All individuals must be educated and led to humanity; otherwise they would not become genuinely human."[57]

The Ambiguity: Aufforderung as Transcendental Fact

Fichte's discussion of the *Aufforderung* is ambiguous. On the one hand, it looks like a regressive argument from conditioned to condition, i.e., a transcendental argument as in the following passage:

> The finite rational being cannot ascribe to itself a freedom efficacious in the world without also ascribing such freedom to others, and without therefore assuming the existence of other finite rational beings besides itself.[58]

Fichte's apparent regress to conditions[59] makes it look as if he is arguing that the other is a transcendental condition of the self-ascription of freedom. But he does not actually regress to a set of transcendental conditions. Fichte is not arguing that since I am free there must be others, for that would only establish the other as a condition of possibility. Instead Fichte argues the opposite: Because another has summoned me, I become explicitly conscious of my freedom and responsibility. In the *Aufforderung*, the other as the occasion for evocation of my consciousness of freedom, has priority over my own activity. This priority of the other limits and inverts the transcendental primacy of subjectivity over being that is the hallmark of Fichte's later development beyond the *Wissenschaftslehre* 1794.[60]

Consequently, *Aufforderung* is not simply a transcendental condition a priori, but a fact, a given.[61] It is not something inferred as a ground, but a fact or starting point. As such, it refers to the prior action of the other. Fichte's discussion is not so much a transcendental argument as it is a description and analysis of the fact of *Aufforderung*, i.e., the fact of being summoned. Grant that fact, and it must also be granted that there is an intelligent rational being that makes the summons. There are several puzzles here. Perhaps the most interesting is that the consciousness of freedom, and thus transcendental freedom itself, depends upon something apparently contingent, namely, a summons or call by another. To formulate the point in Husserlian terminology, transcendental freedom (abstract a priori) has a concrete life-world a priori, namely the a priori of the call. No wonder Weischedel and others think that Fichte approximates Buber's philosophy of dialogue between I and Thou![62] But Fichte is led to such a position as a result of his transcendental argument, and not, as the philosophers of dialogue, by dismissal of transcendental argument.[63]

Recognition (*Anerkennung*)

The discussion of *Aufforderung* in paragraph §3 of the *Naturrecht* establishes intersubjectivity, i.e., that the summons to freedom and responsibility is ethical in nature and requires another intelligent ego as its source. Once the plurality of human beings has been established, the next step is to determine the relations among them.[64] Fichte writes:

> The finite rational being cannot assume still other finite rational beings besides itself, without positing itself as standing with these in a determinate relationship, which is called the relation of right (*das Rechtsverhältniss*).[65]

The concept of right finds expression in an ontology of human existence as ethical and social. This is a concrete ontology involving both contrast and opposition on the one hand, and reciprocity and mutuality on the other. The leading and unifying concept of this concrete ontology is *Anerkennen,* or recognition, acknowledgement.

Aufforderung, although posited as a fact, nevertheless remains somewhat formal. *Anerkennen,* in contrast, is concrete. This has several implications. First, there is a specific interaction between individuals: "The knowledge of one individual by another is conditioned by the fact that the other treats it as free, i.e., the other restricts its freedom through the concept of the freedom of the first."[66]

Second, where *Aufforderung* is asymmetrical, *Anerkennung* involves reciprocity. Action by one is insufficient, for recognition must be reciprocal:

> The relation of free beings to one another is a relation of reciprocity through intelligence and freedom. Neither can recognize the other if both do not mutually recognize each other. And neither can treat the other as a free being if both do not do so mutually and reciprocally.[67]

In contrast to the summons (*Aufforderung*) in which the other has priority over my action, in the case of *Anerkennen* I can influence the recognition which the other grants to me by first recognizing and respecting the other's freedom.[68] Given this constitutive mutual reciprocity it is clear that there can be no absolute primacy of one over the other.[69]

Third, recognition is not simply a matter of knowledge, but a matter of freedom. Through the restriction of freedom the rational being becomes an individual, both contrasting and interdependent with others. Mutual restriction of freedom establishes not only the concept of right, but also the individual as a reciprocal concept, which can be conceived only in relation to other individuals.

Finally, the concreteness of *Anerkennen* is most evident in the fact that the term refers not merely to a concept, but to action. As Fichte points out, what counts is not that I have a concept of another as a rational being, but that I really act in the world.[70] *Anerkennen* is not a merely conceptual matter or inference, but rather an action. Fichte explains:

> The entire described union of concepts was only possible in and through action (*Handlung*).... Actions instead of concepts are what really matter here. And there is no talk here of mere concepts without corresponding actions, for, strictly speaking there could be no talk about such at all.[71]

This point is crucial for Fichte's theory of intersubjectivity. Intersubjectivity is not fundamentally a theoretical problem, or a conceptual problem. It is a problem of ethical action. This transposition of the problem of the other from epistemology to action is perhaps Fichte's most original contribution. Since action is always singular and determinate, *Anerkennung* is, or arises out of, a determinate mode of action or praxis. Accordingly, the problem or concept of intersubjectivity is embedded in consciousness, but consciousness in turn is embedded in various modes of social praxis, not all of which are transparently rational.

Anerkennen is mutual action, that results in reciprocity and community: "The condition was that I recognize the other as a rational being, i.e., that I treat him as such, for only through such action does such mutually valid recognition exist."[72] Here then is Fichte's answer to the question, How do I come to know that there are rational beings besides myself?: I come to know others by recognizing them, and by treating them with the respect due to their freedom, i.e, by acknowledging their freedom as placing limits upon my own.

Through reciprocal recognition, humanity is realized as fundamentally social. Recognition is the concrete existential genesis of social reality, the means for surpassing individualism and solipsism. What surpasses solipsism is not simply an argument or an inference, but rather the action and/or praxis of mutual recognition. In it "we are both through our existence bound to one another and connected with each other."[73] From the vantage point of the socially binding praxis of recognition, Fichte reinterprets the concept of individuality:

> The concept of individuality is a reciprocal concept, that is such that it can only be conceived in relation to another, which in turn stands under the same conditions. This concept of the individual is possible only insofar as it is posited as completed by another. Accordingly it is never a matter of 'mine', but rather my admission, and the admission of the other, 'mine' and 'his', and 'his' and 'mine'. In short, individuality is a social concept, in which two consciousness have become united.... Thus a community is effected, and the further consequences do not depend simply upon me, but also depend on those who stand in solidarity with me.[74]

Thus individuality is a socially conditioned and mediated concept arising out of a social praxis of mutual recognition. In contrast to abstract, pre-reality individuality, genuine individuality depends on, and exists in, intersubjective recognition.

Critical Evaluation

Fichte's account of intersubjectivity in his philosophy of law is not a full discussion in our contemporary sense, and its descriptive component is minimal. Nevertheless, he takes up fundamental issues with which Husserl also struggles.[75] The common difficulty is the balancing and blending of two opposed requirements: on the one hand the other is a fact, a given, an encounter which can only be described. On the other hand, it is the task of philosophy to give an account of this fact, whether a transcendental explanation (Fichte) or transcendental-intentional analysis (Husserl). Fichte's transcendental account is based on the principle that there is nothing *for* the ego which does not exist *through* the ego. These two requirements—the transcendental-idealist-constitutional, and the realistic-descriptive—are in tension with, if not opposition to, each other. For given the transcendental inversion of ordinary consciousness, all givens must be transformed into posits and this seems to make the other derivative from the primary ego.

In his account of the summons of the other (*Aufforderung*), Fichte inverts this relation of dependency. The "primary ego" discovers its own freedom through and before the other. This means that there is reciprocity between the self and the other:

> The relation of free beings to each other is a relation of reciprocity through intelligence and freedom. Neither can recognize the other unless both reciprocally recognize each other, and neither can treat the other as a free being unless both reciprocally do so.[76]

Intersubjectivity is not simply erected on the foundation of perception, viz., the problem of identifying which bodies are those possessing or manifesting freedom and intelligence. It is a practical problem, i.e, an ethical and political one, from the very outset. For Fichte the question of the other coincides with the question of right. The other is not the one who turns me into a mere object by depriving me of my possibilities, but rather the one who summons me to freedom and responsibility.

Yet, Fichte's account is not without puzzles and problems of its own. First, Fichte neglects to provide phenomenological descriptions of ordinary consciousness. This creates the impression that experience has little significance for his system. This impression is strengthened by his formulation of reciprocal *Anerkennung* as a logical opposition or contrast. This formulation suggests that the problem of intersubjective mediation is grasped as a problem of logical opposition between ego and non-ego, and not as a conflict of freedoms.

Second, although Fichte thinks that the concept of right is an original concept of pure reason itself, he holds that existence in community necessarily involves restrictions and limitations of freedom. Indeed community is possible only to the extent that its members restrict their own freedoms. This is a negative concept of intersubjectivity and/or community, that construes the other as a limitation of freedom, rather than as its enhancement or ethical elevation.

Third, although Fichte argues that *Anerkennung* is a transcendental condition of natural right, and conversely that right is grounded in and conferred by mutual recognition and respect, he does not develop his theory of rights concretely out of intersubjective recognition. In fact, recognition plays no role in accounting for the social and historical genesis of right. Moreover, individual acts of recognition do not play any role in securing right in Fichte's theory of the state, and Fichte allows that recognition may be bypassed altogether. Ludwig Siep observes that "The institutions securing rights must, according to Fichte be developed out of the contrary motivation of a universal egoism. In the doctrine of compulsory right (*Zwangsrecht*) and social contract, the principle of self-preservation takes the place of recognition."[77]

While Fichte introduces the important concepts of intersubjectivity and social mediation of individual existence, he fails to think through such concepts systematically. Instead, he separates his ethics from his politics, or *Sittenlehre* from *Naturrecht*. Intersubjectivity and *Anerkennen* are not only obscured and buried by other overriding concerns, they are ultimately superfluous for the concepts of right and social ethics.

NOTES

1. Fichte, *Über die Bestimmung des Gelehrten* (1794), *Werke VI*, Hrsg. I. H. Fichte (Berlin: Walter de Gruyter, 1971), 302. [Hereafter *Fichtes Werke* will be cited as FW VI.]

2. See Heinz Heimsoeth, *Fichte* (München: Reinhardt, 1923), 141. Heimsoeth calls this "Fichte's most original and significant accomplishment." Max Scheler was apparently the only phenomenologist who recognized Fichte's contribution to intersubjectivity (*The Nature and Forms of Sympathy*, 227f). However Scheler did not have direct knowledge of Fichte, and misrepresents the position.

3. FW VI 305.

4. Ibid.

5. Fichte, *Grundlage des Naturrechts nach Principien der Wissenschaftslehre* (1796), FW III 1–385. [Hereafter cited as GNR.]

6. Fichte, *System der Sittenlehre nach Principien der Wissenschaftslehre* (1798) FW IV 1–365.

7. *Wissenschaftslehre*, FW I 280, 279.

8. This is Levinas' interpretation of Fichte. "Not everything that is in consciousness would be posited by consciousness—contrary to the proposition that seemed to Fichte to be fundamental." Emmanuel Levinas, "Substitution," in *The Levinas Reader*, ed. Sean Hand (Oxford: B. Blackwell Ltd., 1989), 91.

9. J. N. Findlay, *Hegel: A Re-Examination* (New York: Collier Macmillan, 1962), 46ff.

10. FW I 281.

11. *Wissenschaftslehre*, FW I 279.

12. Ibid. 282.

13. Tom Rockmore shows that Fichte defends circularity as non-vicious. Circularity arises from the limits of human knowledge. What is an essential limitation is not an eliminable defect, and so must be accepted. Cf. Rockmore, *Hegel's Circular Epistemology* (Bloomington, Ind.: Indiana University Press, 1986), 40f.

14. Ludwig Siep, *Anerkennung als Prinzip der praktischen Philosophie: Untersuchungen zu Hegels Jenaer Philosophie des Geistes* (Freiburg: Alber Verlag, 1979). [Hereafter cited as APP.]

15. APP, 28.

16. Wilhelm Weischedel, *Der frühe Fichte: Aufbruch der Freiheit zur Gemeinschaft* (Stuttgart: Frommann-Holzboog, 1973), 129.

17. Philolenko, *La liberté humaine dans la philosophie de Fichte*, Paris, 1966, 24. "On posera donc—comme première thèse—que Fichte a construit toute sa première philosophie afin de résoudre le problème de l'existence d'autrui." Cited in Edith Düsing, *Intersubjectivität und Selbstbewusstsein* (Köln: Dinter Verlag, 1986), 261n.

18. *Wissenschaftslehre*, FW I 188f.

19. Moreover the assertion, "Kein Du, Kein Ich," is used as an ordinary language illustration of a categorical point, namely the mutual delimitation of ego and non-ego. This scarcely establishes an intersubjective intent, much less a concept, in the absence of which it is difficult to see how the *Wissenschaftslehre* serves as the foundational grounding discipline for the concept of intersubjectivity introduced in *Naturrecht*. For criticism of Philolenko, see Edith Düsing, op. cit. 261n, and Peter Baumanns, *Fichtes Ursprungliches System: Sein Standort zwischen Kant und Hegel* (Stuttgart: Frommann-Holzboog, 1972), 172f.

20. Baumanns, op. cit. 167f.

21. Fichte, GNR FW III 8.

22. Reinhard Lauth, "Le probleme de l'interpersonalite chez J. G. Fichte," *Archives de Philosophie* 26 (1962), 325–344. To be sure, Lauth's observation only establishes that Fichte was aware of the problem of the other at the same time he was

writing the *Wissenschaftslehre* 1794, not that in the latter Fichte sought explicit transcendental-ontological justification for or constitution of the other. Lauth's claim is rejected by Vittorio Hösle (*Hegels System: Der Idealismus der Subjectivität und das Problem der Intersubjectivität*, [Hamburg: Meiner Verlag, 1987], Band II, 380n.). Cf. Fichte, *Some Lectures Concerning the Vocation of the Scholar*, tr. D. Breazeale, *Philosophy of German Idealism*, ed. Ernst Behler, [*The German Library: Volume 23*], (New York: Continuum, 1987), 1–38.

23. Cf. Alfred Schutz, "The Problem of Transcendental Intersubjectivity in Husserl," *Collected Papers*, vol. 3, ed. I. Schutz (The Hague: Martinus Nijhoff, 1966), 51ff. Schutz argues that the problem of intersubjectivity is not a transcendental problem, for, at the transcendental level, subjectivity is indeclinable and singular. Hence the phenomenological problem of intersubjectivity can only be 'located' at the level of the natural attitude. Thus Schutz writes, "It is to be surmised that intersubjectivity is not a problem of constitution which can be solved within the transcendental sphere, but is rather a datum (*Gegebenheit*) of the life-world. It is the fundamental ontological category of human existence in the world, and therefore of all philosophical anthropology." (82)

24. This is a puzzling and tantalizing claim, but its meaning is far from clear. If Fichte identifies the transcendental and empirical subject, does this mean that the transcendental subject is intersubjective? This would have profound implications for the doctrine of the absolute ego of the *Wissenschaftslehre*. It would imply a decentering and pluralizing of the transcendental ego. However, given the regressive nature of transcendental argument to unity as the ultimate condition of possibility, how is a pluralizing of the transcendental possible? Or is the transcendental-empirical 'doublet' retained? Then it would seem that intersubjectivity is a derivative 'constituted' phenomenon, grounded somehow by reference to a transcendental ego. If so, does not this render intersubjective plurality and independence illusory? It may well be that such questions are simply unanswerable.

25. Wolfgang Janke, *Fichte: Sein und Reflexion* (Berlin: Walter de Gruyter, 1970). Ludwig Siep, *Hegel's Fichtekritik und die Wissenschaftslehre von 1804* (Freiburg/München: Verlag Karl Alber, 1970).

26. Fichte, GNR 8.

27. Ibid. 2.

28. Ibid. 8.

29. See Kant, *Foundations of the Metaphysics of Morals,* op. cit.

30. Fichte, GNR 9.

31. Ibid. 11. At least this is the case for the GNR. Fichte of course needs to show this condition actually obtains, and does so in the subsequent exposition of the GNR.

32. Weischedel (op. cit. 192) observes that Kant's interest in the issue of community remains practical and ethical. Although Kant sees that the human being is destined to some sort of unsocial sociability, he does not take up the issue of the ontological status of intersubjectivity and community.

33. Fichte, GNR, FW III 5. [My emphasis.]

34. Ibid. 24.

35. Ibid. 4. This inseparability does not entail the collapse of the object into the subject. Rather the transcendental is both subject and object, or, in Husserlian parlance, the world belongs to the transcendental region as the general correlate of consciousness. This is a Being-in-the-World conception. Cf. Dieter Henrich, "Fichtes ürsprungliche Einsicht," *Subjektivität und Metaphysik,* ed. D. Henrich and H. Wagner (Frankfurt: Klostermann, 1966), 188–232.

36. Ibid. 33.

37. Ibid.

38. Ibid.

39. The term *Aufforderung* is difficult to translate. Kroger translates it as demand. It can also mean "call," "request," and "summon." Demand seems to be too specific and determinate. Fichte's point is that other lays claim upon my freedom by his very presence, and so calls or summons me to freedom, to responsible activity, etc. This is not far from the concept of a "call of conscience," provided that conscience be understood in the etymological sense of intersubjective knowing, or *conscientia.* I shall translate *Aufforderung* sometimes as "summons," and sometimes as "call." For whatever it is worth, Weber's *Aufforderung zum Tanz* is translated as "Invitation to the Dance."

40. *Wissenschaftslehre* FW I 279. The term *Anstoß* means literally a push, or an encounter with an initiative from elsewhere; metaphorically it means an impulse, which in English is burdened with psychological connotations. I have decided to leave it untranslated to communicate its uncanniness.

41. Ibid. This terminology recalls Aristotle's discussion of the first or unmoved mover. It suggests a realistic reading of the *Anstoß.* The *Anstoß* is clearly more than a mere thing in itself, for unlike the latter, the *Anstoß* is portrayed as acting. However Fichte contends that nothing is or can be known about the *Anstoß,* since it is only felt.

42. GNR FW III 33.

43. *Aufforderung* is sometimes translated as 'demand', which is too strong. 'Summons' is not only equally permissible, it brings more clearly into focus the idea of an ethical rather than a physical causality. The other summons me to responsibility. Fichte thus anticipates not so much Heidegger as Levinas: the other is the source of an ethical injunction: freedom is simultaneously elicited and placed under a restriction by the other, namely the prohibition of murder. To be sure, Levinas is highly critical of Fichte (see his essay, "Substitution," op. cit. 90ff.) But for Levinas Fichte's position is represented only by the *Wissenschaftslehre;* Levinas seems unfamiliar with Fichte's *Naturrecht* and *Sittenlehre.* He seems ignorant of Fichte's concept of *Aufforderung* or summons by the other. On the other hand, Levinas seems to be stating Fichte's position when he writes: "The one affected by the other is an anarchic trauma, or an inspiration of one by the other, and not a causality striking mechanical-

ly a matter subject to its energy." Cf. Emmanuel Levinas, "Substitution," op. cit. 113. See also his *Totality and Infinity*, op. cit. Although Fichte does not go as far as Levinas in deriving the specific prohibition of murder from the priority of the other, he agrees with Levinas concerning the priority of the ethical over theoretical ontology, and that *Aufforderung* is not a merely physical causality.

44. Here all the problems concerning the relation between the *Wissenschaftslehre* and *Naturrecht* return: Is the *Aufforderung* a deepening transformation of the *Anstoß* of the *Wissenschaftslehre*? Or is it merely a particular instantiation or application of the *Anstoß*? I follow Lauth, Janke and Baumanns in the former interpretation.

45. The problem is the relation of the *Anstoß* to *Aufforderung*, and the relation of the *Wissenschaftslehre* to the *Naturrecht*. However it should be recalled that even in the *Wissenschaftslehre* the *Anstoß* is an incitement or stimulus to action, and a condition of free self-activity, and so presumably compatible with freedom. Given the distinction between *Anstoß* and *Aufforderung*, which Weischedel stresses, the question is whether he is consistent in also maintaining that the *Naturrecht* is a regional ontology based on the foundational ontology of the *Wissenschaftslehre*.

46. Düsing, op. cit. 251. On the other hand, Weischedel claims that the summons (*Aufforderung*) does not involve physical causality or an influence upon the body, op. cit. 121.

47. Fichte's later development is beyond the scope of this study. See W. Janke, *Fichte: Sein und Reflexion*. Fichte, not unlike the so-called later Heidegger, reversed the relation and priority of the transcendental to Being. Being is prior to thought, and cannot be grasped as relative to or constituted by the transcendental. Fichte's transcendentalism was thus transformed into a speculative theology, whose feeling of absolute dependence was taken up by Friedrich Schleiermacher in his fundamental theology. See Schleiermacher, *Der Christliche Glaube* (Berlin: Walter de Gruyter, 1960), ET *The Christian Faith* (Philadelphia: Fortress Press) §§3–5, 32–35.

48. GNR, FW III 36.

49. This implies that the summons has a linguistic component. Unfortunately Fichte does not spell this out, or provide examples, such as Levinas' analysis of the Face: "You shall not kill."

50. GNR, FW III 36.

51. Fichte observes that in the positing of freedom, I do not appropriate to myself all the freedom that I posit, but leave open freedom for the other. GNR, FW III 8.

52. GNR, FW III 39.

53. Fichte, like Levinas, maintains the primacy of the ethical over the theoretical. There is no neutral ontological conception of freedom as prior to ethics, as in Heidegger.

54. Ibid. "Der Mensch wird nur unter Menschen ein Mensch; und da er nichts

Anderes sein kann, denn ein Mensch, und gar nicht sein würde, wenn er dies nicht wäre—sollen überhaupt Menschen sein, so müssen mehrere sein."

55. NR, FW III 36: "The posited cause of the summons outside of the subject must at least presuppose the possibility that the latter can understand and comprehend it, otherwise the summons has no purpose."

56. Fichte, *System der Sittenlehre* IV, 221.

57. GNR, FW III 39.

58. GNR, FW III 30. This is a transcendental argument not unlike P. F. Strawson's. See Strawson's argument concerning Persons and P-Predicates in *Individuals*.

59. C. K. Hunter characterizes this part of Fichte's argument as an argument for *"intelligibler Interpersonalität,"* which he contrasts with *"wirklich interpersonaler Bestimmung."* See his *Der Interpersonalitätsbeweis in Fichtes früher angewandter praktischer Philosophie* (Meisenheim am Glan: Verlag Anton Hain, 1973), 35ff, 97ff. [Hereafter cited as IPB.]

60. Cf. Levinas, who argues that the relation to the other is asymmetrical: the other is the one who places the I in question. TI, op. cit. 195.

61. Düsing op. cit characterizes *Aufforderung* as a "necessary fact." (247) However a necessary fact is also transcendental in the weaker rather than the stronger sense of transcendental. Cf. also Hunter, IPB 97ff.

62. Weischedel, op. cit. 124ff. See also Hans Duesberg, *Person und Gemeinschaft: Philosophische-Systematische Untersuchungen des Sinnzusammenhangs von personaler Selbstständigkeit und interpersonaler Beziehung an Texten von J. G. Fichte und M. Buber* (Bonn: Bouvier Verlag, 1970).

63. For this antithesis between transcendental philosophy and dialog philosophy, see Michael Theunissen, *Der Andere*, ET: *The Other* (Cambridge, Mass.: MIT Press, 1985). Theunissen's opposition between transcendental approaches to the other and the dialogical approach is dubious. The two are not mutually exclusive opposites but rather complementary levels of analysis.

64. It should be borne in mind that Fichte's account of intersubjectivity is not a full blown theory of intersubjectivity in itself, whatever that might be. Rather Fichte's discussion of intersubjectivity occurs within his ethical and legal theory, i.e., his account of the *Foundations of Natural Law* (*Grundlage des Naturrecht*) and his system of ethics (*System der Sittenlehre*).

65. GNR, FW III 41.

66. Ibid. 44.

67. Ibid.

68. Ibid. 44–45. For a discussion of the issue, cf. Siep, op. cit. 30f.

69. Fichte does not address the question of non-reciprocal recognition. Since he is expounding the concept of right as a form of recognition, he restricts his analysis to the point that I can recognize my own freedom because another has already summoned and recognized me.

70. GNR FW III 45.

71. Ibid. 48.

72. Ibid. 47.

73. GNR, FW III 48: "wir sind beide durch unsere Existenz aneinander *gebunden* und einander *verbunden*."

74. Ibid. 47–48.

75. See Edmund Husserl, *Cartesian Mediations,* tr. Dorion Cairns (The Hague: Martinus Nijhoff, 1960), especially the Fifth Meditation. [Hereafter cited as CM.] For a commentary and discussion, cf. below chapter 12. See also Paul Ricoeur, "Husserl's Fifth Cartesian Meditation," in *Husserl: An Analysis of His Phenomenology,* tr. Ballard and Embree (Evanston, Ill.: Northwestern University Press, 1967), 123ff.

76. Fichte, GNR, FW III 44.

77. Ludwig Siep, op. cit. 35.

PART THREE
HEGEL

FOUR

THE EARLY HEGEL AND FICHTE

Part three focuses on Hegel's appropriation and transformation of the concept of recognition. The relevant literature includes his early writings, chiefly his first book, the *Phenomenology of Spirit*. The present chapter treats Hegel's early, pre-*Phenomenology* social theory and his appropriation of Fichte's concept of recognition. Hegel develops the concept of recognition in a way that allows him to reformulate and integrate his earlier social theory. Chapters 5 and 6 deal with the method and plan of Hegel's *Phenomenology*. Since Hegel's credentials as a phenomenologist have been questioned, I shall seek to show that Hegelian and Husserlian phenomenologies, despite differences, nevertheless communicate with each other on a deeper level. Although it is notoriously difficult to define the term "phenomenology," the term is not a sheer equivocation in its respective Hegelian and Husserlian senses, as Sartre's work has demonstrated.[1] Although Husserl made phenomenological method more explicit than anyone else, Sartre contends that Hegel's treatment of intersubjectivity is superior to and far richer than Husserl's.

After establishing that Hegel's *Phenomenology* is "phenomenology," I shall focus in chapters 7 through 11 on recognition. In the *Phenomenology,* recognition is the existential phenomenological genesis of Hegel's concept of Spirit (*Geist*). This shows that *Geist* has an essential intersubjective-social sense. In other words, Hegel discovers that the interhuman[2] is a dimension of freedom, knowledge, and truth, and sets forth a social conception of reason. Only when its interhuman dimension is understood, is it possible to appreciate Hegel's concept of *Geist*.

Although Hegel found the concept of recognition in Fichte, he did not first discover intersubjectivity by reading Fichte's *Grundlage des Naturrecht.* Before he discovered the concept of recognition, Hegel had already arrived at an understanding of human being as social, and self-consciousness as involving intersubjective mediation. I hasten to point out that Hegel's concern is not to develop a theory of intersubjectivity per se. Like Fichte, he takes up and develops his views of intersubjectivity within the context of a larger project. Hegel began as a social reformer, and it was his social concerns which led him to philosophy and a philosophical biography of spirit (*Geist*).

Lukács observes that Hegel was concerned with the social world and social praxis from the very start, tracing the fortunes of the social subject in the course of history. The 'discussion beneath the discussion' in Hegel's *Early Theological Writings* is "the fragmentation of the collective subject into private individuals of which society will henceforth be the mere 'aggregate'."[3] In social fragmentation and alienation Hegel found the seeds of revolution and the need for philosophy:

> Disunity *[Entzweiung]* is the source of the need of philosophy; and as the culture of the era, it is the given, unfree aspect of the structure. In fragmented disunited culture the appearance of the absolute has been isolated from the absolute, and reified as something independent.[4]

Hegel struggled initially with this issue of disunity or positivity, in the context of religion and morality. He held that religion in general, and Christianity in particular, contributed to cultural disunity and alienation. *The Early Theological Writings* seek to show how Jesus' religion of freedom became corrupted, i.e., underwent a decline into a positive authoritarian religion, or Christianity.[5] Traditional Christianity is a source of alienation and oppression. Hegel came to reassess this interpretation when he discovered that Christianity signifies not only alienation, but also reconciliation which overcomes alienation. Of interest is the fact that Hegel formulates these issues in social-intersubjective terms.

HEGEL'S EARLIEST SOCIAL THEORY

Like Fichte, Hegel's way into intersubjective theory is through a critique and extension of Kant. Whereas Fichte's starting point was the problem of the self-consciousness of freedom, Hegel begins with unfreedom, interpreted in social terms of domination, oppression and alienation. We recall Kant's distinction between autonomy and heteronomy.[6] According to Kant, the will is in a condition of heteronomy whenever something other than it—be it the object of desire, inclination, or another person—determines the end governing its action. Kant elsewhere describes heteronomy as a social condition, as a condition of tutelage, or the "inability to make use of one's understanding without direction from another."[7] Autonomy is a condition in which the rational will determines its own ends out of respect for humanity and for the universality of law. Autonomy signifies self-determination, while heteronomy is a condition of unfreedom. However, despite the implicit assumption of a social-intersubjective context, Kant's discussion of heteronomy and autonomy remains within an individualistic framework.

Heteronomy and Domination in Hegel's Early Theological Writings

In his earliest theological writings, Hegel identifies the religion of Jesus with a moral religion of autonomous freedom in Kant's sense.[8] Unfortunately, after Jesus' death, this religion of freedom degenerated into a positive religion, a heteronomous condition. Heteronomous morality or religion requires a set of rules or beliefs that are positive, i.e., givens accepted and sustained by external authority. A religion becomes positive when it shifts the evidentiary basis of belief from faith's reality-apprehensions to theological authorities. It may construct an absolute self-certifying authority, be it scripture, or tradition, which coerces belief and demands unquestioning assent and obedience. Hegel describes such a faith in terms which elaborate on Kant's concept of heteronomous tutelage: "To shudder before an unknown Being; to renounce one's will in one's conduct; to subject oneself throughout like a machine to given rules, to abandon intellect altogether in action...and to lull oneself into a brief or lifelong insensibility..."[9]

In this first essay, Hegel traces how the moral religion of Jesus declined to a merely positive faith, and thereby contributed to the fragmented, disunited cultural situation. Hegel does not claim that the Christian religion is inherently positive; a decline into authoritarian positivity is an historical fate which can overtake "any doctrine, any precept...since anything can be proclaimed in a forcible way with a suppression of freedom."[10] Moreover, his critique of positive religion does not reduce religion to autonomous human morality: "I am here assuming from the start that human nature of necessity needs to recognize a Being who transcends our consciousness of human agency, to make the intuition of that Being's perfection the animating spirit of human life..."[11]

In the second essay, the "Spirit of Christianity and Its Fate," Hegel's focus is on positivity and heteronomy as social conditions, as configurations of community based on domination and oppression. He contrasts Abraham and Jesus as founders of quite different types of religious communities. Hegel portrays Judaism as a positive or heteronomous religion, its God as an alien transcendent lawgiver, and Abraham, its patriarch as an alienated individual, a stranger to his culture and to the world.[12] Abraham's community is positive and authoritarian; its ideology exhibits a penal vision of the world that portrays God as almighty creditor and administrator of the law, before whom the members are guilty debtors.

A bad conscience they knew only as fear of punishment. Such a conscience, as a consciousness of self in opposition to self, always presupposes an ideal over against a reality which fails to correspond with the ideal.... Their poverty had to serve a being infinitely rich, and by purloining something from him and thereby stealing for themselves a sense of selfhood, these men of bad conscience had made their reality not still poorer but richer. But the result was that they then had to fear the Lord they had robbed; he would let them repay their theft and make sacrifices.... Only by a payment to their almighty creditor would they be free of their debts, and after paying they would be once again without possessions.[13]

The asymmetry between creditor and debtor anticipates Hegel's later famous discussion of mastery and servitude in the *Phenomenology*. These themes are already present in his account of the religion of Abraham:

> Everything was simply under God's mastery. Abraham, as the opposite of the whole world, could have had no higher mode of being than that of the other term of an opposition.... Mastery was the only possible relationship in which Abraham could stand to the infinite world opposed to him, but he was unable to make this mastery actual.[14]

The concept of God as master and the religious as servile, reflect a patriarchal-monarchical metaphor in the conception of religion and divine-human relation.

In contrast, Hegel treats the community founded by Jesus as a community of love and forgiveness. Its ideology exhibits a tragic/comic vision of the world in which tragic conflict is mediated by love. These are the themes which figure prominently in Hegel's mature theory of intersubjectivity and philosophy of religion. What needs stressing is that prior to taking up Fichte's concept of recognition, Hegel had already isolated different kinds and structures of the social, one based upon domination, fear and repression, the other based upon freedom, forgiveness, and reconciliation. These will later appear as the two major levels (*Stufen*) of recognition in the *Phenomenology*.

Love and Reconciliation in the Early Theological Writings

Hegel's reinterpretation of Christianity is influenced by Hölderlin's philosophy of love and unification. Hölderlin helped Hegel see in Christianity, as a religion of love, possibilities for overcoming dualism, disunity and alienation. Hegel conceives love as overcoming the opposition and estrangement constitutive of the legal-penal vision: "...in love all thought of *duties* vanishes."[15] Again, "Love itself pronounces no imperative. It is no universal opposed to a particular, no unity of concept, but a unity of spirit, divinity. To love God is to feel one's self in the 'all' of life, with no restrictions, in the infinite.... Only through love is the might of objectivity [sic. disunity] broken..."[16] It is clear that the religion of love is directed against both authoritarian religions of lordship and bondage, and the tendency towards heteronomy Hegel finds in Kant. "To complete subjection under the law of an alien Lord, Jesus opposed not a particular subjection under a law of one's own— the self-coercion of Kantian virtue, but *virtues without lordship and without submission, i.e., virtues as modifications of love.*"[17]

Hegel now comes to appreciate Christianity as something other than a positive faith reflecting a heteronomous legal-penal vision of the world. Hegel considers Christianity as an alternative to the legal-penal vision of the world because "law and punishment cannot be reconciled, but they can be transcended if fate can be reconciled."[18] The alternative, with which Hegel now identifies Christianity, is a tragic vision whose leading categories are not sin and punishment, but tragic conflict and its resolution in the reconciliation of fate. Thus, the alternative to heteronomy is no longer Kantian moral autonomy and its faith in a moral universe, but rather tragic conflict and its resolution. Hegel's own conception of the tragic is not quite that of classical Greek tragedy.[19] Hegel's tragic vision focuses on conflict with an alien power or fate, and the overcoming of fate through love.

Hegel prefers the tragic interpretation of evil and suffering to the legal-penal vision, because the former does not rest upon the heteronomous dualisms of lawgiver/guilt, and creditor/debtor.

> In the hostile power of fate, the universal is not severed from particular in which the law, as a universal, is opposed to man or his inclinations as the particular.... The trespass of the man regarded as in the toils of fate is therefore not a rebellion of the subject against his ruler, the slave's flight from his master, liberation from subservience.... Hence punishment as fate is the equal reaction of the trespasser's own deed, of a power which he himself has armed, of an enemy made an enemy by himself.[20]

The penal vision presupposes a transcendent alien being who is feared because he can inflict punishment. In the penal vision of the world, the suffering debtor can never satisfy the almighty creditor and administrator of the law. "In fate on the other hand, the hostile power is the power of life made hostile, and the fear of fate is not the fear of an *alien* being.... In fate...the human being recognizes his own [lost] life, and his supplication to it is not a supplication to an alien master, but a reversion and approximation to himself."[21] Thus, tragic suffering is self-inflicted. But a self-inflicted wound is one that can heal, for "life can heal its wounds again."[22] Hegel is attracted to tragic conflict, but he differs from classical tragedy by holding that conflict, while inevitable, can also be overcome and mediated. "Opposition is the possibility of reunification.... This sensing of life, a sensing which finds itself again, is love, and in love fate is reconciled."[23]

HEGEL'S THEORY OF LOVE

Dieter Henrich claims that Hegel's account of love is important for understanding the genesis of Hegel's later system. Henrich writes:

> Once Hegel adopted the concept of love as the basic principle of his thinking, the system came forth without interruption. The theme 'love' was replaced by the richer structure of life—for apparent reasons—and later by the still richer concept of spirit (*Geist*).[24]

The concept of love functions as both an ontological principle and an inter-subjective-social principle. Hegel is influenced by Hölderlin's "*Vereinigungsphilosophie*," in which love is a principle of unification and synthesis rather than a transcendental unity of apperception (Kant) or an absolute ego (Fichte).

Henrich observes that Hölderlin's concept of love differs from Fichte's absolute ego. "Hölderlin's thought replaced Fichte's highest principle with another, and convinced Hegel that it is no longer necessary to begin with consciousness."[25] But Hegel understands the reconciliation of love differently from Hölderlin and the rest of German Idealism.

> Hegel must constantly conceive all structures which Hölderlin understood as deriving from original Being, *as modes of relation which coalesce. The event of coalescence itself, and not a ground out of which coalescence derives, is for Hegel the true absolute, the 'all in all'.* We will see that for this reason Hegel was convinced that the absolute must be conceived as *Geist* and not as Being.[26]

Hegel does not aspire to the holism of a substance metaphysics, or to a mystical unification of all in the One. Instead, Hegel's holism is relational, as Henrich explains: "This is Hegel's distinctive idea, that the *relata* in opposition must, to be sure, derive from a whole. However, this whole does not precede its *relata* as Being, or as intellectual intuition. Rather the whole is only the developed and explicit concept of the *relata* themselves."[27] Hegel inaugurated this novel holism as a result of his appropriation and transformation of Hölderlin's concept of love, and developed it further in his Jena philosophy of *Geist*.[28]

Love as Intersubjective

The concept of love involves two sets of relations, internal and external, or *unio* and *synthesis*. "In love man has found himself again in another. Since love is a unification of life, it presupposes division, a development of life, a developed many-sidedness of life."[29] The basic idea that love overcomes oppositions Hegel now develops as a theory of the interrelation of internal and external relations. Hegel's claim is that the inner relation of the self to itself is more than simple or immediate self-relation; rather it is mediated by an other. Love unites the lover and the beloved. What distinguishes Hegel's conception of love from Plato's Eros is the claim that the self's relation with itself is mediated by the other.[30] In other words, the self depends on the other for overcoming its internal diremption, the filling up of its lack. Thus

> in love life is present as a duplicate of itself and as a single and unified self. Here life has run through the circle of development from an immature to a completely mature unity: when the unity was immature, there still stood over and against it the world and the possibility of a cleavage between itself

and the world. As development proceeded, reflection produced more and more oppositions until it set the whole of man's life in opposition [to objectivity]. Finally love completely destroys objectivity and thereby annuls and transcends reflection, deprives man's opposite of all foreign character...[31]

In the last sentence above there is a formulation of Hegel's point that seems to undermine the very social-intersubjective relation he is concerned to establish. It sounds as if love's overcoming all oppositions eliminates objectivity, and with it, eliminates the other on which it supposedly depends. A common complaint about Hegel's thought is that it "swallows up" or "devours" the other. If so, then Hegel's concept of love would not only be stifling, it would be like the embrace of the Black Widow spider. Fortunately, this is not at all what Hegel has in mind when he claims that the re-union of the self depends on and occurs through the other. When he says that love "destroys" objectivity, he means that it deprives the other of its *foreign* or *alien* character. But this does not mean elimination of the other as such. Hegel continues: "In love the separate does still remain, but as something united and no longer as something separate; life [in the subject] senses life [in the object]."[32]

Moreover, love is more than simply the re-unification of the self with itself mediated by the other. It is also an enhancement and enrichment of the self in a mutual 'giving and taking'. Further, "The lover who takes is not thereby made richer than the other; he is enriched indeed, but only so much as the other is. So, too, the giver does not make himself poorer; by giving to the other he has at the same time and to the same extent enhanced his own treasure" (compare Juliet in *Romeo and Juliet* [ii.1.175-177]: "My bounty is as boundless as the sea, my love is as deep; the more I give to thee, the more I have").[33] Here we find one of the basic ideas of Hegel's social theory: community is not simply a restriction or limitation on freedom, it is a condition and enhancement of life.

But not just any community enhances human life. Hegel distinguishes two conceptions of the "kingdom of God." He observes that the concept of kingship which the Christian movement took over from its predecessor, is a concept of domination and mastery. According to Hegel, Judaism conceives the relation between God and world in terms of a royal metaphor of absolute sovereignty: "Nothing in nature was supposed to have any part in God; everything was simply under God's mastery."[34] Thus the very concept of 'kingdom' "imports something heterogeneous [sic. heteronomous] into the expression of the divine union of men, for it means only a unity through domination, through the power of a stranger over a stranger [*durch Gewalt eines Fremden über ein Fremdes*], a union that must be completely distinguished from the beauty of the divine life of a pure human fellowship, because such a life is the freest possible. This latter idea of a Kingdom of God completes and comprises the whole of the Christian religion as Jesus founded it..."[35] The community Jesus founded is not a community of mastery and domination, and so not, strictly speaking, a kingdom (*Königreich*), but a community founded on the beautiful rule of love.

The kingdom of God in the distinctively Christian sense is a community of love and reconciliation. In such a community "what is common to all is living in God. This is not a mere common character which a concept expresses, but rather a community of love, a living bond which unites the believers. It is the feeling that all oppositions, as pure enmities and also rights...are overcome [*Aufgehoben*]."[36] This community is at another level and of another kind than domination and servitude. Incarnation—which Hegel reformulates as the *mutual recognition* of God and man—replaces the royal metaphor: "The mountain and the eye which sees it are object and subject, but between man and God, between spirit and spirit there is no such cleft of objectivity and subjectivity; one is to the other an other only in that one recognizes the other; both are one."[37] Human intersubjective relations are patterned after the relation of love manifest in incarnation; thus Hegel cites the command to love, and continues: "This friendship of soul [*Seelenfreundschaft*] described in the language of reflection as an essence, as spirit, is the divine spirit, is God who rules the community. Is there an idea more beautiful than that of a people related to one another by love?"[38]

The Limits and Fate of Love

The community of love is profound and beautiful, but it is also limited and incomplete. Hegel asks whether love as a principle of community is incomplete such that fate could still have power over it.[39] His answer appears to be affirmative, namely, that the beautiful community, based on the single principle of love, cannot go beyond love itself, and consequently "there still lies a prodigious field of objectivity which claims activity of many kinds and sets up a fate whose...power is mighty."[40] The Christian community based exclusively on love is radically egalitarian and it can maintain its radical egalitarianism only by opposing it to all relative oppositions and contrasts. Hegel comments that "This restriction of love to itself, its flight from all determinate modes of living...even if they sprang from its spirit, this removal of itself from all fate is just its greatest fate."[41] Jesus defined himself and his movement in a paradoxical relation to the world: extreme purity and flight from the world on the one hand, with political passivity and submission to the powers of the world on the other. The very radicality of the reconciling power of love still leaves love in opposition to the impure world. The reconciliation effected by love is a union in God only, not a reconciliation between individuals themselves, or between individuals and the world.[42] Consequently "the citizens of the kingdom of God become set over and against a hostile state, become private persons excluding themselves from it."[43] Love, conceived as a pure, radically transcendent principle, is in reference to the world, parochial. Therefore, love has limits as a social principle. It does not yet incorporate individual freedom, and differences between individuals.

To be sure, in love individuals are not necessarily eliminated or simply submerged in an ocean of infinity. Love does not eliminate individuals, but preserves the ontological distance and separation between subjects constitutive of finitude even as it overcomes their conflict and opposition.[44] But because reconciliation involves only what is common in the divided elements, and not what is different or individual, Hegel excludes from the bond of love all relations of domination (*Herrschaftsverhältnisse*).[45]

For this reason Siep concludes that individuality, although not excluded, is not yet integrated into Hegel's theory of intersubjectivity. Love cannot take account of, or mediate, assertions of individual differences or rights. Love and right are principles of two distinct spheres that stand in contrast, because reconciliation implies the renunciation of the claims of individuality and its rights. In this respect Hegel's intersubjective theory, based on the concept of love, is incompatible with Fichte's theory that the concept of right is grounded in mutual recognition. Whereas, for Fichte, social intersubjectivity calls for a restriction upon freedom, and community is inherently restrictive and oppressive, for Hegel the intersubjectivity of love transcends the standpoint of right because the standpoint of right is the standpoint of individualism. For Hegel, community is not inherently oppressive, but an enlargement of the self and its freedom.

Hegel's appropriation of Fichte's concept of recognition is an attempt to correct a deficiency in his earlier social theory. For there individuals are subordinate to the universal and social. This means that individuality is conceived negatively. However, the concept of recognition implies a positive conception of individuality and of community. Social relations are not inherently oppressive, but rather secure, enhance and preserve individual freedom.

HEGEL'S CRITIQUE OF FICHTE

Hegel's critique of Fichte is very subtle, and is by no means an absolute rejection. Rather, Hegel learns much from Fichte, and Hegelianism is in part a systematic variation on Fichte.[46] Hegel accepts Fichte's project of reformulating Kant's transcendental philosophy as a system. Hegel considers Kant's transcendental deduction of the categories to be authentic speculative idealism precisely because the categories are *not* subjective, but rather identities of thought and being.[47] Fichte works out the transcendental deduction from the ego as first principle showing that all the categories are modes of action of the ego in its self-constitution. But Fichte is too faithful to Kant, since he preserves the fundamental dualism at the heart of Kant's system.[48]

Hegel complains that Fichte fails to unify the transcendental standpoint with the empirical standpoint, or the transcendental ego with the empirical ego:

> The causal relation between the absolute and its appearance is a false identity.... In the causal relation both opposites have standing, but they are distinct in rank. *The union is forcible. The one subjugates the other. The one rules, the other is subservient.* The unity is forced, and forced into a relative identity. The identity which *ought* to be absolute, *is* incomplete. Contrary to its philosophy, the system has turned into a dogmatism...[49]

Fichte is inconsistent: On the one hand, he holds the idealist position that there is nothing in the ego except what is posited by the ego, and, on the other hand, he maintains that the *Anstoß* influences or summons the ego to action. Fichte claims it is impossible for a finite intellect to escape from this circle.[50] Hegel's point is that Fichte's assumptions make it impossible to have a circle at all. Since the system abandons its fundamental principle, it becomes dualist and fails to revert upon its starting point.[51]

Fichte's fundamental principle is not subjective, nor does it lead to a subjective idealism: "What distinguishes Fichte's idealism is that the identity which it establishes is one that does not deny the objective but puts the subjective and the objective on the same level of reality and certainty—that pure and empirical consciousness are one. For the sake of the identity of subject and object, I posit things outside myself just as surely as I posit myself. The things exist just as surely as I do."[52] Nevertheless, "in Fichte's reconstruction of identity, one ego dominates and the other is dominated.... They stand in a relation of causality...one of them goes into servitude and the sphere of necessity is subordinated to that of freedom. Thus the end of the system is untrue to its beginning, the result is untrue to its principle."[53]

Hegel finds this fundamental problem in evidence throughout Fichte's practical philosophy. Given the 'forcible union' of the dualism at the heart of Fichte's system, it comes as no surprise that Fichte's practical philosophy fails to carry out or implement the freedom which is the logical basis of the system, and the supreme principle of practical philosophy. On the one hand, recognition (*Anerkennung*) is supposed to be a condition of the consciousness of freedom. That is, freedom is socially mediated; the self depends on the recognition of others to become conscious of its own freedom. Yet, Fichte persists in regarding intersubjectivity and community as involving restrictions or negations of freedom. The reciprocal intersubjective mediation of freedom, supposedly the foundation of rights, does not find expression in the practical or applied philosophy. Fichte allows that right may be enforced through coercion if necessary. This is a reversion to domination, mastery, and servitude. For these reasons Hegel criticizes Fichte's view of the social:

> If the community of rational beings were essentially a limitation of true freedom, community would be in and for itself the supreme tyranny. [How-

ever]...the community of a person with others must not be regarded as a limitation of the true freedom of the individual, but essentially as its enlargement. Highest community is highest freedom, both in terms of power and its exercise. But it is precisely in this higher community that freedom as an ideal factor and reason as opposed to nature disappear completely.[54]

Fichte's concept of freedom remains negative and formal, and from this perspective intersubjectivity and community are asymmetrical and restrictive. Consequently, Fichte's concepts of intersubjectivity and community do not overcome heteronomy and coercion. Fichte's ethics remain like Kant's, an internalized conflict of lordship and bondage: "...once the commander is transferred within the human being itself, and the absolute opposition of command and subservience is internalized, the inner harmony is destroyed. Not to be one, but to be an absolute dichotomy constitutes the essence of human nature."[55]

PROBLEMS IN APPROPRIATING *ANERKENNUNG*

We have seen that Hegel already had a theory of intersubjectivity prior to his appropriation of Fichte. That theory is not compatible with Fichte's account of mutual recognition because love reconciles and overcomes the dichotomies of the legal-penal vision. Love signifies a radical egalitarianism that transcends the individualist standpoint of domination. The appropriation of the concept of recognition (*Anerkennung*) compels Hegel to address new issues and problems. At the same time it enables Hegel to fill lacunae in his own views. The general problem is the incorporation of individuality and the accompanying problem of right within his theory of love as reconciliation of opposition. The picture deriving from Kierkegaard's criticism that Hegel forgets existence and the existing individual, is a caricature.[56] Hegel in fact struggles to formulate a theory of individuality, to do justice to the individual and individual freedoms, but in a way that does not relapse into domination and/or alienation. Individuality and difference must be given given their due, without, however, reducing the social to something inherently oppressive, or a mere aggregate, the creation or option of individuals. However, the recognition and incorporation of individuality comes with a price; it means that conflict is an essential element or moment of recognition. Hegel's advance on Fichte is that he sees that, given the ontological distance between individual subjects, recognition requires struggle and issues in tragic conflict.

Given his polemic against Fichte's theory of the *Anstoß*, it comes as no surprise that Hegel does not appropriate Fichte's theory of the other as the summons to freedom and responsibility. That is the language of alienation and Kantian *Moralität*. Instead, Hegel adopts recognition (*Anerkennung*) as the fundamental framework of the theory of intersubjectivity, but modifies it in several important respects.

The most important is its transposition from Fichte's first person problematic into a social problematic and framework. As Harris observes, the 'individuals' Hegel describes in his Jena Manuscripts are, for the most part families, clans, and peoples.[57] Hegel grapples with the transition from the so-called 'state of nature' to the formation of the state or the social itself. The transition from the family, a natural community, to a larger social unit involves the problem of the intersubjective conflict of wills and its resolution. In dealing with this transition, Hegel introduces into recognition elements of alienation, conflict and struggle.

Hegel preserves love as the moment of reconciliation and re-unification. At the same time, he comes to consider love as an incomplete social principle and restricts it to the intimate sphere of the family. In the Jena Manuscripts, he focuses on social or objective spirit, while bracketing consideration of individual spirit and absolute spirit. The Jena Manuscripts—the *System der Sittlichkeit,* the *Philosophie des Geistes* (1803/04) and the *Realphilosophie* (1805/06)—are among the most obscure and difficult that Hegel produced.[58] Incomplete sketches, they point toward the *Phenomenology of Spirit* (1807) as well as toward the later *Philosophy of Right* and *Encyclopedia.* They are difficult to interpret because, in these, Hegel separates his discussion of objective *Geist* from his concept of absolute *Geist.* Moreover, he does not formulate an eidetics of intersubjective recognition until the *Phenomenology of Spirit.* He confines the earlier discussions in the Jena Manuscripts to concrete forms and examples. The ontological structures of intersubjectivity are suggested, but not worked out.

Ludwig Siep attempts to bring some order out of the chaotic materials.[59] Siep distinguishes two levels of recognition, namely, interpersonal recognition, occurring between two individuals, and recognition as a relation between individuals and the spirit of a people (*Volksgeist*), that is expressed in social institutions. The first level (*Stufe*) of recognition is a mutual reciprocal relation in which each self finds itself in another. This most closely approximates to Fichte's discussion of *Anerkennen.* Hegel's specific example is marriage and family. The second level focuses on the relation between persons and social institutions; Hegel develops Fichte's claim that the meaning of right is intersubjectively grounded in recognition. Hegel broadens this to the claim that the relation between persons and social institutions is an intersubjective relation of recognition. That is, the individual self should find its interests reflected in and supported by social institutions. Conversely, if the individual self no longer finds recognition in social institutions, it becomes alienated. Freedom and recognition are inseparable.

While it is useful to distinguish these levels of recognition for purposes of analysis, it is also necessary to realize that there is no sharp distinction, much less separation, between the two. In these essays, Hegel easily passes from one level to the other. Hegel criticizes and rejects the concept of consciousness as a particular, first-person epistemological subject. Without denying the individuality of consciousness, Hegel uncovers its social nature or social infinity, namely, to be both itself and relation to other. He focuses on the family, its origin in desire, its reproductive and educative functions, its passing away, its relation to strangers and to larger social structures.

Siep also shows that Hegel modifies both Fichte's concept of *Anerkennung* and his own theory of intersubjectivity. According to Siep, *Anerkennung* is a synthesis of love and strife (*Liebe und Kampf*). This is an important move. Hegel reformulates love and strife as determinate modes of recognition. This means that recognition becomes the basic ontological structure of Hegel's theory of intersubjectivity, and love and conflict are now taken as determinate instances and shapes of recognition. The term "synthesis" is somewhat misleading. Hegel does not try to synthesize or reconcile love and strife, so much as to show that these are different types or shapes (*Gestalts*) of recognition. Love is the principle of recognition constitutive of marriage and family. Conflict is the principle of recognition constitutive of the state of nature and subsequently of civil society.

TRANSFORMATION OF *ANERKENNUNG*

Love and Anerkennung

Hegel's Jena Manuscripts do not treat love as a metaphysical or theological principle, but as a social principle of union constitutive of the family as a natural social unit. As a principle, "love is recognition without conflict of will."[60] Marriage and family constitute an objective public union of private individual wills, a new corporate personality in which personal and private will is subordinate to the will of the whole. Love conceived here in its natural condition as sexual love, nevertheless elevates desire to the level of an immediate ethical bond or intimate relationship in which the concept of contract—founded upon private individual right—is out of place.

Hegel identifies love explicitly as a form of mutual recognition. He formulates this reciprocity in the fundamental structures of recognition, namely being-for-self and being-for-other: "...each is herself/himself in the being-for-self (*Fürsichsein*) of the other...each is conscious of being-for-self in his/her singularity in the consciousness of the other..."[61] In the *Early Theological Writings*, Hegel characterized love as the mediation of the self to itself by another. Now he makes this synthesis of the 'inner' relations of the self to itself and 'outer' relations between self and other, somewhat more explicit. Each is for himself/herself (*Fürsichsein*, being-for-self) in and through the other. Love signifies a reciprocal recognition: one is 'for-self' through the other, and 'for-other' through being-for-self. Or, being-for-self does not exclude but includes being-for-other, and vice versa. Although these structures are not equivalent in and of themselves, *Fürsichsein* and *Füreinanderssein* become equivalent through love. Siep formulates the issue this way:

> The other...reveals himself to me not as a stranger, but rather as constitutive for my being and of the same kind of being as I am. Therefore the 'loss of self in other' is at the same time a finding-of-self-in-other-as-oneself. In love the difference between being-for-self and being-for-other is sublated.[62]

Nevertheless, Hegel retains the fundamental feature of love in the *Theological Writings,* namely, it is an intersubjective relation expressing the common bond of the partners and not their separate private individuality. Love expresses ethical life in its immediacy and intimacy. Love cannot incorporate and mediate the conflicts of private individual freedoms and property claims arising therefrom. In Hegel's social philosophy, love is confined to the realm of the family, or ethical life in its immediacy. Siep observes that "according to Hegel, the formation of the individual as well as the social-common consciousness comes about not through the oppositionless relation of love and the immediate solidarity of the family, but rather such formation presupposes an element of distance, and the assertion of the independence and differences between individuals. In the struggle for recognition this moment of distance is radicalized."[63] Fichte's account of mutual-reciprocal recognition is radicalized by the introduction of intersubjective distance, alienation, and struggle.

Anerkennung *in the Mode of Conflict*

The second form of recognition is strife (*Kampf*). The Jena Manuscripts provide important background for and alternatives to the famous struggle between Master and Slave, or lordship and bondage of the *Phenomenology.* The 'locus' or background of this form of recognition is not religious positivism and authoritarianism, but the Hobbesian account of the state of nature. Siep explains that the various versions of the struggle for recognition from the *System of Ethical Life* through the *Jena Realphilosophie* are modelled after a duel over honor.[64] According to Harris the 'ethics of honor' is not a purely private matter between two isolated atomic individuals, but is grounded in the family as the fundamental pre-polis social unit. "The independent consciousness that emerges from the family with a full awareness of its responsibility must be prepared to lay down its life for the sake of its independence"[65] or family honor. Thus, the struggle for recognition is situated within the context of the noble, warrior consciousness, the defender of family honor and property. This analysis presupposes the mature development of the will which has been submerged in the immediate unity of the family. This case of recognition focuses on the intersubjective conflict of will with will.

Hegel replaces Fichte's transcendental deduction of right as a pure, a priori concept of reason, with a *phenomenological* account of the genesis of right through a process of conflict and struggle. Struggle is possible, because *Anerkennung* involves intersubjective distance, uncertainty, and opposition. Unlike Fichte, who seems to have assumed that *Anerkennen* is a more or less automatic reciprocal action, Hegel observes that "in freedom the possibility of non-recognition and unfreedom is present just as much as the possibility of recognition and freedom."[66] In other words, mutual recognition is not a given, or necessarily a success story. Rather, struggle is always possible and signifies *Anerkennen* in the mode of failure (*Nichtanerkennen*), refusal, rejection. Conflict is one possible shape of intersubjective relation; it signifies the refusal of recognition, the rejection of relation; or, "the only relation is the nullification of relation."[67]

Hegel's analysis of honor shapes his early account of the struggle for recognition. Honor consists in the capacity and right of appropriation, possession, or having. Hegel identifies a contradiction in the notion of possession: "...in possession there lies the contradiction that something external, a thing, should be under the control of a single man, which is contrary to the nature of the thing as an outward universal."[68] Where honor is at stake, the possession in dispute is not a private, but a family possession. The family seeks to exclude all others from its possession, forging a totality consisting of family and possessions. Within the family totality all members have equal claim to the possessions of the family, and so family honor concerns the capacity of the self (or family) to identify itself as a totality with its external possessions.

This totality of family with its possessions requires acknowledgement, recognition, and confirmation. Only through recognition does possession (*Besitz*) become *property* (*Eigentum*), i.e., the right to exclude others from the possession must be reciprocally acknowledged. But in order to be confirmed, this totality (namely the family plus its possessions) must be recognized by another totality (namely another individual/family). However, the existence of another alien family is an offense, a shock, not unlike Fichte's *Anstoß*. The initial situation is unstable, since the mere presence of the other disturbs each in the security of its possession.

The initial situation can be clarified only through action. Hegel agrees with Fichte that recognition (*Anerkennung*) requires action, for action alone transcends reflection and *accomplishes* recognition (or non-recognition):

> But that my totality as the totality of a single [consciousness] is precisely this independent totality subsisting in the other consciousness as recognized and respected, this I cannot know except through the appearance of the actions [*Handeln*] of the other against my totality...[69]

Since action is always particular and variable, there is no single way in which recognition must come about. In other words, the process of recognition can be endlessly varied. Action may result in non-recognition or conflict as well as in mutual recognition. Moreover, Hegel's Jena accounts of recognition vary considerably. The specific focus of the struggle is sometimes honor, sometimes property. Hegel does not bring the account of the struggle to a single resolution or show the accomplishment of reciprocal recognition. Compared to the later *Phenomenology,* these early accounts are incomplete.

One recurring theme is the struggle to the death. The risk of death shows that recognition is not a process of rational-prudential calculation of interest. For example, recognition's goal or telos is the mutual positing of each totality in the other, or *mutual* recognition. Yet, absolute self-assertion, when confronted by another, seeks the death of the other, and in doing so 'I' must risk my own life and possessions. Thus, I may bring about the exact opposite of what I intend, namely, instead of enjoying my life and possessions, I risk their utter loss. The account in the 1804 *Philosophy of Spirit* is closest to that in the *Phenomenology* (1807):

> Each must have from the other the knowledge whether he [the first] is an absolute consciousness. Each must place himself into such a relation against the other that will bring this to light, i.e, he must injure him. And each can only know of the other whether he is [a] totality if he threatens him to the point of death, and each proves for himself that he is such a totality for himself only if he faces up to death himself. If in his own case he stops short of death, he only proves to the other that he will accept the loss of a part or the whole of his possessions, that he will risk a wound, but not life itself. Then for the other he becomes immediately not a totality...he becomes a slave of other. If on the other hand he stops the conflict short of the death of the other, then he has neither proved himself to be a totality nor has he known the other as such.[70]

The passage is of interest because it is a first attempt at fleshing out the servile consciousness.

In the Jena Manuscripts, Hegel does not show whether mutual-reciprocal recognition is ever accomplished. Yet, mutuality and reciprocity remain the telos of recognition, and it is clear that Hegel believes reciprocity is possible. More important is his claim that in recognition individuality is not so much restricted as 'saved' (*gerettet*).[71]

Here we find Hegel's response to, and transformation of, Fichte's conception of community as a restriction upon freedom. In Hegel's view, community is not inherently oppressive, because it can secure and safeguard recognition of individual freedoms and rights. This claim turns on the possibility of the sublation—transformation and preservation— of individuality and freedom in a social whole. If this were not possible, then Fichte's view of community as inherently heteronomous and repressive would be the only alternative. To be sure, a condition of possibility of community is some restriction of freedom. What Fichte sees is that community must restrict freedom, but he fails to appreciate that it can also safeguard and enhance freedom, and confer upon its members a larger enduring identity and purpose.

Conclusion

Hegel incorporates *Anerkennung* into his social theory. As he appropriates Fichte's concept he tends to reformulate the previous social themes—conflict, domination, reconciliation, etc.—as determinate forms of recognition. But he has not yet formulated a concept of *Anerkennung* in and for itself, i.e., at the level of eidetics. Instead, he discusses his earlier intersubjective themes of love-reconciliation and domination/oppression as distinct forms of *Anerkennung*. He brings to light the different determinate structures of each, as well as the corresponding social or historical locus. His discussion of love and conflict both represent modifications of Fichte's concept.

Hegel does not simply identify intersubjectivity with conflict or alienation. Conflict represents one possibility, love and reconciliation another. In Jena, Hegel stresses and focuses on the *Gestalt* of conflict and opposition. He calls attention to the tragic elements of life, but he does not assert that intersubjectivity is essentially tragic or that it admits only of tragic realization. The point of recognition is not to eliminate the other, but to count for something in the eyes of the other, to be acknowledged and respected by the other. But there is no epistemologically optimistic universal reconciliation and overcoming of alienation and estrangement, for Hegel recognizes the limits of love as a social and ethical principle. Hegel's theory of intersubjectivity is incomplete and sketchy, and its phenomenological character is not yet explicit. He takes that step in his first publication, The *Phenomenology of Spirit,* and to that we now turn.

NOTES

1. Cf. Jean Paul Sartre, *Being and Nothingness,* tr. Hazel Barnes (New York: Philosophical Library, 1956). Even though Sartre does not accept Hegel's concept of *Geist,* Sartre appropriates Hegel's account of intersubjectivity in his own phenomenological ontology, and awards Hegel the palm over Husserl.

2. I use the term "interhuman" as a general one, without any commitment to a particular theory of intersubjectivity. Husserl, Heidegger, Sartre, Levinas—and I would claim Hegel as well—all identify the interhuman as an essential dimension of human existence. All would reject any view of human subjectivity that ignored or

passed over the interhuman, or that sought to restrict human subjectivity to solipsist or purely individualist dimensions. On the other hand, their accounts of the interhuman differ with respect to its interpretation and exact significance.

3. Georg Lukács, *The Young Hegel*, tr. Robert Livingstone (Cambridge, Mass.: MIT Press, 1976), 7.

4. Hegel, *Differenz des Fichteschen und Schellingschen System der Philosophie*, TWA 2, 20ff. ET. *The Difference between and Schelling's System of Philosophy*, tr. W. Cerf and H. S. Harris (Albany, N.Y.: SUNY Press, 1977), 89.

5. Hegel, *Hegels theologische Jugendschriften*, Hrsg. H. Nohl (Tübingen: J. C. B. Mohr, 1907; Tübingen: reprinted Paul Siebeck, 1966). [Hereafter cited as HTJ.] This has been partially reprinted in *Hegels Werke, Theorie Werkausgabe*, Band 1, Frankfurt: Suhrkamp, 1971. ET: *On Christianity: Early Theological Writings*, tr. T. M. Knox and Richard Kroner (New York: Harper Torchbooks, 1948). [Hereafter cited as ETW.] The question how the religion of Jesus became positive Christianity was taken up in the earliest essay, "The Positivity of the Christian Religion" (ETW 67ff). The reassessment of Christianity as a resource for overcoming disunity through reconciliation occurs in the second major essay, "The Spirit of Christianity and Its Fate." For a discussion of positivity, cf. Lukács op. cit. Lukács calls attention to the change in Hegel's view and regards it as ambivalence towards Christianity. (233) Lukács overlooks the subtlety of Hegel's distinctions and manages to miss the point. Hegel is critical of an historical form of Christianity (namely, its positive authoritarian form) on the one hand, and he reformulates and reconstructs it in light of his critique of authoritarianism and heteronomy on the other. To say that Hegel is not a traditional pre-Enlightenment Christian is not to say that he is not a Christian.

6. Kant, *Foundations of the Metaphysics of Morals*, tr. Lewis White Beck (New York: Library of Liberal Arts, 1959), 59ff.

7. Kant,"What is Enlightenment?" op. cit. 85ff.

8. ETW 71.

9. ETW 169–170. For an analysis of the "House of Authority" in traditional Christian theology, see Edward Farley, *Ecclesial Reflection: An Anatomy of Theological Method* (Philadelphia: Fortress Press, 1982).

10. ETW 171–2.

11. ETW 176. Although Hegel describes and interprets alienated religion as a human projection and thus anticipates Feuerbach (ETW 241), he is far from reducing religion per se to a projection. Genuine religion has resources for overcoming alienation, and is not a mere projection.

12. ETW 182ff. Hegel later revised his estimate of Judaism in his *Lectures on the Philosophy of Religion*, ed. Peter C. Hodgson (Berkeley: University of California Press, 1987). There Judaism is identified as a religion of ethical sublimity. The basic structures remain the same, but they are interpreted differently.

13. ETW 241. This passage depicts a legal-penal vision of the world. See also Enz. §194 Zusatz for a parallel discussion. For an account of the penal vision of the world, see Paul Ricoeur, "Original Sin: A Study in Meaning," *Conflict Of Interpretations* (Evanston, Ill.: Northwestern University Press, 1974). See also Ricoeur, *Symbolism of Evil*, tr. Emerson Buchanan (Boston: Beacon Press, 1969). Hegel anticipates Feuerbach's thesis that religion is a projection of human attributes into the divine, Nietzsche's conception of servile morality in *Genealogy of Morals*, and Sartre's analysis of bad faith.

14. ETW 187.

15. ETW 213. This is a polemic against Kant's formal conception of duty and autonomy.

16. ETW 247.

17. ETW 244. [My emphasis.]

18. ETW 228. (HTJ 280)

19. In the classical view, there is no resolution of tragic conflict, but only the terrible spectacle of the destruction of the tragic hero which arouses terror (*phobos*) and pity. For a discussion of the tragic vision and its theology, see Paul Ricoeur, *Symbolism of Evil*, op. cit. Ricoeur shows that the challenge of the Adamic myth is the incorporation of tragic elements without lapsing into the tragic theology pure and simple. This is also Hegel's concern. Cf. below chapter 10.

20. ETW 229–230 (HTJ 280).

21. ETW 231 (HTJ 282).

22. ETW 230 (HTJ 281).

23. ETW 232 (HTJ 282)

24. Henrich, "Hölderlin und Hegel," in *Hegel im Kontext* (Frankfurt: Suhrkamp, 1967), 27.

25. Ibid. 38.

26. Ibid. 28. [My emphasis.]

27. Ibid. 36.

28. Ibid. Henrich observes that the same structure pervades the categories of the logic.

29. ETW 278 (HTJ 322)

30. Hannah Arendt contrasts Platonic rulership with the intersubjective structures of reconciliation. See her *Human Condition* (Chicago: University of Chicago Press, 1958), 237–238. Cf. below Chapter 9.

31. ETW 305. Fragment on Love.

32. Ibid.

33. Ibid. 307.

34. ETW 187 (HTJ 247)

35. ETW 279 (HTJ 320)

36. ETW 279.

37. ETW 265 (HTJ 312).

38. ETW 278 (HTJ 322).

39. ETW 278. (HTJ 322)

40. ETW 280 (HTJ 323)

41. ETW 281 (HTJ 324) For this reason the classical tradition suppresses the tragic dimension of evil and presents a pure divine comedy. Cf. below chapter 10, Hegel's criticism of Dante's *Divine Comedy.*

42. ETW 287 (HTJ 330)

43. ETW 284 (HTJ 327). Hegel means that the unity of the Christian community is parochial, excluding secular concerns, as well as non-Christians, because love is conceived as a purely transcendent principle reconciling individuals to God, but not to each other. The purity and transcendence of love means that it is powerless and passive within the world. Jesus and the community of love thus end up no less alienated from the world than Abraham.

44. This calls for a distinction between finitude, or real plurality of individuals on the one hand, and conflict and opposition as particular forms of relations between individuals on the other.

45. Siep, APP 42.

46. A complete discussion of Hegel's critique of Fichte lies beyond our present task and would require another monograph. However it is interesting that Fichte never replied to Hegel. Cf. Ludwig Siep, *Hegels Fichtekritik und die Wissenschaft-slehre von 1804* (Freiburg: Verlag Karl Alber, 1970). Siep shows that Fichte continued to develop and modify his *Wissenschaftslehre* in such a way that the later position meets many of the objections Hegel raised against the 1794 version, and that this development is largely internal, rather than a response to criticism. If the 1794 *Wissenschaftslehre* is a methodological idealism, it is not surprising that Fichte should proceed to take up the ontological issues which were initially bracketed. On the other hand, Hegel gives little or no evidence that he was familiar with, much less followed or approved of, Fichte's subsequent modification and refinements of position. For additional discussion of Hegel's divergent assessments of Fichte in his early writings, see H. S. Harris' introductions and commentaries in his translations of *The Difference between Fichte's and Schelling's System of Philosophy* (Albany, N.Y.: SUNY Press, 1977) and *Faith and Knowledge* (Albany, N.Y.: SUNY Press, 1977).

47. Hegel, *Difference*, ET 79–80. This suggests that Hegel has a different understanding of transcendental than Kant. Kant's worry about the categories was whether they are subjective or objective, and under what conditions they are objective. Hegel, like Fichte, regards the transcendental categories as identities of thought and being, or subject-object identities. He criticizes Kant for considering thought to be objective in twelve cases only, namely the twelve categories. Kant presents not a pure, but a mixed transcendental theory, one which is limited by the thing in itself. For a discussion of pure versus mixed transcendental theories, cf. Klaus Hartmann, "On Taking the Transcendental Turn," *Review of Metaphysics*, 20.2.78 (December 1966): 223–249.

48. See Hegel's critique of Kant, Fichte, and Jacobi in *Faith and Knowledge*, 61–65. The presupposition common to all three is the concept of reason as affected or tainted by sensibility, which results in the hybrid concept of an "absolute finitude" or contingent absolute.

49. Hegel, *Difference*, ET 115. [My emphasis.]

50. FW I, 279ff.

51. Hegel, *Difference*, ET 81.

52. Ibid. 127–128.

53. Ibid. 138.

54. Ibid. 145.

55. Ibid. 150.

56. See Soren Kierkegaard, *Fear and Trembling*, tr. H. Hong (Princeton, N.J.: Princeton University Press, 1983); *Concluding Unscientific Postscript*, tr. Swenson and Lowrie (Princeton, N.J.: Princeton University Press, 1950).

57. H. S. Harris, "The Concept of Recognition in Hegel's Jena Manuscripts," in *Hegel in Jena*, Hrsg. D. Henrich and K. Düsing, *Hegel Studien Beiheft* (20) (Bonn: Bouvier Verlag, 1980), 229–248.

58. These are available in English Translation. See G. W. F. Hegel, *System of Ethical Life 1802/3 and First Philosophy of Spirit*, tr. H. S. Harris and T. M. Knox (Albany, N.Y.: SUNY Press, 1977); *Hegel and the Human Spirit*, tr. Leo Rauch (Detroit: Wayne State University Press, 1983).

59. Siep, APP 53ff. Siep bases his discussion primarily on the *Jena Realphilosophie* of 1805/1806.

60. Hegel, *Jena Realphilosophie (1805/1806)*, in *G. W. F. Hegel: Frühe politische Systeme*, edited with commentary by Gerhard Göhler (Frankfurt/Berlin: Ullstein, 1974), 229. [Hereafter cited as JR and FPS respectively. Also cited in Siep, APP 55.]

61. Hegel, *Philosophie des Geistes 1803/1804*, Fragment 21 (*Jenaer Systementwürfe I: Das System der spekulativen Philosophie*, Neu herausgegeben von Klaus

Düsing und Heinz Kimmerle, Hamburg: Meiner Verlag). ET *First Philosophy of Spirit*, tr. H. S Harris, op. cit. 231.

62. Siep, APP 59. I am following the convention of translating *aufheben* as sublate.

63. APP 63.

64. APP 63.

65. Harris, *System of Ethical Life*, op. cit. 197.

66. Hegel, *System der Sittlichkeit*, in FPS, 40. ET: *System of Ethical Life*, op. cit. 124.

67. JR 226.

68. *First Philosophy of Spirit 1803/04*, 238; FPS 323.

69. *First Philosophy of Spirit*, 237n; FPS 322n. Hegel denies that recognition is linguistic or verbal, for speech is only an ideal medium, and the requisite recognition is supposed to be real, and that requires the positing of the self as a totality (*Fürsichsein*) in and by the *Fürsichsein* of the other. This is not to deny that language may play a role in recognition. But that role comes at a later stage of development, of society on the one hand, and consciousness on the other.

70. *First Philosophy of Spirit*, 240; FPS 324–5. In this text Hegel shows that the orientation towards one's own death either conceals the self from itself, or first makes the self accessible to itself as a totality. The connection with Heidegger's distinction between authentic and inauthentic *Dasein* is obvious.

71. *First Philosophy of Spirit*, 241; FPS 326.

FIVE

HEGEL AND PHENOMENOLOGY

A history of the concept 'phenomenology' has yet to be written. Spiegelberg's history of the Husserlian phenomenological movement[1] omits the use of phenomenology in earlier German philosophy, and overlooks the first book with *Phenomenology* in its title.[2] Moreover, despite Husserl's strenuous efforts at definition and development of phenomenological method, he produced no less than three different 'introductions' to phenomenology. It is not surprising that consensus concerning phenomenology has been difficult to achieve. The phenomenological movement, as Spiegelberg notes, exhibits not only variety but also opposition to its founder. Husserl did not go far enough when he developed phenomenology as an egology without ontology.[3] The question of being cannot be avoided by the reduction, for some understanding of being guides the reduction and is presupposed by phenomenological inquiry. Thus, Husserl's student Heidegger went beyond his teacher's preoccupation with method to raise the question of being. But while Heidegger was aware of Hegel, he denied that Hegel's book is "phenomenology" in the strict (i.e., Husserlian) sense of the term.[4]

My thesis is that phenomenology in Hegel and in Husserl is not a sheer equivocation. Although they differ in vocabulary and in responses to certain issues, Hegelian and Husserlian phenomenologies nevertheless share common problems and concerns. Both diagnose a crisis in European culture, a crisis involving alienation in the realms of religion, ethics, and politics. Both raise questions concerning the cultural meaning and significance of the sciences. This crisis affects philosophy itself, and involves the collapse of metaphysics. Both raise the problem of philosophizing in the absence of criteria. Finally, both redirect philosophy towards a phenomenology of the life world. Both call for phenomenology to be a critical corrective to philosophy, i.e., a necessary preliminary to ontological reconstruction.

Each seeks to overcome dogmatism, whether that of naturalistic misconstructions such as psychologism and positivism (Husserl), or that of the natural attitude and the related dogmatic metaphysics (Hegel). Both interpret dogmatism as one-sided, incoherent, and self-subverting. Although neither is a skeptical philosopher, each borrows weapons from the skeptical armory, namely, the skeptical epoché. Husserl's phenomenological reduction or epoché is a reformulation of the epoché of classical skepticism.[5] It involves neither affirmation nor negation, but rather a suspension of thesis. Husserl turns the epoché against the naturalistic positivism that displaces and down-grades the life-world as merely subjective. The epoché is a method for uncovering and exploring the life-world as the concrete a priori presupposed by mathematical sciences.

Hegel characterizes his *Phenomenology* as a self-accomplishing skepticism.[6] The phenomenological introduction to his system is shaped by the classical problem of equipollence, or deciding between opposing positions that are equally justified. From the vantage point of ordinary consciousness, equipollence leads to and culminates in the epoché or suspension. However, Hegel thinks that skepticism exhibits a partial and merely negative grasp of dialectic—every position or thesis is self-subverting, veering round into its opposite.[7] But from the standpoint of speculative reason, dialectic is not merely negative, it is also positive. For Hegel, skepticism is not opposed to philosophy; it functions as a critical element or moment in every genuine philosophy. For this reason Hegel calls his phenomenology a self-sublating, self-accomplishing skepticism.

In what follows, I will outline some convergences between Hegelian and Husserlian phenomenologies. The point is not to show convergence for its own sake, but to bring these two phenomenological philosophies into more fruitful relation. To show common problems and elements of method will, in turn, render more plausible the central contention of this study that Hegel's philosophy as a whole, and his treatment of intersubjectivity in particular, is relevant to phenomenological discussions of the other and alterity.

HUSSERL

The Phenomenological Reduction or Epoché

Few topics in Husserl's thought are more central to his method or obscure and controversial than the reduction. Still, it is interesting that Husserl refers to the skeptical epoché in his initial formulation of the reduction in *Ideas*. The epoché is an ancestor of both Husserl's and Hegel's phenomenologies. As we shall see, Husserl's changing accounts of the reduction move away from Descartes and towards Hegel. In Husserl's initial, Cartesian formulation of the reduction, he relates it to Cartesian methodological doubt. This suggests that philosophy, as rigorous science, is to be indubitable and apodictic.[8] The phenomenological reduction (epoché) brackets transcendence and uncovers consciousness as a transcendental field of apodictic certainty. The reduction accordingly appears to be a way of attaining, at a single stroke, the transcendental standpoint of consciousness, or the indubitable *ego-cogito-cogitatum*. Phenomenology seems to be a version of transcendental idealism.

But, although the reduction initially appears to be a form of Cartesian doubt, Husserl distinguishes the reduction from doubt, or negative judgement, by focusing on the element of suspension, or disconnection. Suspension of judgement is neither affirmation nor denial. For example, the reduction is not a Cartesian doubt concerning the existence of the world, but rather a suspension of naive belief in, and complicity with, the world in order to render thematic the thesis of the natural attitude, i.e., the world-directedness of consciousness. Husserl brackets the facticity of the world in order to describe and analyze the meaning of the *world-phenomenon*. To bracket the facticity of the world is not to deny or doubt the existence of the world, or to grasp a worldless transcendental subjectivity as the metaphysical foundation of the world.[9] Consciousness is not invoked as a metaphysical foundation, but only as the medium of access to the world.

Nevertheless, Iso Kern[10] points out that the Cartesian way of reduction obscures rather than discloses its meaning, because: (1) the reduction appears as a loss since it excludes transcendence and facticity; (2) there is the inevitable problem of the residuum after the reduction is effected, namely, transcendental consciousness; (3) the Cartesian way makes the transcendental region seem attainable all at once, at a single stroke, something Husserl later rejects as transcendental naivete; (4) Husserl does not actually follow Descartes in making transcendental consciousness the foundation, but subjects it to critique; (5) the Cartesian way reduces the other to a mere phenomenon, by ignoring or passing over intersubjectivity. Kern summarizes:

> After belief in the existence of the world has been checked along the Cartesian way, Husserl's reader constantly expects that he may return *again* to this belief after an appropriate justification.... Husserl makes no such attempt to secure this belief in the world anew and renounces such attempts as misunderstandings.... The proper meaning of Husserl's transcendental reduction contains nothing of a stepping back behind the belief in the world so that making it valid once again appears as the goal of philosophizing.... The proper meaning of the phenomenological reduction is not to be attained by the Cartesian way.[11]

The Theoretical Inversion of the World of the Natural Attitude

In the *Crisis*, Husserl presents another introduction to phenomenology that reformulates the reduction as a critique of the positivistic conception of science. Husserl's opponent is the same, but there is a shift of emphasis which leads to another formulation of the reduction. Husserl discusses Galileo's thesis of the indirect mathematization of nature. Galileo regards nature as 'in itself' mathematical. Thus, a way is opened for an inversion of the natural attitude. The life-world which is subject-relative and prior to theory, tends to be displaced by theoretical reconstructions which are believed to disclose the world as it is 'in itself' or as "non-subject relative." Truth and reality are no longer ascribed to the life-world, but rather to the world as mathematically measured and constructed by science. Husserl contends that when the life-world is displaced or when theory is identified with the life-world, the originary sense of science as a human enterprise is covered up and obscured. At the end of this obscuring stands positivism, with its reduction of meaning to facts.[12]

Against positivism, Husserl insists that the life-world is the pre-theoretical realm of original self-evidence and self-givenness, that is constantly presupposed by all theoretical cognitive acts, including the mathematical sciences.[13] Although scientific theory redescribes the life-world in mathematical constructs, scientists continue to make use of 'subjective-relative' life-world situations to communicate and critically assess their theoretical constructions and theories. Consequently "while the natural scientist is...interested in the objective...the subjective-relative is still functioning for him, not as something irrelevant that must be passed through, but as that which ultimately grounds the theoretical-ontic validity for all objective verification, i.e., as the source of self-evidence, the source of verification."[14] If ordinary interpersonal communicative acts are 'mere opinion, subjective or invalid', then so are the theoretical claims of science, since the latter tacitly rest upon and presuppose the former. Hence, science cannot invert or displace the life-world without invalidating itself. The critique of positivism leads Husserl to a different conception of the phenomenological reduction, namely, a reversal of the positivistic inversion of the natural attitude.

Reduction as Reversal of the Positivist Reversal

The clue to the shift in the meaning of the phenomenological reduction lies in the shift in meaning of the term 'pre-theoretical'. In *Ideas* Husserl observes that the mathematical sciences presuppose and take for granted the general thesis of the natural standpoint, i.e., belief in the world. Thus, they are appropriately designated as sciences of the natural standpoint. Their goal is to know the world of the natural attitude better and more exactly than the naive lore of experience is able to do. Thus, while science starts with the surrounding world of everyday life, it does not have to remain at home. Husserl regards the natural attitude as something to be overcome and left behind. 'Pre-theoretical' means that the natural attitude is only temporally prior to science, only the starting point, and not a foundation presupposed by theoretical-mathematical inquiry.

In the *Crisis,* however, Husserl maintains that the life-world cannot be left behind because it is prior to science in an ontological sense. Instead of displacing or improving upon the life-world, science and its mathematical constructions are now interpreted as partial abstractions from the life-world.

The sciences constantly presuppose and refer back to the pregiven life-world for their original sense.

Husserl's thought concerning the relation between theoretical reflection and experience undergoes a reversal: the ontological priority of the life-world means that *episteme* is founded upon *doxa.*[15] The reduction likewise undergoes a similar reversal, a *reversal* or *inversion* of the natural attitude:

> The transcendental reduction appears here as a *breaking through limitations*, namely, the limitations of the natural objective cognition, which is shown to be "one-sided," "abstract," "superficial" and "shallow." To use words which hark back to Hegel, it is the transition from the limited character of natural consciousness, which sees objects only positively as static, fixed, foreign things...to philosophical thinking which recognizes the world as the proper achievement of consciousness.... Whenever he tries to grasp the final meaning of the reduction, [Husserl] explains that the reduction is nothing but a change of attitude.[16]

Not only does the *meaning* of the reduction undergo reversal, the *reduction itself* signifies a *reversal,* namely, of the natural attitude. The natural attitude lives in the objective mode, so in the reduction "everything objective is transformed into something subjective."[17] The natural attitude is limited, and has an abstraction all its own. It passes over intentionality and focuses exclusively on the intentional object. The sciences of the natural standpoint presuppose and build upon the abstraction of the natural attitude. Science is an abstraction from the life-world that lifts out only one possible sense, namely the mathematical. Science becomes positivistic when it forgets its abstraction from the life-world and dogmatically declares that objective reality belongs exclusively to the mathematical or the factual.

Properly understood, the reduction is a critique of objectivism that explodes naivete about abstractions and reifications by disclosing the world in the fullness of its possibilities and temporality. The reduction effects a transition from the natural consciousness to a more comprehensive critical consciousness. Kern correctly finds a Hegelian dialectic at work in Husserl: objectifying positivistic science is the negation of the life-world, and phenomenology is the negation of this negation. Kern's formulation suggests that the later version of the phenomenological reduction is oriented towards a holistic perspective which breaks through the narrow dogmatism of the natural attitude. If so, the reference to Hegel is significant. Hegel's thesis is that phenomenology culminates in holism, and this is the only way that it can fulfill its task.

The Abyss of Groundlessness:
Philosophy without Foundations

However, there is a problem beneath the positivistic crisis of science. It is the problem of the interrelation of the life-world and the theoretical worlds of

science, what Husserl calls the problem of the world in general. If the theoretically constructed world(s) of science are abstractions from the pre-given
life-world and life-world evidences which are subjective-relative, what happens to the so-called objective world, or being in itself? How can *episteme* be
founded upon *doxa?*

> The paradoxical interrelationships of the "objectively true world" and the
> "life-world" make enigmatic the manner of being of both. Thus [the idea of
> a] true world in any sense, and within it our own being, becomes an enigma
> with respect to the sense of this being. In our attempts to attain clarity we
> shall suddenly become aware, in the face of emerging paradoxes, that *all of
> our philosophizing up to now has been without a ground.* How can we now
> truly become philosophers?[18]

The second sense of the reduction derives from the critique of science
that traces it to its life-world foundation. The critique reverses the scientific
reversal, that is, it grounds *episteme* in *doxa.* The claim that *episteme* is
grounded in *doxa* is a classical skeptical motif, directed at dogmatism. Even
though Husserl himself does not draw skeptical conclusions from it, he reformulates the skeptical critique of dogmatism:

> ...this phenomenological radicalism...rather than having a ground of things
> taken for granted and ready in advance, as does objective philosophy,
> excludes in principle a ground of this or any other sort. Thus it must begin
> without any underlying ground.[19]

Husserl continues: "But immediately it achieves the possibility of creating a
ground for itself through its own powers, namely, in mastering, through original self-reflection, the naive world as transformed into a phenomenon..."[20]
Husserl, Fichte, and Hegel share, in different ways and degrees, an anti-foundationalist theme: The crisis of philosophy is groundlessness, anarchy, or the
absence of a criterion. If no ground or foundation for philosophy is given,
then one must be created.

Husserl's response to the absence of foundations is ambiguous. He
claims that phenomenology grounds science by providing an ontology of the
life-world. But the priority of the life-world is not foundationalism in any
traditional sense, for *episteme* is founded in *doxa.* In this way, Husserl
departs from and undermines Cartesian foundationalism.[21] The reduction to
life-world leads to a further historical reduction, in which temporality is the
ultimate category. In this interpretation, Husserl is an antifoundationalist
who, despite his intentions to the contrary, undermines the classical idea of
philosophy as a rigorous science.

However, Gadamer advances the opposite view that Husserl introduced
the concept of the life-world, not to undermine philosophy as a rigorous science, but to "make the transcendental reduction flawless."[22] For the ontology

of the life-world can be carried out only from the transcendental standpoint, and not from the natural attitude.[23] In Gadamer's interpretation, the discovery of the life-world does not undermine transcendental philosophy, but serves rather to embody and illustrate it. If the reduction to life-world means that there is no objective foundation, the very grasping of the life-world as relative to consciousness reveals that consciousness must create its own foundation. Husserl never resolved the tension between historicism and a-historical transcendentalism. Instead, he embraced the paradox of subjectivity as something at once transcendental, constituting the world, and empirical, a constituted object in the world.[24] Both sides of the apparent paradox, and its tension, must be preserved.

HEGEL AND HUSSERL?

Let us begin with an objection. It is misleading to bring together Hegelian and Husserlian phenomenologies, because, although each turns to the life-world, it does so for different reasons and with different objectives. Husserl seeks to show that the life-world is the constantly presupposed subsoil of theoretical validity, the concrete a priori presupposed by all forms of praxis. In contrast, Hegel turns to the natural attitude to demonstrate the *untruth* of phenomenal knowledge, i.e., to show that all the *Gestalten* of consciousness self-destruct.[25] Hegel's phenomenology is a massive and progressive attack on the Cartesian primacy of the cogito or subjectivity. The focus of Hegel's critique is consciousness (or the cogito) as a representational system and its presuppositions of immediacy and 'givenness'.

The projects of the two phenomenologies appear incompatible; each seems to refute or undermine the other. If Hegel's phenomenology demonstrates the untruth of life-world consciousness, doesn't it fall under Husserl's critique of the positive sciences for displacing the life-world as subject-relative? And doesn't Husserl's appeal to the 'pre-theoretical immediately pre-given life-world' fall under Hegel's critique of the claim of immediacy to be truth? Where Husserl turns to subjective certainty and presentational immediacy, Hegel undermines these by insisting that there is nothing, including subjectivity, which does not involve mediation. Thus it is pointless to compare the two phenomenologies, because they seem to be mutually exclusive; each subverts the other.

This is a false antithesis. We have seen that Husserl's thought on the reduction underwent a development not unlike Hegelian dialectic. Husserl never rests his claim that the life-world is the foundation of all praxis simply on presentational immediacy, much less on the dogmatic prejudices of the natural attitude. Let us not forget his eidetic inquiry based on free imaginative variation. Imaginative variation not only resembles Hegel's project of identifying unity in opposition; it also involves a critique of immediacy. The claimed primacy of the life-world does not mean an elimination of philosophical reflection in favor of ordinary consciousness: Husserl not only 'discovers' the life-world but calls for an ontology of it. Husserl opposes the positivist confusion of the life-world with mathematical-logical constructs, but he is not opposed to reflection on the life-world per se, for that is what phenomenology is supposed to be. Moreover, Husserl's conception of the reduction as a breaking through limitations is formulated by Kern in Hegelian language: The reduction is an overcoming of abstraction, limitation and one-sidedness. If this is what the reduction is, then Hegel carries out the phenomenological reduction more radically and consistently than any other phenomenological philosopher.[26]

On the other side, Hegel's critique of consciousness and immediacy does not eliminate consciousness per se, but only consciousness as representational.[27] He rejects a world-less, solipsistic subjectivity that relates to an other only through its representations. However, Hegel is so far from "eliminating subjectivity" that he insists that substance is not fully understood until it becomes subject, and he goes on to build subjectivity into the concept of the concept itself.

Further, it is true that Hegel's critique of the natural attitude demonstrates that all the shapes of consciousness self-destruct. But this does not mean that Hegel is *ipso facto* to be identified with the mathematization of the universe and the resulting positivist displacements that Husserl condemns. Nor does Hegel seek to invert and/or displace the life-world as do the mathematical sciences that Husserl criticizes. For example, one of Hegel's many complaints about Kant's philosophy is that Kant sides with empiricism against metaphysics. Kant inverts the proper relation between understanding (*Verstand*) and reason (*Vernunft*). What lies behind this inversion is Kant's effort to justify Newtonian science over and against Hume's skepticism. Kant's so-called 'second Copernican revolution' makes the object correspond to the forms of the understanding, i.e., its mathematical constructs and models of nature.[28]

Hegel maintains that the task of speculative philosophy is to restore reason to its rightful place vis-à-vis the understanding, and thereby make possible a philosophical defense against formal mathematization and potential positivistic reductionism. Speculative philosophy in Hegel's sense neither seeks nor requires any positivistic displacement or downgrading of the life-world. On the contrary, Hegel's philosophy is a defense of the life-world that seeks not to displace it as subject-relative, but to justify it.

For example, Hegel maintains that philosophy and the natural attitude are not antithetical, such that one must displace the other. No less than Husserl, Hegel acknowledges that ordinary consciousness immediately lives in a primordial faith in the world, a faith that precedes reflection and attempts to doubt it: "Philosophy, in its earliest stages, all the sciences and even the daily action and movement...live in this faith."[29] The natural attitude is never really overcome, but rather "is always and at all places to be found."[30] Moreover, although speculative philosophy criticizes the natural attitude, its criticism is not directed at the thesis or content of the natural attitude: "To seek to controvert these maxims of immediate knowledge is the last thing philosophers would think of."[31] Rather it criticizes the natural attitude's dogmatic, exclusive form of truth: "Its distinctive doctrine is that immediate knowledge alone, to the total exclusion of mediation, can possess a knowledge which is true. This exclusiveness is enough to show that the theory is a relapse into the metaphysical understanding, with its pass-words 'either/or'."[32]

Hegel's systematic project is not only sympathetic to Husserl's discovery and defense of the human life-world, his *Logic* carries out a decisive critique of the mathematizing understanding (*Verstand*). For example, Hegel shows that the understanding has to accept the dialectical violations of the law of contradiction that it initially rejects, in order to keep its own enterprise from subverting itself. Joseph C. Flay explains Hegel's speculative dialectical thesis: "...something explicitly denied in the original position is in fact entailed by the original position. The irony is that precisely what was to be avoided, denied or excluded, must, for totally unforeseen reasons, be accepted, affirmed or included."[33] Examples of such ironic reversals include the discovery that the truth of sense certainty is the originally excluded universal, the intersubjective discovery that the truth of the master is manifest in the slave, and the logical discovery that the attempt to utterly dissociate being from nothing and becoming, in fact makes being indistinguishable from nothing and becoming.[34] Thus, knowledge can never be simply a matter of immediate assertion or a priori determinations, but requires the overcoming of one-sidedness, partial insight and error. Truth cannot be simply immediate, although immediacy is a 'moment' of truth. For Hegel truth is always a result in which false consciousness is overcome.[35]

HEGEL'S TREATMENT OF SKEPTICISM

Hegel, unlike most of his contemporaries, seriously studied ancient skepticism, and distinguished it from modern empirical skepticism. He is among the few major philosophers to have treated skepticism seriously and sympathetically. Skepticism, correctly understood, is not an opponent or nemesis of philosophy, but an integral element in philosophical reflection and method. Hegel locates the *philosophical origin* of skepticism in Plato's dialogue *Parmenides*.[36] Skepticism is the negative, critical, introductory aspect of speculative philosophy. Hegel's *Phenomenology,* a "self-accomplishing skepticism,"[37] is intended to reclaim skepticism as a critical aspect inherent in philosophy as such. To say that the *Phenomenology* is self-accomplishing skepticism means that it is an immanent criticism of the various shapes of consciousness (*Gestalten des Bewusstseins*). Phenomenology as such is not skeptical, but the natural attitude is self-subverting. This distinctively Hegelian insight revolutionizes Husserl's concept of the natural attitude, and creates the existential theme of false consciousness.

Hegel thinks that skepticism and speculative philosophy go hand in hand; skepticism can be only as good as its speculative counterpart. In the modern world the fortune of speculative philosophy has been on the decline, which is one reason why Hegel is unimpressed with the modern Cartesian-inspired skepticism of Schulze or Hume.[38] The latter is an anemic partial skepticism about reason, which naively accepts the claims of sense perception. In this respect Hume is not skeptical, but dogmatic. Modern skepticism includes a turn to the subject, and retains immediate certainty as its epistemological foundation.

> The turning of skepticism against philosophy, as soon as philosophy became dogmatism, illustrates how it has kept in step with the common degeneration of philosophy and of the world in general, until finally in these most recent times it has sunk so far in company with dogmatism that for both of them nowadays *the facts of consciousness* have indubitable certainty, and for them both the truth resides in temporality...dogmatism and skepticism coincide with one another *on the underside,* and offer each other the hand of perfect friendship and fraternity.[39]

In Hegel's view, modern skepticism rejects metaphysics, while basing itself on immediate certainty about matters of fact and sense data. Thus it not only betrays its Cartesian heritage, but is insufficiently radical and vulnerable to ancient skepticism. "Ancient skepticism was so far from making feeling and intuition the basis of truth, that it rather turned its attack first of all against sense-certainty."[40] A skepticism which is not radical and thorough is neither genuine nor coherent. It co-exists with the dogmatism of common sense and ordinary consciousness. Hegel reminds modern skepticism that genuine (classical) "skepticism, when a fact is established as certain, understands how to prove that that certainty is nothing."[41]

Classical skepticism formulated two different sets of tropes, one directed primarily against common-sense ordinary consciousness, and the other directed against philosophy. The term "trope" or "turn" expresses the basic skeptical doctrine that to every thesis or argument an equally probable thesis or argument can be opposed. Such opposition is a negative "turn" against, or dialectical reversal of, the first position. An opposing thesis or argument of equal weight and probability shatters dogmatic assurance and certitude. This creates the skeptical problem of equipollence, of deciding between two opposing theses of equal probability.[42] Since both are equally probable, there is no rational basis for choosing one over the other. Equipollence leads to the skeptical suspension of judgement or the epoché.

The various tropes of skepticism pursue this strategy of opposing thesis with antithesis. Hegel thinks the first ten tropes are directed against ordinary consciousness, because they are not expressed in reflective philosophical form.[43] More important is the second group, five tropes aimed not at ordinary consciousness, but at philosophy itself. These are: (1) diversity of philosophical views; (2) infinite regress, or the 'urge towards a ground';[44] (3) relation—that anything standing in relation is limited and cannot be absolute; (4) assumptions—the equipollence or undecidability of two equally probable but opposite theses or arguments; (5) vicious circle. These five tropes are supposed to constitute a comprehensive and exhaustive refutation of claims to objective, public knowledge. They aim at radicalizing the epoché by making it universal, without exception. Hegel comments that "Authentic skepticism has no positive side, as philosophy does, but maintains a pure negativity in relation to knowledge..."[45] Strictly speaking, the skeptical epoché is neither affirmation nor denial, but rather suspension of judgement.[46]

However, Hegel thinks the real target of skepticism is not philosophy, but dogmatism. Hegel distinguishes two senses of dogmatism. First, any philosophy making any claims at all, or having any positive doctrine, may be attacked by skepticism as dogmatic. This is dogmatism in the broad sense. We shall see that Hegel believes skepticism cannot successfully avoid the charge that it has its own dogma or doctrine, that it too is dogmatic in spite of its disclaimers. Its dogma is equipollence, the five tropes etc. So even skepticism is dogmatic in the broad sense.

The second and narrower sense of dogmatism "consists in the tenacity which draws hard and fast lines between certain terms and others opposite to them. We may see this clearly in the strict 'either/or'..."[47] Dogmatism in the narrower sense posits something as absolute by removing it from relation, qualification and conditioning. Dogmatism consists in this abstraction, or removal from context and relation. It lifts its absolute out of context, and seeks to maintain it in fixed opposition to, or abstraction from, everything else.[48] Dogmatism is thus one-sided, exclusive. Dogmatism in the narrower sense is roughly equivalent to the operation of the understanding (*Verstand*) which employs a discursive analytical procedure.[49] Skepticism attacks dogmatism in this narrower sense, and Hegel believes that it is successful.

According to Hegel, the essence of dogmatism is its abstraction from and suppression of relations. In other words, *dogmatism suppresses alterity,* or the other. Hegel prizes the skeptical trope of equipollence, because it corrects the dogmatic suppression of alterity by letting "the opposite moment, from which dogmatism has abstracted, make an appearance and so produce an antinomy."[50] Equipollence shows that the dogmatic 'absolute' is related and depends on the very things it excludes. According to the 3rd trope of relationship, the 'absolute' turns out not to be absolute. Alternatively, if each (the absolute and its excluded other) has its basis in its other, then the 5th trope of circular reasoning applies. If, to avoid the 3rd and 5th tropes, it is claimed that the first is self-grounding or self-evident, this is an immediate, i.e., unproved assumption. But to any immediate assumption, an equally probable opposite assumption can be juxtaposed (4th trope of presuppositions). A final criticism is that the finite absolute of dogmatism must be a universal, and yet, since it is essentially limited, it cannot be universal. In this case the first trope of diversity applies, for what is limited can be set over and against other limited things.[51]

Hegel thinks that the skeptical tropes are effective against dogmatism in the narrower sense, but powerless against philosophy, because they are tropes of reason itself.

> ...these tropes are completely useless against philosophy, since they contain plainly reflective concepts.... Directed against dogmatism, they appear from the point of view where they belong to reason, setting the other term of the necessary antinomy alongside the one asserted by dogmatism; directed against philosophy on the other hand, they appear from the side where they belong to reflection. Against dogmatism they must necessarily be victorious therefore; but in the face of philosophy they fall apart internally, or they are themselves dogmatic.[52]

As the free, critical self-reflective elements implicit in every philosophical system, the tropes are not the exclusive property of skepticism.

Hegel believes that speculative reason includes a skeptical dimension that de-absolutizes the dogmatic claims of the understanding. Hence speculation is not opposed to skepticism. Rather, speculative philosophy joins skepticism in opposing dogmatism in the narrower sense, namely the suppression of alterity and relation. It is worth noting that, for Hegel, abstract identity, first formulated by Parmenides, is the paradigmatic case of such suppression of alterity. Parmenides attempts to separate Being from Nothing, and fix the terms in isolation. "The Being, the One of the Eleatic school, is only an abstraction, a sinking into the abyss of the [abstract] identity of the understanding [*Verstandesidentität*]."[53] This identity excludes alterity, difference. Hegel corrects such suppression of alterity through the principle of equipollence. Equipollence is an example of dialectic, that has positive speculative significance. Specifically, speculative reason accepts equipollence, or the test of alterity, as a requirement of truth. However, skepticism grasps equipollence only negatively, as leading to a suspension or epoché. Skepticism's treatment of equipollence is a degenerate, one-sided form of dialectic. Hegel writes "When the dialectical principle is employed by the understanding separately and independently—especially as seen in its application to philosophical theories—dialectic becomes skepticism, in which the result that ensues from dialectic is presented as sheer negation."[54] The negation in question here is not logical opposition, but rather the skeptical epoché, or suspension (negation) of thesis and antithesis. In contrast, speculative dialectic is the mediation of thesis and antithesis that by relating and qualifying them, suspends the skeptical suspension, or negates the negation.

Hegel develops an alternative reading of the skeptical tropes. Concerning the first trope of diversity, i.e., that pluralism and diversity undermine the claims of reason, Hegel claims that the rational is not a particular, but is universal, everywhere the same.[55] Concerning the trope of relation, the rational is not something in a relation, but is relation itself. The rational is a relation of opposites, an identity of opposites; it is inclusive of difference. The rational has no opposite to be set over and against it as in the fourth trope, inasmuch as it includes both finite opposites, or identity and difference, within itself.[56] Hegel believes that dialectical holism also solves the issues in the second trope of infinite regress, and the fifth trope of vicious circle.

The idea of a coincidence of opposites, or an identity which is constituted by difference, is the way in which speculative philosophy incorporates equipollence, or alterity, into its method and ontology. Hegel comments, "Every...proposition of Reason permits resolution into two strictly contradictory assertions.... Thus, the principle of skepticism [against every argument there is an equal one on the other side] comes on the scene at its full strength."[57] Speculative philosophy is holistic, or, as Hegel later put it, the truth is the whole. But the whole has no opposite; consequently the problem of equipollence does not apply to the whole, because equipollence is the principle of the whole.[58] Hegel's claim is that equipollence opposition is not simply negative, but leads to a holistic conception with an internal triadic structure.[59]

Turning the Tables

Hegel addresses the problem of equipollence by turning the skeptical tropes against skepticism itself. He focuses his attack on the much debated question whether skepticism itself has a dogma. The relevant text runs as follows:

> For whereas the dogmatizer posits the things...as really existent, the Sceptic does not posit these formulae in any absolute sense. For he conceives that, just as the formula 'all things are false' asserts the falsity of itself as well as of everything else, as does the formula 'nothing is true'...and thus [each] cancels itself along with the rest.... If then...the Sceptic enunciates his formulae so that they are virtually cancelled by themselves, he should not be said to dogmatize.... And most important of all, in his enunciation of these formulae he states what appears to himself and announces his own impression in an undogmatic way, without making any positive assertion regarding external realities.[60]

In denying that skepticism has a dogma, Sextus Empiricus interprets the skeptical principles self-referentially, as applying to themselves. Thus, the principle, "All things are false," asserts the falsity of itself as well as everything else. But skepticism becomes incoherent when it says that its assertions are self-referential and cancel themselves. To deny that skepticism has a dogma of its own requires one to pay the price of depriving skeptical assertions of objective significance. They become mere subjective impressions.[61] Skepticism reinterprets all its assertions as subjective statements of the form: 'so it seems to me'. The "is" of judgement thus collapses into subjective "seeming" or mere opinion. But if the thesis, "All things are false," is interpreted subjectively, as meaning "it seems to me that all things are false," then it ceases to assert that "it is the case that all things are false." It is no longer a general thesis or assertion and so it may be controverted as easily as any other subjective opinion:

> This purely negative attitude that wants to remain mere subjectivity and seeming, ceases to be something for knowledge. He who stays holding fast to the vanity of the fact that "it seems so to him," "that he is of the opinion that...," he who wants his utterances never to be taken as objective assertions of thought and judgement at all, must be left alone. His subjectivity concerns no one else, still less does it concern philosophy, nor is philosophy concerned in it.[62]

In summary, skepticism is a philosophy that reflects and makes judgements. However, skepticism, while performing an important service in bringing the tropes to light, misinterprets their significance. Hegel counters the skeptical reading of the tropes as sheer negations, by turning the tropes against skepticism itself. The tropes have positive significance to which skepticism tacitly appeals in order to make its case, but it draws back from positive doctrine, philosophy, etc.

Thus, when skepticism develops its tropes, it has to appropriate the very thing it rejects—namely reason and relativity—in order to make its case. On the other hand, skepticism evades this point by claiming that skeptical judgements are not meant objectively about states of affairs, but are merely statements expressing private subjective feelings and opinions. Then it abandons intersubjective public discourse. When, in order to avoid having a dogma of its own, skepticism retreats into seeming and private individual subjectivity, the result is not *ataraxia* so much as paralysis.[63] This is not a refutation in the strict sense, for the skeptic has retreated to a point where refutation is impossible. Refutation involves public, intersubjective claims, evidence and truth. Practically speaking, however, it comes to a refutation: "To refute a philosophy is to exhibit the dialectical development in its principle..."[64] This is exactly what skepticism does to ordinary consciousness and science by raising the equipollence problem, and what Hegel does in turn to skepticism.

ALTERITY AND TRUTH

The problem of equipollence can take many forms. According to Hegel, Kant's treatment of the antinomies (as signs of the transcendental illusion of knowledge) is the most highly developed contemporary version of skeptical equipollence. Fichte's account of the impasse between dogmatism and idealism in his *First Introduction to Wissenschaftslehre* is another illustration of the same procedure, generalized into a critique of foundationalism and metaphysics. Hegel radicalizes the problem of equipollence and makes the antinomic structure of the tropes central to dialectic. He believes that the five tropes are exhaustive, demolishing all foundationalism, whether the Cartesian cogito, or Reinhold's and Fichte's *Grundsätze*. Moreover, the skeptical tropes make a beginning in philosophy all but impossible: "The difficulty of making a beginning is at the same time obvious, because a beginning, as something immediate, either makes a presupposition or rather is itself a presupposition."[65] These discussions of the problem of the beginning show how seriously Hegel takes classical skepticism. It is an important factor in his abandoning foundationalist transcendental philosophy in favor of holism. He claims that the problem of equipollence is devastating for every partial, finite standpoint, but that it does not apply to the whole. The whole itself has no opposite, although it is constituted by and includes opposition.[66]

However, Hegel criticizes both Fichte and Schelling for dogmatic procedure. He criticizes Fichte's positing of fundamental principles (*Grundsätze*) as the starting point of his *Wissenschaftslehre*. Fichte formulated a version of the equipollence problem in his antithesis between idealism and materialism, but he saw no theoretical solution to it. Only a practical-existential appeal to human interests can guide the decision concerning first principles.[67] Fichte's practical solution is merely a restatement of the problem.[68]

Hegel also criticizes the form of Fichte's philosophy: "A so-called foundation [*Grundsatz*] or first principle of philosophy, if it is true, is also false precisely because it is only a foundation or first principle. It can be easily refuted.... The refutation consists in exhibiting its defect, which is to be merely a first principle, merely a beginning."[69] In this skeptical "turn" one principle is opposed to another, and the chosen first principle dismissed as merely immediate and arbitrary. Moreover, the first principle (*Grundsatz*) as a form of truth is self-defeating, for "truth is not a minted coin that can be given and pocketed ready-made."[70] Such a presumption is dogmatism, a way of thinking that "is nothing else but the view that the true consists in a proposition which is a fixed result, or which is immediately known."[71] In contrast, Hegel's view is that speculative philosophy "...does not express its truth in the form of a proposition; it has no foundational proposition."[72] Consequently, philosophical "science is not that sort of idealism which substitutes for the dogmatism of assertion the dogmatism of assurance or self-certainty."[73]

This same criticism holds against the immediate dogmatic certainty Hegel ascribes to Schelling who, in a moment of enthusiasm, begins his *System of Transcendental Idealism* straightway with absolute knowledge "like a shot from a pistol and makes short work of other standpoints by declaring that he takes no notice of them."[74]

There is an important discussion of equipollence in the *Phenomenology* at the beginning of the chapter on reason (*Vernunft*). This passage contains Hegel's view of the history of post-Kantian idealism and the various appeals to intellectual intuition as the ultimate condition of possibility of transcendental philosophy. Intellectual intuition is reason in an immediate form: "Reason is the certainty of being all reality.... But the consciousness which is this truth, has the path to truth behind it, and has forgotten it...in other words, this reason which comes immediately on the scene, appears only as the certainty of that truth. It immediately assures us that it is the truth, but in fact it does not itself comprehend this, because it is only along that forgotten path that this immediately expressed assertion is comprehended."[75] The problem with the *Grundsatz* is that it suppresses the path to the truth of idealism. Skepticism lies astride that path as a barrier to be surmounted, not by dismissing it but by incorporating its truth. If idealism suppresses or forgets this barrier then it amounts to a non-dialectical immediate assertion.

This immediate form of idealism must confront the problem of equipollence:

> The idealism that does not exhibit that path, but begins with this assertion [of being the certainty of all reality] is therefore itself a pure assurance [*Versicherung*] which does not comprehend itself, nor can it make itself comprehensible to others. It expresses an immediate certainty, which is confronted with other immediate certainties, which have however been lost on that same path. With equal right the assurances of these other certainties stand next to the assurance of that certainty. Reason appeals to the self-consciousness of every other consciousness: I am I, my object and my being is I; and no one will deny reason this truth. However, in grounding itself on this appeal to immediate certainty, reason sanctions the truth of the other certainty, namely when each says "It is otherwise for me; something other than my ego is my object and being..."[76]

If idealism justifies itself by appeal to immediate certainty, it is not only dogmatic, but unable to refute its opponents, or defend its principle. All can claim the same immediate certainty for their own position. One barren assurance is worth as much as any other.

This analysis prepares the way for Hegel's claim that the *Phenomenology* is a self-accomplishing skepticism. "Only if reason comes on the scene as *a reflection from the opposite certainty*, does its assertion stand forth not merely as subjective certainty and assurance, but as *truth*. It does so not as one truth among many, but rather *as the only truth*."[77] Several elements in this passage require elaboration and emphasis. The transition from subjective private certainty to truth must take into account and reflect upon, the opposite standpoint.[78] Certainty can become truth only when it has passed through the alterity, alteration, and otherness of rival certainties. But the initial position is dogmatic. Truth is initially construed as an isolated fact grasped with immediate certainty. However, in the course of experience it is discovered that the original position cannot exclude the other, but rather *depends on* and *requires* the excluded other. Joseph C. Flay makes this point in the following way: "...something explicitly denied in the original position is in fact entailed by the original position. The irony is that precisely what was to be avoided, denied, or excluded, must, for totally unforeseen reasons, be accepted, affirmed, or included."[79] Nothing can stand alone in isolation as an atomic truth; everything involves mediation. Everything is related to everything else. Thus truth cannot take the form of isolated facts or propositions, but requires systematic expression: Truth is the whole.

The demand that alternative and opposing views be confronted and recognized is rational, a demand of self-pluralizing reason itself. Skepticism raises this very demand, but fails to carry it through, and retreats instead into the sheer pluralism of subjective opinions. Thereby it reveals itself to be a fear of truth. After thinking skepticism through, Hegel accepts the equipollence problem as a condition of and an element in justification. Until equipollence is faced, philosophical assertions are dogmatic, barren assurances, incapable of the public universal truth they intend. But when equipollence is faced it leads philosophy to system and holism.

The equipollence problem has an implicit intersubjective dimension. H. S. Harris observes that Hegel applies the concept of recognition to the relation between opposing views of philosophy, and that this is the original occasion for Hegel's use of the concept of recognition.[80] Equipollence implies that *alterity is a fundamental test and requirement of cognition.* Equipollence compels the recognition of alternative opposing positions and points of view. Conversely, equipollence presupposes an intersubjective context of mediation for cognitive claims. Hegel finds an intrinsic connection between the problem of equipollence, and the concept of recognition. Equipollence forcefully brings the concept of recognition, namely, recognition of other, to philosophical attention.

Moreover, "the reflection from the opposite point of view" suggests that mediation is a requirement of public truth. Mediation is not only conceptual and logical, but also intersubjective in principle. The other must be taken into account if there is to be such a thing as public truth in contrast to merely private subjective certainties. Truth is not a simple discovery of something pregiven like a wallet lying in the middle of the street, but rather something jointly brought about, the result of a complex transaction involving the world and intersubjectivity. The variability and fallibility of individuals requires a community of inquiry if truth is to be attained. This means that intersubjectivity is one element in the attainment of truth as universal and objective. The philosophical tradition suppressed or passed over interhuman dimension of truth.

Hegel also claims that the emergence of truth through intersubjective mediations is not to be understood as one truth among others, but rather as the only truth. This contention may appear dogmatic. For how could it be maintained that there is but a single truth, especially in view of the divergence of philosophical views (to cite the first skeptical trope)? This is but an implication of Hegel's thesis that the whole has no opposite. Hegel's dialectical holism maintains that truth emerges as the unity of opposing and conflicting views, and that therefore the truth is the whole.

The larger task of Hegel's *Phenomenology* begins to come into view: Hegel's phenomenological project involves a consideration of all the various standpoints assumed by consciousness (*Gestalten des Bewusstseins*) that shows that they self-destruct and undermine themselves 'from within'.[81] This is the most radical carrying out of the phenomenological reduction in phenomenological philosophy. Hegel intends to demonstrate that there is no alternative to holism. Recognition of the failure of all criteria is the negative side of an argument which leaves Hegel's dialectical holism as the positive side, the only alternative. Emergent holism is not one truth among others, but the only truth there can be.

> Only skepticism directed at the *entire scope* of appearing consciousness [namely *doxa*], makes *Geist* competent to determine what truth is, because it brings about despair concerning all natural representations, thoughts and opinions—whether they are one's own or someone else's. In contrast the consciousness which by-passes such skepticism and begins its examination immediately, is still filled with and hampered by these natural prejudices; consequently it is incapable of accomplishing what it has set out to do.[82]

Critical dialectical holism emerges from the ruins of foundationalist "First Philosophy" and of Skepticism.[83]

NOTES

1. Herbert Spiegelberg, *The Phenomenological Movement* (The Hague: Martinus Nijhoff, 1960).

2. Hegel, *Phänomenologie des Geistes,* Hoffmeister edition (Hamburg: Felix Meiner Verlag, 1952). [Hereafter cited as PhG.] ET: *Phenomenology of Spirit,* tr. A. V Miller (Oxford or New York: Oxford University Press, 1977). [Hereafter cited as PhS.] See also *The Phenomenology of Mind,* tr. J. B. Baillie (New York: Macmillan, 1949). [Hereafter cited as PhM.] [All translations are my own.] Cf. Hoffmeister's

introduction for a discussion of Hegel's pre-cursors in the use of phenomenology, including Lambert and Kant. See above, Chapter 2 for a discussion of Reinhold's conception of phenomenology. See also *Kant and Phenomenology*, ed. Thomas Seebohm and Joseph Kockelmans (Washington, D.C.: Center for Advanced Research in Phenomenology and University Presses of America, 1984); *Dilthey and Phenomenology*, ed. Rudolf Makkreel and John Scanlon (Washington, D. C.: Center for Advanced Research in Phenomenology and University Presses of America, 1987).

3. This is not Husserl's, but Paul Ricoeur's way of characterizing phenomenology. Ricoeur, perhaps the most influential historian of Husserl's thought, characterizes it in the following way: "In this strict sense the question of being, the ontological question, is excluded in advance from phenomenology, either provisionally or definitely. The question of knowing that which *is* in an absolute sense is placed 'between parentheses,' and the manner of appearing is treated as an autonomous problem." (*Husserl: An Analysis of his Phenomenology*, tr. Ballard and Embree [Evanston, Ill.: Northwestern University Press, 1967], 202.) However, Ricoeur's formulation is too extreme and contradicted elsewhere in his own work, where he acknowledges that "the reduction opens, rather than closes, the true problem-set of being." (177–178). The issue of the ontological turn of phenomenology remains a matter of dispute. Heidegger criticizes Husserl for attempting to set aside or postpone the ontological question. Since the ontological question cannot be set aside or postponed, Husserl is naive with respect to ontology, and lapses, against his own intentions, into the metaphysics of presence. (Cf. Heidegger, *History of the Concept of Time*, tr. Theodore Kisiel [Bloomington, Ind.: Indiana University Press, 1985], 108–134.) However, Husserl is not anti-ontology, as his early work on regional ontologies (*Ideen I, II, III*) and his late call for an ontology of the life-world (*Crisis*) attest. Husserl could respond to this 'metaphysics of presence' criticism by pointing out that the "living present" includes absence as well as presence. One such absence is the other.

4. Instead Heidegger maintained that Hegel's *Phenomenology* is the *parousia* of absolute *Geist*, i.e., is a warmed over version of Spinozist metaphysics (Heidegger, *Hegels Begriff der Erfahrung, Holzwege* [Frankfurt: Vittorio Klostermann, 1950], 111–205. ET: *Hegel's Concept of Experience*, tr. K. R. Dove (New York: Harper and Row, 1971). The fact that Heidegger's essay is based on a tendentious reading of the introduction to the *Phänomenologie des Geistes*, severely limits its value as an interpretation. For an account of the complex relation of Heidegger to Hegel, as well as the inconclusiveness of Heidegger's critique, cf. Dennis J. Schmidt, *The Ubiquity of the Finite*, op. cit.

5. This interpretation has been developed at some length by Alfred Schutz. Cf. his *Reflections on the Problem of Relevance* (New Haven, Conn.: Yale University Press, 1970).

6. Hegel, PhG, 67. [My emphasis.] PhS 50; PhM 134. This point needs emphasis, especially in view of Rorty's charge that transcendental philosophy begins by blocking skepticism. (Richard Rorty, *Philosophy and The Mirror of Nature* [Oxford: Blackwell, 1980]). Hegel does not begin by blocking skepticism at all, for skepticism is an element in every genuine philosophy and cannot therefore be blocked. Skepti-

cism's principle of equipollence must not be blocked, but accepted. Hegel's *Phenomenology* is the most thorough exhibition of equipollence in any philosophical literature and for this reason he calls the PhG a self-accomplishing skepticism.

7. "...when the dialectical principle is employed by the understanding separately and independently—especially as seen in its application to philosophical theories—dialectic becomes skepticism, and the result of skepticism is construed as mere negation." Hegel,, TWA Sk 8, §81, ET: *The Logic of Hegel*, tr. W. Wallace (Oxford or New York: Oxford University Press, 1873).

8. Cf. Leslak Kowlakowski, *Husserl's Search For Certitude*, (New Haven, Conn.:Yale University Press).

9. The relativity of the world to consciousness does not decide but allows clarification of the question of its ontological status. Husserl's idealism is methodological, not metaphysical.

10. Iso Kern, "Three Ways to the Phenomenological Reduction" in *Husserl: Expositions and Appraisals*, ed. F. Elliston and P. McCormick (South Bend, Ind.: Notre Dame University Press, 1978). Kern distinguishes the Cartesian way, the way of phenomenological psychology and the way of critique of sciences of the late work, *The Crisis of European Science.*

11. Kern, op. cit. 130. Cf. *Crisis,* 154ff.

12. Husserl regards positivism as a decapitation of philosophy which suppresses its critical problems, the problems of reason, namely the problems of knowledge, ethics and religion. Cf. Husserl, *Crisis,* 9.

13. Ibid. 127f. In other words, the life-world is pre-theoretical not merely in a chronological sense but in an ontological sense. If the life-world were merely chronologically prior to theoretical redescriptions, it would be the starting point of inquiry which is left behind in theoretical inquiry, and displaced in favor of "more adequate" concepts and conceptual schemes. For a defense of this view, cf. Wilfrid Sellars, "Philosophy and the Scientific Image of Man," in *Science Perception and Reality* (New York: Humanities Press, 1963).

14. Husserl, *Crisis,* 126.

15. *Crisis,* 155: The ontology of the life-world must be "a peculiar science...since it concerns the disparaged *doxa,* which now suddenly claims the dignity of a foundation for science, *episteme.*"

16. Kern, op. cit. 144. Kern correctly identifies the critique of scientism as a common theme in both Husserl and Hegel. For Hegel's discussion, cf. his account of the natural attitude in Enz. §§26–36; 65–66. See Merold Westphal, *History and Truth in Hegel's Phenomenology,* (New York: Humanities Press, 1980) for an account of Hegel's critique which makes use of Husserlian moves and terminology.

17. *Crisis,* 178.

18. *Crisis,* 131–132. [My emphasis.]

19. Ibid. 181.

20. Ibid.

21. Cf. Ludwig Landgrebe, "Husserl's Departure from Cartesianism" in *The Phenomenology of Husserl: Selected Critical Readings*, ed. R. O. Elveton (Chicago: Quadrangle Books, 1970). See also David Carr, *Transcendental Phenomenology and the Problem of History* (Evanston, Ill.: Northwestern University Press, 1977).

22. Hans-Georg Gadamer, "The Phenomenological Movement," in *Philosophical Hermeneutics*, tr. and ed. David E. Linge (Berkeley: University of California Press, 1977), 164.

23. Husserl, *Crisis* §38, 147. Husserl observes there are two ways of regarding the life-world: the first through the epoché of objective sciences, which he made use of in his account of the life-world as the pre-theoretical ground of objective validity; the second is through a further epoché which "reduces" the life-world to world-phenomenon, relative to transcendental subjectivity.

24. *Crisis*, 178–185. For a comparable paradox in Fichte, cf. above Chapter 3, the paradoxical immanent and transcendent interpretation of the thing in itself.

25. "Transcendental Philosophy and the Hermeneutic Critique of Consciousness," in J. N. Mohanty, *The Possibility of Transcendental Philosophy [Phaenomenologica Volume 98]* (Dordrecht, The Netherlands: Martinus Nijhoff, 1985), 230. Cf. n. 35 below.

26. For a similar assessment, cf. Kenley R. Dove, "Die Epoché der Phänomenologie des Geistes," *Stuttgarter Hegel-Tage 1970, Hegel Studien Beiheft* (Bonn: Bouvier Verlag, Hrsg. H. G. Gadamer, 1974), 605–622.

27. It is ironic that in the English speaking world representation has come to signify an intermediary between consciousness and world, thereby pushing consciousness into interiority and cutting it off from the world, requiring proofs for the latter. This reflects the influence of Kant's *refutation of idealism*. But it should be pointed out that Hegel is among the first and most trenchant critics of such subjective idealism, and that his doctrine of consciousness exhibits a radical intentionality that, contrary to Heidegger, suspends the idealist-realist debate. Cf. J. N. Mohanty, *The Possibility of Transcendental Philosophy*, op. cit. Essays 5 and 11.

28. Cf. Kant's preface to the second edition of the *Critique of Pure Reason*, "They [viz., Galileo, who, according to Husserl, pioneered the indirect mathematization of nature] learned that reason has insight only into that which it produces after a plan of its own, and that it must not allow itself to be kept, as it were, in nature's leading strings, but must itself show the way with principles of judgement based upon fixed laws, constraining nature to give answer to questions of reason's own determining." (Kant, *Critique of Pure Reason* B xiii, N. K. Smith Translation [New York: St. Martins Press, 1965], 20.)

29. Hegel, *Encyclopedia*, §26; ET 47.

30. Ibid. § 27.

31. Ibid. §64; ET 99. He continues: "The true marvel is that any one could suppose that these principles were opposed to philosophy..."

32. Ibid. §65; ET 101.

33. See Joseph C. Flay's fine article, "Hegel's *Science of Logic:* Ironies of the Understanding" in *Essays on Hegel's Logic,* ed. George di Giovanni (Albany, N.Y.: State University of New York Press, 1990), 160.

34. Flay illustrates the point with reference to the first category of Hegel's *Logic.* (Ibid. 162–166) The original position (*Verstand*) seeks to distinguish and isolate elements, e.g., being and nothing, and fix their meaning in discreteness and separation. This attempt fails, because pure being, as indeterminate, turns out to be indistinguishable from nothing, and vice-versa. Thus, what must be avoided is any absolute separation of being from nothing. If being and nothing are not to be separated, this means that they must be related, and the category that relates them is becoming.

35. J. N. Mohanty formulates the contrast between Hegelian and Husserlian phenomenologies in the following way: Hegel's is a phenomenology of suspicion that emphasizes self-deception and false consciousness, while Husserl's is a phenomenology of respect that does not judge, but seeks to understand. "Transcendental Philosophy and the Hermenueutic Critique of Consciousness," in J. N. Mohanty, *The Possibility of Transcendental Philosophy* [*Phaenomenologica Volume 98*] (Dordrecht, The Netherlands: Martinus Nijhoff, 1985), 230. Mohanty notes that Husserl has the problem of combining respect for evidence with criticism. "Here Husserlian phenomenology has to learn from the Hegelian." "The Destiny of Transcendental Philosophy" (op. cit. 216). This is an acknowledgement that Husserl's phenomenology may be vulnerable to Hegel's critique of immediate knowledge. Because everything contains mediation as well as immediacy, immediacy cannot be simply identified with the truth.

36. "This skepticism that comes on the scene in its pure explicit shape in the *Parmenides,* can, however, be found implicit in every genuine philosophical system; for it is the free side of every genuine philosophy; if in any one proposition that expresses a cognition of reason, its reflected aspect—the concepts that are contained in it—is isolated, and the way that they are bound together is considered, it must become evident that these concepts are together sublated, or in other words they are united in such a way that they contradict each other; otherwise it would not be a proposition of reason but only of understanding." (G. W. F. Hegel, *Verhältnis Skeptizismus zur Philosophie, Werke,* TWA Sk. 2: 229; ET: *On the Relationship of Skepticism to Philosophy,* tr. H. S. Harris, BTKH, op. cit. 324. [Hereafter cited as *Skepticism.*]) It is misleading to associate Hegel and Hegel's systematic conception of skepticism with Descartes and/or Cartesian doubt. Hegel's *Phenomenology* as self-completing skepticism goes far beyond anything envisioned by Descartes. Moreover, Hegel's strategy in employing skepticism as an introduction to philosophical science has nothing to do with the Cartesian "turn to the subject." or quest for subjective certainty. Hegel's concern is not to obtain certainty; rather he agrees with the skeptics "that certainty is nothing." *Skepticism,* 332.

37. G. W. F Hegel, *Phänomenologie des Geistes*, ed. Hoffmeister (Hamburg: Meiner Verlag, 1952), §6, 67. The German is "Dieser sich vollbringende Skeptizismus," which both Baillie and Miller translate misleadingly as "thoroughgoing skepticism." As if Hegel were a thorough skeptic. The verb "vollbringen" does not mean "thorough," but rather "to accomplish, to effect." In view of the reflexive form it is better translated as self-accomplishing.

38. *Skepticism*, 330. For a discussion that supports Hegel's judgement concerning the inferiority of modern skepticism to the ancient, cf. Michael N. Forster, *Hegel and Skepticism* (Cambridge, Mass.: Harvard University Press, 1989), 1–47.

39. Ibid.

40. G. W. F. Hegel, *Enzyklopädie*, (1830) §39 Zusatz. [Hereafter cited as Enz.] ET Enc. Husserl's opponent, namely positivism, is closely related to Humean skepticism, which turns against metaphysics while basing itself upon sense certainty, intuition and feeling.

41. Hegel, *Skepticism*, 332.

42. Kant's discussion of the antinomies and Fichte's account of the theoretically undecidable impasse between dogmatism and idealism in his *First Introduction to Wissenschaftslehre*, are modern examples and instances of the skeptical problem of equipollence.

43. The ten tropes which provide the basis of the skeptical epoché are: (1) the diversity of animals, (2) the diversity of men, (3) diversity in the organization of the senses; (4) diversity of circumstances, (5) diversity of situations, distances and places; (6) muddles in which nothing is clear; (7) diverse sizes and properties of things; (8) relationship: everything stands in relation to everything else; (9) the frequency or rarity of happening; (10) the diversity of education, customs, laws, faiths and prejudices. Not by accident Hegel calls attention to Sextus Empiricus' claim that the ten tropes can be reduced to a triadic formulation: one trope of diversity of the cognitive subject, one trope of the diversity of the cognitive object, and one of both of them put together. Hegel takes these directly from Sextus Empiricus, *Outlines of Pyrrhonism* I, tr. R. G. Bury, *Loeb Classical Library*, (Cambridge, Mass: Harvard University Press, 1976), 36–37 [Hereafter cited as OP.] (Cited by Hegel in *Relationship of Skepticism to Philosophy*, BTKH 331.) H. S. Harris challenges on historical grounds Hegel's view that these tropes are directed against ordinary consciousness. (op. cit. 264). However, even if Hegel's view of the history of skepticism needs correction in light of recent scholarship, Hegel's point—that since the 10 tropes are not reflective but popular in form, they are directed at ordinary consciousness—can still stand.

44. This is the skeptical view of foundationalism. For Hegel the 'urge towards a ground' is more characteristic of *Verstand*, than *Vernunft*.

45. Hegel, *Skepticism*, 330.

46. Ibid. For this reason there is much greater similarity between Husserl's account of the epoché in *Ideas* and the epoché of classical skepticism, than there is

between the former and Cartesian doubt. Doubt is a negation, and still a judgement. But the skeptical epoché is the suspension of all judgement, whether affirmative or negative.

47. *Encyclopedia* §32 Zusatz; ET 52

48. This is where Hegelian and Husserlian phenomenologies coincide, namely as critiques of abstraction, one-sidedness, solipsism.

49. Thus for Hegel, Parmenides and the Eleatic school of philosophy count as dogmatists, because they sought to grasp Being in complete abstraction from and opposition to Nothing. Hegel, *Geschichte der Philosophie*, TWA Sk 18:299.

50. Hegel, *Verhältnis Skeptizismus zur Philosophie*, Werke TWA Sk 2:246; *Skepticism*, 336. [I have altered the translation.]

51. Ibid. 335.

52. *Skepticism*, 335.

53. Hegel, *Geschichte der Philosophie*, TWA Sk 18: 299. Forster's claim that Hegel accepts Parmenides' doctrine of the incoherence of the notion of not-being, and that this is a source of Hegel's claim that the rational has no opposite, must be rejected. (Forster, op. cit. 119f.) Hegel champions Heraclitos against Parmenides; Heraclitos is the only predecessor in the history of philosophy whom Hegel credits with anticipating his own doctrine of becoming (*Werden*) as the dialectical unity of being and nothing. He writes "Here we see land; there is not a single thesis of Heraclitos that I have not incorporated into my logic." (*Geschichte der Philosophie*, TWA Sk 18: 320)

54. Enz. §81. 1.

55. There is of course the universality of fundamental logical principles such as identity, contradiction and sufficient reason. But Hegel makes even stronger claims about the unity of reason itself: "The fact that philosophy is but one, and can only be one, rests on the fact that reason is but one. And just as there cannot be distinct reasons, so too a wall cannot be set up between reason and its self-cognition, through which its self-cognition could become essentially distinguishable from its appearance." (*The Critical Journal*, BTKH, 275)

56. Cf. Forster, op. cit. 103–116.

57. Hegel, *Skepticism*, 324–5.

58. Forster interprets the important thesis that since the rational has no opposite equipollence does not apply to Hegel's philosophy, in a way that slights Hegel's holism and is open to attack. (Op. cit. 107–108.) Hegel's point is not that *his philosophy* is invulnerable to the equipollence problem, but that genuine holism admits no alternative. Hegel concedes that his formulations may yet be deficient in articulating this holism.

59. As Mure points out, triadic holism is for Hegel the *minimum rationale*. (G. R. G. Mure, *A Study of Hegel's Logic* [Oxford or New York: Oxford University Press, 1950], 34–37.) This triadic conception is perhaps first introduced in Plato's *Parmenides*, which Hegel regards as a masterpiece of classical dialectic. Cf. Forster, op. cit. 107–108.

60. In the review article on Skepticism, Hegel refers to Sextus Empiricus, *Outlines of Pyrrhonism* I, VII. (See OP I, VII, 11.) Although Hegel is highly critical of skepticism and ultimately dismisses it, he does not claim or believe that refutation of skepticism is possible, not because no important considerations can be marshalled against it, but because refutation involves public intersubjective truth which the skeptic inconsistently denies.

61. *Skepticism,* 338. Cf. Forster, op. cit. 39–41. Forster gives an oblique defense of Hegel's critique of skepticism.

62. *Skepticism,* 338; TWA 2, 249. In the *Phenomenology,* Hegel identifies skepticism as an oscillation between two different points of view: (1) the universal, essential reflective and (2) the accidental, mere opinion. Skepticism is unable to bring together or reconcile these two contradictory positions on judgements. (157)

63. "If someone absolutely wants to be a skeptic, he cannot be persuaded otherwise to accept philosophy as positive, any more than someone whose limbs are paralyzed can be brought to stand on his own feet. In fact skepticism is such a paralysis, an incapacity for truth, which is capable only of [private] certainty but not the [public] universality of truth, and which remains within the negative and individual subjectivity." *Gesch. der Philosophie,* TWA 19: 359.

64. Enz. §88 Zusatz.

65. Hegel, Enz. Pöggeler ed., §1, 33. Cf. the discussion of the same problem of beginning in the *Science of Logic. Werke* TWA 5: 65f; ET 65ff.

66. For a critical discussion of Hegel's holism, cf. Walter Schulz, "Das Problem der absoluten Reflexion," in *Wissenschaft und Gegenwart Heft 24* (Frankfurt am Main: Klostermann, 1963), 5–31.

67. Cf. *First Introduction to the Wissenschaftslehre.* This formulation in turn reflects Schelling's similar formulation in his *Letters Concerning Philosophical Criticism (1796).* Thus both Fichte and Schelling had come across the problem of equipollence, but neither had been aware of its significance for skepticism in the history of philosophy and neither had made it central to his account of the history of consciousness. That is Hegel's contribution: alterity and equipollence are central to his existential dialectic.

68. That is, the conflict between the first principles of idealism and dogmatism is traced back to the difference of interests, to two different kinds of human being, two radically different assessments of human freedom. Although Fichte believes that idealism, and the underlying interest in freedom, is "true," the question of truth itself has been set aside and is derivative from interest.

69. PhG 23; PhS 13.

70. PhG 33; PhS 22.

71. PhG 34; PhS 23.

72. *Geschichte der Philosophie* TWA 19: 393.

73. Ph G 46; PhS 33.

74. PhG 26; PhS 16. I have altered the text. Hegel ascribes such dogmatism to immediate certainty, and does not mention Schelling here. Cf. Hegel's similar use of the "shot from the pistol" metaphor for immediate knowledge in the *Wissenschaft der Logik:* "The modern embarrassment about the beginning proceeds out of a larger need, which those who proceed dogmatically to demonstrate their principle, or skeptically concerning the discovery of a subjective criterion against dogmatic philosophizing, are not yet cognizant, and which is entirely denied by those who begin like a shot from the pistol with their inner revelation, faith, intellectual intuition etc., and who want to have done with method and logic." W. L. TWA 5:65–66.

75. PhG 177; PhS 140–141.

76. Ibid.

77. Ibid. [Emphasis mine.]

78. Since the skeptic denies certainty and refuses any objective assertion, he undermines intersubjective recognition.

79. Joseph C. Flay, "Hegel's *Science of Logic:* Ironies of the Understanding," in *Essays on Hegel's Logic,* op. cit. 160.

80. "Since *reciprocal recognition* is...suspended, what appears is only two subjectivities in opposition; things that have nothing in common with one another come on stage with equal right for that very reason." (*The Critical Journal,* BTKH, 276) [My emphasis.] Cf. also H. S. Harris' introduction, 253ff.)

81. Cf. Forster, op. cit. 107–8; 119–120; 148–170.

82. PhG 68; PhS 50.

83. J. N. Findlay puts the point in this way: "Hegel thinks...that there is no other satisfactory way of viewing the world than the one just mentioned, and that every other way of looking on that world must lead us, on pain of conflict or intellectual frustration, to the view in question." (*Hegel: A Re-Examination* [New York: Collier Books, 1962], 54) Findlay notes that in the introduction to the *Phenomenology* Hegel "rejects the notion of there being some absolute criterion..." (85) For an antifoundationalist reading of Hegel, see William Maker, "Reason and the Problem of Modernity," *The Philosophical Forum,* vol. XVIII, no. 4 (Summer 1987): 275–303; see also Maker, "Beginning" in *Essays on Hegel's Logic,* op. cit.

Six

Hegelian Phenomenology

The Task of the *Phenomenology of Spirit*

The introduction (which was written before the preface) to the *Phenomenology* sets forth the method and tasks of the work as an introduction to philosophical science (*Wissenschaft*). Philosophy, although autonomous and self-justifying, nevertheless has a pre-philosophical prius, or pre-theoretical presupposition.[1] That is, philosophical science requires an introduction.[2] For Hegel, philosophy has no *Grundsatz*, and no a priori criterion. It cannot begin with immediate certainty or with transcendental intuition like "a shot from a pistol," for that would amount to the philosophical dogmatism for which he takes Fichte and Schelling to task. Such dogmatism succumbs to equipollence objections. On the other hand, philosophy presupposes that consciousness has gotten beyond such objections, i.e., that it is no longer a solipsistic first person cogito, but a universal-social consciousness that is "pure self-knowledge in absolute otherness..."[3] The *Phenomenology's* task is to educate and elevate ordinary consciousness to this universal-social standpoint.

> Philosophical science demands that self-consciousness has already raised itself to this ether in order to be able to live in and with it. Conversely, the individual has the right to demand that philosophical science at least hand him a ladder to its standpoint in order to show him the latter standpoint within his own.[4]

In the previous chapter, it was shown that Hegel's phenomenological project demonstrates that each shape of consciousness is self-subverting. This suggests that the *Phenomenology* has only a negative significance, namely, it demonstrates that all the shapes of consciousness self-destruct. It is a philosophical demolition derby. One interpreter stresses this negative significance when he claims that "all non-scientific viewpoints...*succumb* to equipollence objections. Thus the equipollence method seems to offer an opportunity for *discrediting* all non-scientific viewpoints in a way completely compelling to them on the basis of their own views and criteria."[5] Again, the *Phenomenology* is "an exhaustive *destruction* of all non-scientific claims..."[6] But is the *Phenomenology* simply a *via negativa*?

There is no question that Hegel thinks the *Phenomenology,* as a self-accomplishing skepticism, has some negative significance. Consider the following:

> The natural consciousness will show itself to be only the concept of knowing, not genuine knowledge. But since it immediately takes itself to be genuine knowledge, so the way [the phenomenological traversal of the *Gestalten*] has for it only a negative significance. What is in fact the realization of the *Begriff,* ordinary consciousness takes to be the loss of itself, for on this path it loses its own truth. It can therefore be regarded as the path of doubt, or rather as the highway of despair. This is not a question of mere doubt, which shakes this or that particular truth, so that at the end the matter is understood pretty much the same as before. Rather it is the conscious insight into the untruth of phenomenal knowing [*erscheinende Wissens*]...[7]

This passage makes it sound as if phenomenal knowledge is completely undermined and destroyed on the highway of despair. However this judgement reflects and is true only for a particular standpoint, namely, the naive and dogmatic ordinary consciousness that is wedded to its partial insights. From the perspective of ordinary consciousness, experience is negative. That is because ordinary consciousness is dogmatic in the narrower sense: it assumes its objects are immediate givens and suppresses their mediation and context. But from the perspective of the phenomenological observers, and for the altered and educated ordinary consciousness, the *Phenomenology* is not merely negative. It has a positive result. It demonstrates that there are no immediate fixed absolutes in isolation: The truth is the whole. Moreover, the whole is already implicit in the natural attitude.[8]

Consequently, rather than simply discrediting and destroying ordinary consciousness, it would be more accurate to say that Hegel sublates it.[9] But doesn't sublation (*aufheben*) involve cancellation and negation? On the contrary, sublation also involves a restoration of sense that unmasks and corrects false consciousness. Restoration is the term that fits best with Hegel's early essay on skepticism. The skeptical correction of dogmatism unearths and brings to light what had been there all along, but was suppressed. In Hegel's view, the positive speculative significance of equipollence involves a restoration of something that the natural attitude suppresses or passes over.[10] That is why Hegel is attracted to equipollence, but not to its skeptical interpretation. As Hegel interprets equipollence, it is not sheer negation, but has positive rational significance: "It allows the opposite moment, from which dogmatism has abstracted, to put in an appearance and constitute an antinomy."[11] The positive significance of equipollence is that it restores the suppressed alterity, and thereby makes a transition from a limited partial insight, to a more comprehensive, holistic insight. The original position is shown to depend on the very other it initially denies and excludes. It can maintain its truth only by acknowledging the partial, one-sided character of its original position, and by accepting the validity of what it originally denied or excluded. Thus, ordinary consciousness is not destroyed or discredited, but rather educated: "The series of its shapes and configurations, which consciousness runs through on this path, is in fact the detailed history of the education [*Bildung*] of consciousness itself to the standpoint of science."[12]

Each Gestalt starts out with a presumptive certainty, "good until further notice," that self-destructs in its experiential passage through alterity. The shapes of consciousness (*Gestalten des Bewusstseins*) undergo a concrete skeptical dialectic that purges them of their dogmatic one-sidedness and forces them to confront and incorporate their opposite. The principle of equipollence becomes an element in Hegel's phenomenological method, providing criticism of dogmatism, whether that of ordinary consciousness or traditional metaphysics (*Verstand*). Equipollence becomes the principle of a concrete experiential dialectic.

The *Phenomenology* starts not with philosophy, but with its other, "unphilosophy," the pre-philosophical natural attitude, or *doxa*.[13] This is Hegel's parallel to Husserl's critique of the sciences by regression to the life-world as concrete a priori. Unlike Husserl, Hegel does not accord foundational status to the pre-theoretical natural attitude. The latter is a starting point, not a justification. But neither does Hegel, like the objectifying mathematical sciences, downgrade the life-world to the merely subjective or displace the life-world in favor of a 'more adequate' explanatory framework. That reductive enterprise belongs to the negative analytical power of *Verstand*.[14] Although speculative philosophy appears to ordinary consciousness as an inverted world, and may even stand ordinary consciousness on its head,[15] speculative reason does not seek to undermine, but rather to understand, explain, and justify the truth of natural consciousness.[16] The autonomy of philosophy does not mean that it creates or invents the truth of the natural attitude, but rather purges the latter of its one-sidedness and dogmatism.[17]

<h2>Hegel's Hermeneutical Critique of Critique</h2>

The idea of a critique of reason (by Locke and Kant) involves an examination of the medium or instrument of knowledge *prior to its use,* in order to determine its capacities, limits, and suitability for dealing with certain questions. Hegel contends that this critical enterprise rests upon a presupposition, namely, that knowledge is an instrument:

> It seems natural to suppose that before philosophy gets involved with its subject matter—namely the actual knowledge of what truly is—it is necessary first to come to an understanding concerning knowledge itself, which is regarded as an *instrument* (*Werkzeug*) through which to take possession of the absolute, or as a *medium* (*Mittel*) through which to get sight of it.[18]

The instrumental conception of knowledge plays an important role in the critical hermeneutics of suspicion. Locke believes that knowledge is a passive medium—like a pair of eyeglasses—through which reality may (or may not) reach us. The suspicion is that the medium may introduce a distortion that might not be correctable. Kant believes that knowledge involves the mind as an active instrument—like a particle beam accelerator for studying sub-atomic particles. In this case the suspicion is that the instrument might interfere with or alter the object, making it impossible to apprehend the thing as it is in itself.

Whether or not Kant's critical program is similar to Locke's is not an important issue here.[19] Instead, Hegel, in a brilliant example of hermeneutic phenomenology, focuses on the underlying metaphor of knowledge as an instrument. The instrumental metaphor of knowledge derives from the natural attitude. It has had a long influence in the history of philosophy.[20] It dominates traditional epistemology, and has become explicit in the age of science. But even though it has been pervasive, the instrumental metaphor has implications that make the critical enterprise, *insofar as it depends on that metaphor,*[21] self-defeating:

> For if knowledge is an instrument for taking possession of absolute, the suggestion immediately occurs that the application of an instrument to a state of affairs does not leave it as it is 'in itself', but rather involves a shaping and alteration of that state of affairs. Or, if knowledge is not an instrument of our activity on things, but rather some sort of passive medium through which the light of truth supposedly reaches us, we do not receive it as it is 'in itself', but only as it reaches us through and in this medium. In both cases we make use of a means which immediately brings about the opposite of its own end, or rather the absurdity lies in making use of any means at all.[22]

The critical enterprise wants to examine the 'instrument' of knowing in order to be sure that it can deliver things as they are in themselves. But an instrument interposed between the knower and things cuts the knower off from things in themselves and instead delivers things as they are conditioned by the instrument. Hence the means employed by the critique subvert its end, and bring about the opposite of what is intended. Moreover, if it were possible to correct the alteration imposed by the instrument, or the coloration imposed by the medium, this would presuppose that there is direct access to the things themselves without or apart from the instrument or medium. But with that we are back to the starting point, and the whole critical enterprise becomes "superfluous."[23]

Consequently the critical project contains a fundamental incoherence. Since the examination of knowledge is itself an act of knowledge, critique naively employs the very medium or instrument it is examining. Critique is possible only if it (pre-critically) knows before it (critically) knows. Thus it is naive with respect to its own operative concepts, those of presupposition (that there is such a thing as knowledge, or knowledge as a given) and ground (the search for conditions of possibility of knowledge).

Criticism further shows itself to be uncritical in resting upon some unexamined presuppositions of its own: that knowledge is an instrument and/or medium; and that the absolute or object to be known stands on one side, while knowing stands on the other side—cut off from the absolute, the insoluble problem being how to get to the 'other side'.[24] But with an absolute dichotomy between subject and object, how can knowledge which is outside the absolute and the truth, nevertheless be true? Critique has so determined the conditions of possibility of knowledge that knowledge turns out to be impossible.

Hegel believes that critical philosophy is in fact a form of skepticism, although unaware of this. He characterizes "uncritical criticism" as the fear of truth masquerading as the fear of error.[25] In view of its fundamental incoherence, he counsels a mistrust of the critical mistrust. However this counsel is neither dogmatism nor a rejection of criticism. Instead Hegel, having uncovered the latent skepticism in critical philosophy, proceeds to radicalize skepticism: there are *no* criteria, least of all sense perception, which philosophy can safely take for granted. Hence it is necessary to make a fresh start, by turning to a description of ordinary pre-philosophical consciousness. But Hegel is so far from beginning dogmatically with a life-world a priori that he raises the equipollence problem against all dogmatic assurances. He observes that philosophical science starts out as an appearance, i.e., without any privileged position vis-a-vis the others. Appeals to immediate convictions, first principles and the like, are mere assurances, and "one barren assurance counts just as much [or as little] as another."[26]

The Problem of the Criterion

To deal with the problem of equipollence, Hegel undertakes a phenomenology of knowledge as appearance (*Die Darstellung des erscheinende Wissens*). Far from solving the skeptical problem of the criterion, this only seems to restate it and make it more acute. For philosophical science appears on the scene as one appearance among others; it can only claim equal probability with others. In short, the problem is that of a pre-criteriological selection from equally probable but opposing *doxa*:

> ...a critical examination consists in the application of an accepted criterion, and in determining whether something is right or wrong on the basis of the resulting agreement or disagreement of thing with the standard. Thus the standard as such, and likewise science if it were the criterion, is thereby accepted as the essence or the in itself. But here, where it is a question of

the original appearing of science [*Wissenschaft*] itself, neither science itself nor anything else has been justified as the essence or the in itself. Yet without such a justification and justified criteria, no testing, no critical examination, are possible.[27]

The problem of the criterion of science calls for a *pre-philosophical*, i.e., a phenomenological solution. Hegel's solution—and the reason for turning to the natural attitude—is that ordinary consciousness does not wait for philosophy, but spontaneously provides its own criterion.[28] The criterion consists in what ordinary consciousness itself takes to be the object 'in itself' or *an sich*. Hegel's phenomenology is an immanent criticism of ordinary consciousness. Hegel will seek to show that ordinary consciousness does not conform to its own criteria, and so subverts its own claims to know.

Intentional Analysis of the Gestalts of Consciousness

Hegel apparently borrowed the term *"Gestalt"* from Goethe, who understood by it a living-organic unity, in contrast to a rigid mechanical unity.[29] The paradigm case of *Gestalt* is the human *Gestalt* or shape. In his Jena *Realphilosophie* 1805/6, Hegel identifies life (*Leben*) as a logical structure or *Begriff*.[30] This logical life is in the background of the transition from consciousness to self-consciousness in the *Phenomenology*. Hegel takes a further step beyond Goethe in speaking of *Gestalten des Bewusstseins*. Consciousness itself has a *Gestalt* structure, namely it is "for itself." This suggests a parallel between Hegel's use of the term *"Gestalten des Bewusstseins,"* and Husserl's late concept of ontological types. Both are non-formal ontological conceptions, in contrast with formal-mathematical concepts.[31] Thus, Hegel's phenomenology of *Gestalten des Bewusstseins*, approximates a non-formal, life-world ontology in Husserl's sense. Reinhold Aschenberg characterizes Hegel's phenomenology of the *Gestalten des Bewusstseins* as a pre-categorical ontology,[32] both related to and different from the categorical ontology of the Logic. What is its structure?

A *Gestalt* of consciousness exhibits the following general pattern:

Consciousness simultaneously distinguishes its object from itself, and relates itself to its object, or as this is usually expressed, something exists 'for consciousness'. The determinate aspect of this relation, or *being of something for consciousness*, is knowing. From this *being for another* we distinguish *being in itself*. The latter 'in itself' is distinguished from knowing and posited as existing outside of the cognitive relation. This *being in itself* is *truth*.[33]

The distinction between *being for consciousness* and *being in itself* originates with, and is constitutive of, consciousness; i.e., it is the fundamental structure of consciousness. This structure and its inherent distinction are crucial for

Hegel's project of phenomenology: "The essential point for the entire inquiry is that these several moments: concept and object, being-for-other and being-in-itself, reside within the very knowing which is under investigation."[34] Knowledge and critique are both aspects of Hegel's concept of experience. The distinction between 'in itself' and 'for itself,' while antinomic, is not absolute, but rather involves mediation.

The criterion is provided by ordinary consciousness itself, i.e., the object or "in itself" as it is intended. The intentional object generates and supplies its own criteria. This makes possible the phenomenological investigation and criticism.

> Consciousness provides its own criterion, and the investigation will therefore be a comparison of...consciousness with itself.... At the same time this other is to consciousness not merely for it, but rather exists outside of this relation or is in itself [an sich], i.e., the moment of truth. In that which the ordinary consciousness declares to be the [object] in-itself or the true, we have the criterion (Masstab) which ordinary consciousness itself proposes, against which to measure its knowledge [of the object].[35]

If ordinary consciousness itself supplies the criterion, then no external criteria are necessary: "Consequently it is not necessary for us to bring our own criteria or to apply our own fancy ideas and concepts to the investigation. On the contrary, precisely because we leave these aside and hold them in suspension, we reach our goal of considering things as they are in and for themselves."[36] "Scientific knowledge...requires surrender to the life of the object, or, what is the same thing, confronting and expressing the inner necessity of the object."[37]

Consciousness Tests Itself

The initial generation of criteria by ordinary consciousness does not constitute their justification. It is merely the starting point for their testing. Ordinary consciousness stands at the level of doxa. Doxic immediacy is a form of truth, albeit its poorest form. Hegel denies that immediacy is sufficient justification, even at the pre-theoretical level. Not even ordinary consciousness rests content with its initial immediate positing of the "in itself" as the criterion; it also carries out an examination of the criterion or "in-itself". "But not only is a contribution by us superfluous, since [Begriff] and object [Gegenstand,], criterion [Masstab] and what is to be tested [das zu Prüfende], are already present in consciousness itself, we are also spared the effort of a comparison and the actual testing of the two. Since consciousness tests itself, all that is left for us is pure observation [das reine Zusehen]."[38] Consciousness examines itself and tests its own criterion.

The examination or testing of doxa is a process of comparison between what the object in itself is originally declared to be, and what it subsequently *proves* to be as a result of experience. "Let us call knowing (*Wissen*) the concept (*Begriff*), and being (*Wesen*) or the true, the object (*Gegenstand*). Then the examination (*Prüfung*) will consist in determining whether the concept corresponds to the object."[39] The examination seems to be a straightforward determination of the correspondence of the initial construal of the object, to the object in itself. Truth is apparently understood to be a correspondence between knowledge (representation) and its object. But matters are more complicated, for the testing involves passage of the initial construal of the object "in itself" through the alterity of experience. This will show that the construal is inadequate, partial, and one-sided.

Since the very distinction between being-for-consciousness and being-in itself occurs within consciousness, Hegel can also reverse the terms and the direction of the examination.

> Let us call the being, or the 'in-itself' of the object, the concept (*Begriff*), and conversely let us understand by the object (*Gegenstand*) the object as it is for another [or for the subject]. Then the examination will consist in determining whether the object corresponds to its concept.[40]

In this example the particular object gets measured against its type or genus. An object that corresponds to its concept will be a good example of its type or kind, e.g., "We speak of a true friend, by which we mean a friend whose manner of conduct accords with the concept of friendship."[41]

The examination and testing is simple: a concept that corresponds to the object passes the test. But if experience establishes no correspondence between concept and object, then the concept must be abandoned or altered. Then ordinary consciousness learns through its experience that what it took the "in itself" to be, is in fact only a presumptive certainty, a "subjective in itself." It learns that the proposed "in itself" is only "for it," for consciousness. Neither the original presumptive certainty nor its criterion passes the test. The examination is not merely a testing of *doxa*, but a testing of the doxic criterion. This experiential testing is no calm antiseptic procedure. Far from it! It involves a passage through alterity, including antinomy and contradiction.[42]

The phenomenologist discovers that the truth turns out to be the opposite of what it originally appeared to be. For example, in Hegel's analysis of sense certainty, the truth of the originally intended immediate particular 'this' turns out to be the enduring universal 'this' that was initially rejected.[43] Sense certainty cannot even say what it means without falling into self-contradiction. In the case of master and slave, the truth of mastery turns out to be the dehumanized divided consciousness of the slave. But the recognition received from a mere slave is deficient, and this deficiency produces a false consciousness in the master which brings about his decadence, decline, and fall. Neither of these *Gestalten* survive their passage through alterity. They self-destruct. It is only the observer(s) who learn the lesson of experience.

SELF-ACCOMPLISHING SKEPTICISM: THE HIGHWAY OF DESPAIR

Ordinary consciousness operates immediately with the distinctions "in itself" and "for consciousness." It is familiar with them, but only implicitly aware of their significance. "What is familiar is, precisely because it is familiar, not generally understood."[44] Ordinary consciousness sees only the difference between the "in itself" and the "for-consciousness," but not their mediation. Such one-sided naivete makes ordinary consciousness hostile to mediation. It becomes dogmatic whenever it prefers its presumptive certainties to truth, i.e., posits as absolute something that is finite, limited, and essentially constituted or qualified by opposition. It thinks abstractly by lifting its object out of context, and seeking to maintain it fixed isolation from, or opposition to, everything else.[45]

For example, consider the meaning of the term "in itself." Ordinary consciousness posits the "in itself" as absolute, as existing outside of relation. Thus, it creates a rigid subject-object antithesis, and suppresses one side of the antithesis, namely the "in itself *for consciousness*." Kant's concept of the thing in itself—which is thinkable but not knowable—is but a further hardening of the dogmatic position of ordinary consciousness, one that renders it paradoxical, self-contradictory.[46] The creation of rigid oppositions, and the abstract isolation of the elements from relation, is the cul-de-sac of ordinary consciousness and reflection. In its interpretation of the *Gestalten des Bewusstseins,* ordinary consciousness grasps only the moment of difference, or abstract identity, while suppressing relation and mediation. Thus, ordinary consciousness tends to interpret itself subjectively.

The natural attitude, and the sciences that presuppose and rest upon it, misinterpret the *Gestalt* structure as an *absolute dichotomy*. They regard "being-for-consciousness" and "being-in-itself," as absolutely heterogeneous, and incapable of mediation. This misinterpretation is rooted in the natural attitude, but finds expression in the peculiarly modern cultural situation. Knowledge involves an alienation from the life-world.

> In modern times however, the individual finds the abstract form ready-made.... Hence the present task consists not so much in purging the individual of an immediate sensible mode of apprehension...but rather in the opposite, in freeing determinate thoughts from their fixed rigidity in order to actualize and vivify the universal. But it is far harder to bring fixed thoughts into fluidity, than to purify sense perception.[47]

Hegel employs the principle of equipollence—that to every thesis there is an equal opposing thesis—not as a skeptic but as a critic of dogmatism. The skeptical tropes serve as a critique of abstract rationality (*Verstand*) by restoring suppressed alterity, thereby breaking up fixed abstractions. Where *Verstand* sees only rigid dichotomies and unbridgeable dualisms, *Vernunft* finds that the truth is an organic, interrelated whole.

But such interrelatedness and the attendant qualifications brought to light by experiential testing are for ordinary consciousness a highway of despair:

> The natural consciousness will show itself...not to be genuine knowledge. However, since it immediately takes itself to be genuine knowledge, the way of experience has for it negative significance. The realization of the concept appears to natural consciousness rather as the loss of itself, for in the journey of experience it loses its truth. This way can be viewed as the journey of doubt, or more properly as the highway of despair.[48]

The negative experience of ordinary consciousness is self-inflicted, rooted in its one-sided, dogmatic attitude and in its immediate construals and certainties. Experience, as a passage through antinomic equipollence and alterity, engenders doubts that do not allow of a return to former "truths" and certainties. For ordinary consciousness, experience is "the conscious insight into the untruth of that phenomenal knowledge [*doxa*], which takes the real to be merely the not yet actualized *Begriff.*"[49] Since ordinary consciousness refuses mediation, and identifies the real with fixed entities held apart in abstraction, and since the *Begriff* is the process of breaking up and mediating such abstractions, experience has negative significance for ordinary consciousness. To be torn away from its immediate existence and certainties is death.[50] But this is a self-inflicted wound. For "consciousness is for itself its own concept. Consequently consciousness is immediately transcendence of limitation; and since the limitation belongs to consciousness itself, consciousness transcends itself.... Consciousness suffers this violence, this ruination of every limited satisfaction, at its own hands.... By its very 'nature' it can find no rest..."[51]

Such experience and unrest are the negative aspect of the *Begriff*. However, experience is not merely negative, but constitutes the education or *Bildung* of the ordinary consciousness. The test of experience compels the abandonment of the narrow perspective and the adoption of a larger, holistic perspective which incorporates the opposite point of view. Insight into error presupposes a disclosure, however limited, of an alternative truth.[52] This compels consciousness to alter its conception of the object, and its criterion. The alteration of both consciousness and its object is a reversal or inversion (*Umkehr*). The first 'thing in itself' now turns out to be the opposite of its original meaning, namely a '*subjective thing in itself*'. The experience of this reversal is a second new object (or in itself) for consciousness: "This new object contains the nullification of the first; it is what experience has made of the first."[53] But the partial truth contained in the initial construal is not simply eliminated; it is transformed by confrontation with its opposite and preserved in a larger perspective. This exceedingly formal and abstract sketch is filled in with diverse situations and contents, and repeated on ever more complex levels throughout the *Phenomenology*. The incorporation and mediation of alterity, the opposite point of view, leads to a dialectical holism which suspends the rigid dichotomies and oppositions of consciousness. What begins as a science of the experience of consciousness becomes a phenomenology of *Geist*.

BETWEEN PANLOGISM AND EXISTENTIAL ANTHROPOLOGY

Hegel does not follow Descartes and the transcendental tradition in separating transcendental philosophical consciousness from ordinary consciousness. Nevertheless there are at least two perspectives from which the *Gestalten des Bewusstseins* are considered. The first is the perspective of the ordinary consciousness, which lives in the *Gestalt* and immediately expresses it. This natural consciousness is naive and dogmatic, to some extent a false consciousness because it grasps the *Gestalt* structure immediately as dichotomy or antinomy. But the inadequacy of this *Gestalt* becomes evident only from a second and more adequate perspective, that of the phenomenological observers, whose awareness of the limitations of natural consciousness involves transcendence of them. Is the distinction between these two standpoints simply a distinction between naive and philosophical consciousness? Can consciousness occupy both standpoints at once? Or does the distinction of standpoint require an intersubjective interpretation? Hegel inclines towards the latter, for he speaks of a phenomenological "We."[54]

Klaus Hartmann treats the *Phenomenology* as an extended introduction to transcendental philosophy, one starting with a 'natural' consciousness and watching it change as it realizes its 'truths' are imperfect. But for Hartmann the argument and transitions of the *Phenomenology* are categorically determined, and so depend on the *Logic*. Hence, the phenomenological description of the natural attitude is a mere side show, for it is "only plausible if the right commentary is given, and Hegel in fact introduces an accompanying commentator, the philosopher or ourselves as philosophers, who know the 'logic' of consciousness..."[55] In this view, both the 'natural consciousness' and the 'we' are mere devices deployed by Hegel in his introduction to transcendental philosophy, i.e., the logic. Accordingly, Hegel need not take experience seriously, because "transcendental philosophy is autonomous rather than a result to be reached from the 'ordinary level' in straightforwards steps."[56] According to Hartmann, strictly speaking, there is no *independent* natural consciousness to be educated through experience:

> Whatever consciousness learns it learns under our supervision; it is motivated by what we know are transcendental reasons and thus Hegel, although he merely seems to describe, prescribes from a 'higher' vantage point, or 'deeper' stance, adopted all along.[57]

Natural consciousness and the 'we' are mere devices of transcendental philosophy; they are quasi personifications standing in a relation of tutelage to a transcendental master. Elsewhere Hartmann warns against a realistic reading of the various *Gestalten des Bewusstseins* of the *Phenomenology*.[58]

Were Hartmann's interpretation correct, Hegel's phenomenological project would fail on its own terms. Dialectic would be reducible to purely logical dialectic, and the whole project would be simply an extended monologue of the transcendental philosopher.[59] Feuerbach's complaint that Hegel never allows the natural attitude or sense certainty to speak for itself, would be correct.[60] The *Phenomenology* would be superfluous, a judgment which Hegel himself never made. In my view, Hegel's concept of the *Bildung* of ordinary consciousness presupposes its relative autonomy and independence from philosophy. It further presupposes that the phenomenological development and transitions are accessible not only to the transcendental philosopher and phenomenological We, but to ordinary consciousness as well.[61] Hegel is explicit in granting ordinary consciousness a right to demand and receive a ladder to the standpoint of science, a right "which is grounded in its absolute independence."[62] On Hartmann's view that ordinary consciousness is merely a puppet of transcendental philosophy, its independence and right to education would be denied and the *Logic* would be dogmatically asserted.

Kojève, on the other hand, interprets the *Phenomenology* as an existential philosophical anthropology and considers the descriptions of the natural consciousness in this light. Although Kojève's lectures on Hegel had tremendous impact on the French development of existential phenomenology, his reading is suspect, because it overlooks the point that the *Phenomenology* is to serve as the introduction to Hegel's system. In construing the *Phenomenology* as an existential anthropology, Kojève passes over the logical deep structure and its relation to the *Gestalten des Bewusstseins*. Any reading, however brilliant, that suppresses this basic systematic point, is unreliable. The phenomenological observer must not be collapsed into the natural consciousness, nor phenomenology into anthropology. Hegel's phenomenology of the *Gestalten* is unquestionably relevant to Kojève's anthropological concerns, but it is also more than a philosophical anthropology. Hegel's phenomenological ontology is more than an existential anthropology.

Reinhold Aschenberg provides a middle ground between the 'logical Hegel' and the 'existential-anthropological Hegel' without surrendering the ontological interpretation of the *Phenomenology* : The *Phenomenology* is not a categorical ontology like the logic, but rather "a pre-categorical ontology,"[63] an ontology of the shapes of consciousness (*Gestalten des Bewusstseins*). This is a life-world ontology in Husserl's sense. Each *Gestalt des Bewusstseins* can be considered from two perspectives: that of ordinary consciousness, and that of the phenomenological observer(s). This double consideration comprises a straightforward description of the natural attitude or ordinary consciousness on the one hand (Kojève's existential anthropology), and an eidetic phenomenology of the immanent ontological structure on the other. Hegel indicates the dual standpoints with such locutions as *"für uns"* (the phenomenological observers) and *"für es"* (the ordinary consciousness). Whatever the correct interpretation of the *Phenomenology* may be and regardless of the place of the phenomenological observer within the overall argument, this distinction between the two standpoints of ordinary consciousness and the observer is crucial to Hegel's project and its method.[64] We shall find it central to Hegel's presentation of *Anerkennung* because it is the basis of a distinction between eidetics (analysis of the concept), and empirics (concrete investigations of the concept in determinate form), as it appears in everyday life to ordinary consciousness. Empirics presupposes eidetics; the latter plays a heuristic and hermeneutical role for concrete inquiry. But eidetics without empirics runs the risk of becoming an empty formalism. Although the concept can be isolated and considered in and for itself, it is actual only "at work" in the life-world. It is the living soul of concrete phenomena.

NOTES

1. A central tension in Hegel's thought is whether the logic, as self-explanatory self-justifying transcendental philosophy, admits of a prius, or an introduction at all, or, whether the introduction is part of the system or external to the system. For a discussion of this problem, see H. F. Fulda, *Das Problem einer Einleitung in Hegels Wissenschaft der Logik,* Zweite Auflage (Frankfurt Am Main: Vittorio Klostermann, 1975); Theodor Litt, *Hegel:Versuch einer kritischen Erneurung* (Heidelberg: Quelle and Meyer, 1961); Malcolm Clark, *Logic and System: A Study of the Transition from Vorstellung to Thought in the Philosophy of Hegel* (Loewen, Belgium: Universitaire Werkgemeenschap, 1960); Klaus Hartmann, "On Taking the Transcendental Turn," *Review of Metaphysics,* op cit.; Stanley Rosen, *G. W. F. Hegel; An Introduction to the Science of Wisdom* (New Haven, Conn.: Yale University Press, 1974).

2. On this point Hegel never wavered. Like Husserl he experimented with several different ways of introducing his system, including Logic and Phenomenology. Later in the *Encyclopedia* the system is introduced by the *Vorbegriff,* three attitudes of thought towards objectivity. This *Vorbegriff* is a phenomenology of the history of philosophy.

3. Hegel, *Phänomenologie des Geistes,* Hoffmeister edition (Hamburg, Felix Meiner Verlag, 1952), 25. Hereafter cited as PhG, ET *Phenomenology of Spirit* tr. A. V Miller (Oxford: Oxford University Press, 1977), 15. [Hereafter cited as PhS.] See also *The Phenomenology of Mind,* tr. J. B. Baillie (New York: Macmillan, 1949). [Hereafter cited as PhM.] [Although I have consulted the English translations, all translations are my own.]

4. PhG 24

5. Michael N. Forster, *Hegel and Skepticism*, op. cit. 155. [My italics.]

6. Ibid. 136. [My italics.]

7. PhG. 67; PhS §78.

8. See Joseph C. Flay, *Hegel's Quest For Certainty* (Albany, N.Y.: SUNY Press, 1984), Chap. 1.

9. Recall Hegel's term "aufheben" that signifies both cancellation and preservation. Cf. *Wissenschaft der Logik*, TWA Sk. 5, 113f, the Remark on Becoming as sublation.

10. For example, Hegel shows the putative claims of sense certainty are self-subverting because they involve contradiction. Thus sense certainty means what is particular and excludes the universal, but it cannot express its position without making use of the very universality that it initially rejected.

11. Hegel, *Skepticism*, BTKH, 336; TWA Sk. 2:246.

12. PhG 67; PhS §78.

13. Two interpreters identify Hegel's "natürliche Bewusstsein" with Husserl's natural attitude (*die natürliche Einstellung*). Cf. Merold Westphal, *History and Truth in Hegel's Phenomenology* [New York: Humanities Press 1980]; Joseph C. Flay, *Hegel's Quest For Certainty*, op. cit. As a rough approximation this identification is helpful. It should not be pressed too far however, because there are significant differences. It is not evident that Hegel's natural consciousness has a general thesis, or the thesis of the world, which is central to Husserl's concept. On the other hand, what both the natural attitude and natural consciousness have in common is immediacy, naive immersion in the intentional object. Husserl claims that the general thesis of the natural attitude concerning the world can be treated as an explicit if uninformative judgement, namely, that there is a world out there. Hegel suggests that sense-certainty makes a claim which can be written down, i. e., can be treated as a judgement. For a defense of this claim, cf. Flay's discussion of praxial presuppositions.

14. The understanding subverts itself by generating antinomies and, when these are elevated to consciousness, as in the case of Kant, the result is a sophisticated form of skepticism. PhG 29; Hegel comments that analysis is the transformation (*Aufhebung*) of familiarity. PhS §32, 18.

15. PhG 25; PhS §26, 15.

16. Cf. *Enzyklopädie*, §64; see also Joseph C. Flay, *Hegel's Quest For Certainty*, op. cit. Chap. 1.

17. This is the function of the phenomenological reduction in Husserl's later formulations of it.

18. PhG 63; PhS 46. I am indebted to Robert F. Brown for clarifying the dis-

tinction between knowledge as a passive medium (Locke) and an active instrument (Kant).

19. Cf. J. E. Smith, "Hegel's Critique of Kant" in *Review of Metaphysics*, 1973. Smith observes that Hegel tends to interpret Kant's transcendental program as a psychology.

20. For example Aristotle determines logic as an organon. Locke offers a clear statement of this view. Kant would have liked to offer an organon of pure reason, namely a complete system of all principles for the acquisition of a priori knowledge. (*Critique of Pure Reason*, op. cit. A11 B25, 58) Kant settled for a *Critique* whose purpose, unlike an organon, is not to extend knowledge, but rather to correct and restrict it.

21. Hegel's objection is not to criticism, but rather Kant's view of what a critique of reason is. Hegel's view is that the critique of reason is properly categorial criticism. Categorial criticism is prior to metaphysical constructions, and so goes on 'beneath' the idealist-realist debates.

22. PhG 63–64; PhS 46.

23. PhG 64; PhS 47. The same argument would hold against the representational theory of ideas, which is frequently attributed to Idealism. See Richard Rorty, *Philosophy and The Mirror of Nature* (Princeton, N.J.: Princeton University Press, 1979). For a somewhat inconclusive discussion of Hegel's critique, cf. the essays by Justus Hartnack and W. H. Walsh in Stephen Priest (ed.), *Hegel's Critique of Kant* (Oxford: Clarendon Press, 1987). Hartnack thinks Hegel succeeds in showing that the instrumental conception of knowledge is self-refuting. (81) Walsh acknowledges that Kant thinks of reason as a tool or device (130) but for reasons neither clear nor convincing rejects Hegel's diagnoses of the disastrous implications. Both writers are more concerned with the perennial analytic bugaboo of subjective idealism and the 'thing in itself', i. e., traditional epistemology, than with Hegel's depth-hermeneutical flanking maneuver. Another writer dismisses Hegel because of his alleged neglect of epistemology: "Much of Hegel's metaphysics develops independently of any epistemological basis. He avoids the first person standpoint of Descartes not through any rival theory of knowledge, but by a process of abstraction which, because it abolishes the individual, leaves no evident room for the theory of knowledge at all. This makes Hegel's metaphysics so vulnerable to skeptical attack that it has now little to bequeath us but its poetry." (R. Scruton, *From Descartes to Wittgenstein* [New York: Harper and Row, 1982], 178, cited in Forster, op. cit. 98) Note that for Scruton epistemology is synonymous with an essentially first person, Cartesian enterprise, such that any philosophy which adopts an alternative standpoint such as Hegel's skeptical social holism, has abolished epistemology. From the perspective of Hegel's phenomenology, this understanding of "epistemology" is one shape of consciousness that is shown to self-destruct. As Forster rightly shows, Hegel does not abolish epistemology so much as he transforms it. Scruton's remarks show how an Anglo-American analytic mentality has no inkling, much less comprehension, of what Hegel is up to.

24. Hegel develops these points with especial clarity in his *Skepticism Essay*,

op. cit. 338ff. Kant's critical philosophy sides with *Verstand* against *Vernunft*, it is a phenomenology of consciousness rather than a phenomenology of spirit. (Enz. §415) This means that it elevates non-identity between subject and object to the status of an absolute principle: "This sundering of the rational in which thinking and being are one, and the absolute insistence on this opposition, in other words, the understanding made absolute, constitutes the endlessly repeated and universally applied ground of this dogmatic skepticism." *Skepticism,* 339.

25. PhG 65; PhS 47. Recall that Hegel diagnoses skepticism as an incapacity for truth in the public objective sense.

26. PhG 66; PhS 48.

27. PhG 70.

28. PhG 67; PhS 49.

29. Reinhold Aschenberg, *Der Wahrheitsbegriff in Hegels Phänomenologie des Geistes* in *Die ontologische Option,* Hrsg. Klaus Hartmann (Berlin: Walter de Gruyter, 1976), 229n. I have left untranslated Hegel's term *Gestalt.* This term originated in Hegel's Jena philosophy of life, possibly under Goethe's influence. There it refers to structures and forms of life. In the PhG, Hegel extends the term to consciousness. The PhG considers the *Gestalten des Bewusstseins.* This technical term is usually translated as shapes or figures of consciousness, terminology which does not convey any technical meaning in English. Given the currency of the term Gestalt in phenomenology and psychology, it seems advisable to leave it untranslated.

30. Hegel, *Jena Realphilosophie 1805/06,* (ed. Gerhart Göhler, Berlin/Frankfurt: Ullstein, 1974) 288. This odd expression 'logical life' signifies that life itself is a logical category. In the next chapter we shall discover that logical life signals a decisive break with Cartesian mind-body dualism and Newtonian mechanism in favor of Aristotle's living nature. Otto Pöggeler has called attention to the significance of the Jena Logic which Hegel intended, but never completed, for the structure of the PhG. Cf. Pöggeler, *Grundprobleme der grossen Philosophen,* Hrsg. Josef Speck, UTB 464 (Göttingen: Vandenhoeck and Ruprecht, 1982); see also Pöggeler, *Die Idee einer Phänomenologie des Geistes* (Freiburg: Alber Verlag, 1973).

31. For Husserl's concept of a morphological essence, in contrast to a formal-mathematical essence, cf. *Ideas: A General Introduction to Pure Phenomenology,* tr. W. R. Boyce Gibson (New York: Collier Macmillan, 1962). For a discussion of the issues, see Alfred Schutz, "Type and Eidos in Husserl's Late Philosophy," *Collected Papers,* vol. 3, ed. I. Schutz (The Hague: Martinus Nijhoff, 1966), 92–115.

32. Reinhold Aschenberg, "Die Wahrheitsbegriff in Hegels *Phänomenologie des Geistes,*" in Klaus Hartmann (ed.) *Die ontologische Option,* op. cit. 211–304.

33. PhG 70.

34. PhG 71.

35. PhG 71; PhS 53.

36. PhG 71–72; PhS 53–54.

37. PhG 45; PhS 32.

38. PhG 72; PhS 54.

39. PhG 71. The original *an sich* is only a presumptive certainty, good until further notice, not an objective intersubjectively mediated and confirmed certainty.

40. Ibid.

41. Hegel, Enz. §24 Zusatz. Hegel criticizes the correspondence theory of truth, which he characterizes as mere formal correctness: "Correctness, generally speaking, concerns only the formal coincidence between our conception and its content, whatever the constitution of this content may be. Truth, on the contrary, lies in the correspondence of an object with itself, that is, with its notion. That a person is sick, or that some one has committed a theft, may certainly be correct. But the content is untrue. A sick body is not in harmony with the concept of body, and there is a want of congruity between theft and the concept of human conduct." (Enz. §172 Zusatz).

42. For an example, cf. Thomas Kuhn's discussion of paradigm shifts in the history and philosophy of science (*The Structure of Scientific Revolutions* [Chicago: University of Chicago Press, 1962]). See also Hegel's account of sense certainty and of Mastery and Servitude.

43. PhG 79–89; PhS 58–66. For a discussion of the reversals involved in sensecertainty, and a defense of Hegel against Feuerbach's critique, cf. Merold Westphal, *History and Truth in Hegel's Phenomenology,* (New York: Humanities Press, 1979), 72–80.

44. PhG 28; PhS 17–18.

45. "Dogmatism as a way of thinking, whether in ordinary knowing or in the study of philosophy, is nothing else but the view that the true consists in a proposition which is a fixed result, and is also immediately known." PhG 34; PhS 23.

46. Hegel identified the skepticism implicit in Kant's position: "What our most recent skepticism always brings with it is...the concept of a thing, that lies behind and beneath the phenomenal facts. When ancient skepticism employs the expressions *hypokeimenon, huparchon, adelon,* etc., they signify the objectivity whose essence it is *not* to be expressed; skepticism remains, on its own account, on the subjective side of appearance." *Skepticism,* BTKH 337. [My emphasis]

47. PhG 30; PhS 19–20. For an account of scientific knowledge as involving alienation from the world, cf. Charles Taylor, *Hegel.* (London: Cambridge University Press, 1976), 539–542.

48. PhG 67; PhS 49.

49. PhG 67; PhS 49.

50. PhG 69; PhS 51.

51. PhG 69; PhS 51. This passage reveals Hegel as the prototypical existential-ist. Kierkegaard's infinite passion, and Sartre's bad faith have their philosophical ancestry here.

52. Error arises when what ordinary consciousness declares to be the thing 'in itself', turns out not to correspond to the thing, but rather to be a merely subjective 'in itself', an 'in-itself' relative to consciousness. Cf. Hyppolite, op. cit. 14. See also Josi-ah Royce, "The Possibility of Error," in *The Philosophy of Josiah Royce,* ed. John K. Roth (New York: Crowell Co., 1971).

53. PhG 73; PhS 55. For a reading of this passage in terms of Husserlian phe-nomenology's noesis-noema-Horizon distinctions, cf. Michael Theunissen, *"Begriff und Realität: Hegels Aufhebung des metaphysischen Wahrheitsbegriffs,"* in *Seminar: Dialektik in der Philosophie Hegels,* Hrsg. Rolf-Peter Horstmann (Frankfurt: Suhrkamp, 1978), 324–359. Theunissen claims that the transition from the first *an sich* to the second *an sich* is an expansion of the horizon of consciousness which breaks and shatters the original naivete and provincialism. Narrowly construed, this point is well taken. However, the problem in Theunissen's interpretation is that Hegel does not, within the introduction at least, have a concept of horizon, much less identi-fy it with the world, as Husserl does.

54. For a discussion of the interpretation of the phenomenological "We" cf. Kenley Royce Dove, "Towards An Interpretation of Hegel's *Phänomenologie des Geistes"* (Yale PhD dissertation, 1965).

55. Klaus Hartmann, "On Taking the Transcendental Turn," *Review of Meta-physics,* 20. 2. 78 (December 1966): 237.

56. Ibid.

57. Ibid.

58. Klaus Hartmann, *Sartre's Ontology* (Evanston, Ill.: Northwestern University Press, 1966).

59. Hegel's following remarks may count against any reduction of Hegel's sys-tem to the logic: "Even becoming, however, taken at its best on its own ground, is an extremely poor term; it needs to grow in depth and weight of meaning. Such a deep-ened force we find in Life. Life is a becoming (*Werden*), but becoming does not exhaust the concept of life. A still higher form is found in *Geist.* Here too there is becoming, but richer and more intensive than mere logical becoming. The elements whose unity constitutes *Geist* are not the bare abstracts of Being and Nothing, but the system of the logical Idea and Nature." (Enz. §88 Zusatz)

60. Ludwig Feuerbach, "Towards a Critique of Hegel's Philosophy" (1839) in *The Fiery Brook: Selected Writings of Ludwig Feuerbach,* tr. Zawar Hanfi (New York: Doubleday Anchor Books, 1972), 53ff. For a discussion of Feuerbach's cri-tique of Hegel, see Merold Westphal, op. cit. 73ff.

61. See Forster, op. cit. 151. He comments that ordinary consciousness does not

have to read, much less understand Hegel's logic, in order to understand the development and transitions of the *Phenomenology*.

62. PhG 25; PhS 15.

63. Reinhold Aschenberg, *Der Wahrheitsbegriff in Hegels Phänomenologie des Geistes* in *Die ontologische Option*, op. cit. 230n.

64. Our concern here is not with a commentary on, much less overall interpretation of, the *Phenomenology*, rather our focus is on Hegel's phenomenology of *Anerkennung*. But the latter is a particular application of Hegel's phenomenological method.

SEVEN

HEGEL'S EIDETICS OF INTERSUBJECTIVITY

The dialectical process of the *Phänomenologie des Geistes* is determined by nothing so much as by the problem of the recognition of the 'Thou'. To mention only a few stages of this history: our own self-consciousness, for Hegel, attains to the truth of its self-consciousness only through achieving its recognition by the other person. The immediate relationship between a man and a woman is the natural knowledge of mutual recognition. Beyond this, conscience represents the mental element of being recognized, and mutual self-recognition, in which the mind is absolute, can be attained only via confession and forgiveness. It cannot be denied that the objections of Feuerbach and Kierkegaard are already taken care of in these forms of spirit described by Hegel. H-G. Gadamer, *Truth and Method*[1]

Conventional wisdom maintains that on idealist premisses intersubjectivity is not only lacking, but impossible in principle. Once the *cogito* emerges as the epistemological foundation (*fundamentum inconcussum*), certain of itself by virtue of expelling all mundane content—the body, others, and the world—to the external realm of contingency and dubitability, the issue of solipsism seems inevitable. Thus, intersubjectivity emerges as part of a larger problem: Can the *cogito* grasp anything besides itself? Has the subject-object distinction become an unbridgeable gulf? How can the first person *ego cogito* get to the "other side," gain access to the object? The notorious mind-body problem, and that of other minds exemplify this fundamental dualism.

But is Hegel a Cartesian idealist? This is a matter of dispute. Both sides of the dispute have some justification, for Hegel both praises and criticizes the Cartesian transcendental turn to the subject: "It is the great progress of our times that subjectivity is acknowledged to be an absolute moment; this is an essential determination. However, everything depends on how this determination is made."[2] Descartes' great discovery is transcendental subjectivity. But he falsified his discovery by construing it as a private cogito, a 'for-itself' in contrast to the 'in itself'. Descartes inverts traditional metaphysics while nevertheless remaining on its soil, replacing it with a metaphysics of subjectivity. This metaphysics of subjectivity continues from Descartes through Kant and becomes increasingly self-reflective. Kant turns the distinction between 'for us' and 'in itself' into a rigid skeptical separation.

Although Hegel treats Descartes with respect and approval,[3] he is critical of and breaks with Cartesian reflexion-philosophy:

The one self-certifying certainty [*das an sich und einzig Gewisse*]... is that there exists a thinking subject, a reason affected with finitude; and the whole of philosophy consists in determining the universe with respect to this finite reason. Kant's so-called critique of the cognitive faculties, Fichte's doctrine that consciousness cannot be transcended nor become transcendent, Jacobi's refusal to undertake anything impossible for Reason, all amount to nothing but an absolute restriction of reason to the form of finitude, [an injunction] never to forget the absoluteness of the subject in every rational cognition.... So these philosophies have to be recognized as nothing but the culture of reflection raised to a system.[4]

Hegel accepts the turn to the subject, but not the foundationalist metaphysics of subjectivity. To grasp the cogito as foundation is to suppress alterity and reduce the other to the same. The other must be allowed to be, and this requires the de-absolutization of the cogito. Hegel's departure from Cartesianism consists in the fact that immediate self-consciousness or self-*certainty* is not to be confused with self-*knowledge*. The former is empty, formal, abstract. In such immediate self-presencing, the self is not genuinely present to itself, but rather concealed from itself. Thus, subjective immediacy is only an abstract starting point that requires mediation and development.

The question is, what sort of mediation is involved. Is mediation for Hegel ultimately self-mediation, or does it include intersubjective mediation? If the former is the case, then Hegel represents the culmination of the Cartesian tradition. In this interpretation, the framework requiring mediation is the Cartesian mind-body or mind-nature dualism. Hegel's problem is the removal of the opposition between mind and nature, which is solved by the dialectical self-mediation of mind. In this scheme, nature is deprived of ontological independence and is the self-othering of mind. Mind others itself as nature and then cancels this otherness by recognizing itself in nature (namely, nature as comprehended by modern physics). Hegel's dialectical mediation between mind and other (nature) turns out in the final analysis to be the self-mediation of mind to itself.[5] Nature as the other turns out to be the self-othering of mind, and so reducible to mind. More generally stated, the other is reducible to the same.

My thesis is that a careful reading of Hegel's concept of recognition will show that Hegel does not collapse the other into the same, mediation into self-mediation, and that the latter claims are caricatures of Hegel's position. For Hegel consciousness is not a disembodied, foundational, worldless subjectivity. Rather, consciousness is embodied, situated, and equiprimordial with other subjects and the life-world. Consequently subjectivity is in actuality intersubjectivity, and requires intersubjective mediation. This mediation is not reducible to dialectical self-mediation. Subjectivity is a holist, rather than solipsist concept. Hegel replaces Cartesian atomism with intersubjective holism. For this reason, he breaks with the language and "dramas of subjectivity," and adopts instead the terminology of spirit (*Geist*). *Geist* is not a subject in contrast to object, or a transcendental ego in contrast to the empirical, but an I that is a We and a We that is an I, a social subject.

This chapter consists of a translation and commentary on the first section of chapter four of the *Phenomenology*. This passage includes the famous discussion of master and slave. Since this is one of the most commented upon, familiar and widely known sections of the book, it may be asked, why bother to subject it to such close scrutiny? Why belabor the obvious? There is a good Hegelian answer: What is familiar is not understood precisely because it is familiar (*"Das Bekannte überhaupt ist darum, weil es bekannt ist, nicht erkannt"*).[6] This aphorism applies not merely to naive immediate consciousness, but equally to the passages on recognition. Like many classics, these passages are more often talked about than carefully studied. Many commentators pass over Hegel's analysis of the concept of recognition (§§ 1–8) and focus instead on the derivative discussion of master and slave. The result is a failure to appreciate or understand the *concept* of recognition, which in turn leads to a failure to grasp master and slave as a particular *determinate instance* of recognition. Master and slave cannot be adequately appreciated or understood if recognition is not understood. The mistaken identification of master and slave with Hegel's entire account of intersubjectivity (*Anerkennung*) is a confusion which confirms Hegel's point.

Moreover, these passages are not well translated. A translation is an interpretation of its text. The *Phenomenology* is extremely difficult to understand, much less translate, partly because of its subject matter, partly because of its extremely high level of abstraction.[7] Neither of the existing English translations is reliable unless read together with the German text. Yet another attempt at translation will form the basis of my interpretation. This is one case in which close textual analysis is indispensable.

Finally, it should be noted that the concept of recognition is the phenomenological genesis of spirit (*Geist*). As H. S. Harris notes, "the importance of the concept of recognition can scarcely be overestimated since it is the root element of the concept of *Geist* itself."[8] To unpack and expound recognition is to inquire into the phenomenological origins of *Geist*, a central concept of Hegel's philosophy. Harris contends that "The great arc of Spirit's appearing goes from the mutual recognition of absolute enmity to that of absolute charity. The application of these two extremes to the relation of man and God is what then produces the concept of 'Absolute Knowledge'."[9] For this reason, recognition is an underlying motif running through the *Phenomenology* as the introduction to absolute knowledge. Self-recognition in God constitutes absolute knowledge. Although Hegel is widely known as a social and political philosopher, it is not widely recognized that spirit, even

on its highest levels, results from and presupposes intersubjective reciproci-
ties. For these reasons an inquiry into recognition is long overdue. The end
result of our inquiry, however, may not be a resolution, but rather an intensi-
fication, of major questions of Hegel interpretation.

I shall consider first the background of recognition in Hegel's concept of
logical life. Hegel is an Aristotelian, and the doctrine that subjectivity is
embodied and situated in the world is good Aristotelian doctrine, as well as a
point rediscovered by existential phenomenology. Life and/or the life-world,
not mind-body dualism, is the context of Hegel's concept of self-consciousness as a social infinite. Next, I shall consider Hegel's eidetics of recognition, his exposition of the dialectical development of the concept in itself (or
for us). This is found in the first eight paragraphs of chapter four, section A
of the *Phenomenology*. Eidetics is an exploration of meaning at the general
level of ontology, namely the study of possibility.[10] It brackets determinate
factual questions. The latter are taken up by empirics, which studies the general eidetic structures in their concrete determinate actualization.[11] This will
be the subject of the next chapter.

Life as a Category

Hegel formulated life as a logical category in the Jena logic which he never
completed.[12] Henrich observes that Hegel's early concept of love, which
overcomes and reconciles opposition, subsequently is generalized into the
concept of life, which in turn gets taken up, enriched and transformed in the
concept of *Geist*.[13] Life is a "restless infinite." This general conception Hegel
shared with Schelling and the Romantics. According to Hyppolite, Hegel's
originality lies not in the concept of living and dynamic nature in contrast to
mechanistic conceptions, but in giving the concept of life logical form and
expression.[14] Early in his career, Hegel expressed his fundamental logical
conception in the following way: "...life cannot be considered as union
alone, or as relation alone, but must be regarded as including opposition as
well.... Life is the union [*Verbindung*] of union and non-union."[15]

The above formulation of life as a logical category means that Hegel
sides with Aristotle rather than Descartes: "...if, for Descartes, life is in general no original phenomenon [*Urphänomen*], and if Kant treats it as an
afterthought (in the *Critique of Judgement*), it is clear that for Aristotle the
self-moving motion of life is the original phenomenon of being."[16] However,
"Hegel is less concerned with life as a biological concept than [with] the life
of mind and spirit."[17] Gadamer develops the logical aspect of life: "...what
appears as this undifferentiation of the undifferentiated has life's structure of
splitting in two and becoming identical with itself.... Life is the identity of
identity and difference. *Everything alive is bound to its 'other', the world*

beyond it in the constant exchange of assimilation and secretion. And beyond this, the individual living being does not exist as an individual, but rather only as that mode in which the species preserves itself."[18]

These considerations count against the Cartesian reading of Hegel. Unlike the cogito, consciousness is for Hegel embodied and situated in the world as a member of a species which maintains itself in and through individuals in a continuous process of assimilation and interaction. In contrast, the Cartesian cogito is a pre-reality individual, an abstraction from the fundamental concrete ontological setting in life. Its reflective immediacy is not to be confused or identified with self-knowledge, for such immediacy conceals what it purports to reveal. Moreover, if it is objected that Hegel does not "take the problem of solipsism seriously," the reply is that, owing to the fact that consciousness is embedded and situated within the context of species life and life-world, the other lies deeper than theoretical-reflective or explicitly thematic considerations. When Hegel speaks of an *Anerkennen des Lebens*,[19] he expresses a pre-intentional world-openness and relatedness that has been long forgotten by the intellectual amnesia of the Cartesian cogito.

Hegel takes up the topic of desire (*Begierde*) because he identifies consciousness as living, as a part of living nature. *Begierde* denotes a level of consciousness common to humans and animals. The satisfaction of desire involves experiencing the independence of the object differently from theoretical cognition. Desire is the lowest form of self-consciousness and exhibits the most primitive form of removal of opposition between consciousness and its object, namely the consumption (e.g., eating) or annihilation of the object.[20] Desire is not disinterested contemplation of the object in and for itself; rather the self needs and depends upon the object of desire to fill up its lack. The self coincides with itself (namely, satisfaction) by negating and consuming the independent being of the object. By consuming its object, consciousness is satisfied and reunited with itself. Hegel's uncovering and thematizing desire (*Begierde*) is significant; one of his major contributions— far surpassing Husserl—is to show how intersubjectivity is pervaded by passions and desires that make conflict virtually inevitable.

It should be noted that the basic pattern of consumption is the reduction of the other to the same. Desire is metaphysical: not only does it show the nullity of finite objects (e.g., fruit), it brings them to immediate presence, and then devours and annihilates presence. The question which we will pursue shortly is whether this pattern is also constitutive of recognition (*Anerkennung*). To anticipate, the self is dependent on an other in both cases. However, in the case of recognition, the other cannot be simply eliminated, because the self depends on and requires the continued existence and unforced recognition of the other.

Hegel's assertion that "there is a self-consciousness for a self-consciousness,"[21] announces an apparently abrupt transition which jumps out at the reader. To a Cartesian, it seems to beg the very question raised by the problem of other minds, namely the existence of the other.[22] It seems to imply an immediate encounter between ego and alter ego. However, Hegel does not claim immediate access to others. He denies immediate access. His account will show that there is an immediate confrontation with the other, but no immediate knowledge of the other. The self exists at an epistemological distance both from itself and from its other. For this reason the situation of initial encounter is threatening and intolerable, and leads to a life and death struggle. The latter is an attempt to eliminate the uncertainty by eliminating the other, by reducing the other to the same. But this attempted elimination ends in failure. Instead a reversal occurs when it is discovered that "self-consciousness attains its satisfaction only in another self-consciousness."[23] Both self-knowledge and knowledge of the other are won from struggle and conflict, i.e., mediation.

Consciousness exists concretely in interaction with others and with the world, and finds its satisfaction in another self-consciousness. Such interaction and interdependence means that consciousness is not always subject and never object:

> A self-consciousness confronts another self-consciousness. Only through such confrontation with other is it self-consciousness in fact. Only through such confrontation is the unity of itself in its otherness [Anderssein] for it. The ego, insofar as it is the object of its own conceiving (Begriff), is in fact not an object.... Since a self-consciousness is the object [of desire], it is just as much ego as object. With this the concept of Geist is present for us. What lies ahead for [ordinary] consciousness [is] the experience of what Geist is, this absolute substance as the unity of different independent self-consciousnesses, which, in their opposition, enjoy perfect freedom and independence: I that is We, and We that is I.[24]

Self-consciousness in the explicit sense is not immediate, nor is it a reflective phenomenon, or something that the self can give to itself. We will see that such an immediate being-for-self is a form of false consciousness. Immediacy conceals as well as reveals. Like every immediate claim, it must be put to the test of experience, and undergo a process of mediation which qualifies, deabsolutizes and transforms its original meaning. The self discovers itself only in and through the recognition of others.

Towards an Eidetics of Recognition

In the Phenomenology, Hegel presents a compressed and complex analysis of the concept of recognition.[25] He does not explicitly identify recognition in the title of chapter four or its sections. The discussion of recognition occurs mainly in Section A, "The Dependence and Independence of Self-consciousness; Lordship and Bondage." The preliminary discussion I propose to read as an eidetics, namely a bracketing of fact and an elaboration of meaning. In §§1-7, Hegel focuses on the meaning of recognition: (1) the doubling of consciousness, (2) the double-significations of the moments of recognition, and (3) the two basic stages of recognition, conflict and opposition, and the overcoming of such in mutual reconciliation and releasement. But before examining this in more detail, a difficulty must be removed.

If eidetics involves a bracketing of existence or fact, doesn't that reduce the other to a mere subjective phenomenon immanent in and relative to consciousness?[26] In short, can there be an eidetics of intersubjectivity? Such a question misunderstands eidetics and eidetic abstraction. It is not a subjectivizing reduction of a phenomenon to consciousness. The *eidos* is underdetermined and abstract not because existence or the other are simply eliminated, but rather because only the generic features of both self and other, and not the specific determinate features, are the object of eidetic inquiry. For this reason, eidetic abstraction is puzzling. Heidegger observes, for example, that the expression "*Dasein* is essentially *Mitsein*" has an existential ontological sense, which is not to be confused with empirical assertions such as "I am not alone."[27] As ontological, *Mitsein* determines *Dasein* even when others are empirically absent. Phenomenological ontology is not to be confused with factual claims about others.

Yet, this does not mean that eidetics takes up a merely negative posture towards the existence of others.[28] For example, it is an eidetic insight that a purely transcendental analysis of consciousness and its other is impossible. Eidetics shows that the other cannot be treated fully or adequately at the eidetic level, and that another perspective—an empirics—is required.[29] Since recognition is a non-formal concept, the eidetics of recognition does not simply exclude the empirical, but merely brackets it, i.e., alters consciousness with respect to the empirical, from reality-acceptance to reality-phenomenon. However, eidetic analysis is not empty speculation, but rather an illumination of determinate existence. Hegel's comment on Plato is no less true of his eidetics: "It [The intelligible world of Ideas] is not in heaven or some other place beyond the actual, rather it is the actual world.... The ideal is not metaphysics, but only reality itself brought closer."[30]

Overview of Hegel's Eidetics

Since Hegel's discussion is difficult and obscure, I shall give a summary overview of its major elements. In his Jena period, Hegel identified *Geist* with consciousness, understood as the opposite of itself (*Gegenteil seiner selbst*).[31] Hegel's discussion of the concept of recognition is an analysis of what happens when a self-consciousness (which is the opposite of itself) encounters another self-consciousness (also the opposite of itself). The result, he says, is a complex crossing (*Verschränkung*) with multiple meanings. There are three phases of recognition.[32] These are the phase of abstract parochial universality, the phase of opposition between particulars, and the phase of emergent concrete, i.e., mediated, universality.

The first is the phase of initial confrontation with other. Since the *Phenomenology* sets forth a genetic history of the shapes of consciousness, the starting point is logically and conceptually primitive. This means that each operates with the presumption of being absolute, i.e., exclusive of relation and qualification by other. Each presumes to be universal, but this universality is parochial and abstract since it excludes difference, otherness, and relation. For this reason the confrontation with other is experienced as an abrupt self-transcendence, i.e., a plunge into relation and otherness, that is a loss of self. The presence of the other forces a change or othering that results in a finding of self as other, or as a challenge to and possible loss of the original naive and parochial certitude. Further, the parochial universality of this phase is manifest in the fact that the self is unable to recognize the other as other, and so finds only itself in the other.

It is crucial to note that self-othering or alteration is occasioned by the other. This means that the other is a condition of self-othering, and for this very reason the other cannot be collapsed into the self-othering of the first. Conversely, self-othering, or the self's 'inner' diremption from itself, is a condition of its relation to other. Consequently, self-othering and the other are correlative and should not be confused or identified. The self's alteration (or self-loss) consists in the fact that the self discovers that it is not universal, but is a particular opposed to another particular. This reversal leads to the second moment, namely, opposition between particulars.

The encounter with other shows that the self is not absolutely universal, but a particular in relation to another particular. This 'loss of self' (namely, the transition from presumptive universality to mere particularity) must be overcome. Particularity must be cancelled. This means first of all, that the opposing other must be cancelled or eliminated. Second, it means that the self must demonstrate its transcendence of its particular existence, that it is more than and not tied to its particular existence. Thus the self must risk its life by seeking to eliminate the other. Cancellation of particularity leads to struggle. But the struggle is not simply about elimination of the other; it is about recognition and relation. The 'absolute self' needs the other to recognize and confirm its parochial universality. That is why the death of the opponent is self-defeating. To eliminate the other would be to eliminate a condition of the self's own freedom and self-identity. However, to compel the other's recognition means that the parochial absolute self is no longer unconditionally absolute, but stands in relation to the other and is qualified by its relation. Thus the self now explicitly enters into a process of mediation. The universal must now seek to incorporate rather than exclude its other, the particular.

However such incorporation of other is impossible if it is carried out in a one-sided way. Each side must do something. Joint reciprocal mediation is necessary. The self must 'return' to itself out of its 'othered' state, by winning itself in the other's recognition. This return to self out of otherness is not simply a restoration of the original self-identity qua abstract immediate identity. Rather the original self-identity is enlarged and enriched by the other's recognition. But this enriching return to self is possible only if the self in turn releases the other and allows the other to go free.[33] This mutual releasement of "letting be" connotes not indifference, but granting the other her freedom to be. It is to renounce seizing upon the other's possibilities and freedom. In order for mutual recognition to occur, the other must cease to be the death of my possibilities, and vice-versa. Genuine, as opposed to phony or coerced social solidarity, presupposes such mutual recognition and releasement. Only through such mutual releasement and reciprocal recognition does *Geist,* the universal consciousness and concrete identity, emerge. The concrete universal is generated out of such reciprocal mediation. The universal must incorporate its other, the particular, and the particular must incorporate its other, namely the universal. The attainment of such concrete universality means that being with other is no longer a limitation or restriction on freedom, but rather an enhancement and concrete actualization of freedom. This situation of reciprocal recognition is one of communicative freedom, which Hegel describes as being at home with self in an other.

HEGEL'S EIDETICS: TRANSLATION AND COMMENTARY[34]

Hegel §1

Self-consciousness is in and for itself in and through the fact that it exists in and for itself *for an other.* That is, it exists only as recognized or acknowledged. The concept of this unity in its doubling,[35] the infinity realizing itself in self-consciousness, is a many-sided intersection of and correlation between multiple and diverse meanings. Consequently its elements must, on the one hand, be precisely distinguished and kept separate, and on the other hand these must be taken as *not different* in their differentiation, or they must be taken and known in their *opposite* meaning. The double signification of the distinguished elements lies in the nature of self-consciousness to be infinite, or to be immediately the opposite of the determination in which it is posited. The exposition of this spiritual unity in its doubling will present the movement of recognition [*Anerkennen*].

Commentary: The Doubling of Self-Consciousness

Self-consciousness is in and for itself in and through the fact that it exists in and for itself *for an other.* This formulation contains the Hegelian view of the interhuman in germ. It signifies that consciousness is constituted by two distinguishable, yet inseparable elements. First, consciousness is for itself (*Für-sichsein*). This is not novel, but reflects the modern emphasis on subjectivity. But Hegel's contribution lies in his uncovering a second element, namely consciousness is for an other (*Füreinanderssein*). Consciousness is both at once. Its self-relation is not simply immanent or purely reflective; the self's relation to itself is mediated by its relation to other. Moreover, self-relation conditions relation to other. Self-consciousness thus has a paradoxical structure that explodes the view that it is mere subjectivity exclusive of other.

Hegel's view is an alternative to two others. The first is Cartesian solipsism, that is, the other is completely inaccessible and out of reach in principle. Since Cartesian subjectivity is a "prison," solipsism is the human condition. The second view is that there is direct or immediate access to others, as empathy or sympathy may suggest. In this case, the problem is not how to escape the "prison of subjectivity," but how to achieve individuality and independence, i.e., to break out of the grip of a collective consciousness.[36] Both of these views reflect the standpoint of the understanding (*Verstand*) and its conception of identity as exclusive of difference.[37] The former construes identity as the first-person cogito. Accordingly, the alter ego can only be a duplicate of the primordial ego.[38] The latter view construes identity as an undifferentiated universal. Thus, there can be no real individuation. But no matter whether it is construed as a particular or a universal, identity is here understood as abstract identity, exclusive of difference. In contrast, Hegel's account of intersubjectivity, like his speculative logic, presents a concrete identity or totality inclusive of both identity and difference.

Like Husserl, Hegel denies immediate access to others. However, to deny direct or immediate knowledge of, or access to, the other is not necessarily to embrace solipsism, i.e., the view that intersubjectivity is impossible. At the level of perception, the other is not present, but rather a present-absence. This is important to keep in mind, especially in view of contemporary caricatures of Hegel (and Husserl) as the culmination of metaphysics of presence. Such present-absence constitutes the epistemological distance and intolerable uncertainty concerning the other that leads to conflict. Hegel's view is that the other cannot be brought to immediate or full presence except by reducing the other to self-sameness. He shows that the attempt to do so is inherently one-sided and leads to coercion, the life and death struggle, murder, or enslavement. Who better than Hegel has shown that the project of reducing the other to the same (abstract self-identity) ends in failure? The presence of the other cannot be achieved through the self's own action; the only presence achieved by such is self-presence or self-sameness. That is why intersubjectivity requires a post-idealist move.

However, unlike Husserl, Hegel also denies that the self is immediately present to itself in apodictic self-knowledge. It is well known that Hegel criticizes the claim that immediacy is the truth. This also applies to self-knowledge. Immediate self-consciousness conceals as well as reveals; immediate self-knowledge is in fact false consciousness. Since the self is hidden from itself, it depends on the other for its own self-discovery. That is why self-knowledge for Hegel takes the form of *self-recognition in other*. For Hegel, intersubjectivity means that the self cannot be simply for itself, but needs and depends on the other in its own self-relation. The road to interiority passes through the other. The self is for itself only by being for an other, and the self is for an other only by being for itself. For itself (*Fürsichsein*) and for an other *Füreinanderssein*) are irreducible and inseparable. Their proper relation—that of equivalence such that the self is for itself for other—is the central issue of intersubjectivity. Neither self nor other has any absolute priority or privilege. This is the position Hegel stakes out in the first sentence. All that follows is a further elaboration of this mutual mediation.

Recognition and the Problem of Relation

To be sure, the relation between self and other is elusive. Neither a purely external relation nor a purely internal relation, it is a relation or *correlation* of such relations. An external relation exists between two objects or *relata* that are what they are, independent of the relation. Each is complete in itself and remains the same despite the relation. Hence, external relation does not fundamentally alter, modify or affect the *relata*.The view that everything is externally related presupposes abstract identity (*Verstand*) and finds expression in atomism and pluralism. These are metaphysical views which constitute Hegel's fundamental philosophical opponent, as Horstmann and Harris point out.[39] Hegel's view is that the self, in its internal self-relation, is dependent on and modified by relation to its other. Recognition does not leave the self unaffected by its relation to other; therefore recognition cannot be a merely external relation.

However, the relation between self and other cannot be an "internal" relation either. Internal relations have monist and idealist implications. For example, something internally related to something else, may be reducible to and completely dependent on its other. It would not exist if its other did not exist. In internal relations, the independence of one of the relata is denied. It collapses into the other and exists immediately through the other. This view finds metaphysical expression in monism, pre-eminently Spinoza's analysis of substance/accidents. The construal of *Anerkennung* as an internal relation would imply that the other is merely a duplication or extension of the self. On the other hand, the prevailing view of German Idealism is that it treats the other in terms of negation. But if the other is simply a negation, it can be overcome dialectically in negation of negation. Such a dialectical treatment implies that the other is reducible to the same, and that intersubjective mediation by other is reducible to self-mediation. Hegel rejects these views.

Anerkennung cannot be coherently expressed on the assumptions of either monism or atomistic pluralism. The relation of self to other is neither simply external relation, nor simply internal relation. It involves both in mutual correspondence and correlation. *Anerkennung* requires a third alternative, and it is by no means clear what this would be.[40] My thesis is that community is a distinctive kind or level of being irreducible to monist and pluralist alternatives. Hegel is after an ontology of community and migrates from the monist-pluralist impasse towards his dialectical holism.[41]

However, if we nevertheless speak of "internal" and "external" relations in reference to *Anerkennung*, then it must be said that *Anerkennung* must involve both sets of relations, such that it is at once "internal" and "external." *Anerkennung* is a relation of relations, a coincidence of internal and external relations.[42] The self relates to and coincides with itself through and by means of the other. It is affected by such relation to the other, which is neither eliminated by, nor derivative from, the self. Self-othering and the other are correlative, not identical. The self, in its self-relation (*Fürsichsein, being-for-self*), depends on and requires the other's recognition (*Sein für Andere, being for an other*).

It should be noted that being-for-self or *Fürsichsein* has two distinct senses for Hegel:[43] an immediate or abstract sense, namely the first person "I," and a mediated or more concrete sense, namely the first person plural, or "We." Immediate *Fürsichsein* is abstract, formal and empty.[44] Practically expressed in action it is egoism or *Eigensinn*.[45] For this reason, immediate being-for-self (*Fürsichsein*) is only a starting point for recognition, not its foundation. Recognition is a process of development from simple *immediate Fürsichsein* to intersubjectively *mediated* and qualified *Fürsichsein*, namely, from the I to the We. The We designates the self as mediated and enlarged through the mediation of the other; it is a mutual enrichment and expansion of the initial *Fürsichsein*. The claim that being-for-self (*Fürsichsein*) is reciprocally and intersubjectively mediated, is consistent with Hegel's general critique of immediate knowledge and insistence upon mediation: "There is nothing in heaven, earth, nature or spirit which does not contain both immediacy and mediation, so that these determinations are manifest everywhere together as undivided and indivisible..."[46] Thus, instead of the "I am I" of Fichtean and Schellingian idealism, Hegel speaks of mutual recognition, of two 'I's that become a We. Hegel replaces abstract monism with a concrete social holism.

Hegel §§2–3

§2. Self-consciousness is confronted by another self-consciousness. It has come out of itself. This has a double [equivocal] significance: first, it has lost itself, because it finds itself as an *other being*. Second, it has thereby cancelled *[aufgehoben]* the other, because it does not look upon the other as a being, but rather sees only *itself* in *other*.

§3. It must cancel this its other-being *[Anderssein]*. This is the cancellation of the first equivocal meaning and is itself the creation of a second equivocal meaning. First, it must proceed to cancel the other as an independent being in order thereby to become certain of itself as an independent being. Second, when it cancels this other, it cancels itself, for this other is itself.

Commentary: Othering and the Other

Hegel begins his account of recognition with an analysis of doubling and double-signification. His starting point is an immediate confrontation with an other, starting at the minimal, logically primitive level. The term 'other' is deliberately ambiguous. On the one hand, other means an other independent being; on the other hand, "other" means self-othering, or a relation of the self to itself, or self as other. It is crucial to keep these senses both distinct and correlative.

In confrontation with another self-consciousness, consciousness has come outside of itself. But this self-transcendence has initially a negative significance. It signifies a loss of self, an alteration, or a shattering of immediate being-for-self. The self loses its immediate and naive self-certainty. It is no longer in control of the situation. The presence of the (unknown) other alters and decenters its situation. In this altered situation, the self finds itself as an "othered" being, i.e., as changed and alienated. The epistemologically distant other must at the outset be regarded negatively, as stranger, as threat. Since the other is unknown, the first self finds only itself as other. Nevertheless, despite the change or alteration which it undergoes in confrontation with other, it clings to its immediacy, its immediate being-for-self.

And so "It must cancel this, its other-being *[Anderssein]*." What does *Anderssein* mean? Baillie translates it as "other," Miller as "otherness." Each reflects a limited aspect of Hegel's meaning, while suppressing other aspects. Since the other can refer to another person, Baillie is half-correct. But Miller also has justification: "other" also can mean self-alteration, a becoming other or alien to self. The self's relation to itself, immediate self-sameness or I am I, undergoes a change, an internal diremption in confrontation with other. The presence of the other implies at least the possibility of change that shatters the immediacy of being-for-self and thus modifies and alienates it. The self becomes *other to itself* in confrontation with *other*, and these double significations (other as other v. self as other) are inseparable.[47]

Other-being or self-estrangement, however, is only a temporary terminus. It is also a point of transition because being-other, or not-being-what-one-is, is intolerable, and must be cancelled (*Aufgehoben*).[48] But cancellation has, in turn, a double signification and must be considered from dual perspectives. In the first, to cancel the change or alienation of the self, is to cancel the other as the independent origin of the change. This would be to remain at the level of desire, and to repeat the pattern of desire, namely, the accomplishment of self-coincidence by eliminating the other. The cancellation/elimination of the other would restore immediate being-for-self (*Fürsichsein*). In a second perspective, the cancellation of the other is at the same time a cancellation of the first or "privileged" self, for this other is itself. The self cannot be privileged, because it depends on the recognition of the other. If the other is simply eliminated, the result is a loss of recognition, a condition of freedom. If the other is dominated or subjected to the privileged first, the result is no less satisfactory as the analysis of Mastery and Servitude shows.

Hegel §4

This equivocal sublation of its equivocal other-being is likewise an equivocal return into itself. First, through the sublation of the other-being it gets itself back, because it becomes once more self-same through the sublation of its other-being *[seines Andersseins]*. Second, it gives the other self-consciousness back to itself, for it was conscious of itself in the other; it cancels its being in the other *[sein Sein im Andern]*, and lets the other go free.

Commentary: The Sublation of Otherness and the Other

I use the term "equivocal" to translate "*doppelsinnige*." Equivocal is intended in the literal sense of double signification and not as the logical fallacy of equivocation. Hegel is not guilty of equivocation, or of confusing two different senses of the term, although he does insist they are correlated. The equivocity is grounded in the essential correlation between being-for-self and being-for-other. The return to self (*Ruckkehr in sich*) is the inverse of the initial moment of confrontation or of self-othering. Self-reversion corresponds to the moment of gratification or satisfaction of desire, (*Begierde*). It signifies an overcoming of inner lack or emptiness. But is it the case that in recognition (*Anerkennung*), as in desire, self-coincidence implies or involves an elimination and cancellation of the other? If self-othering must be overcome, the central question is whether this means the *other* is eliminated or reduced to the same. Does Hegel's account privilege unity over plurality, identity over difference, self-sameness over other? Is the other merely a subordinate element in self-identity? I think not. This is the crucial case in which the other must be distinguished from self-othering and otherness.

It has already been pointed out that *Fürsichsein* has two meanings. Prior to recognition, it is immediate, abstract identity or self-sameness. As mediated by conflict, struggle and recognition, *Fürsichsein* is a holistic synthesis of being for self and being for other. In the latter case, self-coincidence is no longer immediate, but is intersubjectively mediated. The elimination of the other (as in *Begierde*) would signify the elimination of a necessary condition of self-mediation.

To claim that the other is *aufgehoben* in recognition does not imply simple cancellation of the other, but also its *preservation*. The relation to other undergoes transformation from alien stranger to friend. But a condition of this preservation and enduring is that the other's recognition be free, and not coerced or manipulated. Thus, in the accomplishment of reciprocal recognition, the other is not eliminated, but rather released and allowed to be (*entlassen*).[49]

The eidetic pattern of recognition differs from desire (*Begierde*). Instead of simple self-coincidence through seizing upon and negating the object (as in desire) recognition is a mediated self-coincidence made possible by and conditioned upon allowing the other to be what it is; letting the other go free. This is Hegel's version of *Gelassenheit*.[50] Genuine reciprocal recognition requires a renunciation of seizing upon the other, stripping him of his possibilities and reducing him to my own possibilities. This renunciation means granting the other freedom to recognize, or to withhold recognition. Not only is the other allowed to be, but the other's free, uncoerced recognition is crucial to the self. The recognition that really counts is the recognition from the other that is not at the disposal of the self.

Recognition (*Anerkennung*), unlike desire, does not essentially involve a reduction of the other to the same.[51] *Anerkennung* involves a search for satisfaction in the *uncoerced* recognition of the other. Although recognition includes self-coincidence or satisfaction, this does not occur through the elimination of the other, but through membership or partnership with Other.

Hegel's German is far from easy, but the English reader is badly served by the translations. Miller obscures the meaning of the last phrase by misconstruing the subject of the sentence.[52] Baillie's is a freer translation which more nearly preserves the meaning of the original: "secondly it likewise gives otherness back to the other self-consciousness, for it was aware of being in the other, it cancels this its own being in the other and thus lets the other again go free."[53] Baillie's translation brings out an important element: in seeing only itself in the other, the one suppresses the other, and denies its otherness. It grasps the other only in terms of its own particular self-identity. In the cancellation of other-being, however, the otherness of the other is not eliminated, but restored. The other is "allowed to be" or to go free.

Thus, the final meaning turns out to be the opposite of that originally intended. Recognition refers to this reversal and inversion of the original meaning and situation. The other whose presence initially alienated the self, and which the self sought to eliminate, turns out to be that on which the self depends, and with whom the self exists in solidarity. Conversely, the self that undergoes loss and alienation before the other, cannot overcome this alienation by itself. Rather such alienation is overcome only in *mutual reciprocal release-ment*. Cancellation of otherness (internal diremption and alienation) is correlative with and conditioned upon letting the other go free. In uncoerced, free recognition, Being-for-other is equivalent to Being-for-self, and vice-versa.

The term "identity" can be used to characterize such emergent solidarity. However this is not an abstract identity that excludes difference, or that recognizes *only* itself in other. It is rather a social identity arising out of reciprocal intersubjective mediation. The "We" is a concrete universal or identity that reflects and is the result of mutual recognition. This concrete identity exhibits what both individuals are, and is their mutual recognition. Hence, if the term identity is used, this is not the abstract identity of the I am I. Rather Hegel reconstructs identity as an I that is a We, i.e., an identity of identity and difference, or as not less than a social subject. As Nicolai Hartmann observes, the concretely universal social subject is Hegel's original discovery.[54]

Hegel §5–6

§5. This movement of self-consciousness in relation to another self-consciousness has been set forth as the doing of the one. But this action has the double significance of being just as much the doing of the one as the doing of the other. For this other is likewise independent, self-determining, and there is nothing in it except what originates through it. The first does not have a merely passive object before it as in the case of desire. Rather the other is an independent being existing for itself. Consequently the first may not use the other for its own ends, unless the other does *for itself* what the first does. The movement [of recognition] is therefore without qualification the doubled movement of both self-consciousnesses. Each sees the other do the same that it does. Each does itself what it requires of the other, and does what it does only insofar as the other does the same. A one-sided action would be useless, since what is supposed to happen can only come about through the joint action of both.

§6. The action has double significance not only because it is an action directed at itself as well as at the other, but also because it is the joint indivisible action of the one as well as the other.

Commentary: Reciprocal Recognition

Paragraph §5 reveals the abstraction from the action of the other in place until this point. Paragraphs §§1–4 distinguished various elements of recognition from the perspective of the one, and kept them methodologically separate from the other. But now it is time to take these in their opposite meaning as joint and reciprocal actions.

The other person is not a merely passive object to be consumed as in the case of desire. The other is another subject, an independent being-for-self. This places limits, both ontological and ethical, upon the freedom of the first: The one may not simply use the other as a mere object for gratification of its own desire. This reminds us of Kant's categorical imperative of respect for humanity. But Hegel's point is mainly ontological: the other is no passive object but being-for-self. Nothing is posited in or for it that is not posited *by* it.[55] To by-pass or ignore this self-positing is to violate the person. However, a joint action is not necessarily a violation of the other.

In a joint action, what the one does, the other must do too, and vice-versa. The action of one is indivisible from the action of the other. In the case of recognition, an action by one alone would be useless. Recognition is essentially a double-sided action. If recognition occurs, it must occur through the mutual and joint action of both, through which the "I's" become a "We." For this reason, the cogito can only be recognition's starting point but not its final perspective. Hegel starts from the individualist standpoint, in order to transcend it. The cogito therefore is not a foundational self-presence. Rather the cogito is equally self-concealment or false consciousness. It discovers its false consciousness through the other. Self-discovery or self-recognition in other is an essentially joint social action.[56]

Recognition is not only a concept and structure, it is also an *action,* a *doing (Tun)*, which is inherently double sided. Recognition is not merely something to be contemplated, but something to be done. As an Aristotelian, Hegel knows that action is always particular and variable. He adds that in this case at least, it must also be double-sided, involving both the one and the other. What is done to the one is done to the other, and what is done to the other is also done to the self.

At this stage of the analysis the brackets are only partially removed; Hegel's analysis remains an eidetics. Eidetics yields transcendental insight into concrete experience, an insight that recognition is more than a mere concept. Action is necessary to recognition. The eidetics show that the requisite action must be two-sided, joint reciprocal action. Eidetic-transcendental insight does not substitute for action but discloses that praxis lies beyond the level of eidetic analysis, and that an empirics of recognition qua action is also necessary.

Hegel §7

In this movement we see a repetition of the same process exhibited in the interplay of forces, but repeated in consciousness. What in that interplay was *for us* the phenomenological observers, here holds true for the extremes themselves. The middle is the self-consciousness which disintegrates into the extremes. Each extreme exchanges its determinacy and makes a complete transition into its opposite. As consciousness it comes outside of itself. However, in its self-transcendence it also abides in itself and it is conscious of its self-transcendence. It is for consciousness that it immediately is and is not another consciousness. Likewise this other is only for itself, when it cancels itself as [pure] being-for-itself and is for itself only in the [independent] being-for-itself of its other [*nur im Fürsichsein des andern für sich ist*]. Each is the mediating term for the other, through which each mediates itself with itself and coincides with itself. Each is for itself and for the other an immediate self-existing being, which at the same time is such only through this mediation. They recognize themselves as reciprocally acknowledging each other.

Commentary: The Interplay of Intersubjectivity

The interplay of forces is the splitting up of force into attraction and repulsion which Hegel discussed in the previous chapter. But the fundamental point of self-diremption is not new. It first appeared in the discussion of perception, and in the words of Hyppolite, is "a step that will appear at every stage of the *Phenomenology*. Force will split itself into two forces, self-consciousness into two self-consciousnesses, etc."[57] Such doubling is ultimately rooted in the dichotomous structure of the *Gestalten des Bewusstseins*. Previously only for the phenomenological observers, (*an sich* or *für uns*) the doubling now repeats itself in and for self-consciousness, which itself is doubled.

Siep explains: "Recognition as a double-sided action of two self-consciousnesses is a relation in which the *relata* relate to themselves through relation to the other, and relate to the other through relation to themselves. The relation to self through other is made possible by the corresponding relation of the other...each of the two *relata* contains the entire relation in itself, and relates to itself as its other [and conversely relates to its other as to itself]."[58] In the doubling of self-consciousness the middle disintegrates into the opposing extremes which exchange their contrasting determinations. Each consciousness both is and is not the other consciousness. Each is for itself only by being for the other, and for the other only by being for itself. Thus, in reciprocal recognition, being-for-other is equivalent to being-for-self, and being-for-self is equivalent to being-for-other. Without free reciprocity, being-for-other and being-for-self do not coincide, and are not equivalent. The result is unequal forms of recognition, e.g., domination and subservience. But this gets ahead of our story.

The crucial point is that the middle not only disintegrates into the extremes, but also comes to self-consciousness and is reconstituted through the joint reciprocal mediation of the extremes. The emergent universal consciousness presupposes the mutual disappearance of each extreme into its opposite. It is the consciousness that has undergone these correlative mutual transitions, that Hegel portrays when he says "It is for consciousness that it immediately is and is not another consciousness." That is why *Geist* is not a subjective, but a holistic concept, and why it must be understood as a complex dialectical identity that presupposes and preserves difference. For these reasons H. S. Harris has considerable justification when he contends that recognition "is the 'absolute Begriff' on its positive side, the concept as life..."[59] Recognition is both a concept with dialectical structure and a concrete experiential dialectic. The eidetics lays out the former, and the empirics displays and examines the latter.

SUMMARY

Paragraphs §§1–7 constitute an eidetics of intersubjectivity, a conceptual analysis of the doubling of subjectivity in intersubjectivity and the resulting ambiguities. Self-consciousness is not simply a Cogito, or reflexive self-identity. Rather it is a self-identity mediated by and dependent on an other. Hence, self-consciousness has two fundamental structures, being-for-self and being-for-other. These structures in turn reflect an intersubjective doubling of consciousness: a self-consciousness *for* a self-consciousness. This doubling shows that the fundamental pattern of recognition is not simply the pattern of desire, i.e., consumption that demonstrates the nullity of the object. This doubling sets up a correlation between internal and external relations, between for-itself and for-an other. The whole analysis presupposes this correlative doubling.

   Hegel identifies two stages of recognition. The first stage is a fruitless replication of the pattern of desire: self-coincidence by elimination of other. This is a one-sided, exclusive self-assertion (*Fürsichsein*) that seeks to suppress or directly appropriate the other and consequently issues in conflict. The eidetics suggests that conflict *of some sort* is an essential structural feature of recognition. But while conflict is necessary, its specific forms—e.g., the life and death struggle, or Mastery and Servitude—are contingent and variable.

   In the second stage, the reversal noted above becomes explicit. Instead of eliminating the other, each turns out to be what it is through mediation by the other. Thus the absolute independence of the extremes has turned out to be illusory, and the rejected alternative of interdependence turns out to be the truth. The alienation or loss of self—but not the internal self-relation—is overcome, not by eliminating other, but through joint action with other. Each must allow the other to be and go free. Such mutual releasement is an eidetic feature, but it can assume different forms, e.g., love (and marriage), forgiveness, and reconciliation.

   This eidetic analysis of recognition recalls the opening categorical moves at the beginning of the logic. For in showing that pure being and pure nothing are fixed and empty abstractions that cannot be successfully isolated from each other and vanish immediately into each other, Hegel deconstructs abstract identity as simple self-sameness that excludes difference. Such abstract identity underlies the immediate non-dialectical view of self-consciousness, in terms of which reality consists in discrete, atomic individuals that are simply self-identical and unrelated to each other.[60] Each must learn that it is necessary to acknowledge the other. This requires a modification of the initial fixed position, a replacement of mutual exclusion with mutual recognition. Acceptance of the other, taking account of and dealing with the other, requires that the self alter its initial construal of the situation. Just as the logical analysis shows that the attempt to isolate pure being fails, and being passes over into its opposite, the immediate *Gestalt* of consciousness self-destructs. This failure establishes that process (*Werden*), relativity and community are the fundamental ontological categories, and that being is dynamic (*Werden*), interrelated and social at the most fundamental level.

This entire exposition and analysis of the concept of recognition is eidetic, or *für uns*. The concern is to lay out the *meaning* of intersubjectivity. However the analysis of the meaning of the other is less than a complete phenomenology of intersubjectivity. This eidetics of intersubjectivity says nothing about how the equivalence of being-for-other and being-for-self becomes *actual*. Intentional analysis can lay out a region or field of experience, and map out problems, including problems of evidence. It can show that recognition must be essentially two-sided, joint and reciprocal. But by itself it does not generate or provide the actual experience.

For this reason Hegel turns from eidetic analysis of the concept to the ordinary consciousness which undergoes the process of recognition (*Anerkennung*). The eidetics prepared for this shift by showing the impossibility of a purely transcendental-eidetic analysis of other. In paragraph five Hegel asserts that the movement of recognition involves a doing (*Tun*) of both parties. The abstraction of the eidetics must now be removed.

Notes

1. Hans-Georg Gadamer, *Truth and Method* (New York: Seabury Press, 1975), 307–308.

2. Hegel, *Vorlesungen über die Philosophie der Religion*, TWA 17: 190. On the other hand, a recent study claims that Hegel is a Cartesian, and bases this claim upon Hegel's discussion of Descartes in the history of philosophy lectures (Cf. Tom Rockmore, *Hegel's Circular Epistemology*, op. cit.). However, Hegel's acknowledgement of Descartes as the founder of modern philosophy does not necessarily mean that he is a Cartesian. While Hegel praises Descartes' introduction of the concept of subjec-

tivity, he observes that everything depends on how such subjectivity is to be understood. Cartesian subjectivity is a one-sided abstraction from intersubjectivity and world. The Cogito is not a foundation, but rather derivative from, or at best equiprimordial with, other subjects and world.

3. Cf. his *Lectures on the History of Philosophy*. (*Geschichte der Philosophie* TWA Sk, 19–20)

4. Hegel, *Faith and Knowledge*, tr. W. Cerf and H. S. Harris (Albany, N.Y.: SUNY Press, 1977), 64. Kojève also emphasizes Hegel's critique of and distanciation from Cartesian doctrines. See his *Introduction to the Reading of Hegel*, ed. A. Bloom, tr. James H. Nichols Jr. (New York: Basic Books, 1969), 33–41.

5. Cf. William Desmond, *Desire, Dialectic and Otherness* (New Haven, Conn.: Yale University Press, 1987), 118–124. Desmond presents here a reading that all mediation is essentially self-mediation. It should be noted that this reading serves a strategic purpose in his argument for metaxological otherness, but as an interpretation of Hegel it requires the qualifications mentioned in the notes.

6. Hegel, PhG 28 .

7. Cf. Gadamer's comments about the difficulties of translating Hegel into foreign languages. ("Hegel and Heidegger," in *Hegel's Dialectic*, tr. P. Christopher Smith (New Haven, Conn.: Yale University Press, 1976), 112ff. Gadamer makes the acute but devastating (for translation at least) observation that Hegel's main terminology is not at all restricted to the conceptual horizons of metaphysics, which in Latin concepts and the elaboration of these, provides the linguistic foundation for the translation of Hegel into Italian, Spanish, French and English. What gets communicated by translation is primarily the metaphysical horizon and core of the Latin background. What is lost in most translations is the German *Umgangsprache*, its simple turns, allusions and puns, upon which Hegel constantly draws. For this reason Gadamer characterizes the Hegel translations as only half successful. It should come as no surprise that the Hegel who is known primarily or only in translation, tends to be the "metaphysical Hegel." What is suppressed is the Hegelian critique of metaphysics and alternative to the metaphysical tradition.

8. H. S. Harris, "The Concept of Recognition in Hegel's Jena Manuscripts," *Hegel Studien* Beiheft 20 (Bonn: Bouvier Verlag, 1979), 229. [Hereafter cited as CR.]

9. Ibid.

10. The term 'eidetics' is controversial, in that it can be taken to suggest a Platonic reading of Husserlian phenomenology, according to which the eidos is a formal-logical concept. This would be a mistake, for Husserl distinguishes between formal-logical-mathematical concepts on the one hand, and non-formal morphologies on the other. (Cf. his *Ideas*, op. cit.) Alfred Schutz reformulated this distinction as Eidos and Type (See Alfred Schutz, "Type and Eidos in Husserl's Late Philosophy," in *Collected Papers III: Studies in Phenomenological Philosophy*, ed. I. Schutz, [*Phaenomenologica*, no. 22] (The Hague: Martinus Nijhoff, 1966), 92–115. The type is an empirical universal; it has not a formal but only a presumptive universality, "good until further

notice." Hegel's phenomenology of the *Gestalten des Bewusstseins* is a non-formal eidetics in this latter sense. For a similar reading, cf. Reinhold Aschenberg, op. cit.; Michael Theunissen, "Begriff und Realität: Hegels Aufhebung des metaphysischen Wahrheitsbegriffs," in *Seminar: Dialektik in der Philosophie Hegels*, op. cit.

11. For a discussion of eidetics and empirics, cf. Paul Ricoeur's multi-volume study of the will. Ricoeur's eidetics of the will is set forth in *Freedom and Nature: The Voluntary and the Involuntary* (Evanston, Ill.: Northwestern University Press). Here Ricoeur sets forth the fundamental ontological structures of the will. Second, Ricoeur's empirics of the will is presented in *Fallible Man*, (Chicago, Regnery); here the will is considered in relation to time and action, and its fallibility is set forth. Finally there is a Poetics of the will, which is set forth in *Symbolism of Evil* (Boston: Beacon Press, 1967); here myths and symbols of evil and the bondage of the will are taken up. The whole project is reminiscent of and is an extension of Hegel's *Lectures on the Philosophy of Religion* and Schelling's *Philosophy of Mythology*.

12. Otto Pöggeler calls attention to the Jena Logic outlined at the end of the *Real-philosophie* 1805/06: the major structures of the Jena logic are "*absolutes Sein, das sich Anderes (Verhältnis wird), Leben und Erkennen; und wissendes Wissen, Geist, Wissen des Geistes von sich.*" (Cited in *Frühe Politische Systeme*, Hrsg. G. Göhler [Frankfurt: Ullstein, 1974]), 288. [Emphasis mine] *Leben* is a distinct category of this logic. Not even Aristotle had gone so far as to identify *Leben* as a logical category. For Pöggeler's discussion cf. *Grundprobleme der grossen Philosophen*, Hrsg. Josef Speck (Göttingen: Vandenhoeck and Ruprecht, 1982), 160ff; see also *Materialien zu Hegels Phänomenologie des Geistes* (Frankfurt: Suhrkamp, 1973), 329–390.

13. Henrich, *Hegel im Kontext*, op cit. 27.

14. Jean Hyppolite, "Life and the Consciousness of Life in the Jena Philosophy," in *Studies on Marx and Hegel*, ed. and tr. by John O'Neill (New York: Harper and Row, 1969), 6.

15. Cf. *Systemfragment* (1800) TWA 1:422, ET ETW 312.

16. Pöggeler observes that Hegel did not succeed in developing life as a logical category in the Jena period, but only much later. "Die Komposition der Phänomenologie des Geistes" in *Materialien zu Hegels Phänomenologie des Geistes* (Frankfurt: Suhrkamp, 1973), 363. Gadamer also mentions Aristotle in passing: "Hegel's Dialectic of Self-Consciousness," in *Hegel's Dialectic*, tr. P. Christopher Smith (New Haven, Conn.: Yale University Press, 1976).

17. Hyppolite, op. cit. 4.

18. H. G. Gadamer, "Hegel's Dialectic of Self-Consciousness," op. cit. 58. [Italics mine.]

19. Hegel, *System der Sittlichkeit*, in *Frühe Politische Systeme*, op. cit. 40. This suggests that recognition is a concept with wider ontological connotations than inter-human relations.

20. On this point, cf. Alexandre Kojève, *Introduction to the Reading of Hegel, Lectures on the Phenomenology of Spirit*, assembled by Raymond Queneau, ed. Allan Bloom, tr. James H. Nichols, Jr. (New York: Basic Books, 1969), 3ff. Desire is the revelation of the nothingness of the subject. For an appreciative critique and caution on Kojève, cf. Gadamer, op. cit. 62, n. 7. Gadamer contends that *Begierde* should not be translated as desire, because it lacks erotic connotations. On the other hand, H. S. Harris claims that in the Jena Manuscripts, *Begierde* is sexual in connotation. This does not necessarily contradict Gadamer's interpretation however, for Harris explains "The extremely enigmatic dialectic of "Leben und Begierde" begins to yield up its secrets when we read it as an account of sexual desire, an account of how the genus appears to the living consciousness that is not yet self-conscious, or as a phenomenology of *animal* awareness." (H. S. Harris, "The Concept of Recognition in Hegel's Jena Manuscripts," *Hegel Studien*, Beiheft 20 [Bonn: Bouvier Verlag, 1979], 232.)

21. PhG 140.

22. Kojève notes that Hegel postulates a plurality of desires, that is undeducible, and given. Ibid. 40.

23. PhG 139. In this text Hegel announces a major thesis of personalist intersubjectivity. This thesis is made further explicit and defended by Feuerbach. (Cf. Ludwig Feuerbach, *The Essence of Christianity*, tr. G. Eliot [New York: Harper and Row, 1957].) It is appropriated from Feuerbach and refined further by Martin Buber in his discussion of "I-Thou" relations. (See Buber, *I and Thou* [New York: Scribners, 1970.]

24. PhG 140.

25. Recent literature on *Anerkennung* includes: Ludwig Siep, *Anerkennung als Prinzip der praktische Philosophie* (Freiburg: Alber Verlag, 1978). [Hereafter cited as APP]; H. S. Harris, "The Concept of Recognition in Hegel's Jena Manuscripts," op. cit. [Hereafter cited as CR]; Andreas Wildt, *Autonomie und Anerkennung* (Stuttgart: Klett-Cotta, 1982); Edith Düsing, *Intersubjektivität und Selbstbewusstsein* (Köln: Jürgen Dinter Verlag, 1986).

26. This interpretation rests on the assumption that the reduction excludes existence. This is the Cartesian version of the reduction that was criticized and rejected above in Chapter 5.

27. Cf. Heidegger's discussion of *Mitdasein* in *Sein und Zeit* (Tübingen: Niemeyer Verlag, 1984), §26.

28. Husserl is often accused of such a formal-mathematical eidetics that separates meaning from fact. It should be noted that even in *Ideas* Husserl distinguished non-formal morphological historical essences from formal-mathematical essences. It is only in the latter case that there can be a question of separation of meaning from fact. The morphological essence is subsequently developed in reference to the Lifeworld. Cf. Alfred Schutz, "Type and Eidos in Husserl's Late Philosophy," op. cit.

29. Cf. Klaus Hartmann "On Taking the Transcendental Turn," *Review of Meta-*

physics, 20. 2. 78 (1966). Hartmann observes that it is a transcendental insight into intersubjectivity that the problem of intersubjectivity cannot be "solved" on the transcendental level. (248) It is likewise a transcendental-categorial insight that contingency is a necessary category, and categorial feature. Cf. Dieter Henrich's discussion of Hegel's theory of contingency. (Henrich, "Hegels Theorie über den Zufall," *Hegel im Kontext,* op. cit. 157–186)

30. Hegel, *Vorlesungen über die Geschichte der Philosophie,* TWA Sk. 19: 39

31. See H. S. Harris, "The Concept of Recognition," op. cit. 237; Ludwig Siep, APP.

32. While this book was in the final stages of production, I received a copy of Edith Düsing's essay "Genesis des Selbstbewusstseins durch Anerkennung und Liebe. Untersuchungen zu Hegels Theorie der knokreten Subjektivität" (in *Hegels Theorie des subjektiven Geistes [Spekulation und Erfahrung II/14]* [Stuttgart: Fromman-Holzboog, 1990], 244–279). Düsing also finds that recognition has three phases. However, since she treats the account of recognition in Hegel's *Encyclopedia* Philosophy of Spirit, she emphasizes other aspects of these phases. This does not alter the fundamental point concerning three phases and the logical deep structure of recognition. This collection of essays demonstrates convergences between Hegelian and Husserlian phenomenologies; cf. especially Lothar Eley's forward.

33. This letting the other go free is reminiscent of *Gelassenheit.* Hegel's concept of the universal as love, that does not dominate its particular, may not be far from Eckhart's vision, but translated into the form and language of holism. (WL TWA 6:277). For a discussion cf. Reiner Schürmann, *Meister Eckhart,* [*Studies In Phenomenology and Existential Philosophy*] (Bloomington, Ind.: Indiana University Press, 1978), 113, 190, 245. See also note 50 below.

34. Hegel's texts form one continuous whole. Here translation of each paragraph is followed immediately by commentary. The first paragraph in my translation corresponds to the first paragraph on page 141 in the PhG (Hoffmeister edition), and paragraph §178 in PhS (The Miller translation).

35. The German term is *Verdoppelung.* Miller and Baillie both translate it as duplication. But duplication suggests that the other is a copy of the one, which implies that it is derivative from the first or primal ego. Duplication is in fact much closer to Husserl's theory of the mediate apprehension of the other in appresentation. In this case, the sense of the other derives from my primal ego as a duplicate of it "over there." Hegel's point is that the other is not a copy, or duplicate, but another member of the same species which exists as a plurality of individuals. Hegel's claim is that the species itself, life, doubles, is a one and a many. This is an objective doubling, not merely a duplication of consciousness. Hegel's starting point, namely with doubled plurality of the species, lies deeper than a potentially contingent transfer of sense. It is Husserl's promised land.

36. For this view, cf. Max Scheler, *The Nature and Forms of Sympathy,* tr. Peter Heath (Hamden, Conn.: The Shoe String Press, 1970) a translation of *Vom Wesen der Sympathiegefühl (1923).* See also Alfred Schutz, "Scheler's Theory of Intersubjectiv-

ity" in *Collected Papers Vol. I: The Problem of Social Reality*, ed. M. Natanson (The Hague: Martinus Nijhoff, 1967), 156–172; See also, Herbert Spiegelberg, *The Phenomenological Movement: A Historical Introduction, Vol. 1* (The Hague: Martinus Nijhoff, 1960), 260ff.

37. Enz, §§115–116.

38. Both English translations are misleading because they represent as Hegel's view the very position(s) he rejects. See note 35 above.

39. See Rolf-Peter Horstmann, *Ontologie und Relationen: Hegel, Bradley, Russell und die Kontroverse über interne und externe Beziehungen* (Hain: Athenäum, 1984); see also Errol E. Harris, *Formal, Transcendental and Dialectical Thinking: Logic and Reality* (Albany, N.Y.: SUNY Press, 1988). These two studies complement each other: Harris shows that atomistic pluralism finds expression in current views concerning formal logic. Horstmann discusses the ontological dimension of the problem in reference to Russell's critique of Bradley, and is critical of Russell's lumping of Hegel together with Bradley. Both agree that Hegel's dialectical logic and holism constitute a third alternative to the impasse between pluralism and monism.

40. From the perspective of *Verstand*, the presumption is that the internal/external dichotomy is exhaustive. But both views of relations turn out to be self-subverting: relations either leave their relata unchanged—they do not qualify or add anything to the relata—or they wind up denying the independence of one of the relata, in which case there is nothing to relate, no "between." Since both theories are self subverting, and appear to exhaust possibilities, Bradley drew the desperate conclusion that relations are impossible and so not real. Levinas on the other hand characterizes intersubjectivity as a relation without terms. This issue continues to provoke discussion. Cf. Edward Halper, "Hegel and the Problem of the Differentia," and the reply by Martin Donougho in *Essays on Hegel's Logic*, ed. G. di Giovanni (1990) op. cit. The problem of the differentia can be framed by a dilemma: if the differentia belongs to the genus it differentiates, it would not explain why the genus is different from other genera. (Ibid. 191) The result would be monism, a reduction of the other to the same. But if the differentia does *not* belong to the genus, then the defining feature of the genus would be transcendent to it. (Ibid. 192) This results in dualism. Donougho thinks that Hegel faces a comparable dilemma. He asks whether the other is one of the determining features of the one (*Etwas*). (Ibid. 210) If it is, then the other appears to collapse into the identity of the one, resulting in monism. If it is not, then the other is completely excluded from identity, and the result is a dualism between the one and the other, or between identity and difference. Both of these dilemmas presuppose abstract identity exclusive of difference and reflect the standpoint of *Verstand*. Hegel rejects both monism and dualism. He shows that identity and difference require each other and are inconceivable except by means of each other. This points to a social conception of being, a unity in difference. Triadic holism is Hegel's alternative to monism and dualism.

41. Horstmann claims that the monist-pluralist debate rests upon a different conception of ontology from Hegel. For Hegel ontology is a theory of categories, and relations are construed as categories. Ultimately, then, it is the Idea which carries the

freight of relations for Hegel. And the Idea has not just one mode, but rather a three-fold mediation. The threefold mediation of the Idea—and the corresponding threefold mediation of the system—constitute Hegel's holistic third alternative to monism and pluralism. (Horstmann *Ontologie,* op. cit. 98ff.)

42. Horstmann observes that Hegel's term *"Übergreifende Subjektivität"* is a metaphor for the whole as a relation of relations. Kierkegaard appropriated this conception and applied it to the theory of the self. Howard Kainz also realizes the significance of this holistic theory, but tends to construe it psychologically as a theory of self-consciousness. (Howard Kainz, *Paradox, Dialectic and System: A Contemporary Reconstruction of the Hegelian Problematic* [University Park, Pa: The Pennsylvania State University Press, 1988], 27.)

43. Emmanuel Levinas fails to observe this distinction, and so interprets Hegelian self-consciousness as a straightforward egological system of identity. In this interpretation the other can only be instrumental to self-coincidence and self-identity. (Cf. Levinas, "Substitution," in *The Levinas Reader,* ed. Sean Hand [Oxford: B. Blackwell Ltd., 1989], 89, 91, 103, 116.) The term *Fürsichsein* is both a *Gestalt des Bewusstseins* and a logical category. Cf. Hegel, *Wissenschaft der Logik,* TWA, SK 5: 174. [Hereafter abbreviated as WL]; ET: *Science of Logic,* tr. A. V. Miller (New York: Humanities Press, 1969), 157. [Hereafter abbreviated as SL.]

44. As a logical concept, being-for-itself (*Fürsichsein*) is similar to Leibniz's concept of a monad in being the center of a network of relations. (*Wissenschaft der Logik,* TWA Sk. 5:174ff; SL 157ff. The monad concept goes back to atomism.) Leibniz's monad has "no windows"; all its apparent interaction with others is due solely to divinely pre-established harmony. Thus, the monad seems to be conceived on Cartesian terms as abstract identity. In contrast, Hegel's being-for-self not only has windows, but the windows are open. Everything is related to and qualified by everything else. The self is *for itself* only by being-for-itself *for an other.* Each is for itself by not being the other, by excluding the other, and yet this apparently exclusive *Fürsichsein* depends on the very other it excludes!

45. See H. S. Harris, CR, 239. Harris notes that Hegel treats *Eigensinn* in a different context in the *Phenomenology* than in the Jena *Philosophy of Spirit.* However this does not alter its fundamental meaning, namely, "the primitive determination of the immature human animal to have its own way." Such an abstraction makes conflict of some sort virtually inevitable.

46. *Wissenschaft der Logik,* TWA Sk. 5:66.

47. Not unlike Plato's dialectical exercises in the *Parmenides,* the term 'other' has several senses. Hegel's account is based on the correlation of the other as independent being with "other" as other-being (*Anderssein*). In both cases, the sharp and rigid distinction between the inner and external senses of the other are broken down and shown to involve transition, namely, from the one to the many (Plato) and from the I to the We (Hegel).

48. This is one passage in which *aufheben* means to cancel, rather than to sublate. The end is not preservation but the cancellation of other-being.

49. It is striking that Hegel uses the same verb (*entlassen*) to refer to reciprocal recognition that he uses to refer to the Idea releasing itself into nature (*Enz* §244).

50. Hegel is no less appreciative of Meister Eckhart than is Heidegger. Reiner Schürmann writes: "It was this very concept of a totality at the beginning and at the end of releasement, unfolding itself without a why, that was to enchant Friedrich Hegel five centuries later." (*Meister Eckhart*, op. cit. 113.) Schürmann also reports the following anecdote: Franz von Baader remarks in his diary (*Sämtliche Werke*, ed. F. Hoffmann [Leipzig, 1851–1860], vol. 15, 159): "Very often at Berlin, I was in the company of Hegel. One day I read him some texts of Meister Eckhart, an author of which he knew only the name. He was so delighted that he gave before me an entire course devoted to Meister Eckhart. At the end he also confided to me: 'Here we have found at last what we were seeking'." quoted by I. Degenhardt, *Studien zum Wandel des Eckhart-Bildes*, (Leiden, 1967), 114. Ibid. 245. Hegel could have and probably did say the same thing about other figures in the history of philosophy, e. g., Heraclitos, Descartes.

51. The life-and death struggle culminating in Master/slave is a futile attempt to reduce the other to the same. But, as we shall see in the next chapter, this attempt is a one-sided unequal recognition that ends in failure, and for essential-eidetic reasons.

52. Miller's translation needlessly creates ambiguity. Miller's translation runs thus: "secondly the other self-consciousness equally gives it back again to itself…" (111). Miller takes as the subject of the clause "das andere Selbstbewusstsein" rather than "es." While this is grammatically possible, it violates the symmetry and the sense of the text. And it overlooks the point that Hegel makes in the next sentence, namely that the initial account of the concept of recognition is restricted to the standpoint of one self-consciousness and represented simply as the action of one. Miller's reading shifts the standpoint to the other self-consciousness, and represents the other as the agent. Baillie's translation on the other hand has the advantage of keeping within the symmetry and the methodological abstraction of the first four paragraphs. Moreover, while it is rather free, it correctly recalls the initial standpoint in paragraph two, in which the self, in regarding the other, sees only itself in the other, and thus suppresses the otherness of the other. It is this otherness of the other which Baillie correctly finds restored in the final moment when the self lets the other go free. Miller also translates this final clause in this way, which makes nonsense of his translation quoted above. If the other were really the agent, then it must set itself free.

53. Hegel: *The Phenomenology of Mind*, rev. ed., tr. J. B. Baillie (New York: Macmillan, 1961), 230.

54. Hartmann writes: "The concept of objective *Geist* is not a consequence of the system or a product of the dialectical train of thought. In fact, it is not a speculative doctrine at all, but a straightforward descriptive concept, a philosophical formulation of a basic phenomenon that allows at any time of demonstration and description independently of [philosophical] standpoint. In a word, it is an original intuition, a discovery on Hegel's part of something which stands on its own two feet. Hegel's conceptualization is a directing of attention to and intellectual formulation of something that simply is. And the only question can be whether one has understood it or

not, or how it is to be interpreted." (Nicolai Hartmann, *Philosophie des deutschen Idealismus,* Zweite Auflage [Berlin: Walter de Gruyter, 1960], 496.)

55. Hegel writes at an obviously high level of abstraction, which includes abstraction from gender; he uses the pronoun "es." For a similar conception of the ego as a self-determining monad into which nothing can come except through its own activity, cf. Fichte, *Wissenschaftslehre, Werke* I, 279–281.

56. Levinas completely ignores Hegel's methodological abstraction from joint action. He presents therefore an interpretation of Hegel that is one-sided and an abstraction from mutual recognition. He thus misinterprets Hegel as attempting to found his whole discussion of intersubjectivity on the self-identity of consciousness, interpreted as ego-substance. See his essay "Substitution" op. cit. 92f.

57. Jean Hyppolite, *Genesis and Structure of Hegel's Phenomenology of Spirit,* tr. Cherniak and Heckman, (Evanston, Ill.: Northwestern University Press, 1974), 115.

58. Siep. op. cit. 138.

59. Harris, CR 236.

60. Cf. Enz. §§86–88; §§115–116. For the suggestion that in the logic Hegel deconstructs *Verstand* and its categories cf. Joseph C. Flay's "Hegel's *Science of Logic:* Ironies of the Understanding" in *Essays on Hegel's Logic,* op. cit.

EIGHT

THE EMPIRICS OF RECOGNITION

Recognition has a speculative, conceptual dimension. As Harris observes, it is the absolute *Begriff* in concrete living form. Recognition also has an experiential dimension, specifically as lived through by ordinary consciousness. The distinction between eidetics and empirics, between *Begriff* and experience is not an absolute one; it would be a mistake to conceive it as an ontological dualism. Eidetics is not some realm apart from or beyond the empirical; rather, as Hegel says, it is only the empirical brought closer, i.e., made explicit and brought into focus. The eidetic structures of being-for-self and being-for-other, reciprocity and reversal, are not actual apart from experience. They are actual only as embedded in experience, and appear in determinate form.[1]

Such empirical actualization is not merely accidental or superfluous. Nor are the empirical appearances to be taken as mere approximations to an ideal that lies in principle beyond experience and history: "Because the Truth is, it must manifest itself, and its manifestation must be an accomplished fact. Truth's self-manifestation is an inseparable part of its own eternal nature, so much so that if it did not manifest itself it would cease to be, that is to say, its content would be reduced to an empty abstraction.... What is in and for itself and what is finite and temporal—these are the two fundamental determinations which must be present in a theory of truth..."[2]

I have previously shown that Hegel's *Phenomenology* employs a skeptical dialectic of tropic reversals. It is an extended application of the principle of equipollence. Each *Gestalt des Bewusstseins* begins with an immediate, naive and one-sided expression. The original *Gestalt* is self-confident, but such self-confidence is only a presumptive certainty that self-destructs under the conditions of experience, the impact of the other. No one has seen this more clearly or expressed the point better and more vividly in English than Josiah Royce:

> The usual character of the biography of any one of these *Gestalten* is as follows. Each expresses an attitude, an idea, and so a mode of behavior, a reaction towards the world.... Any such stage of consciousness presents itself...as inevitable, as rational, as the only way to live and think, as *the* interpretation of life...and of the universe.... Within its own limits, each of these forms is the truth.... As the *Gestalt* thus undertakes the work of its lit-

tle life...it at once must develop what is within and come in conflict with what is without. The result is...either comic or tragic in the resulting dialectic. The calm confidence of its beginning...turns as it proceeds into disappointment, into contradiction.... Its ideas prove to be fantastic, its supposed facts turn out to be dreams, its sincerity is exposed through the experience of life and through a merciless self-criticism and...proves to be sometimes self-deception, sometimes hypocrisy, frequently both.... Its external conflicts with the world that it views as...other than itself, turn out to be also essentially internal conflicts.... On the other hand, its internal diremption, its inner contradiction always expresses itself in external conflicts. *And just this unity of the external and the internal is what furnishes the positive result....* Hence, its failure implies a reconstruction of the view regarding itself and its world with which it had begun. What it had called its own comes to seem foreign to it. What it had called utterly remote, and merely a not-self, turns out to be its own flesh and blood.[3]

In his eidetics of recognition, Hegel presents a special case of the tropic reversals. In this Gestalt, there are two self-consciousnesses involved. Truth is no longer simply a question of the correspondence between concept and object. Here, truth is distinguished from epistemological self-certainty by the requirement of recognition by other. That is, each is the truth of the other. Self-certainty must be made manifest. But how is it to be manifest? It must be manifest in the recognition of an other. Thus, the truth of self-certainty comes to expression in and through the other. The truth of mastery is found in the slave. This truth goes beyond traditional epistemological certainty in that it involves intersubjective mediation. To be sure, the truth of each Gestalt will turn out to be the opposite of what was originally meant. But this reversal must become explicit for the terms, the *relata* themselves.

For this reason, it is misleading to interpret the *Gestalten* as an independent philosophical anthropology as Kojève does. Kojève focuses on specific episodes of the text while missing its plot and structure. Although it cannot be denied that Kojève's reading of Hegel is illuminating and demonstrates Hegel's continuing relevance, his anthropological interpretation does not do justice to the deep structure and systematic argument.[4] Moreover, Kojève's reading collapses recognition into master and slave, and suppresses the fact that the concept of recognition supports alternative possibilities of realization and outcomes.[5] Finally, it distorts the range and continuum of the concept of recognition in the *Phenomenology* as well as in other writings. The life and death struggle, followed immediately by master/slave, are only Hegel's starting point. They represent self-recognition in other in the negative mode of mutual exclusion. But this is not a "realization" of the *concept* of recognition; it is its suppression or perversion. Hegel's discussion proceeds along a continuum from mutual exclusion and refusal, to mutual reciprocal recognition in the determinate modes of forgiveness and love, and culminates in the self-recognition of humanity in God.

Hegel's eidetics establishes that recognition is essentially a two-sided, reciprocal action. But the eidetics, owing to its abstraction, does not consider the "how" of action, the ways recognition is concretely accomplished. When we remove the brackets of eidetic abstraction, we face the classical Aristotelian point that action is always particular and variable. Hegel distinguishes between the *concept* of recognition, or *recognition as such,* and the *determinate forms or actions* of its concrete realization:

> This pure concept of recognition (*Anerkennen*), the doubling of self-consciousness in its unity, is now to be considered as it unfolds for self-consciousness. First, the inequality of both extremes will be exhibited, or the emergence of the middle in the extremes, which as extremes are opposed to each other. The one is only recognized, while the other merely recognizes.[6]

The concept of recognition is universal, general but indeterminate, whereas recognition as action is a particular determinate modification of the general structure. Through action the general structures of recognition—being-for-self and being-for-other, surpassing self in other, reverting upon self and the like—come into play and receive specific shape and determination. Hegel begins his analysis with an examination of conflict, i.e., the inequality of the extremes.

TOWARDS THE LIFE AND DEATH STRUGGLE

Hegel begins with a description of a concrete encounter between two apparently primitive or provincial consciousnesses. Each is what it is by excluding all others, and regarding everything other as merely accidental and inessential. This need not be construed as an elaborate fiction. Harris notes that in the earlier Jena manuscripts the family is the social context for consciousness, and the apparent abrupt encounter may be understood as occurring against the background of the family and clan as primary social units. The other confronting self-consciousness is an outsider, stranger, a representative of another family, defender of its property and honor. The *Gestalt* in the *Phenomenology* may reflect a context and situation that is already irreducibly social.

The question is, does this "clarifying background" give away the epistemological show? It might be objected that Hegel abandons the other as an *epistemological* problem by beginning with the social and political, where the other is already on the scene. But this merely shows that he has no solution to the epistemological problem, and proceeds dogmatically with "epistemological optimism."

I have already shown that in the *Phenomenology* Hegel does not abolish but rather transforms and redefines the epistemological project.[7] Hegel criticizes the solipsistic presuppositions underlying the objection. This objection presupposes the modern Cartesian form of skepticism, namely, privileged access of the ego to itself, and solipsism for everyone else. Hegel claims that this form of skepticism is inferior to ancient skepticism because it is itself dogmatic and succumbs to equipollence objections. Equipollence implies a denial of any privileged position such as that on which solipsism rests. Moreover, the case for solipsism is argued on narrow epistemological grounds which abstract from, while continuing to presuppose, an intersubjective social context of language, as well as mutually agreed criteria of evidence and truth. Alfred Schutz notes the irony in certain philosophical meetings where it is reciprocally and intersubjectively "proven" that "other minds" are unknowable or at best "soft data."[8] If this observation fails to impress the skeptic, that is because he denies having any presuppositions or dogmas of his own. If it were shown that he nevertheless presupposes the life-world, he would apply equipollence to his own assertions. But this means he abandons the field of appearances and retreats into private subjective opinion. Hegel observes that the skeptic really advances no claim, but only a subjective opinion, that need concern no one besides himself.[9]

For Hegel, the problem of the other is not how to "escape the prison" of first-person subjectivity, but rather the exploration of interpersonal interactions from reciprocal exclusion to reciprocal inclusion.

> Self-consciousness is, first of all, simple being-for-self [*Fürsichsein*] i.e., self-identical by the exclusion of every other from itself. Its being and its absolute object is itself [*Ich*], and in this immediate existence of its being-for-itself [*Fürsichsein*] it is a particular. Everything other than it is non-essential, something negative. But the other is also a self-consciousness. Thus, one individual confronts an other.[10]

Prior to recognition, the two individuals are practically solipsists, for each regards himself as absolute or unqualified *Fürsichsein,* and the other as inessential or accidental, a merely mundane object. But they have not yet made themselves known to the other.

> These consciousnesses have not yet jointly accomplished for each other the movement of absolute abstraction which exterminates all immediate being and which is exclusively the pure negative being of self-identical consciousness. They have not yet made themselves known to each other as pure being-for-itself, i.e., as self-conscious. Each is to be sure, certain of itself, but not of the other and this certainty that each has of itself has as yet no truth.[11]

So each is at an epistemological distance from the other. And its self-certainty is not yet truth, but a mere presumption. The truth will turn out to require the inclusion of the suppressed other, and thus will be the opposite of what was originally intended.

Hegel breaks with Cartesian subjectivity when he isolates a second element in self-consciousness, namely being-for-other. Self-consciousness is not simply for itself, but for-itself-for-an other. The self's relation to itself is qualified shaped and mediated by an other. In the very heart of its independence and autonomy, the self nevertheless depends on and needs the recognition of the other. Consequently, in reference to the encounter with the alien stranger, each needs and depends on the other for transforming and elevating its subjective certainty into public intersubjective truth. Prior to recognition, "the self-certainty of each does not yet have truth. For its truth would consist merely in the self-certain claim to be an independent object, or what is the same thing, the object would claim to represent itself as this pure certainty. But in the case of recognition, such claims are impossible, because, as one is for the other, so the other is for the one. Each in itself, through its own doing, together with the other, jointly brings forth this pure abstraction of being-for-itself."[12] Each is what it is by refusal of the other; each seeks to be pure *Fürsichsein*.

But the encounter with the other shatters such a pretension. The presence of the other means that I am no longer in control of the situation. Confrontation with the other shatters the immediate presumption that self-certainty simply is the truth. The other eludes me. Moreover, the presence of the other signifies not merely the possibility of change, but unforeseeable possibilities of change. These call in question the presumptive certainty and abstract self-identity of pure *Fürsichsein*. This situation is intolerable. Each seeks to maintain in the face of the other its presumption to pure being-for-self (*Fürsichsein*).

And so the life or death struggle ensues. This struggle reflects the essential correlation between external and internal relations. As presumptive being-for-self (*Fürsichsein*), each seeks to eliminate the other whose elusive presence calls it into question. But in seeking to eliminate the other, "each places its own life at risk."[13] This is not merely an accident or sheer contingency. The risk of life is crucial to the demonstration of freedom. For being-for-self (*Fürsichsein*) is a claim to transcend facticity, and this is shown by a *willingness* to risk life itself:

> The relation is such that each tests both itself and the other through a life and death struggle. They must undergo this struggle, because they must elevate the private certainty each has of being-for-itself, to *truth in the other* and for itself. It is only in the risking of life that freedom is proved, i.e, that it is proved that the essence of self-consciousness does not consist in mere being, nor in the immediate way that it first appears, nor in the immersion in the expanse of life. Rather *freedom is proved by showing that there is nothing in consciousness which cannot be reduced by it to a vanishing moment*, by showing, in other words, that it is pure being-for-self.[14]

The external negation of the other is correlative with the self's internal negation of its own facticity, risking its own life. Freedom's transcendence of facticity is shown by negation, or the self's willingness to risk the negation of its own existence. Thereby, the self shows that it is not tied to any determinate mundane existence, including its own life.

If the risking of life is avoided, self-recognition in other is less profound: "The individual who has not risked his life may, to be sure, be acknowledged as a person. But he has not attained the truth of such acknowledgement as an independent self-consciousness."[15] Such recognition is abstract. The person is recognized only in an impersonal legal sense, as one unit interchangeable with others. But he is not recognized in his singularity as independent, as being-for-self (*Fürsichsein*). The irony is that the self can fulfill its need to intuit itself as absolute negation of everything fixed, only by seeking to eliminate the other, and yet it depends on the other for recognition of its freedom and negativity. The self cannot demonstrate its freedom and transform its certainty into truth without seeking the elimination of the other, and yet it also depends on the other to confirm its freedom.

This irony points to a reversal of this Gestalt, as Hegel explains:

> This trial by death subverts the very truth that is supposed to issue from it, as well as self-certainty in general. For just as life is the natural situation of consciousness, independence without absolute negation, so death is the natural negation of life, namely, a negation without independence, which therefore remains without the requisite significance of recognition. Death certainly shows that both risked their life and despised life in itself and in the other.... But then the essential element vanishes from their interplay, namely the moment of splitting up into extremes with opposite determinations, and the middle collapses into a lifeless unity...[16]

Going after the death of the other brings about the opposite of what was intended. Prosecution of the struggle to the point of death would not show a genuine transcendence of facticity; it would merely show that both despised life. Cancelling otherness by attempting to kill the other is thus self-subverting. For the point is not to end life, but to secure recognition and intersubjective legitimation of one's own certainty.

This shows that death is a deficient mode of negation. Hegel calls it abstract or simple annihilation. It would establish only a "community of death" based on indifference. Such abstract negation is not the negation of consciousness, which, says Hegel, "cancels in such a way that it maintains and preserves what has been cancelled, so that it survives its cancellation."[17] The negation of consciousness is not abstract, but determinate.[18]

The self-destruction of the life and death struggle is not simply negative. The reversal just noted marks a transition from abstract negation to a more concrete determinate negation, which establishes Mastery and Slavery. The struggle is not taken to the bitter end of annihilation, but is halted short of death. Hegel explains:

> In this experience [of abstract negation] self-consciousness learns that life is just as essential to it as pure self-consciousness [viz., pure *Fürsichsein*].... The dissolution of that simple unity is the result of the first experi-

ence. Through that dissolution there is posited a pure self-consciousness on the one hand, and a consciousness, which is not purely for itself, but for an other, or consciousness in the form of a thing. Both elements are essential. They are first of all unequal and opposed, and their reflection into unity has not yet been achieved. They exist as two opposite figures [*Gestalten*] of self-consciousness: the one is the independent being-for-itself [*Fürsichsein*] the other is the dependent consciousness whose "nature" it is to live or to be for an other. The former is the master, and the latter is the slave.[19]

One side discovers that the life it is about to lose is as essential to it as the need for recognition. It prefers bare survival to annihilation. Thereby it shows that it is bound to facticity and existence. It surrenders its demand for recognition of its freedom, and accepts its status as mere object for the other. It has its existence only at the sufferance of and in dependence on the other. It becomes slave. The other has emerged from the struggle victorious; its claims to being-for-self (*Fürsichsein*) have been validated if not exactly legitimated. It becomes master.

PHENOMENOLOGY OF MASTERY

Through successfully risking his life, the master proves his transcendence of the natural world, his independence of mere existence. The master has no fear of death. Conversely, the slave, in giving up his independence, sinks to the level of a mere commodity. He prefers bare survival to death, which shows that he is in thrall to the fear of death, the absolute master. His very life, and the means of sustaining it, are in the hands of an other. He labors for an other. Thus, the master relates immediately to the slave through the threat and fear of death, and to the world mediately through the slave.

The master relates to the world by interposing the slave between himself and the world. This alters the master's relation to the world. For the prototypical world-relation in the *Phenomenology* is that of desire, i.e., the pursuit and consumption of food. But now the slave labors for the master, procuring objects desired by the master, who is spared the labor necessary to satisfy his desire. "What mere desire cannot do, namely, have done with the thing, the master succeeds in doing, and he achieves the enjoyment of the thing and gratification of his desire. Desire alone could not do this because of the independence of the thing. The master however, has interposed the slave between himself and things, and can appropriate to himself only the dependent aspect of things, and so is pure enjoyment. The independent aspect of things he leaves to the slave who works upon it."[20] The master leads a life of pure enjoyment and satisfaction unsullied by laboring on things. He directly appropriates and enjoys things (i.e., as worked over and pre-shaped by the slave). He becomes a passive consumer. And since the slave works not to satisfy his own desire, but only that of the master, his labor is inessential. What the slave does is actually the doing of the master. The master remains the absolute power before which the independent being of things is negated and reshaped.

The master obtains his recognition under such conditions. The slave has surrendered his claims to being-for-self (*Fürsichsein*) and exists as a commodity or property of the master. Moreover the slave's labor, which shapes the world and satisfies the master's desire, is the master's work. As far as the slave is concerned, his labor is inessential. The slave's doing is actually the doing of the master. Hegel observes that the recognition that the master receives from the slave is deficient. "But for authentic recognition an essential element is still lacking: namely, what the master does to the other, he also does to himself; and what the slave does to himself, he also does to the other. Consequently what has been realized is only a one-sided and unequal recognition."[21]

Hegel expands on the deficiencies in the recognition the master receives from the slave. "The unessential consciousness [of the slave] is merely an object for the master; nevertheless it constitutes the truth of the master's self-certainty. But it is obvious that this object does not correspond to its concept. Rather the object in which the master has accomplished his mastery is quite different than an independent consciousness. What confronts the master now is not an independent, but a dependent consciousness. Therefore, the master is not certain of the truth of his being-for-self, because his truth is found in an unessential consciousness and in an unessential action."[22] The truth of mastery is the servile consciousness, which provides only a distorted and deficient recognition. The other, on whom the master depends for recognition, is regarded by the master as unessential, not an equal. If the slave is no longer an independent being, but merely unessential, so is the recognition the slave bestows.

Moreover, considered from the side of the slave, the latter no longer functions as an independent being, but has accepted and internalized the perspective of the master: "Here is the moment of recognition in which the other consciousness suspends its being-for-self, and rather does to itself what the other does to it."[23] That is, owing to his fear of death, the slave accepts the status of a thing in order to survive. Renouncing his human independence (*Fürsichsein*), he gets it back in mode of dependent thinghood, as the master's property etc. Consequently, the master despises him and holds his recognition to be worthless.

Hegel observes that the praxis of master/slave, omits an eidetic feature of recognition, "namely, what the master does to the other, he also does to himself, and what the slave does to the other, he also does to himself."[24] Reciprocity is not entirely lacking; although the Gestalt is created by the suppression of reciprocity and equality, this very suppression is shown to be in vain, because it leads to a reversal. The master cannot escape the consequences that redound to him as a result of his subjugation of the slave.

Thus, the truth of the master is the slave. The reduction of the slave to a mere commodity makes explicit what mastery is. Moreover, having reduced the other to a slave, to something inessential, the master must now find the *truth* of his self-certainty in the slave. This is impossible. For the slave is no longer an *independent self-consciousness which alone can jointly elevate self-certainty to truth.* Truth requires that the recognition of the other, in order to be genuine and authentic, must be freely bestowed. It cannot be coerced or forced and remain genuine. Since the slave does only what the master wants, the master cannot receive from him a *genuinely independent recognition.* So the master can never be intersubjectively "certain" of his self-certainty: "Therefore the master is not certain of his being-for-self as the truth, because his truth is found in an unessential consciousness and unessential action."[25] Even the slave's confirmation of mastery is worthless because the slave is *for the master* unessential.

Since the slave is unessential, merely an extension of the master, recognition by the slave does not count even for the master. The slave is not genuinely other, it is only "the master's other." Since mastery suppresses the independent other by reducing it to inessential servitude, and omits the eidetic feature that what is done to the other is done to self,[26] it cannot be brought to the level of authentic intersubjective truth. Mastery represents a vain attempt to reduce mediation by other to self-mediation. However, mastery succeeds merely in reducing the other to a slave, only to discover that coerced recognition is both phony and worthless. But phony recognition is the truth of mastery. Thus, mastery turns out to be self-subverting and brings about the opposite of what it intended. Mastery ends in failure, a dead end which can only be maintained by force.

Phenomenology of Servitude

The analysis of servitude is probably the most famous passage in the *Phenomenology.* Hegel observes that servitude as well as mastery proves to be the opposite of what it at first seems to be. "Just as mastery showed that it is the opposite of what it intends to be, so servitude will, in its working out, become the opposite of what it immediately is."[27] Thus, he highlights the reversal of situation (*Umkehr*). At the outset the master is pure being-for-self (*Fürsichsein*) which suppresses being-for-other (*Füreinanderssein*), and conversely the slave is pure being-for-other (*Füreinanderssein*) which suppresses its being-for-self (*Fürsichsein*). What is merely for an other has surrendered any intrinsic being of its own.

Servitude is first considered in its subordination to mastery. The servile consciousness fears death, and surrenders its claim to recognition in order to survive. Anxiety over death is constitutive of the servile consciousness: "The servile consciousness does not have anxiety about this or that particular, or for a few isolated moments. Rather it is 'in Angst' about its entire existence. For it has felt the fear of death, *the absolute master*. It has fallen apart; it has trembled throughout its being and everything firm and fixed in it has been shaken."[28] Fear of the mundane master is the occasion for fear or anxiety (*Angst*) about death, the 'absolute master'. Death is not only a negativity that shakes and dissolves everything solid and substantial, the fear of death compels the renunciation of the need for recognition. This renunciation of being-for-self (*Fürsichsein*) goes hand in hand with the transformation of the slave into a dependent thing, a commodity laboring for the master. The servile transformation is a flight from sheer negativity into objectivity. The flight of the slave from death reveals the slave is in thrall to its existence. Hegel gives a brilliant genetic account of inauthentic existence, i.e., the genesis of the servile consciousness first described by Fichte.[29]

Hegel identifies death and *Fürsichsein*. What both have in common is formless negativity. Death threatens to dissolve everything fixed, but on another level of continued existence, freedom also effects a similar dissolution of fixity. "This pure universal movement, the absolute fluidity of everything solid and permanent, is the simple nature of self-consciousness, the absolute negativity, the *pure being-for-self*, that lies at the heart of this consciousness. This moment of pure being-for-self is also explicit for the servile consciousness, because in the master he finds it as his object."[30] Hegel thus connects consciousness of finitude with death and negativity. Death discloses finitude. But the initial response to such disclosure is flight towards objectivity and dependent, servile existence. The slave first discovers his finitude and the corresponding delimiting negativity, proximately in the master, and ultimately in the threat of death. The slave intuits the master as an alien power over him, but is unaware that he is also the same power of negativity. That is why the slave remains in thrall. He does to himself what the master does, i.e., he internalizes the master's determination of the situation.

But there occurs a reversal. The world-transforming power of negation, or being-for-self (*Fürsichsein*), which is first intuited ultimately in death, externally and proximately in the master, is discovered to be the slave's own power. "Although the fear of the lord is the beginning of wisdom, it has not yet occurred to consciousness that it is *for itself* [autonomous] being-for-self. But through his labor the slave comes to himself, i.e, becomes conscious of what he really is [*Fürsichsein*]."[31] Hegel locates inversion of the Gestalt of the servile consciousness in labor. Through the transformation of the world by his labor, lies the possibility of the liberation of the slave from his thralldom.

Under conditions of involuntary labor, the slave must learn to restrain his desire and postpone gratification. The master, not the slave, immediately appropriates, consumes and enjoys the products of labor. The master leads a life of pleasure. But this leads to decadence: "In the moment which corresponds to desire in the master's consciousness, it seemed that the aspect of the unessential relation to the thing fell to the lot of the slave, since the thing retained its independence. Desire has reserved to itself the pure negating of the object and therein its unmixed self-feeling. This satisfaction of the master is for this reason a vanishing one, for it lacks the objective side [of things] and permanence. In contrast, labor is restrained desire, a delayed vanishing, or, labor shapes and forms."[32] The slave's labor is desire held in check, a delayed gratification.

Although the slave lacks direct enjoyment of the products of his labor, he nevertheless comes to see that the shaping and producing of objects is the key to objective permanence and independence. Thereby the laboring consciousness comes to the intuition of itself in its products, of itself as the power behind its products, or as the genuinely independent being.[33] In laboring, which originally meant only working for another alien being, the servile consciousness comes to an intuition of itself as *Fürsichsein*. "It is precisely in laboring, where it initially seemed to find only an alien significance [namely, working for someone else] that it rediscovers its own mind and independent significance."[34] It becomes *for itself* being-for-self, and when this occurs, the slave has overcome his self-alienation, expressed in the primacy of being-for-other (*Füreinanderssein*).

But does this reversal from dependent servitude to independence have any relevance to or significance for recognition? Does recognition play any role in mediating this sort of independence? It would seem not. Hegel's demonstration that servitude undergoes reversals into its opposite, is not an analysis or description of intersubjectivity, mutual recognition per se. There is self-recognition in otherness, but this is not an intersubjective otherness. Rather it is self-externalization in labor. In service, the slave becomes *for itself Fürsichsein* by laboring on and transforming the independent world. Here it would appear that recognition is merely one route to concrete mediated *Fürsichsein*, and labor is another. If so, how can this be reconciled with Hegel's claim that being-for-self (*Fürsichsein*) is mediated by being-for-other (*Füreinanderssein*)?

In a useful study of Hegel's Jena philosophy of *Geist*, Habermas shows that the concept of *Geist* is shaped by three concrete categories—language, tools and family, which correspond respectively to three patterns of dialectical relation: symbolic representation, labor and interaction.[35] In the Jena *Realphilosophie* these diverse elements appear in a framework Hegel later abandoned. Subsequently, he unified the elements of the philosophy of *Geist* under the concept of intersubjective interaction, thus depriving the concept of labor of its previously independent role.[36] Because the *Phenomenology* reflects Hegel's Jena period, labor appears to be an independent mediation of *Fürsichsein*. But this is a loose end that must be allowed to dangle, for Hegel had not yet brought his views on the nature of labor and intersubjectivity into coherence and unity, or so Habermas contends.[37]

Summary

Hegel's discussion of mastery and servitude revolves around the essential correlation between inner relations (self in relation to itself) and external relations (self in relation to other).[38] The general eidetic principle, that what is done to the other is also, perhaps unintentionally, done to oneself and vice-versa, is evident in both cases. This underlying correlativity supports the reversals that each undergoes. The master, starting out as pure being-for-self (*Fürsichsein*), reduces the slave to a mere object, only to be dehumanized by the inessential recognition of such an object. And the freedom from laboring won by the master, turns into a life of enjoyment and decadence. On the other hand, the slave starts out in abject fear of the master who invokes the threat of death. But the slave gradually discovers the alien power (*Fürsichsein*) of the master to be his own power. He discovers his independence in the transformations of the world wrought by his labor.

The reversals are worked out separately, and their separate occurrences do not add up to mutual recognition or reconciliation between master and slave. There is no reconciliation at this stage of Hegel's phenomenological analysis. Hegel observes that master/slave is a deficient mode of the concept of recognition, that self-destructs and falls apart from its own internal incoherence. Nevertheless, it should be carefully noted that the deficiency does not consist simply in absence of reciprocity. While Hegel characterizes master/slave as an unequal and one-sided form of recognition, it still exhibits a general correlativity, if not reciprocity. Such correlativity underlies the reversals of the *Gestalten*. Thus, we must distinguish the correlative reciprocity that supports and underlies the dialectical tropic reversals, from reciprocal recognition and reconciliation. Master/slave lacks or suppresses the latter, but not the former, for the former is ontological and constitutive.

LOVE AS A FORM OF RECOGNITION

In taking up Hegel's discussion of love, I must interrupt the analysis of the *Phenomenology*, and turn to other writings of Hegel. This may do violence to Hegel's discussions and runs the risk of distortion. Such risks will have to be run. Hegel does not discuss love explicitly in the earlier stages of the *Phenomenology*, and there are good reasons why he did not. The project of the *Phenomenology* is a history of consciousness, beginning with the simplest *Gestalten* and working to the more complex social and historical shapes of *Geist*. Hegel's concern is to show that the *Gestalten des Bewusstseins* self-destruct in the dialectic of equipollence. From the standpoint of ordinary consciousness, the *Phenomenology* is a highway of despair, although it eventually leads us to the promised land of absolute knowledge. But that is the topic and concern of its last chapters. It is evident that love does not fit the overall strategy of the *Phenomenology* because love in Hegel's view is not a one-sided Gestalt that self-destructs in the course of experience. Love is not the failure, but rather the telos, the explicit accomplishment, of mutual recognition. Hegel makes this case later in the *Phenomenology* in the chapters on Spirit and Religion. The point I wish to make here is that it is a mistake to think that the eidetics of recognition supports only conflict and not love. That would confuse the eidetics with one of its particular instances. And it would ignore the origins of Hegel's intersubjective theory in his early discussions of love.

Hegel's most explicit discussions of love are not to be found in the *Phenomenology,* but in the earlier writings and again in the *Philosophy of Right.* Moreover, these discussions, while clearly exhibiting mutual intersubjective recognition, are not as explicit or as fully developed as his discussion of master/slave. That is why the latter has tended to grab all the attention. Yet, to overlook the discussions of love would be to miss the crucial point that Hegel's concept of love is the germ from which the concepts of recognition and *Geist* develop.

My concerns in the following section are two. First I want to show that the concept of recognition has alternative modes of realization besides master/slave. The general concept of recognition supports such, and finds more explicit realization in love than in domination and servitude. Second, I want to examine whether Hegel's formulation of love is consistent with his eidetics. Does he violate his eidetic principle that conflict is a necessary phase of recognition? Does he conceive love in monistic terms, as a unity without opposition? Does he conceive love simply as unity apart from opposition and conflict? Or, if that is impossible, does his vision of love's unity as the principle of reconciliation suppress the ontological differentiation of subjects by reducing mediation to self-mediation? I shall answer these questions in the negative.

The life and death struggle began with consciousness at the level of primitive desire. The pattern of desire is comprised internally by immediate being-for-self (*Fürsichsein*) and externally by the consumption/elimination of the independent object. Insofar as this is a human consciousness at all, it is an absolute particular, alien to, and excluding all others. It is *Eigensinn,* parochial universality, or exclusive particularity, or egoism. Such exclusive particularity is simple; to it any change could only seem a change for the worse. That is why the prospect of being outside self and before other seems catastrophic, a fall into objectivity.[39] Exclusive particularity relates to others only negatively, by excluding and/or cancelling them, or, in the case of mastery, by dominating them. However, the analysis of the *Phenomenology* shows that mastery is self-subverting and ends in failure.

In contrast, love is fundamentally different. Love renounces domination and mastery because it finds intrinsic worth in its object:

*Begreifen ist beherrschen...nur in der Liebe allein ist man eins mit dem
Objekt, es beherrscht nicht und wird nicht beherrscht.*
[To conceive is to dominate...but in love alone one is at-one with the
object, neither dominating it nor dominated by it.][40]

Love seeks a union with its other, in which domination and subordination are
out of place. Love allows the other to be, i.e., it seeks the freedom of the
other. Hegel's conception of love is influenced by Hölderlin and Herder.[41]
What is original is the complex intersubjective formulation Hegel gives to
love because he conceives it to be a determinate form of recognition: "The
beloved is not opposed to us. He/she is one with our very being (Wesen); We
see ourselves in him/her, and nevertheless she/he is not we—a miracle which
we cannot comprehend [*fassen*]."[42]

The early Hegel held that love cannot be *understood*. Hegel writes, "each
intuits itself in the other, but at the same time as something alien, and this is
love. The inconceivability of this self-recognition in other belongs therefore to
nature, not to ethical life. For the latter is the absolute equality of the two in
reference to their differences."[43] This obscure text is found in one of Hegel's
most obscure writings; nevertheless, it is significant for it implies that recognition of self in other is precisely the feature which distinguishes the human
species from pre-human, pre-cultural conditions. Recognition constitutes the
transition from nature to spirit. The transition from nature to spirit is made
concretely when "'*animalische Begierde*' becomes a human relationship."[44]
This occurs when "the woman becomes for the man something existing in her
own right, when she ceases to be [simply] an object of his sexual desire."[45]

The important transition from natural to ethical life occurs in reciprocal
recognition. At the level of nature, self-recognition in other excludes the
other; at the level of *Begierde,* the self recognizes and satisfies only itself.
But spirit and ethical life emerge only when self-recognition in other is reciprocal and the other is also recognized as a freedom requiring respect. This
occurs in the institution of marriage, which sublimates natural *Begierde* into
love, and aims at enduring ethical relationship between the marriage partners, both for themselves and for the sake of potential offspring. Marriage
and family are the elementary units of ethical life (*Sittlichkeit*). From the
standpoint of reciprocal recognition or *Geist,* the comprehension of self in
other is no longer an incomprehensible mystery. For recognition is precisely
this mutual intersubjective comprehension, of man and woman, husband and
wife, and of family members.

But how is this to be comprehended and understood? Here we come to
the systematic issue. When Hegel arrived on the philosophical scene, he
found no philosophical equipment or terminology suitable to this task. The
young Hegel believed that love cannot be understood because he conceived
understanding (*Verstand*) in Kantian terms, whose basic categories are
abstract identity and contradiction. Abstract identity excludes difference and

rules out contradiction.[46] The understanding, by imposing identity and non-contradiction as formal conditions (*Begreifen ist beherrschen*), dominates its object and reduces the other to the same, to presence. Thereby the understanding subverts itself by bringing about the opposite of what it intended: the other, reduced to the presence, or self-sameness, ceases to be other.

Hegel later drew a distinction between two senses of personality that is relevant to the development of his conception of dialectical speculative reason (*Vernunft*) as an alternative to the understanding (*Verstand*). He writes:

> Concerning personality, it is the character of the person, of the subject, to give up its isolation and [abstract] separateness. Ethical life, love, is just this: to give up its particularity, its private personality, and to expand these to universality, i.e., friendship. In friendship and in love I give up my abstract personality and thereby win it back as concrete. The truth of personality is found precisely in winning it back through this immersion, this being immersed in another.[47]

Hegel distinguishes between personality in the first person private sense—which he calls abstract personality—and personality in the concrete sense, namely, as mediated through reciprocal recognition of another, e.g., friendship and love. Abstract personality is formal, reflecting the abstract identity and self-sameness of the understanding (*Verstand*).[48] Hegel observes, "if I treat another in terms of abstract right, I consider him as identical with me."[49] But this is a merely abstract formal anonymous identity that Hegel calls a "*geistlose Gemeinwesen*," a "universal split up into the atoms of a mere aggregate of irreducible individuals"[50] in which all are interchangeable. The significance of abstract I = I is that the I excludes all others. Hegel characterizes this formal legal personality as abstract and without spirit (*geistlose*).[51] It must be contrasted with and distinguished from the concrete personality of love and friendship that is intersubjectively mediated and 'won back' through the releasement and affirmation of another.[52]

The understanding (*Verstand*), governed by abstract identity and contradiction, cannot understand the intersubjectivity of love. On the one hand, recognition signifies an ontological distance between subjects such that there is no direct access to other minds; yet, on the other hand, two human beings transcend their merely particular and private selves and form a corporate person, e.g., friendship, marriage. It is his effort to comprehend this elementary yet universal experience of mutual recognition in love that leads Hegel to develop his speculative conception of dialectical reason (*Vernunft*). Hegel describes love in terms of intersubjective recognition in the *Philosophy of Right,* that recalls his earlier statements and indicates the shift in his position away from Kant:

> Love means generally the consciousness of my unity with an other, so that I am not isolated by myself, but rather gain my self-consciousness only by

giving up my being-for-self *(Fürsichseins)* and by knowing myself in unity with the other and the other in unity with me.... The first moment in love is that I do not wish to be an isolated independent person and that, if I were, I would feel myself lacking and incomplete. The second moment is that I gain myself in and through another person, that I count for something in him/her, and he/she counts for something to me. Love is the most tremendous contradiction, which the understanding cannot solve [lösen]...[53]

What the understanding *(Verstand)* cannot conceive or resolve, speculative reason *(Vernunft)* can, because "Recognition is...the 'absolute *Begriff*' on its positive side, the concept as life, rather than death, or as intelligence rather than nature."[54]

In the above passage on love and marriage, love is described as "the most tremendous contradiction." The contradiction is not that of mutual exclusion, but rather reciprocal inclusion that nevertheless preserves differences. The contradiction of love is that self and other are united without eliminating individuality or difference, without substituting a mystical unity, or a unity of substance, for interpersonal community. "In love the separate does still remain, but as something united and no longer as something separate."[55] The other is no longer a stranger whose gaze strips away possibilities and turns the self into an object. Rather the other is, as Siep observes, "constitutive of my being and essentially similar. Therefore the moment of self-loss in and before the other becomes a finding of self in and through the other. In love the difference between being-for-self [*Fürsichsein*] and being-for-other [*Fureinanderssein*] is sublated."[56]

Love gives up exclusive self-assertion and domination. This leads to a determinate modification of the initial moment of the eidetics, or being outside of self. Self-recognition in other requires objectification by the other. But such objectification seemed to involve an initial loss of self in the life and death struggle and in the ensuing relationship of master/slave, at least for the slave. In love, there is risk, but no loss of self; rather love involves a finding of self in the recognition given by the other. Love renounces coercion and allows the other to be. Thus love is a determinate realization of the generic feature of mutual releasement, of letting the other be. In love, the objectification requisite to self-recognition in other is no longer a loss of freedom *(Fürsichsein)*, but an enhancement and increase of freedom. Each has its being *(Wesen)* through the other, which is not a loss, but a gain or increase.[57] Enrichment of the self *(Fürsichsein)* presupposes the release, letting the other be, acknowledging the other's freedom and incorporating the free recognition of the other. Thus, in love, there is no collapse of intersubjective mediation into self-mediation, much less a reduction of the other to the same.

There is an important text in Hegel's *Aesthetics* that corroborates the intersubjective interpretation of love, and which ties in with the above noted transition from nature to spirit. Hegel begins by observing that Beauty is the ideal of classical art, and that in classical art the other of spirit is the body. The body is the external natural organism which spirit is to pervade and order. The starting point is prior to the emergence of spirit from nature, in which spirit is dominated by and seeks to imitate nature. In contrast, Romantic Art acknowledges spirit and its emergence from and transcendence of nature. In Romantic Art, the ideal is love, a spiritual-personal beauty. Hegel explains that "In contrast to classical art, love means that the other of spirit is not the natural, but rather another spiritual consciousness, another subject. Through such intersubjectivity, *Geist* is realized for itself in its own most proper element."[58] Hegel contends that "The authentic nature of love consists in giving up consciousness of self, in forgetting oneself in another person, and nevertheless only in this self-surpassing and self-forgetting, to discover and to have oneself."[59] Moreover, Hegel explicitly links love with recognition (*Anerkennung*):

> This recognition is true and total when not only my personality—in abstracto or in concrete particular cases—is respected by another, but when I—as this particular individual as I was, am and will be, in my entire subjectivity, together with everything that goes with it—permeate the consciousness of another as the object of his/her desire, knowing and possession. For this other lives [is for him/herself] only in me, as I am present to myself only in him/her. Both exist for themselves in this fulfilled unity, and find their entire soul and world in their identity.[60]

This passage echoes but does not significantly add to the earlier formulations of love previously cited. It does confirm that Hegel conceives love in intersubjective terms that ill accord with the language of self-mediation. Despite Hegel's Romantic language and imagery, the unity of love affords no immediate access to other subjectivity, nor immediate access of subjectivity to itself. This is no metaphysical unity of substance, no collapse of the other into the same, of alterity into egoity, no monism. The other is not eliminated or dominated, but welcomed, accepted as member or partner in an interdependent community.

Previously, I have argued that love is a determinate instance of Hegel's eidetics of recognition, an alternative of mastery and slavery which is equally supported by the underlying eidetic structure. What this section shows however is that recognition is more nearly a generalization from and ontological formulation of Hegel's intersubjective conception of love. However, the examples of love which we have examined thus far do not show that love as a form of recognition includes conflict. Nevertheless, as Hegel understands it, love does not exclude, but presupposes conflict. Love cannot be thought apart from conflict. As the principle of unity and reconciliation, love overcomes conflict and opposition. Thus, love is inseparable from conflict, and this means that love has a tragic realization. This comes out in Hegel's discussion of Spirit at the social-historical level, and in Religion.

NOTES

1. For example, it will be shown that master/slave is a contingent instance, a determinate modification of the concept of recognition. However, it is not the only possible outcome, nor does it exhaust the *possibilities* of the concept.

2. Hegel, Foreword to H. Fr. W. Hinrichs' *Die Religion im inneren Verhältnisse zur Wissenschaft* (1822), tr. A. V. Miller, *Beyond Epistemology: New Studies in the Philosophy of Hegel,* ed. F. Weiss (The Hague: Martinus Nijhoff, 1974), 230, 234.

3. Josiah Royce, *Lectures on Modern Idealism* (New Haven, Conn.: Yale University Press, 1919, 1964), 151–153.[Emphasis mine.]

4. For criticisms of the existential anthropological reading, cf. Joseph C. Flay, *Hegel's Quest for Certainty* (Albany, N.Y.: SUNY Press, 1984); see also Klaus Hartmann, *Sartre's Ontology* (Evanston, Ill.: Northwestern University Press, 1966), 114–125. This issue, the question whether phenomenological ontology is anthropology, also surfaces in the phenomenological tradition. It was debated by Husserl and Heidegger, again by Heidegger against Sartre. The common element that keeps the issue alive is the modern turn to the subject, that subjectivity in some sense—whether transcendental egology or Dasein, or the Cogito—is a necessary critical condition and seems inescapable. The question turns on the ontological interpretation and reference of the ego. Although there has been a retreat from the claim of the primacy of subjectivity, few accept the proposals concerning the elimination of subjectivity altogether. The issues involved in Hegel's critique and decentering of subjective idealism (Kant, Jacobi, Fichte) are still with us.

5. Cf. H. S. Harris: "The clear statement regarding the logically possible outcomes of 'Krieg' in the *System der Sittlichkeit* is the only key that we need. The struggle can end in a standoff, or a victory that is not decisive..." CR 242.

6. Hegel, PhG, 143.

7. See above Chapter 6, Section II.

8. Solipsism is a theoretical conviction belied by practice. How is this anomaly to be assessed? If ordinary actions of interpersonal communication are merely subjective or invalid, then theoretical science, which presupposes and makes use of such in demonstrating and communicating its position, is also invalid, merely subjective, etc. On the other hand, if solipsism is a theoretical posture derivative from and presupposing a concrete social-intersubjective linguistic context, it appears to lack seriousness and degenerates into a mere intellectual game.

9. See above Chapter 5.

10. PhG 143.

11. Ibid. Note the uncertainty concerning the other; this is not utter skepticism in the solipsistic sense, but rather epistemological distance.

12. Ibid.

13. PhG 144.

14. PhG 144. [My emphasis.]

15. Ibid.

16. PhG 145

17. Ibid.

18. This is related to Hegel's well-known observation that *Aufheben* involves both cancellation and preservation.

19. PhG 145–146.

20. PhG 146.

21. PhG 147. This comment shows that Hegel himself distinguishes between the concept of recognition, which includes reciprocity, and master/slave as a particular contingent instance, namely unequal non-reciprocal recognition.

22. PhG 147–8.

23. Ibid.

24. Ibid.

25. Master/slave can also be read as a demonstration of the futility of conceiving intersubjective praxis in terms of a metaphysical substance/accidents scheme (e.g., Spinoza), or in terms of the ontological primacy of the ego (Descartes, Husserl, Sartre).

26. J. M. Bernstein translates and expresses this in the following way: "For recognition proper the moment is lacking, that what the lord does to the other he also does to himself [but he does not] and what the bondsman does to himself he should also do to the other [but he does not]." From "Self-Consciousness to Community: Act and Recognition in the Master-Slave Relationship," in *The State and Civil Society: Studies in Hegel's Political Philosophy,* ed. Z. A. Pelczynski (Cambridge: Cambridge University Press, 1984), 22. This proposal raises an interesting question: Can an eidetic feature be omitted? In what does the deficiency of master/slave as a form of recognition lie? does it lie in the reciprocal correlation between master and slave? or in the absence of correlation, namely the master omits doing to himself (reducing to thinghood and rendering dependent) what he does to the slave. This seems to be Bernstein's meaning. But this makes it sound as if the master or slave *should* do what they omit doing. In the case of mastery, with its objectification of the slave, this seems absurd. To say that the master does not do to himself what he does to the slave means that he seeks to reject any dependence on the slave. But Hegel's point seems to be that (*an sich* or *für uns*) eidetic reciprocity obtains whether consciously acknowledged or not, and so each winds up doing to itself what it does to the other. Thus the master cannot avoid doing to himself what he does to the slave, namely, rendering himself a dependent being. The point is that the master cannot escape relation and qualification.

27. PhG 147–148.

28. PhG 148. Kojève has no trouble in demonstrating that Hegel anticipates Heidegger's existential analysis of finitude, and that in certain respects Hegel's analysis is superior in that it situates death anxiety in a socio-ontological matrix. On the ontological level Dasein is being towards death, but it is the master which brings this ontological possibility to light and plays it against the slave.

29. See his First Introduction to the *Wissenschaftslehre*. There Fichte isolates a strange consciousness that thinks of itself as a mere thing. It is not yet conscious of its freedom, but depends on external things to give it self-identity and solidity. This deficient mode of self-consciousness has many philosophical progeny: it becomes Hegel's servile consciousness, Kierkegaard's aesthetic stage of existence, Heidegger's inauthentic existence, and Sartre's bad faith.

30. PhG 148.

31. Ibid.

32. Ibid.

33. "In this way the laboring consciousness comes to an intuition of the independent being as itself [i. e., the independent being is no longer a given, but the result of labor]." PhG 148.

34. PhG 149.

35. Jurgen Habermas, *"Arbeit und Interaktion: Bemerkungen zu Hegels Jena Philosophie des Geistes"* cited in *Frühe politische Systeme,* Hrsg. G. Göhler (Frankfurt: Ullstein, 1974), 786ff. English Translation: "Labor and Interaction: Remarks on Hegel's Jena *Philosophy of Mind,"* in *Theory and Practice,* tr. John Viertel (Boston: Beacon Press, 1974), 142–169.

36. Habermas, op. cit. 807–812; ET 162–167.

37. This may be a false antithesis, since Hegel treats labor and economic relations—at least in the modern state—as involving complex forms of recognition. On the other hand, Harris contends that even in the Jena manuscripts, including the *System der Sittlichkeit* (1801), recognition is medium of social existence, although it is not always as clearly phenomenologically displayed as it is in the *Phenomenology.* In the *Philosophie des Geistes 1803/04,* recognition is the general medium of political existence. See H. S. Harris, CR 234ff.

38. One commentator claims that mastery and servitude are modalities of a single consciousness, and consequently that independence and dependence, or master and slave, refer to consciousness in relation to itself. (George Armstrong Kelly, "Notes on Hegel's 'Lordship and Bondage'" in *Hegel: A Collection of Critical Essays,* ed. Alasdair MacIntyre (Garden City, N.Y.: Anchor Books, 1972), 191, 196.) In countering Kojève's predominantly social anthropological reading, Kelly claims that the terminology self and other, independence and dependence, master and slave can have a psychological immanent sense as well as a social sense. If consciousness

itself is both dependent and independent, there is no need to interpret master/slave intersubjectively, for self-consciousness itself is both master and slave. Kelly is not entirely incorrect in grasping the reciprocal correlations, but he is wrong in focusing on only one side of the correlation in abstraction from the other. My view is that the internal relations cannot be separated from the external. In Kelly's view, consciousness is both master (i.e., legislator of duties) and slave (subordinate to the legislated duties). Since Hegel criticizes Kant's theory as heteronomous—to wit, that each person is slave to his own self-legislated duties—it would be surprising to find Hegel himself holding such a view.

39. Cf. Sartre, *Being and Nothingness*, tr. Hazel Barnes (New York: Philosophical Library, 1956), 263.

40. Hegel, *Entwürfe über die Religion und Liebe* (1797/8), TWA 1: 242. This is obviously very close to the concluding moment in the eidetics, namely that each self lets the other be, go free, etc.

41. Siep, op. cit. 42; Henrich, *Hegel im Kontext* op. cit. 26–27. Cf. also Chapter 7 for the comments on Hegel's discovery of Eckhart's *Gelassenheit*.

42. Hegel, *Theologische Jugendschriften*, (Nohl) 377, cited in Siep. op cit. 43. For an English translation by H. S. Harris, cf. CLIO 8:2 (Winter 1979), 257–265. These issues have not disappeared. They also emerge in Levinas' account of alterity and love: "It is only by showing in what way eros differs from possession and power that I can acknowledge a communication in eros. It is neither a struggle, nor a fusion, nor a knowledge. One must recognize its exceptional place among relationships. It is a relationship with alterity...with what is never there.... Love is not a possibility, is not due to our initiative, is without reason; it invades and wounds us, and nevertheless the I survives in it." Emmanuel Levinas, *Time and the Other*, tr. R. Cohen (Pittsburgh: Duquesne University Press, 1987), 88.

43. Hegel, *System der Sittlichkeit*, ed. Lasson (Hamburg, 1967), 17–18. [Cited by H. S. Harris in CR 233.]

44. Harris, CR 240.

45. Ibid.

46. Enz. §115 Zusatz. Hegel also observes that abstract identity can tend either towards Spinoza's monism or towards atomism which construes everything as an isolated atomic unit cut off from relation.

47. G. W. F. Hegel, *Vorlesungen Über die Philosophie der Religion, Teil 3: Die vollendete Religion*, Hrsg. Walter Jaeschke (Hamburg: Meiner Verlag, 1984), 211. [Hereafter cited as VPR III], ET: Hegel, *Lectures on the Philosophy of Religion Vol. III: The Consummate Religion*, tr. and ed. by Peter C. Hodgson (Berkeley: University of California Press, 1985), 285–286. [Hereafter cited as LPR III.]

48. Hegel, *Grundlinien der Philosophie des Rechts*, §35, TWA Sk. 7:93. This is a formal conception of equality before the law, which abstracts from existential determinacy and particularities. In the *Phenomenology* Hegel discusses this under the

Roman empire as an early example of the levelling of individual differences and the creation of mass society. Cf. PhG 342ff, "Rechtszustand," (Legal Status).

49. VPR III 211n.; LPR III 285n.

50. PhG 342; PhS 290.

51. PhG 342ff; PhS 290ff (§§477–480). This bloodless abstraction is the conception of subjectivity and identity that is naively taken up in the Cartesian Cogito, and Kant's transcendentalism with its formal *Moralität*.

52. See Wolfhart Pannenberg, "Die Bedeutung des Christentums in der Philosophie Hegels," in *Stuttgarter Hegel-Tage 1970. Hegel Studien* Beiheft 11, (Bonn: Bouvier Verlag, 1974), 193.

53. Hegel, *Grundlinien der Philosophie des Rechts*, §158 Zusatz, TWA 7: 307–308. The difference between the early and the later analyses of love is that what the understanding could not resolve or understand, the later speculative dialectical reason can.

54. H. S. Harris, CR 236.

55. Hegel, *Early Theological Writings*, tr. Knox, op cit. 305.

56. APP 59

57. Siep, op. cit. 57; cf. Hegel, *Jena Realphilosophie 1805/06*, Göhler, op. cit. 223.

58. Hegel, *Vorlesungen über die Aesthetik*, TWA 7:156. Once again we must observe that although the claim that all mediation is self-mediation might be plausible as an interpretation of classical art, for which the other of spirit is the body, this is not a plausible interpretation of what Hegel has to say about love in Romantic Art, which exhibits a social-intersubjective principle.

59. Ibid. 7:155.

60. Ibid. 7:182.

NINE

RECOGNITION AND *GEIST*

Recognition is the existential-phenomenological genesis of *Geist;* conversely, *Geist* is the result, the accomplishment, of reciprocal recognition. My thesis is that recognition is '*aufgehoben*' and therefore preserved in the concept of *Geist.* Consequently, *Geist* is essentially a holistic social-intersubjective conception. It should not be confused with a transcendental ego, because the latter, as the 'I think' that must be able to accompany and unify all my representations, is a residual individualist conception. The transcendental subject is at most a phase (*Stufe*) in the development of *Geist;* but it must not be identified with *Geist.* Rather it is an abstraction from the larger, concrete social whole. I want to sketch this transformation of philosophy which Hegel introduces in the concept of *Geist.* In many ways this initial statement, although sketchy and inchoate, remains unsurpassed in its suggestiveness.

The *Phenomenology* opens up new areas of inquiry and possibilities of philosophical reconstruction that Hegel himself may have left undeveloped in his subsequent writings. What happens to philosophical inquiry when it is acknowledged that reason is intersubjective and embedded in a social-intersubjective context? Truth is inextricably related to the interhuman sphere; it does not exist apart from interhuman recognition. It is socially shaped and conditioned. Yet this does not imply a relativistic dissolution of truth into certainties or ideology. Truth has many dimensions; it involves an original rising into presence, and judgments which articulate that presence.[1] However, judgment tends to be viewed in the context of individualism. But truth, in contrast to private certainty, requires and involves intersubjective mediation. For only in this way is certainty elevated to public truth. I am aware that such assertions create perplexity if not disorientation. Although they call for analysis and clarification, an appropriate vocabulary to discuss these issues in English does not yet exist. Hegel's migration from transcendental philosophy and idealism to the language of *Geist* remains one of the pioneering efforts in this direction.

What follows is not a full treatment, much less solution to the systematic problems in themselves, but rather an uncovering of Hegel's vision of this strange new world. The first part focuses on the social mediation and the social dimension of reason. Recognition is the gateway to the social, which in turn is a depth dimension and presupposition of rationality. The second part takes up some of the determinate historical shapes of recognition that

Hegel treats. Recognition has roots in Greek ethical life (*Sittlichkeit*), namely, tragedy. However, in the modern world shaped by Christianity, recognition comes to expression in the determinate shape of reconciliation. This is reflected in Hegel's discussion of conscience and forgiveness.

THE SOCIAL DIMENSION OF RECOGNITION

Two Levels of Recognition

Ludwig Siep distinguishes two levels (*Stufen*) of recognition: the interpersonal and the social.[2] Whereas interpersonal recognition is roughly the domain of face to face relations, social recognition, or the relation between persons and institutions can be either abstract or concrete, either impersonal-formal or personal. Hegel does not confine recognition to the "other minds problem" or descriptions of face to face situations. Instead he counts as forms of recognition such apparently diverse phenomena as contracts, laws, family and intrafamily relations; certain forms of community (the classical Greek polis, as an historical example), criminal actions and their punishment by the state, and finally, religion or divine-human relation.

The two levels are distinct yet interconnected. The second level (*Stufe*) repeats on a higher plane and in different forms and contexts, patterns of recognition exhibited on the first level. The general feature of conflict can take the form of duels, life and death struggle, on the interpersonal level, and war on the social level. Siep acknowledges that the two levels are not neatly separable. Yet to whittle *Geist* down to a first person Cogito or a third person status is to pass over the first person plural, and with it the social element so important for Hegel. The standard first person/third person categories of the philosophy of mind betray an atomized individualism that is only one phase in the development of *Geist* and a specific target of Hegel's phenomenological critique.[3] It assumes a nominalist interpretation of human reality, according to which individuals, in their atomic separateness and isolation, are primary, and the social world is a derivative aggregate.[4]

Hegel rejects such nominalist individualism:

> ...in dealing with ethical life only two standpoints are possible: either we start from the substantiality [i.e., the substantive intersubjectivity] of the ethical order, or else we proceed atomistically and build on the basis of single individuals. The latter point of view excludes *Geist* because it leads only to an externally related aggregate. However *Geist* is not something single, but rather a unity of the particular and the universal.[5]

The first person approach is inadequate for a philosophy of *Geist* since, as socially *Geistlos,* it excludes in principle the very subject matter to be investigated. Hegel's *Phenomenology* is not a first person, but rather, a social phenomenology. Subjectivity and freedom are social realities that cannot be adequately understood in terms of atomistic individualism. For example, freedom has an intersubjective structure of being at home with self in other, and has its actuality not in a disembodied cogito, but rather in community.[6]

Now for some qualifications. Hegel is not concerned to explain how the second or social level of recognition arises out of the first, as if the social were the deliberate creation of individual interactions, as if individuals were ontologically prior to the social. This view is precisely what Hegel calls into question.[7] Self-recognition in other is the distinctive feature of human consciousness. Real individuals, as far as we can know them, are already social, i.e., embedded within, and dependent on, a social matrix and context. Hegel's concern is with the *meaning* of the social, not with its genesis: "the *Phenomenology* is not concerned with specific forms and institutions of right, but with the critique of concepts of what right and justice are."[8] These concepts belong not to psychology (individual mind) but to objective *Geist*.

The concept of objective *Geist* is easy to caricature as mystical, or worse, a group mind. Such caricatures fail to comprehend its significance and importance. Nicolai Hartmann responds to these misrepresentations by offering the following clarification:

> What is "objective *Geist*"? One thinks here first of all of objectivity, which is a characteristic of all mental intentional life. All consciousness has its object, and the content of the object points to an objective world. This is not what objective *Geist* means. Such intentionality is characteristic of subjective *Geist*, for the latter is a consciousness. The objective *Geist* is not a consciousness. There is to be sure a consciousness of objective *Geist*, and every human consciousness includes such. But *Geist* itself is not this consciousness. It has another mode of being, namely an objective mode.
>
> Nevertheless objective *Geist* is far from being something hidden, mysterious or mystical, nor does it designate a particular psychological attitude. On the contrary it is something well known, an element of life in which we all stand, outside of which we have no existence, the spiritual air, as it were, in which we breathe. It is the sphere in which we are situated and nurtured by birth, education and historical influence. It is the all pervasive reality that we know in culture, customs, language, thought forms, prejudices, dominant values—all as supra-individual and nevertheless real powers, in the face of which the individual stands virtually powerless and defenseless, because his own being no less than all the others is permeated, carried along and shaped by these.[9]

Hegel's Departure from Transcendental Philosophy

Transcendental philosophy is concerned with securing the objective validity and necessity of knowledge. It secures validity by radically separating the transcendental from the empirical subject.[10] The relation between the transcendental and the empirical must be asymmetrical. As the condition of possible objects of experience, the transcendental subject is not itself a mundane object. It must be distinguished from these, be complete a priori, and related non-reciprocally to experience. This requirement raises problems. The ground, or transcendental constituting stratum, must be non-reciprocally related to the consequent, or constituted stratum. If the transcendental were identified with the empirical, it would lose its foundational a priori status. For example, there is an asymmetry in the fact that, while time is "in" the transcendental subject, the latter itself is not "in time." This implies that the transcendental subject, its categories and rules, must be a-historical. As an a priori condition of objects, the transcendental must always be subject and never object. Otherwise it could not serve as foundation or condition of the empirical, but would itself require a foundation or ground.

Hegel seeks to overcome such an abstract separation between the transcendental and empirical subjects. This requires breaking up the rigid distinction between transcendental subject on the one hand, and objectivity on the other. Ground and consequent stand in relation of dialectical reciprocity.[11] This means that, contrary to the attempt to secure conditions of knowledge a priori through the transcendental turn, "there is nowhere a firm footing to be found: everything bears an aspect of relativity."[12] There is no reason why *Geist* should not be at once subject and object. *Geist* signifies a post-transcendental move to the social and historical. The issue is not, who is the transcendental subject? Hegel does not try to answer this question, but rather demolishes the presuppositions that give rise to it.[13] He pluralizes and historicizes the asymmetrical transcendental subject. The latter turns out to be an abstraction from *Geist*.

The Social Context and Mediation of Reason

I begin with an apparent ambiguity in Hegel's discussion of reason in the *Phenomenology*.[14] Hegel discusses idealism's thesis that reason is certain of being all reality, or more simply, that self-consciousness and being coincide. This sounds like transcendental philosophy with a vengeance. But Hegel also asserts that reason and truth are socially mediated, and that the fundamental stratum and embodiment of reason and rationality is not the cogito, but a social spirit (*Geist*) that finds expression in the life of a people. This tension is at least partially mitigated by noting that Hegel is both a representative and a critic of idealism. It is his criticism of idealism that points towards the necessity of a social dimension and mediation of reason.

Idealism initially appears on the scene like all other *Gestalten*, namely, as an immediate certainty.[15] However, idealism's thesis—that reason is certain of being the whole of reality—expressed as an immediate certainty, not only appears incredible, it is indefensible in this immediate form. Idealism, qua immediate, succumbs to equipollence objections. For this reason the validity and plausibility of idealism's thesis do not reside in the immediate claim by itself. That claim is a mere assurance which passes over the labor of thought, i.e, *mediations,* from which the claim emerged. Its plausibility and justification are to be found in that passed over and forgotten path which alone makes intelligible the claim that actuality is not other than reason.[16]

> The idealism that does not exhibit that path, but begins with this assertion [of being the certainty of all reality] is therefore itself a pure assurance [*Versicherung*] which does not comprehend itself, nor can it make itself comprehensible to others. It expresses an immediate certainty, which is confronted with other immediate certainties, which have however been lost on that same path. With equal right the assurances of these other certainties stand next to the assurance of that certainty. Reason appeals to the self-consciousness of every other consciousness: I am I, my object and my being is I; and no one will deny reason this truth. However, in grounding itself on this appeal to immediate certainty, reason sanctions the truth of the other certainty, namely when each says "It is otherwise for me; something other than my ego is my object and being..."[17]

The initial statement of idealism is defective because it is immediate and one-sided. "Only a poor one-sided idealism allows the unity of a category to appear as mere consciousness on the one side, in opposition to a [transcendent] 'in itself'."[18] Such idealism has a transcendent other that stands over and against it. This idealism has to acknowledge other views, and when it does so, it succumbs to equipollence objections, i.e., to skepticism.

In his *Phenomenology,* Hegel undertakes to answer these objections. His strategy is to subject every position, including idealism, to the test of equipollence objections. This test is not and cannot be met or passed at a single blow, or with a few deft maneuvers on the theme of doubt as Cartesian transcendentalism tries to do. Rather, equipollence must be faced step by step, by traversing every Gestalt in the history of consciousness. To those who charge that Hegel fails to do justice to otherness, it must be pointed out that Hegel imposes the equipollence demand that critical philosophy confront *every* other and thus demonstrate that its thesis is not just another barren assurance. The goal is to show that the other, which the equipollence objection raises, is not other, and thereby to demonstrate that there is no alternative to reason.[19]

> The fact that self-consciousness has emerged as reason transforms its previously negative relation to otherness (*Anderssein*) into a positive one. Up until now self-consciousness had been concerned only with its own independence and freedom, concerned to save and preserve itself at the expense of the world, or of its own actuality. Both of these appeared to it to be the opposite of its being. But as reason assured of itself, it is at peace with them and can

endure them; for it is certain that it is itself this reality, or that all actuality is not other than it.... It is as if it had experienced the world for the first time.[20]

Reason develops and moves beyond the solipsistic transcendental level of the understanding (*Verstand*) to the social level. It comprehends the world as a public world there for everyone, and so experiences the world for the first time.

Specifically, the transition to reason, or rational self-consciousness, represents the attainment of a universal self-consciousness. This universal self-consciousness is the result of reciprocal mediation with the world (on its theoretical side) and reciprocal intersubjective mediations (on its practical side). That is, the universal rational self-consciousness is both subject and object, the result of reciprocal mediation. The equipollence dialectic transforms "idealism" from an implausible one-sided immediate assertion into dialectical social holism. Hegel expresses the thesis of such holism succinctly: Reason has no opposite; rather reason is its own opposite: "Every...proposition of Reason permits resolution into two strictly contradictory assertions.... Thus the principle of skepticism [against every argument there is an equal one on the other side] comes on the scene at its full strength."[21] Since opposition is the very principle of speculative reason, then equipollence objections do not apply. As Hegel later put it, the truth is the whole. But since the whole embraces and includes all opposition, it has no opposite.[22]

Reason is a dialectical unity of opposites. It cannot be conceived in terms of abstract identity that excludes difference. Rather, the speculative identity of reason is an identity that requires difference and mediation. The structure of reason, in the light of equipollence, is determined as *self-recognition in other:* "This *category*, or *the unity of self-consciousness and being,* already implicitly includes the difference. For its nature is to be equivalent to itself in otherness or in absolute difference to remain the same."[23] Self-recognition in other is the universal, relational structure that pervades all aspects of reason in its concrete actuality. This structure signals a transformation in the relation of reason to the world (as is evident from the passage above) and to its other. The world is no longer alien, but is not other than reason, or better, reason is already present in the world prior to and independent of human subjectivity.

Practically, this implies that the relational aspect and dimension of intersubjectivity is not contingent, but rather part of the structure of rationality itself. In other words, instead of the abstract, immediate 'I am I' of idealism, Hegel advances the claims of recognition, that the 'I' exists concretely as self-recognition in other.[24] Instead of a purely formal opposition between ego and non-ego, Hegel advances the concept of the doubling of consciousness and the mutual self- recognition in other. Röttges observes that this means freedom is intersubjective, social: "I am free only if I am at home with myself with the other in the determinacy of my will."[25]

Social mediation is required in order for reason to elevate its certainty to universal truth. We have already seen that consciousness starts out as an exclusive particular (*Begierde*) with presumptions of universality. As such, it can bring to expression its own private certainty, but not truth. Truth requires reflection from an opposite standpoint, which is another certainty. Master and slave are each the truth of the other. But this relationship rests upon a one-sided, coerced, phony recognition and so self-destructs. In our consideration of love, we found that according to Hegel, human consciousness is transformed from exclusive particularity (the I) to inclusive universality (We) through reciprocal recognition. Thus, recognition is necessary for reason to acquire genuine universality. Reason must undergo reciprocal intersubjective mediation, and apart from such, it remains abstractly universal. Consider the following passage:

> What the general stations of this (viz., Reason's) actualization will be apparent from a comparison with the patterns previously exhibited. Just as reason, in the role of observer, repeated, in the element of the category, the movement of *consciousness,* namely sense-certainty, perception and understanding, so will reason also run through the *doubled movement of self consciousness,* and pass over from independence into its freedom. *First of all this active reason is conscious of itself merely as an individual, and as such must both demand and bring forth its actuality in an other.* In this way its consciousness is elevated to universality. It becomes universal reason, and is conscious of itself as a reason *recognized* in and for itself, and which, in its pure consciousness unites all self-consciousness.[26]

Without intersubjective mediation, reason is mere subjective assurance; it exists as an abstract particular in a solipsist mode. But the latter is only a starting point. A private certainty that claims to be true becomes true by the recognition of another. Each is the truth of the other, and only in reciprocal recognition is it possible for the common element, namely public truth or universal reason, to emerge. The goal towards which reason strives is a "self-consciousness that is recognized, that has its certainty in another free self-consciousness and possesses its truth precisely in that other..."[27]

In Hegel's view, reason is fundamentally social. "It is in the life of a people that self-conscious reason—of beholding in the independence of the other, my complete unity with him, or having for my object the free thinghood of the other which confronts me and is the negative of my self as being-for-myself—that the concept (*Begriff*) of reason has its actualization and complete reality."[28] Reason's epistemological claims to universality and objectivity, i.e., its certainty of being all reality, are rooted in and inextricably bound up with an intersubjective and social universality. Intersubjective mediation is crucial to the idealist claim that reason is objective in the world: "In the universal *Geist* therefore, each has only the certainty of himself, of finding in the actual world nothing other than himself. He is as certain of the others as he is of himself.—I recognize in all of them that they are for themselves only these independent beings, just as I am. I recognize in them the free unity with others so that, just as that free unity with other exists through me, it exists through the others as well, they as me, and me as they.... There is nothing that would not be recipro-cal.... In a free people therefore the truth of reason is realized."[29] This belies the conventional view that idealism excludes intersubjectivity. On the con-trary. The truth of idealism requires and reflects social mediation.

The dependence of the epistemological subject—including its transcen-dental versions—on intersubjective mediation, and its inclusion (*aufheben*) in *Geist* is briefly summarized at the opening of chapter 6. "*Geist* is thus the enduring self-sustaining real being. All previous *Gestalten* of consciousness are abstractions from, and abstract forms of, *Geist*. It is *Geist* that has ana-lyzed and distinguished its moments, and tarries at each individual element in turn. The discriminating and isolating of these moments [viz., sense-cer-tainty, perception, consciousness, self-consciousness, unhappy conscious-ness] presupposes *Geist* itself and requires *Geist* for its subsistence; in other words, this isolation of *Gestalten* goes on only within *Geist, which* is the concrete existence. Taken in isolation, each appears to stand on its own. But their advance and return into their ground and being, shows that they are only moments or vanishing quantities, and their essence is shown to be pre-cisely this movement and resolution of these moments."[30]

Hegel's claim that reason is socially mediated and actualized has an important qualification: "Reason is realized in truth in a *free* people."[31] Hegel distinguishes between two different sorts of community: The first is community as conceived by reflection (*Verstand*), namely as an aggregate of atomic individuals capable of existing in isolation. Social unity must be coerced or compelled. This sort of community is a heteronomous limitation of freedom. Hegel finds this view represented in Fichte's *Naturrecht:*

> Freedom is the characteristic mark of rationality; it is that which in itself suspends all limitation.... In a community with others, however, freedom must be surrendered in order to make possible the freedom of all rational beings living in community. Conversely community is a condition of free-dom. So freedom must suspend itself in order to be free. Freedom here is something merely negative, namely absolute indeterminateness...freedom [is] regarded from the standpoint of reflection.[32]

What troubles Hegel is Fichte's conception of community as merely a limita-tion of freedom and rationality: "If the community of rational beings were essentially a limitation of true freedom, community (*Gemeinschaft*) would be in and for itself the supreme form of tyranny. But only indeterminate free-dom...is limited by community..."[33] Hegel rejects the view of community as limit: "...the community of a person with others must not be regarded as a lim-itation of the true freedom of the individual, but essentially as its enlargement. Highest community is highest freedom, both in terms of power and of its exer-cise. But it is precisely in this highest community that freedom as an [indeter-minate] ideal factor, and reason as opposed to nature, disappear completely."[34]

Truth and rationality thus depend upon a positive community of freedom, or free communicative praxis. This is the community of freedom or spirit.[35] Hegel describes the community of freedom impressionistically as follows: "...to suspend this endless determination and domination in the true infinity of a beautiful community where laws are made superfluous by customs, the excesses of an unsatisfied life by hallowed joys, and the crimes of oppressed forces by the possibility of activities directed towards great endeavors."[36] Reason as a social infinite involves a unity in which individuality is not suppressed or eliminated, but elevated to a higher cause (*die Sache Selbst*), that of freedom and truth.

The *Sache Selbst* is perhaps best translated, following Royce, as a social cause that is an end in itself, an absorbing life-task greater than any individual and commanding the loyalty, devotion and efforts of individuals who serve it. It is a social doing of all individuals who cooperate as one. The cause is "the doing of all and each, a being that is the common spiritual being of all. Consciousness experiences that no one of the moments is subject, but rather that each is dissolved into the universal cause."[37] Royce comments, "Here then are the conditions of an ideal society. Here subject and object are...on equal terms. We who pursue a common calling exist as servants of our *Sache;* and this cause...exists by virtue of our choice, our work.... Our cause is indeed objective; we serve it; we sacrifice for it; but it is its own excuse for being."[38] But is there such a cause? Or is this too a *Gestalt* which self-destructs? Hegel emphasizes the self-deception and self-destructive aspects in his discussion of *das geistige Tierreich.* However, Royce observes that this is due to the overall plan of the *Phenomenology* as skepticism. But this is not the end of the matter as far as Hegel is concerned. Royce continues: "Suppose that there is indeed a task which is not arbitrarily selected by me as my task, and then hypocritically treated as if it were the universal task which I impersonally serve. Suppose that the genuine task is one forced upon us by our common nature and social needs. This then will be *die Sache Selbst,* our work, our life.... Is there such a task, such a *Sache?* Hegel replies in effect, 'Yes, the consciousness of a free people, of a *Volk.*... Here...in the consciousness of a free people we have no longer crude self-consciousness, no longer lonely seeking of impossible ideals, and no longer the centering of the world about the demands of any one individual. In the consciousness of a free people each individual self is in unity with the spirit of the entire community.' And here the world of *Geist* begins."[39]

Spirit and the World

Geist is no longer a subjectivity in contrast with or in opposition to objectivity; rather it is the form of a world. "Reason has therefore now a general interest in the world, because it is certain of having presence in the world, or that the present is rational. Reason seeks its other, because it knows that therein it possesses nothing besides itself; it seeks only its own infinity."[40] *Geist,* as the structure of the world, is at once subjective and objective, the concrete realization of reason's claim to presence in the world. As the form (Gestalt) of the world, *Geist* is both ethical substance and ethical subjectivity.[41] It is an ontological concept of community as a social unity that is both result and 'cause' of individuals.[42] For Hegel, community is a distinct level of being that cannot be treated within a dyadic oppositional subject-object scheme such as transcendental philosophy. Hegel seeks to eliminate the subjectivism haunting Kant's and Fichte's transcendental idealism as subjective idealism, and to overcome the domination and mastery over the world in the transcendental conception of reason.[43] If reason itself is not in the world, but imposed on it by transcendental subjectivity, then without human subjectivity, the world would have no intelligible structure and goodness. Hegel rejects such one-sided transcendentalism.[44] *Geist* is not a *Gestalt* of consciousness, but the *Gestalt* of the world: "It [*Geist*] is the soul of the individual consciousness, to which it is contrasted, or rather which it opposes to itself as an objective actual world, a world which has completely lost the significance of something alien to consciousness, just as the self has completely lost the significance of a being-for-self [*Fürsichsein*] separated from the world."[45] The "subjective structures" of *Geist* are "in-the-world" structures; they are real spirits, actual world-historical epochs—not merely shapes of [subjective] consciousness but shapes of the world itself.[46]

Although not a philosophy of history, the *Phenomenology* takes up the manifestation of *Geist* in three historical-cultural forms of ethical life: Greek *Sittlichkeit,* alienated *Geist,* and *Geist* certain of itself. *Geist,* as the ethical life of a people,[47] is both a result, and a starting point. First, *Geist* begins historically in a state of immediacy in Greek ethical life. Second, *Geist* cancels its immediacy by plunging into diremption and alienation, including the Roman-Medieval world, as well as the struggle between faith and Enlightenment. Third, *Geist* advances to self-consciousness in intersubjective conscience, which reconciles faith and Enlightenment, and dissolves the moral view of the world in a new form of tragic vision.

RECOGNITION IN ITS TRAGIC REALIZATION

Geist has an immediate phase. Ethical substance is implicitly, but not yet actually, spirit. Ethical substance is merely the starting point, a potential to be realized through action. It is *Geist* in the form of abstract immediacy. For *Geist* must annul its immediacy. It must be realized through action wherein it becomes subject, and actualizes Spirit (*Geist*). "*Geist* must proceed to become conscious of what it is immediately, cancel the beautiful ethical life and acquire self-knowledge through a series of shapes."[48]

Hegel initially formulates the realization of ethical substance in Aristotelian terms: ethical substance *an sich* (potential) is brought to actualization (*Fürsichsein*) as the telos and work of all. Spirit translates ethical substance into ethical actuality,[49] leaving behind it the beauty of ethical life and traversing a new series of historical and cultural shapes. But there is no hint of any "disturbance" of the transition from potential to actual—at least in the initial formulations.

Upon closer examination, however, the historical actualization of *Geist* is not a success story. Hegel combines his eidetics of ethical substance (intersubjectivity) with a tragic view of its realization. *Geist* recapitulates on a higher level the pattern of conflict present in the eidetics and first levels (*Stufen*) of recognition. The ontological distance between subjects, and the concealment of the self from itself, while not itself evil or tragic, makes tragic realization virtually inevitable. Royce observes that for Hegel the realization of *Geist* is even more tragic than that of individual lives.[50] Hegel's discussion of Greek *Sittlichkeit*—the first Gestalt of *Geist*—reflects Greek tragedy. Hegel's discussion of *Antigone* illustrates the concept of recognition against the background of Greek *Sittlichkeit* and tragedy.

Tragic Recognition: Antigone

Antigone is an exemplary embodiment of Hegel's theory of tragedy. Kurt von Fritz writes:

> The splitting of the ethical into two laws, the collision of duties which results, the guilt stemming from the fact that in acting one of the two laws is made the sole rule of conduct—guilt which once action is performed is unavoidable—reconciliation through the agents' fall or limitation: all these basic features of Hegel's interpretation of tragedy are illustrated first and foremost in the *Antigone*.[51]

Antigone is also important because Hegel makes heuristic use of the concept of recognition in his interpretation and translation. This suggests that Hegel was quite possibly led to the concept of recognition because of his interest in Greek tragedy.[52] There recognition corresponds to the moment of self-discovery on the part of the tragic hero/heroine, that involves a sudden reversal in the situation. Recognition is the dramatic moment in which what had been hidden is made manifest, the tragic heroine recognizes herself in otherness, and the situation turns out to be the opposite of what it was initially taken to be. This means that recognition is the lived, dramatic form of equipollence. It is the existential form of the equipollence dialectic, that shatters dogmatic certitude and its parochial universality. I shall focus not on Hegel's theory of tragedy, or on Hegel's interpretation of *Antigone*,[53] but on the underlying concepts of Spirit and recognition.

Like consciousness, Spirit too must come to self-consciousness. Spirit begins with a state of immediacy that must be cancelled. Cancellation of immediacy requires action (*Handlung*). Action divides and separates spirit into ethical substance and ethical consciousness.[54] Ethical substance divides itself into a human and divine law.[55] The former is the law of the state, the latter the unwritten law or customs of the family. Conversely, ethical subjectivity is also divided. It is a blind immediate knowing that is ignorant of what it does—but not totally ignorant, hence a false consciousness (*ein betrogenes Wissen*).[56] Once again, immediacy is not Cartesian self-transparency, but rather, both disclosure and concealment. Thus, the human and divine law are held in false consciousness. These are historical conditions which make for a tragic realization of ethical substance. "Self-consciousness learns through its own action the contradiction of those powers into which ethical substance divided itself and their mutual destruction, as well as the contradiction between its knowledge of the ethical character of its action and what the ethical is in and for itself, and so finds its own downfall *[Untergang]*. In fact, ethical substance has through this development become actual self-consciousness, i.e., ethical substance in and for itself; but in this same development the [pre-conscious] ethical order itself has been ruined and perishes."[57] This tragic internal conflict of the classical ethical-social order is epitomized in Sophocles' play *Antigone*.

We are concerned mainly with Hegel's social ontology, and only secondarily with the play *Antigone*, or Hegel's understanding and interpretation of it. The tragic conflict occurs between essential elements of ethical substance, namely, the government of the state, which promulgates and enforces explicit human laws, and the natural-ethical institution of the family which follows the unwritten divine law—expressing an ethical bond among family members, living and dead. Although these two realms are really one in the unity of Greek ethical life, they constitute relatively independent and separate modes of *Geist*, each obeying a logic of its own. This creates the objective conditions of conflict. Although the state depends on and respects the family as an institution, it is also the power which seeks to animate and unify the whole. As such, it seeks to counteract factionalism and tendencies towards individualism; lest the communal spirit atrophy and evaporate, the government shakes matters up by resorting to war as a means of restoring unity. In so doing, the state, like the master in the life and death struggle, invokes and imposes death, or the fear of death—the absolute master—on members of the community, i.e., upon individuals and their families. Although this works hardship on families, the state is concerned not with the individual as such but only with the preservation of the whole. The intimate "blood relation" between family members is not part of the concept of a citizen.[58] Hence, the state treats individuals as means to the preservation of the whole; the individual, insofar as he is more than a citizen, i.e., as belonging to a family, is only an unreal featureless shadow.[59]

In contrast, the family of blood relatives is concerned with the individual, not in the role of citizen, but as a family member. Relatives have duties towards family members, and these duties constitute the content of the unwritten divine law. Hegel presents an elaborate analysis of the family and divine law, as well as of family relations as determinate modes of recognition. We have previously examined marriage and family as determinate forms of intersubjective recognition. Love seeks an enduring relationship, which finds expression in marriage. Hegel analyzes marriage as a corporate personality, an ethical intersubjectivity; the relation of husband and wife is the first form of reciprocal recognition. But marriage aims at an enduring relation which includes offspring. Thus, marriage tends naturally to become a larger family. This leads to a second form of recognition, namely, between parents and children. Their child is the other in which husband and wife behold and recognize their love, the "return into self" or objective reality of their recognition.[60]

However, the family as an ethical intersubjectivity is not exhausted in the marriage relation between husband and wife, or the recognition between parents and children. There is a third form of recognition that exhibits the eidetic structure in its purity. That is, the purest form of recognition, free from the emotions and passions that pervade relations of marriage partners and of children to parents, Hegel finds in the brother/sister relation: "They are the same blood which has, however, in them, reached a state of rest and equilibrium. Therefore, they do not desire one another, nor have they given to or received from one another this independent being-for-self; on the contrary they are free individualities with respect to each other."[61] The recognition which sister obtains from brother and vice versa is not bound up with any particular desire; it seeks no advantage or exploitation. Such considerations are irrelevant and out of place. The reciprocal recognition between brother and sister is a unique exemplification of the eidetic structure of mutual releasement and allowing of the other to be. This form of recognition is not tragic, or torn by conflict. Hegel observes that within this relationship, "the individual self, recognizing and recognized, can here assert its right because it is connected with the equality of blood and relation, and is devoid of desire [Begierde]. Consequently, the loss of the brother is irreplaceable to the sister, and her duty towards him is the highest."[62] This duty, grounded in the mutual recognition constitutive of the ethical unity of the family, makes Antigone the avenger, the Erinys of her dead brother and brings her into conflict with state power.

Hegel analyzes the conflict between family and state power, represented by Antigone and Creon respectively, as a case of tragic recognition. Each character has a false consciousness, a one-sided grasp of the whole which leads him/her to identify entirely with his/her particular social role and its duties while denying validity to the claims of the other. Both of these are, within their respective limits, justified and right. However, they are limited and partial, and for this reason they cannot and do not recognize the other, much less its legitimacy:

> The ethical consciousness, because it is decisively for one of these two powers [namely family-divine law or state-human law], is essentially character. It does not accept that both [unwritten divine law and written human law] are fundamentally the same. For this reason the opposition between them appears as an unfortunate collision of duty with a reality that has no ethical claims of its own.... Since it sees right only on one side and wrong on the other, that consciousness which belongs to the divine law sees in the other side only capricious human violence, while that which holds to the human law sees in the other only the self-will and disobedience of private being-for-self *[Fürsichsein]*. For the commands of government have a universal public meaning open to the light of day; the other [unwritten] law is locked up in the darkness of the nether regions, and in its outer existence appears only as the will of an isolated individual, which, as contradicting the first, is an outrage.[63]

Creon regards Antigone as arbitrarily and capriciously violating the rules he has established. Antigone sees Creon as treating the state as subject to his merely private whim. Each fails to recognize the other as a legitimate aspect of ethical life and order (*Sittlichkeit*). Each is in false consciousness.

In Hegel's view, the classical world had a deficient conception of subjectivity and freedom. This deficiency finds expression in the provincial consciousness of Antigone and Creon, and underlies their immediate identification with their respective social roles. Hegel terms such limited subjectivity "character." In it, freedom is not yet explicit, but subordinate to, and a function of, social role. Given such provincial false consciousness, there is no emergent middle, and each is unable to find self-recognition in the other. Thus, the social order comes into tragic conflict with itself.

Antigone's tragic suffering prompts her to say *"pathontes an suggnoimen harmartekotes,"* which Hegel translates: *"weil wir leiden, anerkennen wir, dass wir gefehlt"* ("Because we suffer, we recognize that we have erred.")[64] His rendition suggests that Hegel finds the origin of the concept of recognition in Greek tragedy. Recognition here involves tragic pathos in that there is no emergent middle. Suffering is a symptom of something hidden, concealed; suffering reveals estrangement, which is constitutive of tragic recognition. This form of recognition is tragic in that discovery occurs too late, after the deed, which is, in retrospect, trespass. Tragic self-recognition in other is accompanied by the demise of the self. The limited discovery or self-recognition in other leads to an acknowledgement of fault, sufficient to constitute tragic guilt, but not sufficient to overcome the conflict within the ethical realm or between the characters.[65] Each recognizes itself belatedly as part of a larger whole, to which the other also legitimately belongs. The mutual personal tragedies of Antigone and Creon anticipate the larger social-political tragedy of the downfall of Greek *Sittlichkeit*.

Tragedy in Estranged Spirit

A similar pattern emerges in the discussion of the next two historical-cultural worlds of *Geist*.[66] Greek *Sittlichkeit* divided itself into the contrasting world-structures of the unwritten divine law of the family, and the written law of the state. So, too, in the next section, alienated *Geist* divides into the opposition between this world and the beyond, or immanence and transcendence, the realms of culture and faith respectively. Each realm is opposed to the other, alien realm.[67] The realm of culture grasps everything as relative to the self and denies intrinsic worth to the world. Everything mundane—including the self—faces reduction to a merely instrumental value or its utility relative to the self. In contrast, the realm of faith is flight from the here and now into a beyond of absolute being,[68] where the self is relative to true, self-sufficient being. Each sub-world is the inverse of the other. Similarly the self-consciousness of this *Geist* initially appears in the form of parochial false consciousness divided into knowing and not knowing. Each realm is thus opposed to and alien to the other, but in false consciousness about itself. Yet, at a deeper level, there is an underlying identity of the two realms. This raises the fundamental problem of overcoming the divisions in culture and consciousness. Hegel specifies it as the problem of *self-recognition in otherness.*

Although Hegel's eidetics has established the possibility of reciprocal recognition *in principle,* his concrete phenomenological analyses show that *Geist* does not attain self-recognition without tragedy. This becomes evident in the section on the struggle of the Enlightenment with faith. Enlightenment 'pure reason' is a false consciousness because it fails to see that Spirit both conceals as well as reveals itself.[69] Thus, Hegel shows how Enlightenment rationality becomes irrationality, and how, in attacking faith in absolute being, it is at the same time attacking its own concealed faith in rationality. "It entangles itself in this contradiction through engaging in dispute, and imagines that what it is attacking is something other than itself. It only *imagines* this, for its essence as absolute negativity implies that it contains that otherness within itself.... Consequently, what pure insight pronounces to be its other, what it asserts to be an error or lie, can be nothing else but its own self; it can condemn only what it is itself.... When therefore reason speaks of something other than itself, it speaks in fact only of itself; so doing, it does not go outside of itself."[70]

Enlightenment rationality does not recognize itself in faith, its other—and declares faith to be in error. It says that what for faith is the absolute being, is merely "a creation of consciousness itself. However, what Enlightenment declares to be an error and a fiction—namely a creation of consciousness—is the very same thing as Enlightenment itself is."[71] This reflects the eidetic correlation and principle, that what is done to the other is, at the same time, done to oneself. On the other hand, faith cannot deny to Enlightenment rationality the right of subjectivity and individual interpretation, for this is also what faith is. Hence, between faith and Enlightenment there is a tragic failure of recognition: faith turns out to be dissatisfied Enlightenment, while its opposite is complacent, satisfied Enlightenment. The impasse between Enlightenment and Faith dissolves into the French Revolution and the ensuing terror. Such cultural collapse shows that pure reason, pure freedom, etc., can find direct expression only in negation and destruction. The result is a return to the chaotic conflict of the life and death struggle.

Is then recognition for Hegel necessarily tragic loss and suffering? Is reciprocal recognition concretely possible at all? The patterns of conflict, domination, and even death, are repeated and transformed on higher levels of *Geist*'s development. These patterns appear to dominate the exposition of the *Phenomenology* to such an extent that a recent study claims "It is not only that the *actuality* of reciprocal recognition is missing from Hegel's world; its *possibility* is missing from his argument."[72] But this interpretation is wrong in denying even the *possibility* of reciprocal recognition. According to Hegel's eidetics, reciprocal recognition is at least possible in principle. Moreover, his treatment of the family, especially the brother/sister relation, as well as forgiveness, demonstrates the actuality of reciprocal recognition. On the other hand, Hegel believes that the actualization of recognition and *Geist* at the world-historical level is primarily tragic—a point that should not be forgotten, especially in view of Sartre's charge of ontological optimism.

BEYOND TRAGEDY: CONSCIENCE AND FORGIVENESS

The world-historical failure of recognition between Enlightenment and Faith results from a one-sided dogmatic absolutizing of being-for-self (e.g., Enlightenment) and a dogmatic absolutizing of being-for-other (e.g., Faith). Such dogmatism leads each to exclude its opposite. Hegel criticizes both the abstract atomic individualism and humanism of the Enlightenment (viz., abstract being-for-self) and the abstract theology of faith (viz., abstract being-for-other). His third alternative is conscience (*das Gewissen*). Conscience is introduced in Hegel's critique of Kantian morality.

There is an antinomy within the moral view of the world as set forth by Kant and Fichte. On the one hand, virtue must be possible, and so moral perfection must be possible. On the other hand, a perfect moral agent would be holy and no longer subject to the moral law; so morality depends on the non-actualization of virtue, on the gap between ought and is. If the gap between 'ought' and 'is' were finally closed through moral action and excellence, morality would be abolished in its very realization! Moral action would be the elimination of moral action. Sensing the paradox but unable to resolve it, Kant postulates God as the guarantor standing above moral struggle, and Fichte falls back on infinite moral striving itself. Hegel regards both as subterfuges that conceal rather than resolve the antinomy.

Conscience cancels and suspends the opposing principles, not at the conceptual level but at the level of action. Whether or not Hegel successfully replies to Kant, he introduces the intersubjective structure of conscience as a form of recognition. In noting that the self, qua consciousness, is constituted by the contrast between being-for-self and being-for-other, Hegel retrieves the fundamental concept of conscience as *con-scientia,* i.e., knowing-with. "Conscience is the common element of the two self-consciousnesses, and this element is the substance in which action has an enduring reality, namely the moment of being recognized by others. The moral self-consciousness lacks the concrete totality of recognition by others. For this reason, the moral consciousness does not act, and is not concretely actual."[73] Conscience is the emergent middle that was lacking or delayed in tragic recognition. Thus, *conscience is the intersubjective completion of morality in reciprocal recognition. Conscience, as the universal consciousness common to two (or more) self-consciousnesses, is constituted through mutual recognition.*

Conscience is the "Sache Selbst" or social cause become explicit.[74] In the reciprocity constitutive of universal consciousness or the We, mutually exclusive being-for-self and being-for-other undergo mediation and qualification: "Conscience, when it proceeds to action, enters into relation with the many aspects of the case.... Conscience knows that it has to choose between them, and to make a decision; *for none of them...is absolute.... Conscience does not recognize the absoluteness of any content, since it is the absolute negativity of everything determinate.*"[75] The meaning of duty shifts from the abstract formal universality of *Moralität* to active participation in a social cause, i.e., duty becomes a function of social station. In the social mediation between universal and particular, "...this distinction between universal consciousness and the individual self is just what has been superseded, and the supersession, as such, is conscience. The self's immediate knowing that is certain of itself is law and duty...all that is required is that it should know this and state its conviction. The declaration of this assurance rids the form of particularity.... In calling itself conscience, it calls itself pure knowledge of itself...i.e., it calls itself a universal knowing and willing which recognizes and acknowledges others...and for that reason is also recognized and acknowledged by them."[76]

But this is only a solution *in principle* to the antinomy of morality. Conscience develops an opposition between the beautiful soul and the active consciousness which, because it acts, compromises the purity of its principles. Each takes up a different attitude towards the pure universal constitutive of conscience. The acting consciousness, by virtue of its action, has to make compromises that taint the universal with particularity. Such particularity and determinacy are viewed by the ethical purist as corruptions. On the other hand, the ethical purist preserves his moral purity by abstaining from action, for action is the source of impure determinacy. He becomes the beautiful soul too fine to act or commit himself to anything, fleeing actuality and expressing himself in fine sentiments. But talk without deeds is meaningless. In seeking to preserve its moral purity by abstaining from action, the beautiful soul either vanishes or degenerates into moral hypocrisy when it condemns the actor as impure.

In contrast, the person of action makes compromises that are, of necessity, impure.[77] For action is always particular, and so actions fall short of and are measured by their corresponding universal. However, by confessing its compromises as impure, the active consciousness seeks recognition, i.e., a vision of itself in the other. The acting consciousness, in confessing the necessary imperfections of its compromises, shows that it recognizes the ethical universal. However, the ethical purist refuses such a confession. In seeking to maintain his 'universal' moral purity, the purist, in fact, shows himself to be a stubborn particular. He is a hypocrite who wants his fine sentiments and words without deeds to be recognized as moral excellence. Moralism's hypocritical condemnation of action is a *failure of recognition*. But the inequality—moral confession of sins on the one side, and hypocritical airs of moral superiority on the other—undergoes a reversal.[78] The pentitent sees himself repulsed, but discovers that the "pure one" is in the wrong. The one who preserves his purity by abstaining from action wastes away yearning for recognition. However, in hypocritically condemning the actor for doing what the "pure one" fails to do, he shows himself to be neither pure nor universal, but a stubborn particular and so forfeits the very purity to which he clings.[79]

This failure of unequal recognition can be remedied. The wounds of the spirit can heal without leaving scars.[80] Reciprocal recognition can occur if each "gives a little." The "evil" man of action must acknowledge the impurity of his compromises, and the moralist must overcome his hard-hearted rigidity and set aside his one-sided judgement on the actor. Each can attain its self-recognition in the other only by a mutual act of forgiveness: "The word of reconciliation is the objectively existing *Geist*, which beholds the pure knowledge of itself qua universal consciousness in and through its opposite...[This is] *a reciprocal recognition which is the absolute Geist*."[81] It is difficult to overestimate the significance of the preceding passage. It contains the first explicit mention of *reciprocal* recognition and absolute *Geist* in the *Phenomenology*. Forgiveness is the determinate form which reciprocal recognition assumes, the determinate historical shape taken by the eidetic feature of mutual releasement.

Hannah Arendt makes explicit the connection between forgiveness and action.[82] Specifically, forgiving is the "remedy against the irreversibility and unpredictability of...action..."[83] Owing to such irreversibility and contingency, injury or trespass against others is a virtually inevitable accompaniment of action. Thus, action, to the extent it involves unavoidable injury to another, requires forgiveness. Forgiveness is the capability of undoing what has been done. Arendt observes, "The possible redemption from the predicament of irreversibility—of being able to undo what one has done though one did not, and could not, have known what he was doing—is the faculty of forgiving.... Without being forgiven, released from the consequences of what we have done, our capacity to act would, as it were, be confined to one single deed from which we could never recover; we would be victims of its consequences forever..."[84] Hegel also notes that the element of reversibility, of being able to undo what one has done, is central to the concept of reconciliation, and is the reason why the wounds of *Geist* can be healed without leaving scars.[85]

Arendt makes explicit the connection between forgiveness and releasement: "Only through the constant mutual *release* from what they do can men remain free agents, only by constant willingness to change their minds and start again can they be trusted with so great a power as that to begin something new. In this respect, forgiveness is the exact opposite of vengeance, which acts in the form of re-acting against an original trespassing, whereby far from putting an end to the consequences of the first misdeed, everybody remains bound to the process..."[86]

Moreover, Arendt observes that forgiveness/releasement is possible only under the conditions of intersubjective plurality. This is important in light of the claim that Hegel's discussion of forgiveness and reconciliation is not intersubjective, but monosubjectival. This claim rests on such texts as the following: "The reconciling 'Yes' in which the two 'I's renounce their exclusive and opposing existence, is the existence of the I which has been expanded into a duality, and therein remains identical with itself."[87] However, as Arendt points out—and as Hegel himself well understands throughout his discussion of forgiveness—forgiveness depends "on plurality, on the presence and acting of others, for no one can forgive himself..."[88] She distinguishes forgiveness from the Platonic conception of rulership. The latter "draws its guiding principles...from a relation established between me and myself, so that the right and wrong of relationships with others are determined by attitudes towards oneself.... The moral code, on the other hand, inferred from...forgiving...rests upon experiences which nobody could ever have with himself, which, on the contrary are entirely based on the presence of others.[89] The I which is expanded to duality in the above text signifies, not the domination of the other by incorporation within my experience and ego, but rather the spirit of community expressing itself as the power of forgiveness. Forgiveness constitutes the transition to absolute *Geist* and has theological implications.

The preceding discussion of reconciliation and forgiveness is Hegel's first mention of absolute *Geist* in the *Phenomenology*. It is significant that forgiveness is identified as a mutual recognition that *is* absolute *Geist*. Kroner writes, "Insofar as *Geist* realizes its absoluteness in an act of pardon, it becomes an appearing God and is elevated to the level of religion."[90] Reciprocal recognition implies an emergent common element; the passage suggests that either God is the event of reciprocal forgiveness, or accompanies the event of forgiveness as its basis. Forgiveness involves an affirmation of the person in spite of his deed. As Arendt points out, forgiveness overlooks or "undoes" the deed for the sake of the person. Thus, forgiveness presupposes that the person has intrinsic worth, despite his transgressions. That is why forgiveness presupposes and is grounded in love. For love values the worth of the person, and divine love is the basis of the absolute or infinite worth of the person as Hegel often points out.[91]

Hegel reiterates this identification of absolute *Geist* with reciprocal recognition in the concluding paragraph on Spirit: "The reconciling 'Yes' in which the two 'I's renounce their exclusive and opposing existence, is the existence of the I which has been expanded into a duality, and therein remains identical with itself. In its complete externalization and opposite, it possesses the certainty of itself. It is God appearing in the midst of those who know even as they are known."[92] This passage is the first explicit accomplishment and manifestation of the eidetic feature of mutual releasement. Phenomenologically, God is a mediating third, namely, the power of pardoning, forgiving, or the power of releasement and reconciliation itself that is grounded in love. Each releases the other from its vengeful counterclaim and affirms the worth of the the other in spite of the offense. Forgiveness renounces revenge and domination. Each must renounce its exclusive, vengeful claims and allow the other to be, i.e., release the other from his transgressions (in the case of acting consciousness) or hypocrisy (the pure soul).

Such releasement of the other recalls Hegel's conception of love, which is in turn the origin of his speculative conception of *Geist* and identity. In light of this "allowing the other to be" (*Gelassenheit*), let us recall some of the texts on love. These texts suggest that what is distinctive about Hegel's speculative identity is its renunciation of domination. It is not to be confused with the abstract identity of the understanding *(Verstand)* that excludes difference or that dominates the other by reducing it to the same. In the early Frankfurt fragments there is the following passage:

> *Begreifen ist beherrschen...nur in der Liebe allein ist man eins mit dem Objekt, es beherrscht nicht und wird nicht beherrscht.*
> [To conceive is to dominate...but only in love one is at-one with the object, neither dominating it nor dominated by it.][93]

In his *Early Theological Writings*, Hegel writes "In love the separate does still remain, but as something in union and no longer as something separate; life [in the subject] senses life [in the object]."[94] Love does not eliminate the other, but affirms and preserves it. Finally, a text from the *Logic:*

> The universal is therefore the free power; it is itself and overreaches its other, but not in a dominating or forceful way [*aber nicht als ein Gewaltsames*]. Rather it is quiet and at home with itself in its other. As it has been called free power, so it could also be called free love and limitless blessedness, for it is a relating to its other [*zu dem Unterschiedenen*] only as itself. In its other it has returned to itself.[95]

Love transcends the standpoint of domination, and allows the other to be free. In such absolving love, there is no reduction of the other to the same or exclusion of difference from totality, but rather solidarity with the other. Self-recognition in other presupposes and requires that the other remains distinct, even as it is no longer purely other. Love transforms identity into a holistic conception that not only preserves, but requires otherness.

These considerations show that recognition retains its religious and theological dimension in the *Phenomenology*. Reconciliation through forgiveness points beyond tragic recognition, but is no ontological optimism or metaphysical triumphalism. Hegel has incorporated too much of the tragic view into recognition for a return to optimism. In its career, *Geist* learns that defect, error, sin, contradiction are constitutive of experience. The rational self cannot be expressed without irrationality, the pure self cannot be expressed without impurity. Self recognition in other can only be realized through a continual conflict and a constant overcoming of failures.

NOTES

1. Hegel's concept of truth is complex and is by no means reducible to correspondence. Hegel rejects the correspondence theory of truth as mere technical correctness (Cf. Enz. §§24, Zusatz 172). For helpful studies of Hegel's concept of truth see Reinhold Aschenberg, "Der Wahrheitsbegriff in Hegels Phänomenologie des Geistes," in *Die ontologische Option*, Hrsg. Klaus Hartmann (Berlin: Walter de Gruyter, 1976), 215–305; see also Czeslaw Prokopczyk, *Truth and Reality in Marx and Hegel*, (Amherst, Mass.: The University of Massachusetts Press, 1980); Werner Marx, *Heidegger and The Tradition*, tr. T. Kisiel (Evanston, Ill.: Northwestern University Press, 1971).

2. Siep, APP, op. cit. 54ff.

3. Husserlian phenomenology takes a first person approach to others, from Husserl's *Ideas* through Sartre's *Being and Nothingness.* So does Buber's account of I-Thou relation. This approach runs the risk of never getting to the social level, or of

making the second level of recognition or *Geist* into a mere construct derived from the person to person, face-to-face situation. Cf. below, Chapter 12.

4. This somewhat unusual usage of the term *nominalist* comes from Klaus Hartmann, who adapts it to social philosophy. See his "Towards a New Systematic Reading of Hegel's *Philosophy of Right*" in *The State and Civil Society,* ed. Z. A. Pelczynski (Cambridge: Cambridge University Press, 1984), 114–136.

5. Hegel, *Philosophie des Rechts,* §156 Zusatz, TWA Sk 7: 305; ET *Philosophy of Right,* tr. T. M. Knox (Oxford: Clarendon Press 1952), 261.

6. Cf. Hegel, *Philosophy of Right,* §57. Hegel is after a conception of the social which recognizes individual subjectivity: "The right of the subject's particularity, his right to be satisfied, or in other words, the right of subjective freedom, is the pivot and center of the difference between antiquity and modern times. This right in its infinity is given expression in Christianity and it has become the universal effective principle of a new form of civilization. Among the primary shapes which this right assumes are love, romanticism, the quest for the eternal salvation of the individual etc., and next come moral convictions and conscience...the principle of civil society..." Ibid. §124, ET: 84.

7. Klaus Hartmann distinguishes Hegel from "Hobbes, Locke and many others, including Rousseau, who wish to explain the genetic question of how the atomic individuals in the state of nature establish a state. Hegel on the other hand is interested in what the state is, regardless of how it arose." "Towards a New Systematic Reading of Hegel's *Philosophy of Right*" op. cit. 120. "Hegel does not make the mistake of the classical (English, French, German) theory which linked the concept of the state with its genesis and so tried to picture the transition from...the state of nature, to political organization." Ibid. 127.

8. Siep, op. cit. 103.

9. N. Hartmann, op. cit. 497.

10. Some interpreters view *Geist* as equivalent to Kant's transcendental ego, or transcendental unity of apperception; cf. J. N. Findlay's Forward to *Hegel's Philosophy of Mind,* the English translation of Part III of Hegel's *Encyclopedia,* tr. W. Wallace and A. V. Miller, (Oxford: Clarendon Press, 1971); R. C. Solomon, "Hegel's Concept of Geist," in *Hegel: A Collection of Critical Essays,* ed. A. MacIntyre (New York: Doubleday Anchor, 1972).

11. Hegel, Enz. §§112–124.

12. Ibid. §123 Zusatz.

13. An indication of how murky the conceptual problems are may be gathered from Merold Westphal's *History and Truth in Hegel's Phenomenology* (op. cit). Westphal notes Hegel's move from subjectivity to intersubjectivity, from the exclusive first person cogito to the spirit or the We. However Westphal remains conceptually close to such a problematic when he repeatedly raises the question, Who is the

Transcendental Subject? (96, 136). If it is the case, as Westphal acknowledges, that a philosophy oriented towards the ego is abstract and incomplete until it becomes a philosophy of Spirit, that transcendental philosophy in the Cartesian and Kantian sense finds its own foundation beyond itself (137–138), why retain the transcendental terminology, concept and problematic when Hegel himself does not? The transcendental is but a one-sided expression of spirit, and is perpetually haunted by solipsism and subjective idealism; this is precisely Hegel's complaint against Fichte: the form of Fichte's system, as transcendental, contradicts the content and spirit of the system. Cf. Hegel, *Differenzschrift; Difference,* passim.

14. This is found in PhG, Chapters 5 and 6, 175–182, 255–261, and 313–316.

15. "Its thinking is immediately itself actuality; its relation to the actual is idealism." PhG 176.

16. PhG 177.

17. Ibid.

18. PhG 178.

19. J. N. Findlay comments: "Hegel thinks...that there is no *other* satisfactory way of viewing the world than the one just mentioned, and that every other way of looking on the world must lead us, on pain of conflict or intellectual frustration, to the view in question." Findlay, *Hegel: A Re-Examination* (New York: Collier Books, 1962), 54.

20. PhG 176. Cf. 183: "Reason has therefore now a general interest in the world, because it is certain of having presence in the world, or that the present is rational. Reason seeks its other, because it knows that therein it possesses nothing besides itself; it seeks only its own infinity." The infinity in question is a social infinite.

21. Hegel, *Skepticism,* 324–5.

22. To demonstrate this claim requires the detailed step by step traversal of the *Gestalten* that Hegel undertakes in the PhG.

23. PhG 178. [My emphasis.] This passage also shows the distinctive Hegelian meaning of the term category, namely, the unity of self-consciousness and being, or the identity of thought and being, or identity of identity and difference. These are all equivalent formulations. But the one that is distinctive phenomenologically is the first. It shows that Hegelian categories, unlike traditional categories, include subjectivity or have it built into their very meaning. That is why Hegel's thought does not, like some versions of traditional metaphysical thought, end in positivism.

24. Cf. Heinz Röttges, *Dialektik und Skeptizismus: Die Rolle des Skeptizismus für Genese, Selbstverständnis und Kritik der Dialektik* [Monographien zur philosophischen Forschung] (Athenäum: Hain Verlag, 1986). Röttges writes "In place of the Ich = Ich recognition appears as the concrete existence [*Dasein*] of self-consciousness." (155). He explains that the unity of the ego with itself, is possible only as non-identity, as doubling. This connection of non-identity with *doubling,* sug-

gests a transformation of the merely formal logical opposition inherited from Fichte, namely the opposition between ego and non-ego.

25. Ibid. It should be recalled that one of Hegel's earliest mentions of recognition occurs as a statement concerning the relation of various philosophies to each other. Hegel applies the concept of recognition to the relation between opposing views of philosophy in his opening introduction to *The Critical Journal of Philosophy* (1802), BTKH 276. Cf. also H. S. Harris' introduction, 253ff. This is to construe the history of philosophy, not as a set of warm up exercises for contemporary "great minds," but rather as a dialectical development of philosophy. Hegel rejects the view that "the preceding philosophical systems would...be nothing but practice studies for the big brains. But if the Absolute, like Reason which is its appearance, is eternally one and the same—as indeed it is—then every Reason that is directed towards itself and comes to *recognize* itself, produces a true philosophy and solves for itself the problem which, like its solution, is at all times the same. In philosophy, Reason comes to know itself, and deals only with itself so that its whole work and activity are grounded in itself, and *with respect to the inner essence of philosophy there are neither predecessors nor successors.*" (*Difference*, ET 87 [emphasis mine].) Hegel returns to this same theme in his *Encyclopedia*: "In the history of philosophy, the different stages of the logical Idea assume the shape of successive systems.... The relation too of earlier to the later systems of philosophy is much like the relation of the corresponding stages of the logical Idea: ...the earlier are preserved in the later, but subordinated.... Now although it may be admitted that every philosophy has been refuted, it must in an equal degree be maintained that no philosophy has ever been refuted, or can be refuted. The refutation of a philosophy only means that its barriers are crossed, and its special principle reduced to a factor in the more complete principle that follows. Thus, the history of philosophy, in its true meaning, deals not with a past, but with an eternal and veritable present: and, in its results, resembles not a museum of aberrations of the human intellect, but a pantheon of Godlike figures." (§86 Zusatz)

26. PhG 255–256. [Italics mine.]

27. PhG 256.

28. PhG 256–257.

29. PhG 257, 258. Miller's translation is misleading: he translates "*nichts anders in der seienden Wirklichkeit zu finden als sich selbst,*" as "finding in the actual world nothing *but* himself." The translation makes it appear as if the individual person literally finds only himself or herself in the world. Hegel's point is quite different. It is that reason in the individual finds in the world nothing *other* than or utterly alien to itself. The rationality already at work in the actual world, is not other than the rationality active and coming to explicit self-consciousness in human beings. Hegel had made this point earlier when he wrote, "[reason] is certain of itself as reality or that everything actual is nothing other than it." (PhG 176) Moreover, the world does not have to wait for human beings to confer intelligible structure upon it—which is the case in the merely anthropological reading of Kant's transcendental ego—rather it already has a rational structure. This rational structure is the element common to human beings (subjective, self-conscious rationality) and the world. This universal

rational structure becomes explicit through a highly complex social interaction with the world, namely, recognition.

30. PhG 314–315.

31. PhG 258.

32. Hegel, *Difference*, 145.

33. Ibid.

34. Ibid. Cf. Aristotle: "The man who is isolated—who is unable to share in the benefits of political association, or has no need to share because he is already self-sufficient—is not part of the polis and must therefore be either a beast or a god." *Politics* 1253a, tr. E. Barker (Oxford: Oxford University Press, 1958), 6.

35. Hegel makes such a distinction in his discussion of Fichte's *Naturrecht*. Cf. *Difference* ET 144ff.

36. Ibid. 146.

37. PhG 300.

38. Royce, *Lectures on Modern Idealism*, op cit., 197.

39. Ibid. 200.

40. PhG 183.

41. PhG 313–314. As world-Gestalt, *Geist* is clearly related to and anticipates the later phenomenological concepts of life-world (Husserl) and Being-in-the-world (Heidegger).

42. The family is an example of a social unity, viz., an immediate natural unity.

43. Kant is explicit on this point: "...reason has insight only into that which it produces after a plan of its own, and...it must not be kept, as it were, in nature's leading strings, but must itself show the way...constraining nature to give answers to questions of reason's own determining.... Reason, holding in one hand its principles, according to which alone concordant appearances can be admitted as equivalent to laws, and in the other hand the experiment which it has devised in conformity with these principles, must approach nature in order to be taught by it. It must not, however do so in the character of a pupil who listens to everything that the teacher chooses to say, but of an appointed judge who compels the witness to answer questions which he has himself formulated." *Critique of Pure Reason*, Preface to Second edition, tr. N. K. Smith (New York: St. Martin's Press, 1958), 20.

44. See his critique of the is-ought distinction in *Tugend und der Weltlauf* (PhG 274–282; PhS 228–235), and of dualism in general.

45. PhG 314; PhS 263f.

46. PhG 315; PhS 263ff. Hegel's concept of *Geist* bears at least a family resem-

blance to Heidegger's concept of being-in-the-world, and must be understood likewise as an in-the-world structure.

47. PhG 315; cf. 256, 258.

48. PhG 315.

49. PhG 313–317; PhS 263–266.

50. Royce, op. cit. 201.

51. Kurt von Fritz, *"Tragische Schuld und poetische Gerechtigkeit in der Griechischen Tragödie,"* in his *Antike und Moderne Tragödie: Neun Abhandlungen* (Berlin: Walter de Gruyter, 1962), 90–91; cited by Martin Donougho, "The Woman in White: On the Reception of Hegel's Antigone, in *OWL of Minerva,* vol. 21, no. 1 (Fall 1989): 65f.

52. See Eliot L. Jurist, "Hegel's Concept of Recognition: Its Origins, Development and Significance" (Doctoral dissertation, Columbia University, 1983). Jurist contends that an important source of Hegel's concept of recognition is Aristotle's theory of tragedy set forth in the *Poetics,* Chapter 11. It is the moment of *discovery* that sweeps away tragic ignorance or false consciousness, and the situation of the tragic hero/heroine is revealed to be the opposite of what it was initially and blindly taken to be.

53. Donougho's essay cited in the previous note is a useful survey of the complex controversy surrounding Hegel's *Antigone* interpretation.

54. PhG 317; PhS 266. This text counts against those interpretations which attempt to draw a clear and sharp distinction between *Geist* and consciousness. However consciousness here does not mean the cogito, but is rather a collective concept, the We. Mure observes that action for Hegel involves both separation and reconciliation. Cf. G. R. G Mure, op. cit.

55. Ibid. Hegel speaks of ethical substance here in pre-conscious terms; yet he also maintains that ethical substance exhibits distinctions within itself that only consciousness can make, namely, articulating itself as a world with distinct regions. The temptation to read "Spinoza" into every mention of ethical substance must be resisted. For ethical substance is itself a socially mediated result, the previous work of all that is received and requires appropriation and interpretation. It should be noted that Hegel is not yet considering absolute spirit, but only objective spirit. Absolute Spirit is bracketed in the present chapter—an essential qualification of the so-called concrete actuality of spirit which bears all previous *Gestalten* of consciousness. The concept of Absolute Spirit is taken up in the following chapter of the *Phenomenology.*

56. PhG 317; PhS 266.

57. PhG 317–318; PhS 266.

58. PhG 321; PhS 269.

59. PhG 321.

60. PhG 325; PhS 273.

61. PhG 326; PhS 274. This passage shows that recognition and love can acknowledge individuality, i.e., concrete individuals, as in Hegel's analysis of the relation between Antigone and Polynices. Wilfried Goossens notes that "Brother and sister are however the same blood in a specific manner: they remain inviolably *distinct* from one another. The text alludes to this when it makes a comparison with the man-woman relationship. This latter lacks precisely the singularity of terms necessary.... The universality which the 'I' gains in love is fatal to the singularity of the 'I': the sides of the relationship are combined within their transition into one another. In contrast, brother and sister recognize themselves in one another, but the other is immediately recognized as the other and retains its singularity. Singularity as such prevails in the brother and the sister..." "Ethical Life and Family in the *Phenomenology of Spirit*," in *Hegel On the Ethical Life, Religion and Philosophy*, ed. A. Wylleman, *Louvain Philosophical Studies 3* (Dordrecht: Kluwer Academic Publishers, 1989), 188. This counts against Kierkegaard's caricature of Hegel as unable to deal with individual existence. What is at issue is what concrete individual existence means. Instead of Kierkegaard's abstraction of "the individual," Hegel stresses the threefold mediation of individuality by the family as ethical intersubjectivity.

62. Ibid.

63. PhG 332; PhS 280.

64. PhG 336; PhS 284.

65. Donougho comments that "despite her universality of purpose (*pace* Goethe and others) [Antigone] has revealed the individualism—the particularity at the foundations of the polis.... What she uncovers is the individualism at the heart of the polis, its male chauvinism, its overemphasis on the male principle, its pretense that this is universal and natural." (Ibid. 85–86). Antigone reveals the allegedly common *Sittlichkeit* to be a Warrior ethic, which is not only in conflict with the family, but is founded on force and will perish by force.

66. Again, our focus is primarily on the concept of recognition, and not on a detailed commentary or exegesis of the *Phenomenology*.

67. PhG 347ff; PhS 294ff. This particular world-historical shape of *Geist* constructs for itself a world that is doubled, divided and opposed to itself.

68. PhG 380f; PhS 325f.

69. PhG 388;PhS 332.

70. PhG 389f; PhS 333.

71. PhG 390; PhS 334.

72. Merold Westphal, *History and Truth in Hegel's Phenomenology* (New York: Humanities Press, 1978), 226. [Italics mine.]

73. PhG 450; PhS 388.

74. Ibid.

75. Ibid. [My emphasis.] Universal norms are not simply abolished, but require interpretation, appropriation and application to situation. That is what conscience is supposed to do, not unlike Aristotle's *phronesis* and the *phronimos,* or man of practical wisdom.

76. PhG 460; PhS 397. Hegel here emphasizes the importance of language as the *Dasein des Geistes* (PhG 458; PhS 396). Unlike sense certainty and the unwritten divine law, conscience as intersubjective, can, must and does find linguistic expression. Language is the explicit medium of intersubjectivity, "the middle term, mediating between the independent and the recognized consciousnesses, and the existing self is immediately in a condition of universal recognition and acknowledgement..." (PhG 459: PhS 396)

77. PhG 463ff; PhS 400ff.

78. PhG 469; PhS 405.

79. PhG 470; PhS 407.

80. Ibid.

81. PhG 471; PhS 408. [My emphasis.]

82. Hannah Arendt, *The Human Condition,* (Chicago: University of Chicago Press, 1958), 236ff.

83. Ibid.

84. Ibid. 237.

85. Hegel: VPR II 559; LPR II 667; PhG 470; PhS 407.

86. Ibid. 240. Arendt comments on the New Testament Greek terms, and shows that the root meaning of forgive is to dismiss and release, namely, from the consequences of one's actions.

87. PhG 472; PhS 409.

88. Arendt, op. cit. 237.

89. Ibid. 238.

90. Richard Kroner, *Von Kant Bis Hegel,* vol. 2 (Tübingen: J. C. B. Mohr, 1921–24), 394.

91. Cf. the following discussion from the *Encyclopedia:* "...the Christian religion is to be regarded as the religion of consolation, and even of absolute consolation. Christianity, we know, teaches that God wishes all men to be saved. That teaching declares that subjectivity has an infinite value. And that consoling power of Christianity just lies in the fact that God himself is known in it as the absolute subjectivity, so that, inasmuch as subjectivity involves the element of particularity, our particular personality too is recognized not merely as something to be solely and simply nullified, but as at the same time something to be preserved." Hegel, *Encyclopedia,* §147 Zusatz. See also §163 Zusatz.

92. PhG 472; PhS 409.

93. Hegel, *Entwürfe über die Religion und Liebe* (1797/8), TWA 1: 242. This is obviously very close to the concluding moment in the eidetics, namely that each self lets the other be, go free etc. Note that Hegel later changed his mind about *Begreifen*, as he discovered and developed his speculative dialectical conception of the *Begriff* that is like love in not dominating but rather allowing the other to be. Recognition is an important element in Hegel's discovery.

94. TWA 1: 246; ETW 305. Fragment on Love. This text exhibits Hegel's later interpretation of *aufheben* as a technical term meaning both to cancel and to preserve. Love overcomes the alienation from the other, and this cannot be an elimination of the other, but rather is an affirmation of and solidarity with the other.

95. Hegel, *Wissenschaft der Logik*, TWA Sk. 6: 277.

TEN

ABSOLUTE SPIRIT, RECOGNITION, AND TRAGEDY

A full discussion of Hegel's philosophy of religion in light of new critical editions would require a separate monograph.[1] Instead, I intend to focus on the discussion of religion in the *Phenomenology* from the perspective of recognition, and to refer to the *Lectures on the Philosophy of Religion* as they supplement and clarify certain issues.[2] Recognition is a theme in Hegel's treatment of religion from his earliest writings. In the *Phenomenology*, self-recognition in other is treated on a continuum which begins with mutual exclusion (master/slave) and culminates in human self-recognition in God, constitutive of absolute knowledge.[3] Indeed, the concept of absolute *Geist* is first introduced as a reciprocal recognition qualified as forgiveness.

Religion cannot be properly understood in merely individualist or merely interpersonal terms. Hegel's thesis that religion is the self-consciousness of spirit must be understood as a social interpretation of religion. Josiah Royce observes, "Religion as such appears in the *Phänomenologie* as a social and not as an individual life."[4] Instead of a solitary ego cogito, religious subjectivity is intersubjectivity, and the relation to the divine is socially mediated. "Religion is for Hegel an interpretation of the world by the social self, and by the individual man only insofar as he identifies himself with the social self.... Religion as a purely private and personal experience could only consist of such forms as the unhappy consciousness has already exemplified."[5] Self-consciousness involves self-recognition in other, a finding of self in an other, a being at home with self in and through an other. Religion is the culmination of this quest for mutual recognition in a divine-human community, in which the self-consciousness of each side is mediated through the recognition of the other.

The divine-human relation is not one of direct interpersonal recognition, for God is not simply an interpersonal other. It is as social that the human being is religious. The divine human relation is socially mediated and shaped by interpersonal recognition. It is not merely private, but occurs on the inter-subjective-social level. On the other hand, the divine human relation is not merely social; theology for Hegel is not reducible to anthropology. God is more than human society. But the religious relation is not less than a social-interpersonal one. It too involves reciprocal recognition. God is no exception to the fundamental social ontology or holism that Hegel develops, but its chief exemplification. Hegel presents a philosophical interpretation of the Christian doctrine of incarnation as divine-human relation of recognition; God's absoluteness does not exclude relation, but essentially involves relation. Since God requires an other, but no other can be given to God, God is his own other. Dualism is excluded, or in theological terms, incarnation requires trinity. God thus exemplifies the fundamental structure of spirit (*Geist*) namely, self-recognition in other.[6] For this reason God is social and personal. As such, God secures the worth and validity of human freedom and personality. Phenomenologically God 'appears' as the basis and power of interpersonal forgiveness, whereby the tragic consequences of action are reversed.

But divine-human recognition does not occur without tragic conflict and suffering. We have already found that, owing to the epistemological distance between subjects, recognition involves conflict. Since recognition includes ambiguity and the possibility of false consciousness, it is open to tragic realization. As divine-human recognition, religion too displays tragic features. However, Hegel's views on tragedy appear to undergo change. In the early essay on *Natural Law,* he holds that "the absolute relation is set forth in tragedy."[7] Tragedy is superior to comedy, and tragic religion is superior to divine comedy. In the *Phenomenology* the revelatory or consummate religion appears superior to tragedy. Further, Hegel appears to depart from classical Christian orthodoxy because he interprets Christianity tragically by introducing the theme of the death of God. The latter is Hegel's christological speculation that not only involves a criticism of classical theism's conception of divine eternity and immutability, it makes explicit the suppressed Christian motif of tragic suffering in God. This chapter will seek to sort out these issues.

ANOMALIES IN HEGEL'S TREATMENT OF RELIGION IN
THE *PHENOMENOLOGY*

Hegel's speculative treatment of recognition and elements of his social theory originated in his early theological writings. It is not surprising to find recognition and the themes of love and reconciliation in Hegel's mature treatment of religion. However, Hegel's treatment of religion in the *Phenomenology* is elusive. In the introduction, he almost casually lets slip the remark that the absolute is already present (*das absolute ist schon bei uns*). Hegel seeks to justify the assumption that the absolute is present, while conceiving that presence as tragic.[8] The tragic motif is implicit throughout the *Phenomenology* as self-accomplishing skepticism, namely, the "destruction" (through equipollence) of all alternate claims to truth, and shows that there is no alternative to the whole, the emergent absolute. The tragic motif is explicit in the sections on unhappy consciousness, Antigone, the struggle between Enlightenment and Faith, and the death of God.

In the preliminary discussions of religion, Hegel brackets religion as such and treats only a limited aspect or dimension of it,[9] namely its individualistic expression in the unhappy consciousness. This procedure resembles the phenomenological method (*epoché*).[10] But the individualistic unhappy consciousness is not the whole story, because the individual per se is an abstraction from a larger concrete whole. Hence, to focus only on religion in the individual amounts to an abstract treatment of religion. Hegel underscores this abstraction when he comments on the unhappy consciousness as an immediate shape of reason: "The immediate existence of reason and its distinctive shapes...have no religion, because self-consciousness knows or seeks itself only in the immediate present."[11] Hegel does not remove the brackets until the chapter on religion.

There Hegel recalls the previous limited and abstract discussions of religion:

> In the previous *Gestalten* (which are distinguished in general as consciousness, self-consciousness, reason and Spirit), religion, as the consciousness of the absolute being, has been a topic under consideration. But religion has been considered only from the standpoint of the consciousness of the absolute being. However, the absolute being in and for itself, the self-consciousness of Spirit, has not appeared in those previous forms.[12]

Hegel's procedure involves a method of bracketing, an abstraction analogous to that practiced in the eidetics. The above passage refers to the fact that the self-consciousness of spirit, i.e., its development from substance to subject, has been bracketed. The result is a conception of the absolute merely as substance; the latter is one-sided because it intends the eternal or absolute as devoid of self. This is the abstract universal, "which is a long way from being the Spirit that knows itself as Spirit."[13] Under such conditions, mutual recognition is not yet actual. Religious consciousness is dominated by fear and relates to the divine as slave to master.[14] In contrast, Hegel thinks genuine religious experience involves a consciousness of the divine not as an impersonal substance, but rather as a subject in which the human being can find recognition.[15] Self-recognition in other requires that the other be subject because only a subject can recognize another subject.

AN INTERSUBJECTIVE-SOCIAL CONCEPTION
OF RELIGION

Most studies of recognition note that for Hegel the telos of reciprocal recognition is realized in religion, and that recognition is integrally bound up with the overall argument of the *Phenomenology*.[16] There, mutual forgiveness of sins is the realization of reciprocal recognition, which Hegel identifies as the absolute *Geist,* the "appearance of God." This suggests that recognition is of central systematic importance. And it surely is. Religion is inherently social, and not purely private individual life. As Royce puts it, "religion is, for Hegel, an interpretation of the world by the social self, and by the individual man only insofar as he identifies himself with the social self."[17]

Religion is the human attempt to find recognition in, and unity with, the divine. This is the view "from below." Viewed from "above" religion is the divine becoming self-conscious in and through human recognition. The telos of reciprocal recognition—to be at home with self in an other, or love—is also the structure of absolute *Geist.* The absolute ethical substance becomes subject by means of recognition. The absolute is understood in social and personal terms, namely as self-determining and self-specifying. So, on the one hand, Hegel thinks of religion in social terms, i.e., as the self-consciousness of *Geist.* On the other hand, he reconstructs the traditional doctrines of incarnation and trinity as general social forms of religion. Specifically, incarnation is reconstructed as the consummate form of divine-human community or *Geist.* "This incarnation of the divine being, or that it essentially and immediately has the form of a self, is the simple content of the absolute religion."[18] If the absolute has the form of a self, then it is no immediate I am I, but rather self-recognition in other. The absolute does not exclude relation, but is relation itself.

Hegel's social conception of the absolute is an ontological reconstruction of two Christian doctrines, incarnation and trinity.[19] Incarnation (*Menschwerdung*) is a determinate form of recognition, the consummation of reciprocal recognition or reconciliation.[20] Incarnation is the determinate way that substance becomes subject.[21] Hegel does not dream up this speculative principle, but claims to find it implicit as a general principle in world religions, explicit in the religion of art, and consummate in the Christian religion.[22] For this reason, Hegel treats classical christological and trinitarian doctrines not merely as subjective confessional statements, but as having some experiential basis and as expressions of states of affairs. The supreme principle of speculative philosophy—that the absolute is *Geist*—is not merely foreshadowed, but pre-given in the Christian religion. It is only because Christianity grasps the absolute as *Geist* that Hegel identifies it as the "true religion."[23]

Trinity, the other key doctrine, addresses the fundamental intersubjective and speculative problem, namely self-recognition in other, or being at home with self in an other.[24] A condition of being-for-other is being-for-self, and vice-versa. The task of reciprocal recognition is to render the two sets of relations equivalent, namely, to relate to other in such a way that the difference between self-relation and relation to other—but not the other per se—vanishes. This occurs in mutual releasement and consummates reciprocal recognition and reconciliation. The triad signifies the achievement of equivalence between being-for-self and being-for-other. This equivalence, or social unity and solidarity, is another description of *Geist.*[25] For Hegel, the triad is not only the structure of reciprocal recognition and *Geist*, it is also the structure of reason itself.[26] This signifies that the absolute must not be conceived as monopolar substance, but rather as having multiple modes of being. The triad constitutes a unity in difference, or tri-unity. So understood, triadic tri-unity becomes the principle of a speculative social ontology, which underlies and forms the framework of Hegel's philosophy of religion.[27]

RELIGION AS QUEST FOR RECOGNITION

In the *Phenomenology*, the transition from the chapter on *Geist* to the chapter on religion is not a transition from immanence to transcendence—from anthropology to metaphysical theology—but from substance to subject, from an abstract impersonal conception of the absolute to the recognition that the absolute is *Geist*.[28] This transition is highly complex. It does not occur "all at once," but in several stages or *Stufen*, which constitute Hegel's threefold history and philosophy of religion, namely, the Nature Religions, the Religions of Beauty and Sublimity, and the Consummate religion.[29] According to Hegel's phenomenology of religion, nature religions exhibit an immediate unity of the spiritual and the natural, and so belong to a phase of cultural development in which the consciousness of freedom is only implicit.[30] Spiritual religions are those in which freedom emerges, or becomes explicit, and the spiritual is superior to the merely natural, which becomes instrumental to the unfolding spiritual teleology of freedom. These *Stufen* parallel the fundamental divisions or levels of the preceding *Gestalten*, namely consciousness, self-consciousness and reason-*Geist*.

There is a correlation between the stages of self-consciousness and the stages of religion: "The principle by which God is defined for human beings is also the principle for how humanity defines itself inwardly, or for humanity in its own spirit. An inferior God or a nature god has inferior, natural, unfree human beings as its correlates; the pure concept of God has as its correlate spirit that is free...and...actually knows God."[31] Thus, on the first level of nature religions, the sacred tends to be understood as pre-ethical power, or as natural powers. On the second level of spiritual religions, the sacred is no longer regarded as sheer power, or as arbitrary freedom. Both the Greek religions of humanity and beauty and the Jewish religion of sublimity, tend to subordinate the natural to the ethical.[32] But this subordination is not absolute; Hegel points to Greek tragedy as recognizing fate as a blind power to which the gods, as ethical powers, are subject. And although for Judaism God is absolute subject, this subjectivity is so transcendent to the world that it cannot be affected by the world or a result of interaction with the world.[33] It is an awesome sublimity that goes hand in hand with domination, alienation and patriarchalism.

Under what conditions is the finding of self in the divine possible? An impersonal absolute, or a conception of the divine merely as substance, undermines the possibility of divine-human recognition because it incites fear that the absolute simply swallows up or annuls subjectivity, or that freedom has no basis in the absolute.[34] If the absolute lacks subjectivity (*fürsichsein*), it tends to be only a negative impersonal conception that is subject to a higher necessity or fate. Hegel's answer is that self-recognition in the absolute is possible only if the absolute is or becomes subject, for only a subject is capable of recognizing another subject. The much debated questions whether God is subject, and whether such "subjectivity" is personal, would require a separate monograph and lie beyond the scope of this study.[35]

Nevertheless, it is significant that Hegel uses the same terminology to refer to the transition from the Logical Idea to Nature, as he uses in his account of reciprocal recognition, namely "to allow the other to be, to go free."[36] This suggests that Hegel may well have been implicitly thinking of the former in personal terms. Fichte first raised the objection that personhood cannot be ascribed to God, because personhood requires reference to and limitation by other. In other words, personhood is essentially finite, an individualist notion. But God, as infinite, can have no limit and no other; consequently, personality does not apply to God. Hegel replies to Fichte by denying that relation to other is simply a limitation. His alternative conception of recognition shows that self-recognition in other is the enhancement and fulfillment of personhood: "Logic shows that the category of unity is a poor category, the wholly abstract [atomic] unit. If I say 'one' of God, I must also say this of everything else. But as far as personality is concerned, it is the character of the person, of the subject, to give up its isolation and separateness. Ethical life, love is just this, to give up particularity, private personality and to elevate it to universality, e.g., friendship. In friendship and love I give up my abstract personality and win it back as concrete. The truth of personality is found precisely in winning it back through this immersion, this being immersed in the other."[37] Personhood cannot be understood in merely abstract individualist terms; rather to be personal is to exist through recognition of and by others. Thus, personhood is a fundamentally social conception, a social infinite. There is no reason why this concept of a social infinite may not be applied to God. Hegel conceives God's absoluteness not as excluding relation, but as inclusive of relation, as universal relativity. At the very least, this implies that God is social, which is what trinity means for Hegel.[38]

We recall that self-consciousness attains its satisfaction only in another self-consciousness.[39] Human self-recognition in the divine is possible only if both the divine and the human are capable of recognition and entering into community. This becomes explicit in the revelatory or consummate religion. Prior to or apart from this level (*Stufe*), the divine appears in one-sided and abstract forms: "But the supersensible, eternal or however one may wish to designate it, is devoid of self [*selbstlos*]; it is only the [abstract] universal, and that is still far from being *Geist* knowing itself as *Geist*."[40] In the revelatory or consummate religion, incarnation, the general religious principle of divine-human community, finds consummate realization and expression in a particular historical individual.[41] For this reason, Hegel characterizes the consummate religion as a religion of consolation (*Trost*). The claim that God is subject, and not merely substance, constitutes the revelatory element in the Christian, or revelatory, religion.

In Hegel's view, the inner logic of the concept of religion requires a developing divine human community which culminates in incarnation (*Menschwerdung*). Stages of this development include divine-human relations in the form of master/slave, tragedy, but also love and reconciliation. Hegel's 'history of religion' parallels his social and intersubjective analyses.[42] Domination, oppression and tragedy are found in world religions and in the revelatory religion as well. Incarnation, when consummated, transforms and reconciles such conflict. It is a distinctive form of divine-human community in which both the human being and 'the absolute' are at home with self in other (*bei sich im andern*). "Spirit is actual as absolute *Geist* only when it is also for itself in its truth as it is in its certainty of itself, or when in the extremes into which it as consciousness divides itself, *are for each other in the form of Geist*."[43] Although religion is more than a social anthropology, it is also not less than an interpersonal relation of recognition. Neither the divine nor the human is a solitary atom complete in itself apart from relation.[44] But this is not yet explicit in the earlier, one-sided forms of religion.

TRAGIC RECOGNITION

The Religion of Art

Tragedy is no merely private or solipsistic phenomenon, but a social vision of the world, including the complex relations of the divine and the human, the state and family. Tragedy expresses a people's religious sense of the world.[45] Hegel takes tragedy far more seriously than either Enlightenment or Romantic thinkers; he prefers it to the shallow optimism of the Enlightenment, and to the divine comedy of classical Christianity (as in Dante).

Hegel discusses tragedy a second time in the religion chapter of the *Phenomenology*. The earlier patterns—the division of unwritten divine law and human law, and the problem of false consciousness—are repeated. In addition, Hegel provides hints of a tragic theology of the unknown God whose oracles speak ambiguously in riddles. Greek tragedy is a religion of art, differing from religions of nature. It requires a different mode of expression, or language: "...the god [requires] another mode of coming forth than this, which, out of the depths of his creative night, he descends into the opposite.... This element is language...the complete separation into independent selves is at the same time the fluidity and the universally communicated unity of the many selves; language is the soul existing as soul."[46] But language can conceal as well as reveal.

Tragedy exploits the possibilities of concealment. As is well known, the utterances of the oracle turn out to mean the opposite of what they appear to say. This reversal of situation reveals the false consciousness of the tragic hero. He is blinded to truth of the situation, and discovers (recognizes) the full complexity of the situation, including his transgression, too late. The religious dimension of Greek ethical life is a divided realm, with a divided, false consciousness: "The doer finds himself in the contrast of knowing and not-knowing. He takes his purpose from his character and knows it as ethical necessity. But through the determinacy of character he knows only one power of ethical substance, and the other is concealed from him. The present reality is therefore one thing in itself, and another for consciousness. The upper and lower law signify [respectively] the power that knows and reveals itself to consciousness and the power that conceals itself and lies in ambush."[47] Behind the ambiguous utterance of the oracle is the self-concealing tragic god.[48]

The tragic hero's action leads to a discovery, a reversal of situation, from naively presuming to act rightly, to being guilty of violating the hidden law. "In following the god that knows, it really got hold of what was *not revealed,* and pays the penalty for trusting a knowledge whose ambiguity...also becomes explicit for consciousness and a warning to it."[49] If the tragic God is concealed and hostile, then the ambiguity in its oracles cannot be reliably deciphered. Since the oracles mean the opposite of what they say, self-recognition in other—human or divine—can only be tragic.

Hegel's Changing Assessment of Tragedy

Hegel's view of tragedy apparently undergoes a change. In the *Natural Law* essay he holds that tragedy is superior to comedy because comedy lacks fate, and so is without genuine struggle or conflict. Hegel refers to classical Christian thought as one example of comedy. "Dante's *Divine Comedy* is without fate and without genuine struggle, because absolute confidence and assurance of the reality of the Absolute exist in it without opposition, and whatever opposition brings movement into this perfect security and calm is merely opposition without seriousness or inner truth."[50] Consequently, when Hegel says that tragedy is superior to comedy, he appears to be distancing himself from classical Christian doctrine. He claims that conflict is the tragic principle and that "the absolute relation...is set forth in tragedy."[51]

In the *Phenomenology,* however, Hegel portrays comedy as the superior, post-tragic level (*Stufe*) of religion. Comedy dissolves the plurality of gods into a higher fate and prepares for the next stage of religious development, namely the revelatory religion. In the *Phenomenology,* tragedy passes over into comedy, in which "self-consciousness exhibits itself as the fate of the gods."[52] In comedy, the individual self is the negative power through which and in which the gods vanish. "They are clouds, an evanescent mist..."[53] The gods die when they cease to be taken seriously, and when they are grasped critically as relative to the subjectivity which is supposedly subject to them.

In the *Phenomenology,* comedy is a higher form than tragedy, but it does not include divine-human *reconciliation.* Rather it signifies the return or collapse of the gods into religious consciousness. The comic consciousness degenerates into empty skepticism and vanity, and becomes unhappy consciousness when it becomes aware of the loss of divine reality. Hegel expresses this with the phrase "God is dead," which first refers to the self-subversion of the religion of art, namely, the surpassing of tragedy by comedy in which the gods all disappear into subjectivity, i.e., are shown to be projections relative to subjectivity.[54]

Comedy involves not only loss of fear of the gods, but also loss of essential being by everything other than consciousness. As Hegel interprets it, comedy is a form of unhappy consciousness, because the self into which everything returns and which is superior to everything alien, is an empty individual.[55] "This unhappy consciousness constitutes the counterpart and completion of the comic consciousness that is perfectly happy within itself. Into the latter, all divine being returns. The comic consciousness is the complete alienation of [divine] substance."[56]

Self-consciousness is the fate of the gods because "these elementary beings are, as universal moments, *not a self* and *are not actual.* They are fitted out with the form of individuality, to be sure, but this is only in imagination and does not really belong to them."[57] Actual consciousness is human; it cannot find itself recognized in such deities, or rather, it finds nothing but itself in them. It turns to irony and comedy to express its transcendence of the gods, and their relativity to consciousness. But although comedy is a higher stage of religious development than tragedy, both are one-sided forms. Neither exhibits reconciliation or a fulfilled reciprocal recognition. These are accomplished only at a higher level of the revelatory religion, where the absolute is apprehended as itself subject, as *Geist.*

The Revelatory Religion

Hegel works out the development of substance to subject explicitly in the section on revelatory religion. What is "revelatory" is the recognition that God is subject, and as such, self-manifesting and self-specifying.[58] In other words, God is not a mere impersonal substance to which predicates are ascribed in external reflection. That culminates in the view that all theological predicates, as external, apply to God only negatively. This is tantamount to declaring that God cannot be known. But if God cannot be known, this returns us to the ancient tragic theology according to which God is envious and jealous.

However, revelatory religion surpasses tragedy and the ambiguous oracles of the tragic theology. "If God is not posited in a mere subjective belief, but rather it is taken seriously that God is and is for us, that God from God's side has a relation to us...it is implied that God communicates with the human being, that God is not jealous."[59] Hegel sides with Plato and Aristotle against the tragic theology of the concealed hostile, jealous God. But he goes beyond them, for he claims that the absolute gives itself the form of self-consciousness and is present as an actual human being.[60] God is not jealous, but self-communicating and thus social. Moreover, the specific form of God's self-communication is that of a servant (*Knechtsgestalt*).[61] For Hegel, God is not a master, but rather identifies with and takes the form of a servant. In this lowly other, God is recognized (*erkannt*): "Consciousness does not proceed out of its inwardness from its own thoughts, in order (in its own thought) to connect synthetically the concept of God with existence. Rather it proceeds from the immediate presence of this existence and recognizes God in him.... This God is immediately and sensibly intuited as self, as an actual individual human being. Only so is God self-consciousness. This incarnation of the divine being, or that it immediately and in itself has the form of self-consciousness, is the simple content of the absolute religion."[62]

The revelatory religion cannot be reduced to a one-sided relation as if only human consciousness relates to the divine, but not vice-versa. A one-sided relation would be merely an ideal or subjective one, projected by imagination, a mere anthropology, as Feuerbach made clear. Instead, in religion both sides are reciprocally related to and mediated by the other, religion and theology are correlative. Hegel explains:

> In such relation, there is at least this much implied, namely, not only do we stand in relation to God, but also that God stands in relation to us.... A one-sided relation is no relation at all. If in fact religion should be understood only as a relation running from us to God, an independent being of God would not be possible. In religion, God would only be something posited and produced. The much used and much censured expression that God is only in religion, has a great and true sense, that it belongs to the nature of God in complete independence existing in and for itself, [nevertheless] to be for the human being and to communicate with the human being. But the meaning of this is quite different from the meaning implicit in the preceding remarks, according to which God is merely a postulate, a belief. Rather God is, and gives himself a relation to the human being.[63]

Although the term *Anerkennung* does not appear in this passage, its sense is very much in evidence in the requirement of reciprocal relation.[64] For here, as in the eidetics of recognition, a one-sided action is useless. To be actual, religion requires reciprocal action and relation. Religion, as divine-human community, consists in a two-sided reciprocal relation. Christianity is the revelatory religion because it grasps the absolute as social, revelatory, or *Geist*.[65]

The tragic view of the absolute is one-sided, as is evident from its naive false consciousness, and from tragic recognition. In the tragic reversal, the other, destructive aspect of the absolute, which had hitherto been concealed or suppressed, is made manifest. In contrast, revelatory religion exhibits a two-sided reciprocal relation. Its incarnational principle is a social one, with some positive result, namely the establishment of reciprocity, or divine-human community.[66] Hegel formulates the divine self-communication in the now familiar terms of recognition, namely, self-recognition in other. Conversely, the human need for recognition finds its highest interest and expression: "The hopes and expectations of the preceding world reached forward towards this revelation in order to intuit what the absolute is and to find itself in the absolute."[67]

Absolute Geist and Tragedy

In his early essay on *Natural Law*, Hegel presents a dialectical concept of infinity: "since it is the principle of movement and change, its essence is nothing but to be the immediate opposite of itself. In other words, it is the negatively absolute, the abstraction of form which, as pure identity, is immediately [also] pure non-identity or absolute opposition which, as pure ideality, is with equal immediacy pure reality; as the infinite, is the absolutely finite; as the indeterminate, is absolute determinacy...absolute transition into its contradictory...is its essence..."[68] The infinite, as immediate opposite to itself, is not infinite by contrast to finitude, but is itself both infinite and finite.[69] That is, Hegel does not begin with an abstract infinite existing by itself in isolation, and then ask how this abstract transcendent principle comes to have a second alongside it; rather Hegel begins with the infinite-finite. *This* infinite does not exclude relation, but is rather absolute as and in relation, as the act of coincidence with and transition into opposite.[70] The infinite exists only as doubled, as bi-polar; it is not merely a One, but a One *and* a Many. The absolute is not a being that suddenly comes to have contingent relations, but *is relation,* or an absolute of relation.

Hegel conceives this self-relating absolute tragically, as "the tragedy which the absolute eternally enacts with itself, by eternally bringing itself forth into objectivity, submitting in this objective form to suffering and death, and rising from its ashes into glory."[71] This is an elusive passage. In the essay on *Natural Law*, Hegel's examples of the tragic play of the absolute come from Greek tragedy. On the other hand, his underlying conception of the absolute is triadic. The living absolute is the unity of the opposing natures. The absolute is not a one-dimensional, monopolar substance, but consists in multiple (triadic) modes of being.

Hegel determines that the natures so distinguished are in opposition, that is, in tragic conflict. The absolute relation is not a tranquil calm of sheer self-sameness, but rather suffering. One aspect of the absolute is the death of the other, "since that life is only in connection with this other life, and yet just as absolutely is resurrected out of it, since in this death (as the sacrifice of the second nature), death is mastered."[72] This tragic concept of the absolute anticipates Hegel's subsequent discussion of the death of God in the *Phenomenology* and *Lectures on the Philosophy of Religion*.

The Death of God: Hegel's Theological Atheism

Hegel is the first philosopher to formulate the death of God motif, and one of the few to realize its theological origin and significance.[73] No atheism pure and simple, it is a *theological* critique of traditional metaphysical theology from the perspective of Christology.[74] Hegel cites a Lutheran hymn in which the phrase "God himself lies dead" occurs. Debate about this hymn revived classical theological discussions about the suffering and death of Jesus.[75] The orthodox held that Christ's human nature suffers and dies, but not the divine nature, which, as immutable and self-same, is incapable of suffering and death. Eternal self-sameness and immutability imply impassibility, i.e., that God is incapable of suffering. In contrast, the phrase "God himself lies dead" departs from classical metaphysical theism, for it signifies that suffering and death pertain to the divine as well. God, and not merely the human Jesus, suffers. Against the classical conception of divine immutability, Hegel defends the view that the God incarnate must be capable of change and suffering.[76]

Hegel's concept of the death of God gathers the ancient tragic experience, including the deaths of Socrates and Jesus, and the modern experience of the desacralization of nature, the Enlightenment reduction of the sacred grove to mere timber.[77] Theological thinking must incorporate the theme of desacralization or divine absence. Hegel reformulates the incarnation as a general principle of divine self-othering and self-divestment (*Entäusserung*). God renounces absolute, exclusive being-for-self (*fürsichsein*) and exists in relation with other. Concretely, God identifies with finitude to its limit, namely death. The death of Jesus is God's highest self-divestment (*Entäusserung*): in it "God has died, God himself is dead. This fearful picture brings before the imagination the deepest abyss of alienation."[78]

God's self-alienation is motivated by, and expresses love. "For love [consists] in giving up one's personality, all that is one's own. [It is] a self-conscious activity, the supreme surrender [of oneself] in other, even in this most extrinsic other-being of death.... The death of Christ [is] the vision of this love itself—not [love merely] for or on behalf of others, but precisely divinity in this universal identity with other-being, death. The tremendous unity of these absolute extremes is love itself—this is the speculative intuition."[79] The content of the speculative intuition is *Geist,* a triadic concept which is self-identical in its self-differentiation;[80] the unity of the divine and the human is the concrete content of absolute *Geist.*[81] Although this is a dialectical formulation, Hegel immediately passes to an intersubjective expression of the same idea: "Spirit, love [is] the intuition of self in another..."[82] Thus, the themes of recognition, including the life and death struggle and its reconciliation in divine love, return in transformation on the highest level of *Geist.* The self-abandonment of the divine to its other—finitude—to the point of death, is perhaps the supreme exemplification of releasement (*Gelassenheit*).

In the *Phenomenology* Hegel formulates the death of the mediator as a death affecting both his human and divine natures.

> The death of the mediator grasped by the self is the cancellation *[Aufheben]* of his objectivity or his particular being-for-self *[Fürsichseins];* this particular being-for-self has become universal self-consciousness. On the other side, the universal has likewise become self-consciousness and the pure or inactive *Geist* of mere thinking has become actual. The death of the mediator is the death not only of his natural side or his particular being-for-self, not only of the already dead husk stripped of its essential being, but also the abstraction of the divine being itself.[83]

This formulation is a critique of abstract substance metaphysics and theology. It is a theological criticism of abstract eternity and transcendence. What dies is not the divine being per se, but its abstraction, i.e., abstract transcendence, the infinite that, since it is opposed to the finite, is itself finite.

Hegel develops further his critique of classical metaphysical theology.

> The death of this representation contains at the same time the death of the abstraction of the divine being, that is not posited as self. It is the painful feeling of the unhappy consciousness, that God himself is dead. This hard word is the expression of the innermost simple self-knowledge, the return of consciousness into the depths of the night of the I = I, which distinguishes and knows nothing besides itself. This feeling is therefore in fact the loss of substance and its standing over and against consciousness; but at the same time it is the pure subjectivity of substance, or the pure certainty of itself, which, as object, or immediate, or as pure being, it lacks. This knowing therefore is the inspiration through which substance has become subject, its abstraction and lifelessness perishes, and it becomes actual, simple and universal self-consciousness.[84]

In this passage, the death of God refers to a theological and not an atheistic critique of traditional theology. Hegel speaks here of the death, the nullity of abstract substance. But this nullity, or "loss of substance" is not necessarily an anti-theistic or atheist thesis.[85] It is a critique of the onto-theological abstraction of classical metaphysics which conceived God as actual apart from relation, or as involved in relations that have no influence or effect on the divine. However, when substance becomes subject, and stands in relation to other subjects, it does not simply vanish. If it did, the result would be a subjective idealism, or Feuerbach's reduction of theology to anthropology. Hegel's critique of foundationalist ontotheology does not culminate in its inversion, namely, foundationalist anthropo-ontology.

Hegel's suggestion is that the loss or 'death' of abstract substance parallels the renunciation of immediate and exclusive being-for-self (*Fürsichsein*) required by reciprocal recognition, as a precondition of *Geist*. Incarnation requires a cancellation of immediate *Fürsichsein*. Similarly, the "death of abstract substance" points to a critique of its abstract immediacy. The renunciation or qualification of such abstract immediacy is a condition of the formation of a divine-human community.[86] The divine too must renounce abstract immediacy, i.e., immediate *Fürsichsein*, in order to enter into relation and to be at home with itself in an other.

The Death of God and Tragedy

It has been noted that Hegel's estimate of tragedy and comedy undergoes change between his *Natural Law* essay and the *Phenomenology*. The *Natural Law* essay distinguishes between comedy and tragedy. Tragedy is marked by conflict, comedy by the dissolution of conflict. Comedy can take two forms, ancient or modern. The ancient form is found in classical Christian theism. Hegel characterizes the classical Christianity of Dante's *Divine Comedy* as "without fate and without a genuine struggle, because absolute confidence and assurance of the reality of the absolute exist in it without opposition, and whatever opposition brings movement into this perfect security and calm is merely opposition without seriousness or inner truth."[87] The *Divine Comedy* expresses the dissolution of opposition and conflict in an undifferentiated absolute. The modern form of comedy presents the absolute itself as an illusion.[88] Comedy points either to classical theism (Dante), of which Spinoza's infinite substance is perhaps the ultimate metaphysical expression, or to atheism, in which human subjectivity is the fate of the gods.[89] However, Hegel thinks tragedy is superior to the comedy of classical theism because it exhibits the absolute relation, namely conflict and suffering: "...the true and absolute relation is that the one [nature] really does illumine the other; each [nature] has a living bearing on the other, and each is the other's serious fate. The absolute relation, then, is set forth in tragedy."[90]

In the *Phenomenology*, Hegel apparently revises his previous estimate of the superiority of tragedy to comedy. Here, comedy provides the transition to the revelatory religion, which places mutual recognition, forgiveness of sins and reconciliation (*Versöhnung*) at the center. Otto Pöggeler claims this means that Hegel changes his mind about the relation of tragedy to comedy, and shifts from tragic to teleological principles of thought. "The result of our considerations is that a dialectical-teleological thinking infiltrates and usurps Hegel's relation to Greek tragedy."[91] Tragedy is thus restricted and confined to a lower level of development than the revelatory or Christian religion; it no longer exhibits the absolute relation, now conceived as reconciliation or unity. Tragic conflict, no longer the absolute relation, becomes instead a means to reconciliation and unity. Hegel's emphasis on teleology, whether driven by the influence of Aristotle or the concept of reconciliation, allegedly undermines and eliminates his earlier emphasis on tragedy in religion. Opposition and conflict, instead of being permanent features, are reinterpreted as *means* to a final telos, namely reconciliation and unity.[92] The absolute, in its transition from substance to subject, both excludes and stands above tragic conflict.[93] Reconciliation and tragedy are mutually exclusive.

Pöggeler spells out the incompatibility in the following way:

> The absolute as independent Spirit does not coincide with itself in tragic conflict or reconciliation, but in a dialectical teleological syllogism. In the Preface to the *Phenomenology*, before he calls attention to Aristotelian teleology, Hegel warns us not to forget the seriousness, the pain, the patience and the labor of the negative, in considering the life of God as a play of love with itself. But doesn't Hegel himself forget this seriousness when he later says "God is love, i.e., the making of distinctions and the nullifying of such distinctions, a play of distinctions which is not serious; distinctions which are annulled as soon as they are posited, the eternal simple Idea."? It is significant that these comments explicate the Christian doctrine of trinity, and that Hegel carries out this analysis with aristotelian concepts.[94]

In shifting from tragic disunity to triumphal teleological self-coincidence, Hegel sides with Plato and Aristotle *against* the tragic view of existence. Hegel comes to interpret tragedy from comic premises, i.e., from the presupposition of a reconciliation which lies *beyond* tragedy.[95] Stated in terms of equipollence, Hegel's thesis that equipollence does not apply to the absolute because the absolute has no opposite, would likewise appear to point to a comic ontotheological interpretation.

But does Hegel's account of the revelatory religion exclude tragedy as Pöggeler contends? Specifically, does reconciliation exclude tragedy? If so, then Hegel would simply offer another version of classical *Divine Comedy*, which is not serious about opposition, conflict, suffering and evil, since these do not apply to the absolute. And this would show that Hegel is not an alternative to, but rather the culmination of, the metaphysical tradition according to which the absolute has no opposite. On the other hand, the question is whether reconciliation, far from suppressing, rather *presupposes* tragedy and tragic conflict? If reconciliation and Hegel's absolute include tragic elements, this would show that he departs from classical Christian theological assumptions.[96]

We must turn now to ask whether Hegel's account of the death of God incorporates tragic features. Hegel has a peculiar view of tragedy. Pöggeler notes that, despite his fascination with tragedy, Hegel never interpreted it as excluding mediation and reconciliation. And this is precisely the issue. Goethe attacked Hegel on the grounds that tragedy and reconciliation are mutually exclusive.[97] *Antigone* is a tragedy precisely because there is no possible solution, no mediation of conflict. Tragedy means inescapable conflict with no possible reconciliation, no soteriology. It ends in the downfall or destruction of the tragic hero/heroine. As soon as the actuality or possibility of balancing and mediation is admitted, tragedy in the strict sense disappears.[98] It must be conceded that tragic conflict for Hegel is not absolutely irreconcilable. But all that this shows is that Hegel has a different interpretation of tragedy than the classical one.

If Hegel's conception of the death of God is not tragic in the strict classical sense, is it comic? Hegel characterizes Dante's *Divine Comedy* as without fate or a genuine struggle, because the absolute exists in it as sheer presence without opposition. This view of comedy belongs to the metaphysics of pure light and transparency. Werner Marx charges Hegel with the same conception. Marx acknowledges that from the time of his youth Hegel was convinced that "reality in itself is in the deepest sense rent, sundered, estranged, full of contradiction...that there is...darkness in the form of untruth, error, evil and death."[99] Nevertheless, says Marx, Hegel subordinates this conviction to the optimistic rationalism of Aristotle that reason can heal and reconcile all oppositions, and overcome all estrangement. Hence, light prevails over darkness. Although the absolute may contain the harshest internal opposition, it nevertheless overcomes it. Hegel's teleological thinking thus "guarantees conclusive victory to the light, to the truth undisguised by the untruth."[100] Marx's talk of "conclusive victory for the light" makes it appear as if opposition is finally non-serious, excluded in principle from the absolute. If that were so, then Hegel would be serving up another version of the *Divine Comedy*.

Marx's judgment cannot stand. It is the metaphysical theological tradition and not Hegel, that upholds the metaphysics of pure light, of the unopposed absolute, by interpreting the death of Jesus as the death of the human nature only. This death does not affect the divine nature, and so the tradition upheld divine impassibility. Therefore, Hegel is correct in characterizing the *tradition* as comedy. Its absolute excludes opposition and renders the opposition non-serious. Given its acceptance of the categories of abstract eternity and identity, the tradition could not acknowledge or incorporate tragedy or tragic suffering in its conception of God.

In emphasizing the death of God, Hegel parts company with the tradition. The death of God means that there is suffering, pain, and negation in God, there is suffering and tragedy in the divine itself. This point is made explicit in several texts, early as well as late,[101] especially the *Lectures on the Philosophy of Religion.* The 1824 Lectures read thus: "It [the death of God] must not then be represented merely as the death of this individual...what it means is rather that *God* has died, that *God himself is dead.* God has died: this is negation, which is accordingly a moment of the divine nature, of God himself."[102] The next is from the 1827 lectures:

> "God himself is dead," it says in a Lutheran hymn, expressing an awareness that the human, the finite, the weak, the negative, are themselves a moment of the divine, that they are within God himself, that finitude, negativity, otherness are not outside of God and do not, as otherness, hinder unity with God. Otherness, the negative, is known to be a moment of the divine nature itself. This involves the highest idea of spirit.[103]

And from the 1831 Lectures: "God has died, God is dead, this is the most frightful of all thoughts, that everything eternal and true is not, that negation itself is found in God. The deepest anguish, the feeling of complete irretrievability, the annulling of everything that is elevated, are bound up with this thought."[104] The theme of tragic suffering and negation in God is clear and consistent.

Hegel's view, while Christian, diverges significantly from classical orthodoxy. Feuerbach's expression for it is apt: theological atheism. It must be noted that Hegel's theological atheism is not simply atheistic, but rather involves a triadic-trinitarian conception. God has multiple modes of being, and death pertains to one of these modes.[105] Further, if death pertains to one mode, this is a negation that affects the other modes. In denying negation in God, classical Christian thought obscured one of its must profound insights into suffering. To correct the tradition, Christian thought must uncover its suppressed elements, and acknowledge that there is tragic suffering in God. This acknowledgement signals a revision of the classical metaphysical tradition.

It might be objected that Hegel is not really serious about the death of God, because of his emphasis on teleology. As Pöggeler observes, Hegel's emphasis on teleology suggests that there is a final unity which overwhelms and excludes tragic suffering. At the ultimate level, Hegel's thought reverts from the early pantragedism to teleological panlogism. And that reversion to self-sameness implies the exclusion of any serious otherness.

While there is little doubt that Hegel draws close to Aristotle, it would be a mistake to find him in complete agreement with Aristotle on this crucial point. For the criticism of panlogism that Pöggeler levels at Hegel is made by Hegel himself against certain forms of the metaphysical tradition:

> "The life of God and divine knowledge may well be spoken of as a play of love with itself. But this idea sinks into mere edification, even insipidity if

it lacks the seriousness, the suffering, the patience and the labor of the negative. In itself (*an sich*) that life is indeed one of untroubled equality and unity with itself, which is not serious about otherness [*Anderssein*], alienation, and the overcoming of alienation. But this in itself is *abstract universality*, in which the nature of divine life to be for itself...is left altogether out of account."[106]

Hegel parts company with the Aristotelian version of pure thought thinking itself, because it lacks the labor of the negative. Aristotle's *noesis noeseos* may well be another version of divine comedy, the final teleological triumph of light over darkness. Nevertheless, it manages to co-exist with slavery and oppression. This means that although Aristotle's God is not jealous like the tragic God, nevertheless, like the master, Aristotle's God does not recognize its other. It does not recognize human worth or acknowledge a right to consolation.

In comparison with Aristotle, Hegel is a Christian tragedian who acknowledges the right of subjectivity to consolation. He writes

"In the creed of the ancients...necessity figured as Destiny. The modern point of view on the contrary, is that of consolation. And consolation means that, if we renounce our aims and interests, we do so only in prospect of receiving consolation. Destiny, on the contrary, leaves no room for consolation...it is a frame of mind that needs no consolation, so long as personal subjectivity has not acquired its infinite significance. It is this point on which special stress should be laid in comparing the ancient sentiment with that of the modern and Christian world.... It is in this sense that the Christian religion is to be regarded as a religion of consolation, even absolute consolation. Christianity...teaches that God wishes all men to be saved. That teaching declares that subjectivity has infinite value. And that consoling power of Christianity lies in the fact that God himself is in it known as the absolute subjectivity, so that, inasmuch as subjectivity involves the element of particularity, our particular personality too is recognized not merely as something to be merely nullified, but rather as worthy of preservation."[107]

Consolation presupposes recognition of subjectivity and granting subjectivity its right. This requires (1) acknowledgement that self-recognition in other is the basic structure of subjectivity, and (2) that the absolute itself is subject, not merely known, but self-knowing, and whose self-knowing has the structure of self-recognition in other. Hegel explains: "In the ancient creeds not only men, but even gods, were represented as subject to destiny, a destiny which we must conceive as necessity not unveiled, and thus as something wholly impersonal, self-less and blind. On the other hand, the Christian God is God not merely known, but also self-knowing; he is a personality not merely figured in our minds, but rather absolutely actual."[108]

Although it cannot be denied that Hegel remains close to Aristotle, there is an important difference. Aristotle gives priority to the object which God thinks, which must be the best. But Aristotle does not thematize subjectivity adequately. For him it is sheer transparency and actuality. Hegel, on the contrary, sees that subjectivity involves recognition, and that recognition is a disclosure of what was previously hidden. Self-recognition in other presupposes prior hiddenness or concealment and involves a critique of immediacy as concealment or false consciousness. Consequently, if God is subject, this involves hiddenness, epistemological distance, alienation and the possibility of suffering. The epistemological distancing of subjectivity from itself and from others is not evil, but rather an ontological condition of freedom, self-disclosure, and self-recognition in other. These conditions underlie evil as tragic aspects of existence, but equally underlie and condition reconciliation.[109]

Further, Hegel stresses that the infinite grief of the death of God must be incorporated as a moment of the supreme idea.[110] Thus, Hegel imposes an additional requirement, namely speculative philosophy "must re-establish for philosophy the Idea of absolute freedom, and along with it, the absolute Passion, the speculative Good Friday in place of the historic Good Friday. Good Friday must be speculatively re-established in the whole truth and harshness of its God-forsakenness."[111] In other words, the death of God must be incorporated into theology, and when it is, it signifies tragic suffering in the absolute. Hegel never abandoned his conception of the tragic absolute, even if tragedy is no longer simply equated with the absolute relation.

If this infinite grief, the tragic element in the absolute is suppressed, then Pöggeler would be correct that Hegel gives priority to Aristotle's teleology over tragedy. Then suffering would be merely instrumental to a teleological reinstatement of identity and self-sameness. Hegel would have to be regarded as culminating in some version of classical metaphysics, and offering another version of divine comedy. It cannot be denied that some texts point in this direction.[112]

My thesis is that Hegel is after an alternative to tragedy and to the divine comedy of classical metaphysics, and this alternative is the triadic conception of the absolute. The Hegelian trinity is an alternative to the dyadic subject-object identity of idealism. It incorporates tragedy even as it seeks to reconcile tragic conflict. Hegel says to his critics that the idea of reconciliation "makes no sense if God is not known as the triune God, if it is not recognized that God is, but also is as the other, as self-distinguishing, so that this other is God himself."[113] In other words, Hegel's concept of reconciliation does not entail either teleological elimination of tragedy (Pöggeler) or relapse into being as self-sameness (Marx).

Hegel thinks reconciliation without conflict makes no sense. For this reason he conceives divine love itself in tragic terms. He identifies divine love not with reconciliation so much as with death: "Death is what reconciles. Death is love itself; in it absolute love is envisaged."[114] The identity of the divine with the human in this death means that the divine has a tragic presence. In tragic suffering "God is at home with himself in humanity...and in its death this finitude is itself a determination of God."[115] The so-called Hegelian parousia of the absolute is not sheer presence, but includes negation, death and suffering.[116] There is tragedy in God, although tragedy does not overwhelm God, nor is it the only word. Hegel's concept of *Geist in seiner Gemeinde,* signifies a divine society that can tarry with the negative and look it in the face. To conceive God as inherently social is to go beyond the divine comedy inherent in the tradition's royal metaphor for the relation between God and world.[117] According to Hegel, the incarnation signifies that God renounces mastery and rather identifies with servitude, the poor and the oppressed. God transforms servitude by assuming the form of a servant, even to the point of death. Although Hegel himself may not have thought through his analysis to the end, its clear implication is that the concept of divine sovereignty as divine mastery over the world must be abandoned. It is rather manifest in the opposite of mastery, namely, forgiveness and the power of enduring suffering at the hands of its other.

NOTES

1. Fortunately, this discussion has already begun. See Walter Jaeschke *Vernunft in der Religion: Studien zur Grundlegung der Religionsphilosophie Hegels* [*Spekulation und Erfahrung: Texte und Untersuchungen zum Deutschen Idealismus* Band 4] (Stuttgart: Frommann-Holzboog, 1986). [Hereafter cited as VR]; English translation: *Reason in Religion: The Foundations of Hegel's Philosophy of Religion,* tr. J. Michael Stewart and Peter C. Hodgson (Berkeley: University of California Press, 1990). [Hereafter cited as RR]

2. Sources for Hegel's philosophy of religion include *Faith and Knowledge* (1802), the *System of Ethical Life,* and culminate in the *Phenomenology Spirit* (1807); the *Encyclopedia* (1830), and the *Lectures on the Philosophy of Religion* (1821, 1824, 1827, 1831). The most complete discussion among Hegel's published works is the *Phenomenology.* The most complete discussion of all is found in the *Lectures On the Philosophy of Religion;* even though the latter were never published and are in part reconstructions from students' notes, they are indispensable. Fortunately they have recently appeared in translation a new critical edition. See below, notes 19 and 29.

3. H. S. Harris, "The Concept of Recognition in Hegel's Jena Manuscripts," *Hegel-Studien* Beiheft 20 (Bonn: Bouvier Verlag, 1979), 229.

4. Josiah Royce, *Lectures on Modern Idealism* (New Haven, Conn.: Yale University Press, 1919), 180–1. Royce is one of the few English speaking philosophers who appreciates the ontological significance of the social in Hegel's thought. His writing on the *Phenomenology* still ranks among the very best in English.

5. Ibid. 210.

6. Jaeschke, VR 323–5; RR 311–313.

7. Hegel, *Über die wissenschaftlichen Behandlungsarten des Naturrechts,* TWA, Sk: 2: 499; ET: *Natural Law,* tr. T. M. Knox (Philadelphia: University of Pennsylvania Press, 1975), 108. [Hereafter cited as NR and NL respectively.]

8. Otto Pöggeler, *Hegels Idee einer Phänomenologie des Geistes* (Freiburg: Alber Verlag, 1973), 85, 90. For a discussion of how the absolute can already be present, without involving dogmatism, see Joseph C. Flay, *Hegel's Quest for Certainty* (Albany, N.Y.: SUNY Press, 1984), Chapter 2.

9. Thus, in the first treatment of unhappy consciousness, Hegel indicates that he is taking up only the unchangeable as the unchangeable of consciousness, and "not the unchangeable as it is in and for itself." (PhG 161–162) It should be noted that the unhappy consciousness represents a consciousness turned within, i.e., privatistic. From this it is but a short step to the subsequent discussion of faith as privatistic flight from the world (PhG, 350), which Hegel likewise characterizes as an abstraction from religion as such, and as an abstract consciousness of the absolute being, not the absolute being as it is in and for itself (cf. 377).

10. Those who might challenge this claim should note that Hegel explicitly characterizes the earlier sections of the *Phenomenology* (consciousness, self-consciousness and reason) as abstractions from *Geist.* (PhG, 314) Therefore, the discussion of religion in these earlier sections could only reflect this abstraction. But religion, as the self-conciousness of *Geist,* can be explicitly treated only after *Geist* itself is introduced, and this is Hegel's procedure.

11. PhG 473.

12. PhG 473; PhS 410.

13. Ibid. Cf. Jaeschke, VR 240ff; RR 229ff.

14. "If God is conceived as the one substance…, this supports the instinctive fear that in such an absolute, self-consciousness goes under and is not preserved…" PhG, 19. Cf. Enz. §194 Zusatz: "Fichte in modern times has especially and with justice insisted that the theory which regards the absolute or God as the Object, and stops there, expresses the point of view taken by superstition and slavish fear."

15. Ibid..

16. Siep, Düsing, and Harris all make this point.

17. Royce, op. cit. 210.

18. PhG 527–528.

19. Hegel treats trinity and incarnation more broadly than as specifically Christian doctrines. As doctrines of the philosophy of religion rather than Christian theology, they are, Hegel believes, ontological structures more general than Christian reli-

gion, belonging to the general essence of religion, and are therefore found in different forms and shapes in other religions. Cf. Hegel, *Lectures on the Philosophy of Religion Vol. III: The Consummate Religion*, tr. and ed. by Peter C. Hodgson (Berkeley: University of California Press, 1985), 314n. [Hereafter cited as LPR III.] The German Edition: G. W. F. Hegel, *Vorlesungen Über die Philosophie der Religion, Teil 3: Die vollendete Religion*, Hrsg. Walter Jaeschke (Hamburg: Meiner Verlag, 1984), 238. [Hereafter cited as VPR III.] Walter Jaeschke observes that Hegel's philosophy of religion lends itself to both theological and philosophical interpretation, and this creates considerable complexity for interpreters. Nevertheless, Jaeschke is correct to insist that Hegel's thought, even though treating theological material, nevertheless must be understood as philosophy: "Hegel's Philosophy of Religion can be of interest to philosophy as well as theology, only when it is understood as philosophy: as a remarkable attempt to revise and renew the philosophical concepts of God and philosophy of religion in fruitful dialogue with the Enlightenment critique." Walter Jaeschke, VR 300; RR 289.

20. Although Jaeschke does not put the point in this way, his study of Hegel's speculative Christology and Pneumatology confirms it. Thus, God's son is conceived as God's other (VR 323; RR 313), and incarnation has its material condition in the concept of divine-human community. (VR 348ff; RR 337ff.)

21. PhG 528. This clarifies the sense in which the divine is dependent on the human. God does not depend on human beings in order to *be*, but is so dependent for recognition, concrete mediated self-consciousness, etc.

22. PhG 527–8; PhS 458. Hegel indicates that speculative knowledge has the same content as the revelatory religion. (PhG 530; PhS: 461; he makes the same point in the opening paragraph of the *Encyclopedia* 1830) This shows that it is difficult, if not impossible to separate Hegel's phenomenology from theology. The *Phenomenology* is a phenomenological theology. The theology in question should not be confused with traditional metaphysical theology (*metaphysica specialis*). Hegel's phenomenological theology presupposes and accepts the truth of the central Christian doctrines of incarnation and trinity. These doctrines are reconstructed by Hegel via the social conception and categories of *Geist*. Hegel's reconstruction has as its fundamental principles (1) that it belongs to *Geist*—whether divine or human—to manifest itself, and *Geist* can manifest itself only to *Geist*. A *Geist* that failed to manifest itself would be a jealous *Geist*, a return to the theological presuppositions of Greek tragedy. (2) The relation between the divine and human is something like a relation of recognition: "God is God only so far as he knows himself: his self-knowledge is, further, a self-consciousness in man and man's knowledge of God, which proceeds to man's self-knowledge in God." (Enz. §564. These propositions are taken from Hegel's review of C. G. Göschel, *Aphorisms on Knowing and not-Knowing*, [Berlin, 1829]).

23. Jaeschke, VR 197; RR 184.

24. Jaeschke, VR 322; RR 311.

25. Dieter Henrich observes that "Hegel must continually re-interpret the structures which Hölderlin understood as deriving from the original being, as modes of

relatedness which coalesce. The occurrence or event of union rather than a ground from which unity is to be derived, is the true absolute, the all in all. We will see that for this reason Hegel came to the conclusion that the absolute must be understood as *Geist* and not as Being." Dieter Henrich, "Hegel und Hölderlin," in *Hegel im Kontext,* (Frankfurt: Suhrkamp, 1981), 28.

26. As Mure puts it, the triad is for Hegel the *minimum rationale.* Cf. G. R. G Mure, *A Study of Hegel's Logic* (Oxford: Clarendon Press, 1950), 34ff. Cf. Enz. §187 Zusatz.

27. Jaeschke, VR 319; RR 311. Trinity, as a principle of social ontology, addresses the classical problem of the One and the Many. It hearkens back to Plato's *Parmenides* and *Sophist,* where the fundamental principle that the triad is the *minimum rationale* is first laid down and given dialectical treatment. Although the explicit doctrine of God as triune belongs to the consummate religion (identified by Hegel with Christianity), Hegel employs the triadic structure throughout the *Lectures on the Philosophy of Religion.* Cf. the editorial introduction to the *Lectures on the Philosophy of Religion,* one volume edition (The 1827 Lectures) by Peter C. Hodgson, (Berkeley: University of California Press, 1988), 16ff. Hodgson observes that by 1831 the distinctive Hegelian concept of God as triune had become the "centerpiece" of the Philosophy of Religion. Moreover, in these lectures "trinity" is conceived as a statement of social relations.

28. Hyppolite believes that there is a fundamental incompatibility in Hegel's thought here. He thinks that the alternatives are either phenomenology and anthropology on the one hand, or noumenology and metaphysics on the other. He writes "Is religion the portrait that a finite spirit, man, draws of God, or is it the knowledge that God has of himself? For Hegel the solution to this problem...is not in doubt.... Religion is simultaneously the one and the other." Jean Hyppolite, *Genesis and Structure of Hegel's Phenomenology of Spirit,* tr. Cherniak and Heckman (Evanston, Ill.: Northwestern University Press, 1974), 541. However, Hyppolite poses an abstract either/or: either phenomenology or noumenology. He finds the noumenological interpretation tending towards theosophical mysticism (Eckhart), and the phenomenological-anthropological interpretation tending towards Feuerbach. While Hyppolite recognizes that Hegel's position cannot be reduced to either of these, he overlooks that Hegel's alternative is characterized by (1) a speculative reconstruction of christology and trinity, and (2) recognition as a central concept in this speculative reconstruction. If there is such a thing as divine-human recognition—and Hegel believes that such recognition is historically given in the history of religion and consummated in Christian faith, the revelatory religion—this would constitute an alternative to Hyppolite's dilemma that phenomenology is possible only as anthropology and theology is possible only as metaphysics and/or mysticism. See my article, "Phenomenology and Theology" in *Essays on Phenomenological Theology,* ed. J. Hart and S. Laycock (Albany, N.Y.: SUNY Press, 1986).

29. Hegel notes that the term Natural Religion is ambiguous and can refer either to so-called primitive religions, i.e., the immediate unity of spirit with nature, or to religion in a universal rational sense. Cf. *Lectures on the Philosophy of Religion Vol-*

ume II: Determinate Religion, ed. Peter C. Hodgson, tr. R. F. Brown (Berkeley: University of California Press, 1987), 517ff. [Hereafter cited as LPR. II.] This apparently linear progressive development from one level (*Stufe*) to another, is misleading. It occurs only in the 1824 lectures, but is abandoned in the others. In these, determinate religion has its own threefold structure, differently conceived each time, and there is no unambiguous linear advance through the *Stufen* to the consummate religion. Rather, determinate religion appears to circle back upon itself; it does not make any linear historical progress, for it culminates in Roman religion, a religion of utility and expediency. Given Hegel's view that the Roman period, including its religion, is a cultural disaster that overtakes Greek *Sittlichkeit,* going hand in hand with domination and bondage, Roman religion cannot be regarded either as the culmination or synthesis of Greek and Jewish Religions. Rather it represents the *Untergang* of determinate religions, including the religions of beauty (Greek Religion) and ethical sublimity (Judaism). Consummate religion appears not as a development of, but rather as a break with, Roman religion. Walter Jaeschke observes that Hegel does not succeed in offering a coherent unitary historical development of religion, but at best a typology and geography of religions. (VR 283–294; RR 272ff) See also Peter C. Hodgson's editorial introduction to LPR. II. Hodgson observes that whenever Hegel attempts to lay out the stages of consciousness of freedom in any sort of historical ordering and sequence, he gets into trouble. Moreover, Hegel's changing accounts of Determinate Religion shows that he was aware of the difficulties involved.

30. Ibid.

31. Ibid. 515.

32. Hegel points to the practice of animal sacrifice as involving a desacralization of nature, and observes that Zeus is above all a political god. Ibid., 643ff

33. R 673; VPR II 565. Hegel remarks that "if divine subjectivity were determined as result...then it would be grasped as concrete spirit." This is a triadic conception of the absolute as *Geist,* which is manifest in the revelatory or consummate religion.

34. Cf. PhG 19.

35. For an overview of the issues, cf. Jaeschke, VR 377ff; RR 365ff.

36. In the *Phenomenology* Hegel writes: "...es hebt dies sein Sein im andern auf, entläßt also das andere wieder frei." (PhG 142) In the *Encyclopedia* he says: "Die absolute Freiheit der Idee aber ist...in der absoluten Wahrheit ihrer selbst sich entschließt, das Moment ihrer Besonderheit oder des ersten Bestimmens und Andersseins, die unmittelbare Idee als ihren Widerschein, sich als Natur frei aus sich zu entlassen." (Enz §244)

37. VPR III 210–211; LPR III 285–286.

38. Whether this implies that God is a person is another question. Some claim that this fundamentally relational conception of personhood implies that God is supremely personal, the absolute person. See Karl Barth, *Church Dogmatics,* vol. 2

(Edinburgh: T&T Clark, 1957). For a discussion of the complex philosophical and theological issues, see Falk Wagner, *Der Gedanke der Persönlichkeit Gottes bei Fichte und Hegel* (Gutersloh: Gerd Mohn, 1971); see also Wolfhart Pannenberg, "Die Bedeutung des Christentums in der Philosophie Hegels," in *Stuttgarter Hegel-Tage 1970*. *Hegel Studien* Beiheft 11 (Bonn: Bouvier Verlag, 1974), 175–202; Dale M. Schlitt, *Hegel's Trinitarian Claim: A Critical Reflection* (Leiden: E. J. Brill, 1984); Walter Jaeschke, "Absolute Idee—Absolute Subjektivität: Zum Problem der Persönlichkeit Gottes in der Logik und in der Religionsphilosophie," *Zeitschrift für philosophische Forschung*, Band 35, Heft 3/4, (Meisenheim/Glan: Verlag Anton Hain, 1981), 385–416; Jaeschke, VR 377ff, RR 365ff.

39. PhG 139; PhS 110.

40. PhG 473; PhS 410; cf. PhG 479; PhS 415.

41. Hegel acknowledges that incarnation as a principle has no truth for eastern religions, because the concept of reconciliation does not play a central role in their *Geist*. PhG 482; PhS 418.

42. Thus the natural religions correspond to the analysis of consciousness; in them the forces of light and darkness contend for mastery. Here Hegel locates master/slave as a form of divine-human relation, which will re-appear in higher more complex forms. (PhG 483; PhS 419).

43. PhG 479; PhS 415. [Emphasis mine.]

44. This claim distances Hegel from classical theistic metaphysics. Cf. his sketch of such metaphysics in the *Encyclopedia* (1830) §32 Zusatz. Cf. also §§28–36.

45. See Martin Donougho, "The Woman in White: On the Reception of Hegel's Antigone," *Owl of Minerva*, vol. 21 no. 1 (Fall 1989): 80.

46. PhG 496; PhS 430.

47. PhG 512; PhS 446.

48. See Paul Ricoeur, *The Symbolism of Evil*, tr. E. Buchanan (Boston: Beacon Press, 1969), 211ff.

49. PhG 515; PhS 448.

50. NR TWA Sk. 2: 496f; NL 105–6.

51. NR TWA Sk. 2:499; NL 108.

52. PhG 517; PhS 450.

53. PhG 519; PhS 451.

54. That is, comedy rests upon the acknowledgement of subjectivity. The gods are grasped as relative to subjectivity, and thus as projections. Feuerbach applies Hegel's comic interpretation of religion to Christianity itself. Here lies an important difference between Hegel and Feuerbach. Both agree that classical Christianity is

comic. But, for Hegel it is a *divine* comedy and no projection, whereas Feuerbach identifies Christianity with its classical form, and so announces a post-Christian anthropological development of religion. Hegel distinguishes between Christianity as such (or the idea of Christianity) and its classical historical forms. This distinction implies the possibility of an internal theological criticism of Christianity which makes theological reconstruction both possible and necessary. Hegel's reconstructed Christianity incorporates tragic features. See *Glauben und Wissen* (TWA Sk 2), ET *Faith and Knowledge*, tr. Cerf and Harris (Albany, N.Y.: SUNY Press, 1977), 190–191.

55. PhG 517, 523; PhS 450, 455.

56. PhG 523; PhS 455.

57. PhG 518; PhS 450. There is an error in the translation: Miller's term "equal" is a mistranslation for "actual" (*wirkliche*), and in this context makes no sense. Hegel advances this claim in the context of a detailed discussion of tragic plot structure. He is not making a dogmatic claim concerning "true" versus "false" religion, Christianity versus paganism.

58. Jaeschke observes that this involves transcendence of mere human representations: for in religion *Geist* itself, and not merely a representation of it, is the object of religious consciousness. (VR 205; RR 193) A condition of such self-manifestation is that God has the shape of subjectivity, i.e., actually incarnates Godself. (VR 215; RR 204)

59. Hegel, *Vorlesungen über die Beweise vom Dasein Gottes*, Hrsg. G. Lasson (Hamburg: Meiner Verlag, 1930, 1973), 47. The claim that God is jealous is of course the tragic theology, which is criticized by Plato, Aristotle and Hegel. See Enz. §564: "If the word 'God' is taken seriously in religion at all, it is from Him, the theme and center of religion, that the method of divine knowledge may and must begin: and if self-revelation is refused Him, then the only thing left to constitute his nature would be to ascribe envy to Him. But clearly if the word '*Geist*' is to have a meaning, it implies the revelation of Him." (ET *Hegel's Philosophy of Mind*, 298.) *Geist* is essentially social, and therefore self-revelatory.

60. PhG 527. This shows how intimately Hegel's thought is connected with and is a philosophical interpretation of, Christian thought.

61. Hegel, *Beweise*, 47.

62. PhG 527–528. It should also be noted that Hegel explicitly denies that this content is produced by or a projection reducible to, human subjectivity and thought.

63. Hegel, *Beweise vom Dasein Gottes*, Hamburg: Meiner Verlag, 1973, 46.

64. Edith Düsing (op. cit.) also believes that this passage implies *Anerkennung* although the term itself does not appear.

65. PhG 529: "This is the true form of *Geist*, to be revelatory according to its very concept…" That is, *Geist* is revelatory because it is fundamentally social, the coincidence or equivalence between being-for-other and being-for-self. Incarnation as

a divine-human community, initially appears as a kenosis (*herabsteigen*); but it is also the consummation of the concept of spirit. Cf. Jaeschke, VR 197; RR 184, 204.

66. PhG 541. Cf. Jaeschke VR 348ff; RR 337ff: "The community forms the material prerequisite of Christology."

67. PhG 530.

68. NR TWA Sk 2: 454; NL 71.

69. This is obviously related to Hegel's contrast between the false and the genuine infinite. The false infinite is a Beyond set in absolute contrast and opposition to the finite. However, by virtue of its opposition to finitude, the infinite is itself reduced to something finite and limited. In the preceding quotations Hegel employs his concept of genuine infinity, a social-holistic concept. Cf. *Encyclopedia* §28 Zusatz.

70. This same point emerges in the very first category of the *Logic*. The determinacy of being is to have no determinacy, and thus being is an immediate transition into its opposite, nothing. Cf. WL. TWA, Sk 5: 82ff; SL 82ff.

71. Hegel, *Natural Law*, ET 104.

72. Ibid.

73. Stephen Crites observes "The horrendous notion that God himself has died on the cross, which has been obscured by harmless conventional renderings of the story, is here restored not merely as an historical event but as a supreme speculative insight restored in all its original force and pitiless severity..." "The Golgotha of Absolute Spirit" in *Method and Speculation in Hegel's Phenomenology*, ed. M. Westphal (New York: Humanities Press, 1982), 51.

74. Feuerbach believes that it signifies a theological criticism of theology; he complains that Hegel's treatment of the death of God theme is a theological negation of theology, i.e., a negation of theology that is itself theology. Cf. Ludwig Feuerbach, "Principles of the Philosophy of the Future," in *The Fiery Brook: Selected Writings of Ludwig Feuerbach*, tr. Z. Hanfi (New York: Doubleday, 1972), 168, 204. For a Feuerbachian reading of Hegel, see Merold Westphal, op. cit. If Westphal were correct that Hegel really maintained a reduction of theology to anthropology, this would constitute an ironic twist for Feuerbach, who devoted much effort correcting Hegel on just this issue.

75. Cited in Hegel, LPR. III 125n, 163: "O grosse Not, Gott selbst liegt tot. Am Kreuz ist er gestorben; hat dadurch das Himmelreich uns aus Lieb' erworben." The hymn was written by Johannes Rist. For a discussion of the Lutheran debate, cf. Eberhard Jüngel, *God as the Mystery of the World*, tr. Darrell L. Guder (Grand Rapids, Mich.: Eerdmans Publishing Company, 1983), 64. The theological dispute in Lutheran circles revived the ancient debate over divine impassibility and suffering, i.e., whether God suffers and dies (Patripassianism), or only the human nature of the second person of the trinity.

76. The *Phenomenology* focuses on the death of God as a multi-leveled christological statement and critique of abstract substance metaphysics. The *Philosophy of*

Religion Lectures, on the other hand, make explicit the connection between the christological and triadic aspects of the theme.

77. Cf. Hegel, *Faith and Knowledge,* op. cit. 57–8.

78. Hegel, LPR III. 125; VPR 60. Texts are from Hegel's Lecture Manuscript (1821). Cf. NL 71, 104; NR 104; TWA Sk. 2: 454, 495.

79. LPR III. 125; VPR III. 60. [I have modified the English translation.]

80. LPR III. 78; VPR III. 16.

81. LPR III. 66; VPR III. 6.

82. LPR III. 78; VPR III. 16–17.

83. PhG 546.

84. Ibid. The imagery is not unlike the opening discussion of Being in the *Wissenschaft der Logik.* Pure being cannot be isolated, for its determinacy is to have no determinacy, and so it "vanishes," i.e., passes over into its opposite, namely nothing.

85. Unless of course one simply identifies theology with classical metaphysics and metaphysical theology (Aristotle). One interpreter who makes such an identification is Alan White (*Absolute Knowledge: Hegel and the Problem of Metaphysics* [Ohio University Press, 1983], 70ff.) But that identification begs the question with which Hegel is struggling, namely in the light of the critique of foundationalism, is theology simply ontotheology? Although Hegel's thought is not free from ambiguity, there are motifs in it, such as love, forgiveness and releasement (*Gelassenheit*) which point beyond ontotheology in a non-foundationalist direction.

86. PhG 540–1.

87. NL 105–6.

88. Ibid.

89. Feuerbach's reduction of theology to anthropology is a modern expression of comedy.

90. NL 108.

91. Pöggeler, op. cit. 99.

92. To extrapolate this line of reasoning further, the other would be merely instrumental to self-sameness and unity, rather than an end in itself.

93. Pöggeler thinks that Hegel's "Christianity" is, in its conception of God nothing more than a facade for "the God of the philosophers," namely Aristotelian teleological pure thought thinking itself. Hegel's account of trinity would thus reduce to Aristotle's. (Ibid. 100)

94. Otto Pöggeler, op. cit. 98.

95. Pöggeler, op. cit. 99.

96. Paul Ricoeur demonstrates that the Adamic myth of classical Christian theology involves a critique and rejection of tragic presuppositions, e.g., the tragic God who blinds, existence as tragically flawed (Cf. Ricoeur, *Symbolism of Evil*, op. cit.). Instead of tracing the origin of evil to a tragic flaw, the Adamic myth sets forth an anthropological origin of evil, which occurs within a world already created good. But the classical doctrine is susceptible to a moralizing pelagian interpretation that suppresses and conceals the tragic depths of evil present in the Adamic myth. For this reason, the classical doctrine, although not the Adamic myth per se, has been eclipsed in the modern world as a theory of evil, forcing contemporary theology to re-open and struggle with the tragic myth. Hegel is important here because he incorporates tragic elements in his reconstruction of Christianity. Cf. my essay, "Sin and Evil" in *Christian Theology: An Introduction to its Traditions and Tasks*, ed. Peter Hodgson and Robert King (Philadelphia: Fortress Press, 1982), 168–193.

97. Pöggeler, op. cit. 99. For a critique of Goethe's attack on Hegel, see Donougho, "The Woman In White" op. cit.

98. Goethe to Mueller, cited in Pöggeler op. cit. 99n. Ricoeur's discussion of the tragic myth tends to confirm Goethe's claim. Cf. *Symbolism of Evil*, op. cit. The Adamic myth involves a de-mythologization of the tragic myth. However, Ricoeur notes that, understood at a deeper level, the Adamic myth is not tragic, but nevertheless incorporates certain tragic features. For example it does not collapse evil entirely into the Adam figure; Adam finds evil already there and yields to it. This mitigates the stark opposition between tragedy and reconciliation formulated by Goethe and seconded by Pöggeler, and is much closer to Hegel's view.

99. Werner Marx, *Heidegger and the Tradition*, tr. Theodore Kisiel (Evanston, Ill.: Northwestern University Press, 1971), 55.

100. Ibid. 57. Marx cites the Logic for the claim that the absolute "eternally overcomes" opposition. TWA 6: 467–8. However his quoting is highly selective, and makes it appear as if Hegel holds the same position as Dante, namely that the absolute exists above and/or without opposition, that opposition is excluded in principle from the absolute.

101. See *Faith and Knowledge*, 190–191. Hegel speaks of the necessity of incorporating infinite grief into the absolute divine idea.

102. Hegel, *Lectures on the Philosophy of Religion III*, 219.

103. Ibid. 326.

104. Ibid. 323n.

105. This was Hegel's conception as early as *Natural Law*. Cf. NR TWA Sk. 2: 495; NL 104: "...the movement of the absolute contradiction between these two natures presents itself in the Divine nature as courage, whereby the first nature frees itself from the death inherent in the other conflicting nature."

106. PhG 20; PhS §19, 10.

107. *Enz.* §147 Zusatz. ET, *The Logic of Hegel*, 209–210.

108. Ibid. 210–211.

109. Hegel rejects the traditional theological account of Creation and Fall, by means of which the tradition sought to distinguish finitude from sin and evil. Hegel thus confronts the problem, if the temporal distinction between Creation and Fall is rejected, how to maintain the *non-coincidence of sin with finitude?* Instead of locating evil in the Fall as an event, Hegel finds its conditions in the epistemological distancing of subjectivity from itself and others, the restlessness of spirit, and the ontological anxiety that accompanies the self-consciousness of freedom. Such conditions are not evil, or causes of evil, for they also underlie and shape reconciliation as well. Nevertheless the recognition of such conditions is at the same time the recognition of a tragic or at least shadow side of existence. (On the crucial distinction between sin and finitude, cf. Hegel, *The Philosophy of Right*, §139.) Moreover, although finitude is a moment of the absolute logical Idea, it is not to be equated with sin. Hence, in God there is otherness, but not evil. Evil occurs at the level of history, occasioned but not caused by the ontological restlessness and anxiety constitutive of human freedom. Hegel's *Philosophy of Religion* is not simply an instantiation, but a determinate qualification and modification of the logical categories.

110. Hegel, *Faith and Knowledge*, op. cit. 190.

111. Ibid. 190–191.

112. Consider the following formulation: "However, the process does not come to an end at this point [viz., the death of God, the loss of everything eternal and true]; rather a reversal *[Umkehrung]* takes place: God, that is to say, maintains himself in this process, and the latter is only the death of death. God rises again to life and thus things are reversed." (*Lectures on Philosophy of Religion III*, 323.) The question is, what does this reversal mean? It seems to imply that the death of God is finally transformed into a death of death. But does this imply a return to the metaphysics of light? an exclusion of otherness from identity, the exclusion of infinite grief from the divine Idea? I doubt it. For Hegel speaks of the need to incorporate infinite grief into the divine Idea, and this belies any reduction of the triad to a sheer undifferentiated unity.

113. Ibid. 327.

114. LPR III 220; VP. III 150.

115. Ibid.

116. Pöggeler overlooks such negation and suffering in God when he charges that in Hegel's thought teleology overtakes and excludes tragedy. Similarly, Marx suppresses these features in his account of Hegel. Marx selectively quotes Hegel's *Logic* and makes it appear as if Hegel returns to the classical metaphysical tradition. Marx says that, although the absolute "contains, in Hegel's words, 'even the harshest opposition,'" it nevertheless 'eternally overcomes' it. The dialectical order thereby guarantees the conclusive victory to the light, to the truth undisguised by untruth." (Marx, op. cit. 57) This is a selective quotation out of context which distorts Hegel's

meaning by suppressing the timeless triadic structure which includes opposition as well as mediation. The passage which Marx misquotes runs as follows: "*die Idee hat um der Freiheit willen, die der Begriff in ihr erreicht, auch den härtesten Gegensatz in sich; ihre Ruhe besteht in der Sicherheit und Gewissheit, womit sie ihn ewig erzeugt und ewig überwindet und in ihm mit sich selbst zusammengeht.*" [The idea includes for the sake of the freedom which the concept attains in it, the hardest opposition in itself. Its rest consists in the security and certainty with which it eternally *produces* opposition, eternally *overcomes* opposition and in opposition *coincides* with itself.] TWA 6: 468. [Emphasis mine.] The self-coincidence is not that of the I = I, but rather has a triadic structure. It is the triadic structure which is crucial to Hegel's concrete identity.

117. The royal metaphor supports the reading of classical Christianity as a divine comedy. The royal metaphor portrays God as absolutely sovereign, abstract from all relation and constraints. It implies a logic of divine sovereignty or mastery over the world. For a discussion of this classical conception, cf. Edward Farley, *Ecclesial Reflection: An Anatomy of Theological Method* (Philadelphia: Fortress Press, 1982).

ELEVEN

RECOGNITION AND ABSOLUTE KNOWLEDGE

Not without reason, commentators find the final chapter on absolute knowledge in the *Phenomenology* one of the most compressed and difficult. Hyppolite concludes his massive commentary by complaining that "absolute knowledge...is presented to us in a form so vague as to open the path to diverse interpretations; we are unable to indicate exactly which interpretation constitutes the authentic heritage of Hegelianism."[1] The difficulty does not lie merely in the supposed haste with which the *Phenomenology* was written, but in the very conception of absolute knowing itself. Absolute knowing is not simply a super-intellectualist epistemology or knowledge of knowledge. In absolute knowing, epistemology and ontology are inseparable; it is at once epistemology and ontology.

But what does this mean? Here interpretations diverge, and there is little consensus.[2] Some hold that absolute knowledge is a metaphysical pantheist monism of I = I.[3] This view interprets Hegel as an abstract metaphysician, and absolute knowledge is about a large supersensible entity. Others hold a phenomenological view, namely that absolute knowledge does not involve any metaphysical transcendence of experience.[4] But this view divides further into those who interpret the absolute as anthropology (Kojève, Westphal), and those who interpret absolute knowing as in some sense dialogical (Ludwig, Flay). One way to sort this out is along the lines marked out by Hyppolite: phenomenology or noumenology, phenomenological anthropology or metaphysical theology.

The view that I propose is another version of the phenomenological-dialogical reading, but one which rejects the division between phenomenology and noumenology, or between phenomenology and theology. That is, absolute knowledge means not only the human knowledge of the absolute, but also the absolute's self-knowledge. The latter is inclusive of the former. Whatever else it means, absolute knowing involves a novel conception of divine-human self-recognition in other. Recall Göschel's aphorisms which Hegel cites with approval: "God is God only insofar as he knows himself; his self-knowing is further his self-consciousness in human beings, and the human knowledge of God, that advances to human self-knowledge in God."[5] This suggests that Hegel conceives the divine-human relation as one of mutual-reciprocal self-recognition in other.

The central interpretive issue concerning absolute knowledge may be stated as follows: On the one hand, absolute knowing is the complete and final transformation of substance into subject, the transparency of I = I. On the other hand, Hegel develops and puts forth a social-intersubjective concept of *Geist*. The question is, are these compatible? If not, does he finally override or undermine his social conception at the ultimate level of absolute knowledge? If such were the case, it would mean that Hegel's absolute *Geist* lapses into idealism and falls below the level of his doctrine of subjective and objective *Geist*. If the absolute *Geist* overrides or eliminates otherness, then it would in the final analysis be life-less, solitary and alone. This is exactly what Hegel denies. Not only is the intersubjective model of spirit retained, in the *Phenomenology* it is the comprehensive formulation of *Geist*.

But when interpreting Hegel, matters are seldom clear cut. A further complication is that absolute knowing is both logical and historical. There is a tension between these two requirements: on the one hand Hegel's system is open to history and *Geist* exhibits a restlessness and dynamism that incessantly propels it; on the other hand Hegel also describes the movement of *Geist* in terms of the metaphor of the circle that attains its beginning only as it reaches its end.[6] The former tendency requires that the system be open to otherness, while the latter suggests that the system reverts upon or returns to its beginning in closure, thus eliminating otherness.

Hegel rejects any forced choice between rationality and history; as a post-Enlightenment thinker, he affirms both.[7] He conceives the transition from substance to subject not as purely theoretical or a-historical, but also as existential-historical, as Kroner has pointed out.[8] This creates the anomaly that absolute knowledge, as the final Gestalt of *Geist,* has existential and historical presuppositions. It is no merely speculative construction, since its content is already given in religion, i.e., the revelatory religion.[9] Since Absolute *Geist* emerges concretely in and through reciprocal recognition of forgiveness, the transition from substance to subject has a temporal-historical dimension or aspect. Absolute knowledge arises out of and is the final form of divine-human recognition. Its structure is self-recognition in other. As self-recognition in other, absolute knowledge includes mediation by other. It is not simply a subject-object relation but a subject's relation to itself mediated by another subject.

Yet absolute knowledge is also knowledge. It allegedly overcomes the separation between subject and object constitutive of representation (*Vorstellung*). This dichotomy between subject and object pervades consciousness (*Bewusstsein*) and its representations (*Vorstellungen*). The dichotomy is constitutive of religious consciousness, and prevents the latter from being fully self-conscious. Religion fails to recognize that its object (other) is in some sense its own doing: "The doing of the self retains a negative significance for it [religious consciousness] because the self-divestment of substance is taken to be an action implicit in substance. But religious consciousness does not comprehend this action, nor does it find its own doing therein."[10] When *Vorstellung* is transformed into *Begriff*, the separation between subject and object constitutive of representations is supposed to be overcome, and the content (*Inhalt*) is supposed to receive its final form, the truth in the form of the true, or in the form of self.[11] The transcending of the dichotomies between subject and object, thought and being, means that absolute knowing (the I = I), and not religion, is the final Gestalt of the *Phenomenology*.[12]

The juxtaposition of these two apparently quite different views of absolute knowledge—the social and the absolute reflection—brings before us the problem of the unity and coherence of Hegel's thought. It appears that each view generates a different interpretation of the Other. In the first, the Other is essential to and a requirement of self-knowledge. This points to holism. In the latter, the Other is a phase to be passed through and overcome, eliminated in a final unity. If so, then these two views appear to be exclusive. Can these two views be brought together? We do well to heed Hyppolite's remark that "It is meaningless to say that a philosopher is an absolute idealist if we cannot see the exact meaning of this idealism."[13]

In what follows, I shall attempt to show that absolute knowledge recalls and preserves the fundamental structure of reciprocal recognition. I shall show that Hegel does not eliminate the other or reduce self-recognition in other to sheer self-sameness. Subjectivity finds its culmination in intersubjectivity. This is not to maintain that Hegel's thought is entirely free from ambiguity. Far from it. I shall begin by confronting the ambiguity, which unfolds in terms of two apparently different models of absolute knowledge, the social and the idealist. These two may be compatible, but only with certain qualifications. My thesis is that the idealist model cannot account for the social, but the social can include and incorporate the idealist model. Moreover, Hegel concludes the *Phenomenology* with the social model.

ABSOLUTE KNOWLEDGE

Two Models

Let us begin by fleshing out and clarifying the two different models of absolute knowledge.[14] The first model is the idealist conception. In this view, absolute knowledge results from substance becoming subject. Subjectivity emerges as the final Gestalt, reducing all preceding *Gestalten* to instrumentalities of its self-positing. Self-consciousness is a bending back of subjectivity upon itself, recapturing its substance and history in complete transparency. It is the absolute ego become fully transparent to itself, or I = I. "This subject is truly actual only as it is the movement of self-positing, or the mediation of self-othering with itself...only this self-restoring identity or reflexion in oth-erness is the true, and not some original unity as such, or the immediate as such."[15] From this vantage point, the fundamental oppositions and contrasts of consciousness, including the other, are overcome. The other turns out to be the self-othering of the ego, subordinate to the ego's identity and unity.

Such is the received view. Hegel is supposed to be an idealist, and the idealist interpretation of the other is that it is a form of the self, or self-other-ing. Feuerbach complains that the *Phenomenology* "begins...not with the 'other-being' of thought, but with the *idea of the 'other being' of thought*."[16] In other words, Hegel confuses "the other" with the "*thought* of the other." This enables him to treat the other as a negation. The other is the result of the negation (*Ur-teil*) of unity and identity. As such, it is a subordinate element derivative from identity and not equiprimordial or co-constitutive of identity. Once the other is identified as derivative from negation, it can be eliminated by the next step—negation of negation—which restores self-identity and self-sameness.

Self-recognition in *other*, being at home with self in an other, are, on the idealist model, interpreted simply as *self*-recognition. Thus, in dealing with its other, spirit is only dealing with itself. What gets recognized is not the other, but the self. Strictly speaking, there is no other, the other is only the self or self-othering.[17] On this view, the process whereby substance becomes subject is the unfolding of an a-historical identity. The speculative development from substance to subject is timeless and requires no historical or social mediation.

A second possible interpretation of absolute knowledge is the intersub-jective model. By this I mean that the concept of substance become subject is not to be interpreted solipsistically, but as social, as involving self-recogni-tion in other.[18] To interpret *Geist* as a solitary subject is to overlook Hegel's major contribution that *Geist* is an I that is a We, and a We that is an I. So understood, *Geist* cannot be collapsed into immediate self-transparency of the I = I, but rather has a triadic social structure with threefold mediation.[19] That is why Hegel appreciates the structure, if not the symbolism, of the classical Christian doctrine of trinity: it articulates and resolves the funda-mental speculative-social problem, namely the equivalence between being-for-other and being-for-self. The social, as a relation of internal and external relations, necessarily has a triadic structure. I believe this is the authentically Hegelian interpretation of idealism's I = I, that explodes the latter's abstract undifferentiated identity and solipsism, and transforms it into an identity that requires difference.

The Problem of Relating the Two Models

It is beyond dispute that both models of absolute spirit and knowledge are present in Hegel's discussion. What is in dispute is the relation between the two, whether one is prior to the other, and if so, which takes priority. My claim is that the triadic social model (I = We) can incorporate the dyadic idealist model (I = I). However, many interpreters claim that the idealist model subsumes the social. Although these interpreters would concede that Hegel treats intersubjectivity, they claim that in the final analysis he undermines it by incorporating and subordinating it to his idealism, i.e., the other is reducible to the same.[20] The dialectical treatment of otherness means that otherness is instrumental to the development of identity and unity. Thus intersubjective mediation by other turns out, in the final analysis, to be self-mediation. The other is merely a subordinate negative phase of the unity of the subject, the I = I.

Moreover, some would contend that the intersubjective reading of Hegel interprets his thought too existentially and realistically.[21] The intersubjective reading disregards absolute knowledge's programmatic reduction of the dichotomous *Vorstellung* (or consciousness as a representational system) to the unity of the *Begriff*. The same objection can be brought against Hegel's treatment of religion. For Hegel religion remains at the level of *Vorstellung*, which is not the ultimate, but only the penultimate in Hegel's system. Religion too must be interpreted by and subordinate to the *Begriff*.

From Vorstellung *to* Begriff

According to Hegel, *Vorstellung* is based upon and constituted by the dichotomy between subject and object. The 'problem of the other" arises at this level, because consciousness (*Bewusstsein*) views itself and the other as bare immediate particulars. As such, they are independent, transcendent and irreducible, and incapable of mediation. The other is and remains other, not unlike the thing in itself.[22] Consciousness is initially naive and positive, i.e., it is unaware that the other on which the self depends for recognition, is, from the higher standpoint of the *Begriff*, the self's own dialectical self-mediation. Once this higher level is appreciated and understood, the central problem that absolute knowledge poses for the entire phenomenological project becomes clear. The culmination of the *Phenomenology* in absolute knowing shows that the phenomenological project is self-subverting, because it calls into question and abolishes its own fundamental presupposition, namely, the transcendence and independence of its object. Absolute knowing seems to collapse the distinction between consciousness and its object on which consciousness, and the phenomenology of consciousness, depend. Thus the final undermining of Hegelian phenomenology is idealist absolute knowledge itself. The latter imposes a set of reflective demands and conditions that undermine the claim that idealism can deal non-reductively with intersubjectivity. Hegel manages to avoid equipollence only by undermining the other: absolute knowing has no other.[23]

The idealist reading requires that what at the level of consciousness (*Bewusstsein*) appears as a given, must be transformed into, or regarded as, a *posit* of the (emergent) subject. All the previous *Gestalten des Bewusstseins* are to be understood from the final teleological perspective as instrumentalities of the subject's own becoming. Therefore, what appears as a given must be re-conceived as the doing of the subject, the subject's own act. "What goes on outside of the ego and appears opposed to the ego, is its own doing; thereby it shows itself to be essentially subject."[24] Mediation by other turns out to be self-mediation. Hegel, on the ultimate level of absolute knowledge, reduces the other to the same.

These same considerations lead to the conclusion that religion is undermined by absolute knowledge. Religion views its object as the Beyond, or Transcendent. Religious consciousness operates at the level of *Vorstellung* because it takes its object as a given, i.e., religion accepts its object in positive and figurate form.[25] And it tends to separate its object from experience and from the world.[26] Feuerbach formulated the reversal of religion in absolute knowledge thus: "the object of any subject is nothing but the subject's own nature taken objectively."[27] The religious object, when revealed to be a posit of the subject, loses its independence and transcendence. Consequently, the religious object turns out to be a projection of the religious consciousness, and so theology is, in the final perspective, reducible to anthropology.[28] Thus, neither intersubjectivity nor religion survives its translation into absolute knowledge: the other is a projection of the subject, and so the other is reducible to the same. William James' characterization is apt: Absolute knowledge is like a bear's cave where countless animal tracks are seen going in, but none coming back out. On the idealist reading, absolute knowledge devours all phenomena.

TOWARDS A NON-FOUNDATIONAL ABSOLUTE KNOWLEDGE

The foregoing reading rests upon a particular interpretation of the term "posit" (*setzen*). It presupposes that posit (*setzen*) is equivalent to metaphysical creation. To have all givens transformed into posits of absolute subjectivity, is to grasp them as relative to and metaphysically derivative from subjectivity. On this reading, Hegel's phenomenological project is an extended argument for metaphysical idealism, in which substance is shown to be derivative from subjectivity. Absolute knowledge makes explicit this inversion, and it does so in reference to religion and the other: "What religious consciousness takes to be its content, or the representation of an other, is here the self's own doing."[29] One commentator interprets this to mean "Absolute knowing allows for the comprehension of phenomenology as the science of experiencing consciousness insofar as the content of consciousness—and this is ultimately spirit—is *brought forth* by consciousness in the element of the concept."[30]

To be sure, it is far from clear what posit (*setzen*) means. Perhaps it is a term without clear equivalent or even appropriate translation. Even in English the term is far from clear; it includes such diverse meanings as "presume," "postulate," and "presuppose." The philosophical use of the term posit (*setzen*) apparently derives from Fichte. According to Fichte, the essence of dogmatism is the claim that there is but a single posit, a single first principle, a single type of explanation, e.g., the causal.[31] However, dogmatism fails to account for a second sense of posit, namely the presentation itself, or consciousness of—. But the presentation is not a cause, rather it is a medium of access to things that is prior to and presupposed by causal explanation. In Fichte's view, both naturalistic materialism and metaphysical idealism are dogmatic, because each seeks to reduce the other (causally) to its first principle. It is just this reductive dogmatic procedure that Fichte seeks to overcome. The presentation, phenomenologically understood, provides access to the world, that makes possible the question concerning origins, while leaving open the question of metaphysical interpretation. Fichte's is not a metaphysical, but a critical idealism. However, if there are two contrasting and opposite senses, then there must be a third which unites them. Thus, Fichte arrived at a scheme of threefold positing, namely thesis, antithesis and synthesis.[32]

Hegel took over and modified this scheme. For Hegel posit does not mean or imply causal-metaphysical explanation. He criticizes such explanations as one-sided. Hegel identifies three orientations of thought towards objectivity: the metaphysical, the transcendental, and the post-transcendental.[33] Hegel observes that in metaphysical thinking everything is interpreted as a thing, an entity. The soul is a thing, and God is the most real thing (*ens realissimum*). Thus, metaphysics tends to interpret everything as a given, a mundane entity capable of explanation in terms of the traditional categories, including causality. Here, thought must conform to a pre-given object or structure. Critical Idealism inverts traditional substance metaphysics by shifting the foundation from substance to subject. Now it is things which must conform to conditions laid down by thought. Nevertheless idealism, as an inversion of metaphysical foundationalism, remains on the same ground as metaphysics. But the task is to suspend the concept of positing as metaphysical and foundational.

Hegel's post-metaphysical conception finds initial expression in his analysis of love as beyond domination.

> *Begreifen ist beherrschen...nur in der Liebe allein ist man eins mit dem Objekt, es beherrscht nicht und wird nicht beherrscht.*
> [To conceive is to dominate...but only in love one is at-one with the object, neither dominating it nor dominated by it.][34]

Hegel's concept of love implies releasement, i.e., the other is set free and allowed to be. This is possible only if domination is renounced in favor of recognition. Self-recognition in other thus replaces positing. The lesson of recognition is that absolute or single positing is self-subverting and plunges the self into life and death struggle. In the course of the struggle, each learns that it must renounce its immediacy. A further corollary of such self-renunciation is the releasement (*Gelassenheit*) of the other which allows the other to be, to go free.[35] Each side must renounce its immediacy and enter into a process of mutual-reciprocal mediation.

It is not Hegel's alleged idealism, but his critique of abstract atomism and insistence upon universal relativity, that leads him to reject the claim of the unmediated totally other. The totally other is only the nullpoint, the starting point of mediation, which begins with absolute enmity and rejection, i.e., the life and death struggle. But there is no remaining in the posture of total exclusion, for that leads to, or involves the acceptance of, murder and death. The problem with master and slave is not that there is too much mediation, but rather that there is not enough. Hegel's account of recognition unfolds, not without conflict, from minimal recognition to reciprocal recognition in forgiveness. The 'We' emerging through reciprocal recognition is no reduction of the other to the same, because domination of the other has been abandoned in favor of releasement, reciprocity and holism.

But can the same be said of Hegel's treatment of absolute knowing? How are we to interpret Hegel's remark, "Thus, what religion takes to be the content (*Inhalt*) or the form of representation of an other, is here the self's own doing; the *Begriff* makes the connection that the content is the doing of the self"?[36] The transition from *Vorstellung* to *Begriff*, which overcomes the oppositions of consciousness, appears to make the other relative to the self, and thus to collapse the other into the self. Absolute knowledge can have no givens; all givens are reducible to the self's own posits. The transcendence and independence of the other seem to be undermined. Absolute *knowledge*, insofar as this is supposed to have an intersubjective or a theological-religious content, seems to be the end of *absolute* knowledge. This is Heidegger's reading. The absolute, as utterly autonomous and self-grounding, can have no givens presented to it from elsewhere; its self-grounding wrests it away from and 'absolves' it from all givens.[37]

Such a radical transcendental reading, while possible, is mistaken. Hegel himself cautions against such a one-sided reductive reading at the beginning of his discussion of absolute knowing: "This overcoming of the object of consciousness is not to be taken in the one-sided sense that the object shows itself returning into the self."[38] In other words, to posit does *not* mean to reduce, or to interpret the [posited] content as the effect and result of the agent. This is a one-sided oppositional form that reflects the unresolved dichotomies of *Verstand*, and not absolute knowledge.[39]

Heidegger interprets the term "absolute" from its Latin root (*absolvere*), meaning "to loose," "absolve" or "release." Heidegger takes *absolvere* in a foundationalist sense: The absolute can have no givens, but absolves itself from all givens. Absolute knowledge therefore means a knowledge 'absolved' from dependence on givens in assuring itself of truth. "The conventional notion of the absolute is something that itself is absolved from or independent of everything finite and relative."[40] Thus, what is absolute is excluded from relation and qualification. Heidegger emphasizes this conventional reading, and, not surprisingly, interprets Hegel as the culmination of onto-theological foundationalist metaphysics.

But such a reading of the absolute as excluding relations is susceptible to equipollence objections, as Hegel observes: "The essence of dogmatism consists in this, that it posits something finite, something burdened with an opposition (e.g., pure subject, or pure object, or in dualism the duality as opposed to the identity) as the Absolute; hence Reason shows with respect to this Absolute, that it has a relation to what is excluded from it, and only exists through and in this relation to an other..."[41] Hegel's equipollence critique lays to rest the foundationalist connotations of the absolute, as exclusive of relation and as abstract identity. Moreover, equipollence points to a second, non-foundationalist sense of absolute and *absolvere,* namely, the absolute as relation, or relativity itself. Hegel writes: "...the rational...is itself nothing but the relationship. Since the rational is relation itself, the terms stand in relation to each other which are supposed to ground one another..."[42] A relation presupposes that its *relata* cannot be collapsed into each other, but remain distinct. How is their distinction to be maintained? Hegel's comments point to a second sense of *absolvere,* namely, releasement (*Gelassenheit*), or letting the other be.[43] The rational is an absolute of relation that releases its terms and allows them to be.

This clarification of *absolvere* permits a further clarification of absolute knowing. It is frequently said that the absolute has no other, or that absolute knowing has no other. In view of the ambiguity in '*absolvere*' these assertions are likewise ambiguous. When it is said that the absolute has no other, does this mean that the absolute eliminates otherness and the other? This is the conventional reading that culminates in abstract identity and metaphysics. On the other hand, these assertions may also mean that the absolute allows the other to be. The result is not dualism that renders the infinite finite (the so-called bad infinity), but an ontological concept of being as community in which the other loses its alien character, but not its independence. The social reading reflects Hegel's concept of recognition and antifoundational critique of metaphysics.

The following passage illustrates this point *apropos* the question of a reduction of religion to the social, of theology to anthropology:

...the absolute being of faith is essentially not the abstract being, the Beyond of believing consciousness. Rather it is the *Geist* of the community, the unity of the abstract being and self-consciousness. That this *Geist* is the *Geist* of the community depends essentially on the doing of the community. For this *Geist* exists only through the productive action of consciousness—or rather, *it is not without having been brought forth by consciousness. For although such doing is essential, it is nevertheless not the sole essential ground of that being, but merely one moment. At the same time, the being [of faith] exists in and for itself.*[44]

The first part of this text sounds like Feuerbach, as if posit were equivalent to metaphysical-causal production, i.e., *Geist* results from the doing of the community and is purely anthropological. But this interpretation can be sustained only by suppressing the last part of the text.[45] To say that *Geist* does not exist without its having been brought forth by consciousness does not mean that its content can be collapsed into (human) consciousness. What is posited by consciousness is posited as existing in and for itself (*zugleich an und für sich selbst*). That is, positing does not have a metaphysical foundationalist sense. Hegel makes the same point in another place: "The concept to be sure produces the truth—for such is subjective freedom—but at the same time it recognizes this truth not as something produced, but as the true existing in and for itself."[46]

Hegel's Critique of Positivity

In chapter 4 we noted that Hegel's attitude towards Christian faith underwent a change from a negative to a somewhat more favorable, positive assessment. The negative attitude reflected Hegel's earlier Kantian period, while the positive attitude reflects his overcoming metaphysics and replacing the abstract identity with concrete identity as self-recognition in other. Central to this change of attitude are three fundamental questions: Can Christianity be distinguished from its traditional historical forms? Second, Can reason support positivity, historical contingency and particularity? Can reason be actual in history? Hegel answers these questions in the affirmative. He distinguishes the "essence of Christianity" from its positive authoritarian forms.[47] This distinction implies that Christianity as such is a religion of freedom, and is not *essentially* positive in the alienating, authoritarian sense.

At the same time Hegel makes another discovery: the Enlightenment's negative assessment of positivity depends on its abstract formal rationalism, its mania for universality evident in its preference for natural religion rather than the positive or sectarian. But this concept of reason is formal, and can find only negative rather than positive expression in history. For example, the reign of terror in the name of freedom following the French Revolution and Kantian formalism in ethics, show in different ways the inability of

Enlightenment formal rationalism to be concretely normative. Thus, not only the traditional form of Christianity, but also the Enlightenment's a-historical formal rationalism, are sources of the alienation of modern life that must be overcome.

Hegel formulates an alternative conception of reason—the speculative—which makes possible a fresh appraisal and critical re-appropriation of history and positivity. Speculative reason is not simply universal to the exclusion of the historically positive, particular, and contingent. An infinite that excludes the finite and particular is itself finite and particular. For Hegel, reason itself is positive and actual (*wirkliche*), and the universal does not exclude but rather includes and depends on its particulars.[48] Positivity is no longer opposed to reason, but an essential element in the development and self-manifestation of speculative holism. This new conception of reason makes it possible for Hegel to affirm historical consciousness, to adopt a more favorable attitude towards Christianity, to distinguish it from its decadent forms, and to find in it a resource for overcoming of alienation and cultural decadence. That is why Hegel identifies the logical development whereby substance becomes subject with the Christian history of the incarnation and death of God that is the basis of the community of forgiveness.[49]

Hegel breaks with those who identify Christianity with its traditional forms and doctrines and maintain that these cannot be changed or reconstructed.[50] He also breaks with those who identify Christianity with its historical forms and doctrines and maintain that these cannot be salvaged or translated into alternative conceptualities.[51] Both are wrong; both deny in different ways and for different reasons Hegel's claim that "...what religion takes to be content (*Inhalt*) or the form of representation of an other, is here the self's own doing." The meaning of this assertion is not that the content of Christian doctrines is a mere projection or human creation. Rather, Hegel means that Christian faith is an historical phenomenon that cannot be apprehended or appropriated without mediation, namely, self-recognition in other. Further, the Christian religion not only can but should be distinguished from its traditional forms, and be reformulated—through the self's own doing—in different terms and historical situations.

For example, Hegel maintains that the Christian religion and philosophy have the same content, which is the content of absolute knowledge. That is why the Christian religion can be translated into the language of philosophy and regenerated, not out of alien positive historical forms, but out of the concrete concept (*Begriff*). Thus, philosophy reconstructs and re-presents the experience of the death of God:

> By marking this feeling [that God himself is dead] as a moment of the supreme idea, the pure concept...must reestablish for philosophy the Idea of absolute freedom and along with it the absolute passion, the speculative Good Friday in place of the historic Good Friday. Good Friday must be

speculatively reestablished in the whole truth and harshness of its God-for-sakenness.[52]

The historical God-man introduces a new principle of divine-human community into history that is a socially and historically mediated extension of the original founding event. "Just as the individual divine man has an implicit (*ansichseienden Vater*) father and only an actual mother, in like manner the universal divine man—the religious community—has as its father its own doing and knowing, while its mother is eternal love which it only feels..."[53] When Hegel says that the content of religion is to be regarded as the subject's own doing, he does not mean a reduction of theology to anthropology, but rather the historical appropriation, correction and reformulation of religion reflecting self-recognition in other. A *critical* appropriation is one that does not simply repeat an immutable a-historical tradition, but criticizes and reformulates it in response to problems in the tradition's own self-understanding.[54]

At the conclusion of the *Phenomenology,* Hegel sets forth an outline of history as a successive series of spiritual worlds (*Geisterreich*), "of which each is outfitted with the complete riches of *Geist.*"[55] This is additional evidence of Hegel's departure from the I = I of idealism. Instead of an absolute ego coming to self-consciousness in complete self-transparency, Hegel speaks here of the recollection and reminiscence of absolute spirit.[56] Without the diverse worlds of spirit, the absolute would be a bloodless abstraction—solitary, lifeless, and alone like Aristotle's unmoved mover or the Neo-Platonic One. Hegel does not continue abstract metaphysical theism, i.e., ontotheology's pure abstract being without relations, nor does he insist upon relativity to the subject (in the foundationalist sense of critical idealism that inverts the metaphysical tradition while remaining on its ground) that reduces theology to anthropology. His thought reaches beyond the impasse between abstract metaphysics and its idealist inversion.

THE TRIADIC STRUCTURE OF ABSOLUTE SPIRIT

Hegel is attracted to the triadic form not on traditional theological grounds,[57] but because the triadic structure articulates and makes possible a holistic equivalence between being for other and being for self. In such equivalence there is no reduction of the other to the same. The triadic *equivalence* or reciprocity between being-for-other and being-for-self constitutive of the We, is an alternative to abstract undifferentiated *identity* of the I = I.

Walter Jaeschke has called attention to this point: "For Hegel the concept of trinity is not restricted to the *Religionsphilosophie.* It appears as a historically pre-given solution of a fundamental problem of speculative philosophy: to conceive the relation to self as a relation to an other, to conceive how freedom is possible. For this is also the structure of Hegel's concept of freedom: to be at home with self in an other."[58] Freedom is not an individualist, but a social reality achieved through mutual recognition. Not only historical positivity and alienation, but also freedom, knowledge and truth, have the fundamental structure of self-recognition in other. Hegel's doctrine of three-fold mediation and corresponding triadic structure, is an ontological general-ization of his doctrine of intersubjectivity.

Within this triadic structure, the equivalence between being-for-other and being-for-self is not sheer identity or unity. It is a mutual correspondence between internal and external relations that is constitutive of *Geist*. Hegel rejects purely external relations because these do not affect or influence the *relata*. To stand in relation is to be open to influence and the possibility of change. He insists that the relation between self and other is internal and, as such, affects the *relata*. But Hegel does not fall into the opposite trap of purely internal relations, that reduce one of the *relata* to the other (monism). Bradley, who could see no alternative to external or internal, wound up deny-ing that relations are real; instead he claimed they are merely apparent.[59] *Geist* reflects an alternative, namely a correspondence or triadic relation of 'internal' and 'external' relations.

Hegel formulates a universal ontological pattern of threefold media-tion,[60] present not only in intersubjective recognition, but on all levels of being. This point is stressed by Theunissen, who interprets Hegel's logic as a general theory of communicative freedom: "in his logic, Hegel discerns structures which place the whole of reality, and not merely interhuman rela-tions, under the requirement of absolute reciprocity."[61] This implies that self-recognition in other is a universal ontological structure of the absolute Idea, and not limited to interhuman recognition.[62]

This universality is the direct result of Hegel's effort to rethink sub-stance as subject,[63] the absolute Idea as Aristotle's pure thought thinking itself. Jaeschke observes that "Here, references to Aristotle's concept of *noe-sis noeseos* are not to be overlooked. They are not accidental. For Hegel's aim is nothing less than to show that in the concept of trinity everything is conceived in the unity of *nous* and *noeton:* In the identity of concept and reality as thought thinking itself, the trinity is also thought, and the reverse is also true."[64] Jaeschke's formulation suggests an equivalence between Hegel's triadic holism and Aristotle's *noesis noeseos*. There is textual evi-dence for this identification, since Hegel himself cites Aristotle at the conclu-sion of his *Encyclopedia Philosophy of Spirit*.[65] Nevertheless, the exact meaning of this equivalence is far from clear. The citation of Aristotle at the end of the *Philosophy of Spirit* seems to indicate that the trinity is a *Vorstel-lung* inferior to the logical *Begriff*, the form of which is set forth finally in Aristotle's *noesis noeseos*. The latter is the final form of truth, the philosoph-ical, or truth in the form of truth, the truth in the form of a self.

The question is whether Hegel ultimately rejoins the dyadic concept of abstract identity (I = I) of the metaphysical tradition. Does the fact that Hegel cites Aristotle's *noesis noeseos* make him an Aristotelian, such that the major features of the Aristotelian conception are also to be ascribed to Hegel?[66] I think not. Although Hegel cites Aristotle's *noesis noeseos,* he also criticizes it. The criticism turns on the possibility that Aristotle's *noesis noeseos* may end up as immediate knowing.[67] Pure thought must think only of the best, i.e., itself. If subject and object are identical, as in this case they surely are, then the knower coincides immediately with the known. Aristotle's *noesis noeseos* may not be an exception to but rather an illustration of an immediate direct grasp of being as self-sameness. It may turn out to be another version of immediate knowing, or Schelling's undifferentiated identity. Aristotle's *noesis* seems to exclude alterity and collapses into immediate identity. Hegel's point is that if thought simply eliminated its other or collapsed its other into self-sameness, it would fail. For to eliminate the other is to remove the possibility of mediation on which all knowledge depends.[68]

In addition, I have pointed out that Hegel incorporates the notion of releasement in his conception of knowledge. Absolute knowledge does not seize upon, restrict or eliminate the other's possibilities, but renounces domination of other. This signifies a renunciation of the possession of the object on which Aristotle insists.[69] If metaphysical thinking is a manifestation of the will to power, to dominate and to possess, Hegel's releasement (*Gelassenheit*) points beyond metaphysical foundationalism.[70] Absolute knowledge involves a self-coincidence in other that requires releasement and allows the other to be. The 'otherness' of the other, but *not the other itself,* is overcome.[71]

Aristotle's *noesis noeseos* excludes any serious concept of other and otherness such as Hegel speaks of when he writes:

> But that an accident as such, when cut loose from its environment—an acci-
> dent that is essentially bound up with and has existence only in connection
> with something else—should obtain an existence of its own and gain free-
> dom and independence on its own account—this is the tremendous power of
> the negative; it is the energy of thought, of the pure ego. Death, if we want to
> so designate that unreality, is the most fearsome, and to keep and hold fast
> what is dead demands the greatest force of all. Beauty, powerless and help-
> less, hates the understanding, because it demands from it what it cannot do.
> But the life of Spirit (*Geist*) is not one that shuns death and preserves itself
> from destruction; rather it endures death and maintains its being in death. It
> gains its truth only when it finds itself in utter dismemberment.[72]

In comparison with Hegel's fearsome images, Aristotle's self-knowing knower amounts to immediate knowledge or abstract identity. In the passage above, Hegel incorporates tragic elements that Aristotle and the tradition suppress.

Hegel directs similar criticisms against the then-current metaphysical versions of identity. He calls Schelling's abstract undifferentiated identity "the night in which all cows are black." He thinks such a concept of the absolute is an abyss, which cannot account for determinacy and determinate, differentiated existence.[73] Immediate abstract identity is like a black hole into which knowing and being disappear. This is the result of any view which gives priority to unity or identity over difference. The task is to give difference its due.

HEGEL'S TRIADIC HOLISM: TWO POSSIBILITIES

G. R. G. Mure observes that Hegel's position concerning thought and its other is ambiguous.[74] Mure observes that the empirical—the other of thought—has two meanings in Hegel's philosophy, it is (1) a term for what is non-rational, and (2) an element in pure thought. Mure correctly points out that, although the empirical element, or the other, is ultimately thought, it is not reducible to the pure thought of the logical categories. Critics of Hegel tend to separate these two meanings and play one off against the other: either the other is totally other, in which case it cannot be thought at all, or else the other is merely immanent in thought and so not-other. Mure's point, however, is that these two senses are inseparable, and should not be played off against each other.

Nevertheless, Mure concedes that Hegel's thought allows two somewhat divergent readings. One possibility is that thought and sense are one, i.e., thought. This reading emphasizes monosubjectival unity and identifies the system with the logic, which is transcendental philosophy with a vengeance.[75] The *Realphilosophie* refers to no autonomous or independent sphere of being, but is merely a further extension of the logical categories. The other turns out, as Feuerbach complained, to be merely *thought* of the other. Thus, the system is closed, a-historical.

A second possibility is that reason and sense cannot be wholly unified, i.e, reduced to identity. This means that thought stands in a relation of reciprocity to experience. Philosophy, or pure thought, depends on the empirical disciplines—natural sciences—religious experience and history, and reconstructs these.[76] In philosophical reconstruction, there is an imperfect sublation of empirical materials, including the data of natural science, the materials of philosophy of religion and philosophy of history. In this reading, the Hegelian system cannot be entirely or simply identified with the logic, but consists in a correspondence between the logic as transcendental philosophy and the *Realphilosophie* (Nature and Spirit). The system is both closed in respect to its categorical structure (the logic) and open with respect to its correspondences with the empirical realm, even to the point of allowing the latter's contingencies to reflect back into the former. Mure inclines towards this second reading, and my reading of Hegel is indebted to his.

In working out the implications of this second interpretation for the other, Mure shows that the other which thought thinks is not simply pure thought itself in the guise of alterity. *"This 'other', which, taken simply in the act of severance and apart from the process of reconciliation,...is...at once thought and the opposite of thought."*[77] Mure's nuanced formulation of the other as *both* thought and the other of thought captures the complexity of Hegel's thought and distinguishes it from Feuerbach's caricature. Several important consequences follow from this:

> Qua the opposite of thought, it [i.e., the other] is the utter privation of self-centered system, utter self-externality. For that reason we cannot, as we might be tempted to do, identify it with the first category of the Logic, with the Pure Being which is equally Not-being. Pure Being could be regarded as the utter opposite of the Idea only within the dialectical circle of pure thought, for Pure Being is a form of pure thought. *But this 'other' of thought is beyond pure thought.* It is the being to which the original unity of thought and being refers.... *The full nature of thought as containing its 'other' within itself is more than pure thought, and only Philosophy as the culmination of concrete Spirit, the content of which is the whole circle of the super-triad, expresses this full nature of thought.*[78]

If the other is both thought and the other of thought, then the problem of the other is not simply a categorical problem, and cannot be resolved within the 'pure thought' of the logic.[79] The "other of thought" does not constitute a dialectical opposite whose otherness is totally sublated in the *Ruckkehr,* the reversion upon self. This other is released from categorial sublation and allowed to be. The other is both categorial and extracategorial, in the same sense that contingency is both a category and yet points beyond itself.

On the other hand, Mure is not claiming that this other cannot be thought at all, for that is self-refuting. Rather the thought that apprehends the other is not the pure thought of the logic, but the concrete thought of the whole. In other words, the Hegelian system consists in the super-triad of Logic, Nature, and *Geist,* which stand in a non-foundationalist threefold mutual mediation. This threefold mediation includes and presupposes the releasement of the logical Idea into otherness.

Mure thus isolates two senses of other that we can characterize as the logical (other as self-othering) and the empirical, or the other "broken free in utter dismemberment." My thesis is that it is impossible to account for the latter, much less *unify it non-reductively* with the former, on the grounds of Aristotle's *noesis noeseos.* That path returns to abstract, immediate identity, the I = I, and reduces the other to the same. It is not Aristotle's dyadic *noesis noeseos* that subsumes trinity as an example, nor is it the ultimate form of truth to which the trinity conforms, but rather the other way around. The triad cannot be reduced to abstract identity (I = I), but identity can be thought as a triadic holistic concept. For it is the whole that articulates the concrete identity that gives difference its due.

Aristotle's *noesis noeseos* may be read as an account of what the tradition called the immanent triad,[80] in which no serious opposition arises. Hegel writes:

> The life of God and divine knowledge may be characterized as a play [*Spiel*] of love with itself, but this idea falls into mere edification and insipidity if it lacks the seriousness, the suffering and the labor of the negative. In itself the divine life is no doubt undisturbed identity and unity with itself which finds no serious obstacle in otherness [*Anderssein*] and estrangement.... But this "in itself" is the abstract universality in which the nature of the divine life to be for itself is left altogether out of account.[81]

Aristotle's (and classical theism's) commitment to divine simplicity makes it problematic that God could know or be related to an other. As I = I, Aristotle's God does not have an other; it does not know, and is not related to, the world. Hegel's point is that internal complexity is a condition of external relations. Only such an inwardly complex being can be affected by an other without being destroyed by such influence and the concomitant possibility of change.

The abstract universal is only one moment of the *Begriff*. It should not be confused with the whole in its full concrete development.[82] We have already noted Hegel's distinction between absolute as substance and absolute as *Geist*.[83] In contrast to the abstract Logical Idea, or immanent triad, the economic triad exhibits the full power of negative that dismembers the Idea and compels *Geist* to "look the negative in the face and tarry with it."[84] The latter refers to history, the consciousness of death, and to the death of God. Hegel's treatment of the death of God motif goes far beyond the tradition because it finds negativity, death, suffering in the absolute.[85] The external relations or economic triad, both presuppose and modify the immanent triad. Unlike the tradition, the economic trinity subsumes or includes the immanent trinity (the logic), and is the result of mediation.[86] In this way, the other, difference, and negativity are taken seriously and given their due.

Despite his praise of Aristotle, Hegel differs from Aristotle in important respects by incorporating tragic suffering into divine bliss. The latter may not cease to be bliss, but it surely ceases to be pure transparent light or immediate bliss, because of the other and the negative. Hegel does not end in immediate knowledge, or collapse of the object into the subject, the known into the knower, because the immanent relations are affected and modified by the external, and the whole includes both sets of relations. Hegel expresses this in triadic-trinitarian language:

> We say that God eternally begets his Son, that God distinguishes himself from himself...and is completely at home with himself [*schlechthin bei sich selbst in dem gesetzten Anderen*] in the other whom he has posited (in the form of love). But at the same time we must know that God is himself this entire activity. God is the beginning...but he is likewise the end, the totali-

ty, and it is as totality that God is *Geist*.... The fact that this is the truth, and the absolute truth, may have the form of something given. But that this should be known as the truth in and for itself is the task of philosophy and the entire content of philosophy.[87]

Hegel's self-differentiating holism must include both identity and difference. As such, difference and the other cannot be eliminated, because these are the ordering and structuring principles of the whole. Deprived of such—as in the pure noetic vision of *noesis noeseos*—the whole would collapse upon itself. Moreover, the difference principle cannot remain merely implicit as if the so-called "immanent trinity" were all that there is. It must issue in an ordered whole[88] which includes external relations as well, or both a one and a many.[89] Otherwise, it is not genuine difference. This is not due merely to human epistemological requirements, but is required by the whole itself. Errol Harris has pointed out that

> Hegel's logic is...the self-differentiation of organic wholeness.... In that there is, of course, an element (or moment) of necessity, for the whole is immanent throughout and the principle of organization governs the structure of the constituent parts as well as the succession of developmental phases. But just because the concreteness of the whole requires radical differentiation, it necessarily involves the opposite moment of finitude and contingency.[90]

CONCLUSION

In his earliest philosophical publication Hegel tells us that difference must be given its due.[91] This is Hegel's project, which leads him to replace the theory of abstract identity with recognition (*Anerkennen*) and to generalize the structure of self-recognition in other and incorporate it in his concept of absolute *Geist*. Difference cannot be excluded from identity as the understanding (*Verstand*) would have it; rather difference is intrinsic to identity. For this reason the hegelian system is a holism involving complex articulation. Such articulation does not mean that the other is progressively swallowed up by or flattened into logical immanence. Although the logic articulates the structure of the whole, it is nevertheless not the whole *system*. Although the logic is supposed to provide the fundamental categories for the other parts of the system, it is crucial to understand that the logic is abstract, and requires mediation.[92] This requirement prevents the logic from being a merely formal set of categories. The logic presupposes that its categories are not empty, and have instantiation in the world. It is not a supra-historical speculation or ballet of bloodless thought-forms.

Consequently, the Hegelian system takes the form of a "super triad" involving multiple modes of being and requiring threefold mediation. In such a holism there is no absolute primacy. The issues of primacy and priority, founding and grounding, are suspended. When foundationalism is suspended, so is the related issue of the reduction of the other to the same. All such reductions violate the fundamental systematic requirement of mediation and relativity. For this reason Hegel's system cannot be adequately characterized as idealism in the modern subjective sense, because the latter is one-sided and reductive.

The basic systematic problem is the relation between thought and the other. If, as in dualism, thought fails to attain its other, then no knowledge is possible, and skeptical silence before the void is the result. But if, as in monism, thought consumes or eliminates its other, or reduces the other to the same, this reduction also means that knowledge is impossible, or merely formal. Who has made this point more forcefully than Hegel? Thought cannot be either entirely separated from or immediately identical with its other. Hegel unites identity and difference without collapsing difference into identity, or the other into self-sameness: "We must be careful when we say that the ground is the unity of identity and difference, not to understand by this unity an abstract identity. Otherwise we only change the name, while we still think this identity (of the understanding) already seen to be false. To avoid this misconception, we may say that the ground, besides being the *unity,* is also the *difference* of identity and difference."[93]

Such considerations seem far removed from a phenomenology of the other. Yet, these issues are raised when the problems inherent in such accounts are pushed to the ontological level.[94] They are not settled simply by perception, for perception is shaped and guided by such fundamental considerations. Once the structures of being for self and being for others are acknowledged, the task is to bring these into relation without subordinating or reducing one to the other. Hegel's task is to formulate a concept of being as a community, an ordered whole. Hegel's thesis is that triadic holism is the most adequate ontology of the social. Hegel can express this concept abstractly when he says that "everything rational is manifested as a triple syllogism; that is to say, each one of the members takes in turn the place of the extremes, as well as of the mean which reconciles them. Such for example is the case with the three branches of philosophy: the logical Idea, Nature and *Geist.*"[95] But he makes the same point in his more poetic utterance which brings the *Phenomenology* to a close:

> The telos, absolute knowledge, or *Geist* that knows itself as *Geist,* has for its path the recollection of spirits as they are in themselves and as they bring about the organization of their realm. Their preservation, regarded from the side of their free existence appearing in the form of contingency, is *history.* Regarded from the side of their [philosophically] comprehended organization, it is the *science* of phenomenal knowledge [*die Wissenschaft des erscheinenden Wissens*]. The two together, *comprehended history,* form

the recollection and the Golgotha of absolute *Geist,* the actuality, truth and certainty of his throne, without which he would be the lifeless Alone. Only:
from the chalice of this realm of spirits
foams forth for Him his infinitude.[96]

NOTES

1. Jean Hyppolite, *Genesis and Structure of Hegel's Phenomenology of Spirit,* tr. Cherniak and Heckman (Evanston, Ill.: Northwestern University Press, 1974) 600.

2. See Walter Ludwig, "Hegel's Conception of Absolute Knowing," *Owl of Minerva,* vol. 21, no. 1 (Fall 1989): 5–19.

3. J. N. Findlay, *Hegel: A Re-examination* (New York: Collier Macmillan, 1958); Charles Taylor, *Hegel* (Cambridge: Cambridge University Press, 1975).

4. Kojève, op. cit.; Hyppolite, op. cit. ; Quentin Lauer, *A Reading of Hegel's Phenomenology of Spirit* (New York: Fordham University Press, 1976); Merold Westphal *History and Truth in Hegel's Phenomenology of Spirit* (New York: Humanities Press, 1979); Joseph C. Flay, *Hegel's Quest for Certainty* (Albany, N.Y.: SUNY Press, 1984).

5. *Enz* §564 Zusatz. For a translation of Hegel's review of Göschel's book from which these aphorisms are taken, see "G. W. F. Hegel: Review of C. F. Göschel's Aphorisms" translated by Clark Butler in *CLIO* 17:4 (1988), 369–393.

6. Hyppolite observes that Hegel makes both claims, but maintains that these are incompatible. See his "Anmerkungen zur Vorrede der Phänomenologie des Geistes und zum Thema: das Absolute ist Subjekt," in *Materialien zu Hegels Phänomenologie des Geistes,* Hrsg. H. F. Fulda und D. Henrich (Frankfurt am Main: Suhrkamp Taschenbuch Verlag, 1973), 47. Daniel Berthold-Bond (*Hegel's Grand Synthesis: A Study of Being, Thought and History* [Albany, N.Y.: SUNY Press, 1989]) contends that Hegel and his interpreters are confronted with a forced choice between absolute *Geist* and history, because Hegel's absolute allegedly undermines the very conditions of knowledge and spirit. (Ibid. 143) But this assumes that Hegel's absolute is a timeless Parmenidean undifferentiated identity and unity. This is false. Bond's proposal to make Hegel "consistent" by jettisoning the concept of absolute spirit is a dubious "interpretation" and itself incoherent. The significance of absolute spirit is that art, religion and philosophy are historical phenomena that nevertheless have enduring, trans-historical and supra-temporal validity. It is precisely such validity that Berthold-Bond tacitly invokes for his epochal theory of history as an interpretation of Hegel. Bond's theory is a philosophical thesis in Hegel's sense of absolute spirit. For a similar rejection of and tacit borrowing from Hegel, cf. Paul Ricoeur, *Time and Narrative,* vol. 3, (tr. K Blamey and D. Pellauer [Chicago: University of Chicago Press,1988)], Chaps. 9–10.

7. See Hegel, *Lectures on the Philosophy of Religion,* vol. III, 253: "Positivity

does not in any way detract from its character as rational and therefore as something that is our own." This places the oft quoted "The rational is actual" in a somewhat different light. In Hegel's view reason (in contrast to *Verstand*) is itself positive. For this reason the rational is self-actualizing, and therefore actual.

8. Richard Kroner, *Von Kant bis Hegel*, op. cit. II, 415: "The reconciling word, which absolute knowledge speaks, does not arise out of a one-sidedly conceived intellect, or out of a practical reason opposed to the theoretical, but out of the concrete *Geist* that comprehends itself as concrete in its self-knowledge. Absolute knowledge is therefore not an alternative to faith, for it is a believing knowledge or a self-conscious faith, a self-recognitive will, a self-comprehending life." See also H. S. Harris, *Hegel's Development: Night Thoughts* (Oxford: Clarendon Press, 1983), 519ff. Harris shows that Hegel identifies logical development and historical processes. In his introduction to the history of philosophy, Hegel advances the claim that the history of philosophy follows in temporally successive order the conceptual-logical order of positions laid down in the logic. This does not mean that Hegel simply identifies the logical and the historical order, although there are texts that lean in this direction. Rather, Hegel's system is structured by a distinction and correlation between logic and *Realphilosophie*, or between thought and experience. Mure, *A Study of Hegel's Logic*, op. cit. Hyppolite (op. cit), Emil Fackenheim, *The Religious Dimension in Hegel's Thought* (Chicago: University of Chicago Press, 1967), Shlomo Avinieri, *Hegel's Theory of the Modern State* (Cambridge: Cambridge University Press, 1972), and Peter C. Hodgson, *God and History* (Nashville: Abingdon Press, 1989) emphasize this irreducible duality in Hegel's thought.

9. Cf Hegel, *Enz.* §1: "The objects of philosophy, it is true, are upon the whole the same as those of religion. In both the object is truth, in that supreme sense in which God and God only is the truth." For a different view, cf. Lu De Vos, "Absolute Knowing in the Phenomenology" in *Hegel On the Ethical Life, Religion and Philosophy*, ed. A. Wylleman (Leuven, Belgium: Leuven University Press [Kluwer Academic Publishers], 1989), 231–270. De Vos believes that absolute knowledge is a construction imposed on the phenomena by speculative philosophy.

10. Hegel PhG 547; PhS §787, 477–478.

11. PhG 556.

12. The *Phenomenology*, writes Hyppolite, "culminates in the conception of a science which is simultaneously the science of being and the position of the self in Being. Being thinks itself as self, and self thinks itself as being. This thought of the self, this ontologic, which is the thought of thought at the same time it is the thought of all things, constitutes absolute knowledge." Jean Hyppolite, *Genesis*, op. cit. 574. See also Wolfhart Pannenberg, "Der Geist und sein Anderes," in *Hegels Logik der Philosophie*, ed. D. Henrich and R. Horstmann (Stuttgart: Klett-Kotta Verlag, 1984), 152.

13. Ibid. The label of idealism is a red herring, more misleading than helpful.

14. Jürgen Habermas suggests such a distinction in his "Arbeit und Interaktion: Bemerkungen zu Hegels Jenaer Philosophie des Geistes" Göhler, *Hegel: Frühe poli-*

tische Systeme, op. cit., ET, "Labor and Interaction" in *Theory and Praxis,* tr. John Viertel (Boston: Beacon Press, 1973.) Habermas reiterates the same interpretation of Hegel in his later *Philosophical Discourse of Modernity* (Cambridge, Mass.: MIT Press, 1987). See below, n. 20.

15. PhG 20.

16. Ludwig Feuerbach, "Towards a Critique of Hegel's Philosophy," tr. in *The Fiery Brook,* 79. Feuerbach refers to the chapter on Sense Certainty, and not Hegel's account of recognition. Nevertheless, his point holds also as a more general criticism of Hegel's account of the other. For a critique of Feuerbach's reading of sense certainty, and a defense of Hegel, cf. Merold Westphal, *History and Truth in Hegel's Phenomenology,* op. cit.

17. This is the way William Desmond formulates the criticism in his *Desire Dialectic and Otherness* (New Haven, Conn.: Yale University Press, 1987), 120. However, it should be noted that despite his criticism that Hegel reduces mediation to self-mediation, this criticism is qualified, and Desmond allows that other readings are possible. He draws on these in his defense of Hegel against deconstructionist criticism that Hegel reduces the other to the same. See his *Art and the Absolute* (Albany, N.Y.: SUNY Press, 1986), Chapter 5.

18. cf. Heinz Röttges, *Dialektik und Skeptizismus* (op. cit) who writes "in place of the I = I, recognition [*Anerkennen*] appears as the concrete existence of self-consciousness." (155)

19. For the doctrine of threefold mediation at the basis of Hegel's system, cf. *Enz.* §187 Zusatz.

20. Cf. Levinas, op. cit. See also Habermas, who thinks the early writings of Hegel hold out the possibility of an ethical totality as a communicative reason embodied in intersubjective life-contexts. But the later Hegel of the logic places emphasis on a single absolute subject conceiving itself, and this "makes the institutionalism of a strong state necessary." See Jürgen Habermas, *The Philosophical Discourse of Modernity,* op. cit. 40. Habermas serves up the old story of the radical early Hegel of the *Phenomenology* versus the conservative later Hegel of the logic. See also William Desmond, op. cit. Desmond isolates the crucial axiom on which this line of interpretation rests: "For self-consciousness, Hegel holds, is such that the object of the subject is the subject himself objectified." 120. This is a restatement of Feuerbach's one-sided grasp of mediation: "the object of any subject is nothing but the subject's own nature taken objectively" (*The Essence of Christianity,* tr. G. Eliot [New York: Harper & Row, 1957], 12.). From this axiom Desmond draws the conclusion that "self-mediation seems to encompass the self and the other, and all differences are caught up within this self-contained circle." (p. 120)

21. See Klaus Hartmann, *Sartre's Ontology,* (Evanston, Ill.: Northwestern University Press, 1966): "The *Phenomenology of Spirit,* although designed to unfold the principle of the subject in a conceptual dialectic, permits, in its oppositional stages, the substitution of real pluralities as illustrations. It is therefore tempting to interpret it in terms of a real dialectic or a metaphysical hypostasis.... These oppositions are not

existent pluralities but dialectical oppositions. What Hegel intends to show is that spirit as such, or the subject as such, have to be regarded as mediated with opposites on the level of the determinatenesses concerned. How this is possible in real terms is not Hegel's problem." (118). Hartmann is correct to deny—as a corrective to Kojève—that the *Phenomenology* is anthropology. Joseph Flay urges similar considerations against Kojève's reading of the *Phenomenology*. (Flay, *Hegel's Quest for Certainty,* op. cit.) I agree with this criticism of Kojève. However the question is whether this settles the issue of the existential presuppositions of the logic. I think not. The logic presupposes that its categories are not empty. The *Phenomenology* remains relevant to establishing this presupposition, as does the *Realphilosophie*. But then it follows that the logic is in some sense mediated, and requires an other.

22. Cf. *Enz.* §415. Hegel criticizes Kant for grasping *Geist* only at the level of consciousness, and so as in opposition to a transcendent beyond. Speculative reason needs to cancel the very appearance of otherness. Here Hegelian phenomenology seems to be anti-Husserlian phenomenology.

23. Pannenberg, *"Der Geist und sein Anderes,"* op. cit. 155.

24. PhG 32.

25. See Hegel's critique of positivity in his *Early Theological Writings;* see also his critical discussion of metaphysical theology in the "Three Attitudes of 'Thought Towards Objectivity" in his *Encyclopedia* §§25–85. See especially §30: "These totalities—God, the Soul and World—were taken by the metaphysician as subjects ready-made, to form the basis for an application of the categories of the understanding. They were assumed from popular conception. Accordingly, popular conception was the only canon for settling whether or not the predicates were suitable and sufficient."

26. Hegel criticizes the traditional doctrine of creation because it separates God from world. In maintaining this dualist ontological separation, the tradition reveals that its *Vorstellungen* are conceived at the level of *Verstand,* by means of its abstract concepts of identity, difference and contradiction. Against this categorial scheme, Hegel often observes that an infinite separated from and standing over and against the finite, is itself finite. The logical forms of the traditional *Vorstellungen* thus subverted and concealed what the tradition meant to say.

27. See Ludwig Feuerbach, *The Essence of Christianity,* op. cit. 12.

28. Cf. Kojève: "Now according to Hegel, one can realize the Christian *anthropological* ideal (which he accepts in full) only by 'overcoming' the Christian *theology:* Christian man can really become what he would like to be only by becoming a man without God—or if you will, a God-Man.... In other words, he must eliminate the Christian idea of transcendence." (op. cit. 67). Westphal's recent study, *History and Truth in Hegel's* Phenomenology of Spirit, offers a left-Hegelian reading that reduces theology to anthropology (195ff). Westphal asserts both that religion is for Hegel a projection and that nevertheless it is not a mere figment of the imagination, thereby attempting to differentiate Hegel from Feuerbach. But this differentiation is a distinction without a difference.

29. PhG. 556.

30. Lu De Vos, "Absolute Knowing in the *Phenomenology*," *Hegel On The Ethical Life, Religion and Philosophy*, ed. A Wylleman, *Louvain Philosophical Studies* 3 (Leuven, Belgium: Leuven University Press and Kluwer Academic Publishers, 1989), 256. Emphasis mine. For a similar formulation and interpretation, cf. the preceding essay concerning religion by R. Devos, 214.

31. Fichte, *First Introduction to Wissenschaftslehre*, ET 16–21.

32. Fichte, *Grundlage der gesammten Wissenschaftslehre 1794*, FW I 206.

33. See his "Three Attitudes of Thought Towards Objectivity" in *Enz.* §§26–85.

34. Hegel, *Entwürfe über die Religion und Liebe* (1797/8), TWA 1: 242. This is obviously very close to the concluding moment in the eidetics, namely that each self lets the other be, go free, etc.

35. Hegel's term is *entlassen*, which means release, set free. It is significant that this term is used both in Hegel's eidetics of recognition (as the culmination of reciprocal recognition) and in his account of the important and vexing transition from Logic to Nature. The logical Idea, he says, releases nature. (*Enz.* §244)

36. PhG 556; PhS §797, 485.

37. See his "Hegels Begriff der Erfahrung," *Holzwege* (Frankfurt am Main: Klostermann, 1980), 134; ET, *Hegel's Concept of Experience* (New York: Harper & Row, 1989). See also his *Hegels Phänomenologie des Geistes* (Frankfurt: Klostermann, 1980), 72; ET. *Hegel's Phenomenology of Spirit*, tr. Emad and K. Maly (Bloomington, Ind.: Indiana University Press, 1988), 51. A major study of Heidegger's thought, William J. Richardson, *Heidegger: Through Phenomenology to Thought* (The Hague: Martinus Nijhoff, 1963), 331–361, repeats and embellishes Heidegger's foundationalist Cartesian reading of Hegel.

38. PhG 549.

39. See Donald Philip Verene, *Hegel's Recollection: A Study of the Images in the Phenomenology of Spirit* (Albany, N.Y.: SUNY Press, 1985), Chapter 9. Verene notes that absolute knowledge has the form of a conjunction of *ansichsein* and *fürsichsein;* in contrast, ordinary consciousness is self-subverting because it forgets about the "and." (106–107)

40. Peter C. Hodgson, *God in History* (Nashville, Tenn.: Abingdon Press, 1989), 172. The English translators of Heidegger's book, *Hegel's Phenomenology of Spirit*, faithfully capture this conventional sense of absolute as Heidegger develops it. Thus "das Absolute" means "literally: not relative." (op. cit. 154) And Heidegger's neologism, absolvent, means "detaching…the process of becoming absolute" (154), i.e., freed from all relation.

41. Hegel, *Skepticism*, BTKH 335.

42. *Skepticism*, op. cit. 336.

43. See above Chapter 7 §§5–6. In this connection Hodgson observes that "the word *absolute* derives from the Latin *absolvere*, meaning 'to loosen (*solvere*) from (*ab*)', hence 'to release', 'to set free'" (Hodgson, op. cit. 172). This is not far from releasement (*Gelassenheit*). Verene observes "Absolute knowing...just accepts what is there. It accepts the absolute distance between the in itself and the for itself. It accepts the circle that is formed through the *and*. This acceptance leaves the world as it is and in this way appearance is conquered." (op. cit. 109) I agree with Verene up to his final comment, which is baffling. To speak of conquering appearances reflects the idealist metaphysical model rather than *Gelassenheit*.

44. PhG 391. [Italics mine.] Walter Jaeschke observes that although Hegel develops a social theory of religion, this does not mean that he reduces the content (Inhalt) of religion to anthropology. The content of religion—Absolute *Geist*—is distinguished from, and is to be liberated from, the spirit of a people (*Volksgeist*). See Walter Jaeschke, VR 191; RR 179. Moreover, even where Hegel characterizes certain Greek deities as projections of human consciousness, he denies that they are mere fictions or arbitrary creations. The concept of projection pertains only to the form, but not to the content (*Inhalt*) of religious consciousness. See LPR II 658. Projection is not originary, but a response to the prior sacred.

45. Westphal can sustain his Feuerbachian reading of Hegel only by suppressing the last part of the text. Cf. Westphal, op. cit. 192.

46. Hegel, *Vorlesungen über die Philosophie der Religion, Teil 3 Die vollendete Religion*, Hrsg. von Walter Jaeschke (Hamburg: Meiner Verlag, 1984), 268. ET, *Lectures on the Philosophy of Religion Vol. III. The Consummate Religion*, ed. Peter C. Hodgson, tr. R. Brown, Hodgson, J. Stewart, with the assistance of H. S. Harris (Berkeley: University of California Press, 1985), 345.

47. Hegel does not use the term "essence of Christianity" (*das Wesen des Christentums*), but he does formulate the *Begriff der Religion*, which, like the former, is an historical concept or historical-morphological essence. Cf. W. Jaeschke, VR 227; RR 217f, 231f.

48. Beside the famous preface to the *Philosophy of Right* where Hegel asserts that the rational is actual, other relevant texts include the following: "What is in and for itself, and what is finitely and temporally—these are the two fundamental determinations (*Grundbestimmungen*) which must be present in any satisfactory theory of truth." (Hegel's "Vorrede zu Hinrichs Religionsphilosophie" (1822) TWA Sk. 11:52; ET *Beyond Epistemology*, ed. F. Weiss [The Hague: Martinus Nijhoff, 1974], 234) These two requirements constitute the concept of concrete or determinate universality. All attempts to separate these opposing requirements result in failures. A universal which is abstractly opposed to the concrete and particular is a false infinite, for by virtue of its opposition to particulars, it is itself a particular. Hence, Hegel sides with Aristotle against Plato. The universal must become, and when it undergoes change it becomes other than itself. Hegel describes the determinate universal in the following terms: "The universal, even though posited in a determination, remains what it is. It is the soul of the concrete in which it indwells unhindered and identical with itself in its multiplicity and differences." (*Wissenschaft der Logik*, TWA Sk. 6, 276) See also Jaeschke, VR 227; RR 217.

49. This shows the close connection between Hegel's philosophy and Christian thought. It also shows Hegel to be a post-Enlightenment thinker. Hegel "does philosophy" out of an explicit particular historical perspective and religious tradition. Although absolute knowledge is the context of a universal or general ontology (*metaphysica generalis*), it is nevertheless not a "view from nowhere."

50. Westphal appears to identify Christianity with its classical doctrinal package. He writes "Where God has become society's projected self-image and the incarnation means that mankind is universally divine, how can one speak any longer of Christianity?... Does not Kierkegaard have the right to be deeply offended...?" (op. cit. 204) Although he caricatures Hegel's christological reconstruction as a reduction of theology to anthropology, Westphal correctly senses that Hegel embraces historical consciousness and does not repeat, but criticizes and reconstructs traditional Christian doctrines. However, Westphal's rhetorical question, "how can one speak any longer of Christianity?" presupposes an identification of Christianity with its tradition, and a view of that tradition as a-historical. He dismisses Hegel as the first of "countless variations on this theme of salvation through a post-Christian Christianity." (206) The problem with such a view is that it is *post*-Christian, i.e., the claim of "post" here seems to make Christianity a "wholly historical phenomenon like feudalism or capitalism. Since it has always claimed to be more than that, its fulfillment could only be in the confirmation and not in the falsification of that claim." (207) This last sentence seems to imply an a-historical view of the tradition that makes the tradition incompatible with historical consciousness, and beyond historical criticism, correction or reconstruction.

51. An example of such a claim is Kojève's assertion that the Christian *anthropological* ideal can be realized only by rejecting and overcoming Christian *theology*. Op. cit. 67.

52. Hegel, *Faith and Knowledge*, tr. W. Cerf and H. S. Harris (Albany, N.Y.: SUNY Press, 1977), 190–1. See also the appendix supplied by Karl Rosenkranz to Hegel's *System of Ethical Life*, in G. W. F. Hegel, *System of Ethical Life and First Philosophy of Spirit*, ed. and tr. H. S. Harris and T. M. Knox (Albany, N.Y.: SUNY Press, 1979), 179–186. For a discussion, see H. S. Harris's commentary, 81–85.

53. PhG 548; PhM 784. This strange terminology refers not to the reduction of theology to anthropology, but rather to Hegel's interest in reconstructing Christian faith in a new form that suspends the antithesis of Protestantism and Catholicism. See Hegel, *System of Ethical Life*, op. cit. 183–185; cf. Harris' discussion 84–5.

54. The traditional exclusion of tragic evil and suffering is one example. Hegel makes tragedy a central issue in his theological reconstruction. For additional discussions which seek to incorporate the tragic into theological reconstruction, see Paul Ricoeur, *The Symbolism of Evil*, tr. E. Buchanan (Boston: Beacon Press, 1967), 211–346; see also Robert R. Williams, "Sin and Evil" in *Christian Thought: An Introduction to its Traditions and Its Tasks* (Philadelphia: Fortress Press, 1982).

55. PhG 563f. H. S. Harris points out the significant development of Hegel's thought during the Jena period when Hegel rethinks the absolute identity theory

(Schelling) as the final phase of his philosophy of Spirit. Hegel's bringing identity within a phenomenological and historical framework signals a change in his system and the transformation of identity into a socio-historical concept. Harris observes "The continuity between the temporal and eternal was established by transforming the theory of 'absolute identity' into the final phase of the philosophy of spirit itself." (See H. S. Harris, Introduction and Commentary on Hegel's *System of Ethical Life,* op. cit. 64f.) This involves a change in Hegel's conception of philosophy, namely, "...the upgrading of the practical social function of philosophy which the philosophy of identity might very well lead us to despise." (Ibid. 64–65; See also Harris, *Hegel's Development: Night Thoughts,* op. cit. 226, 234.) Religion is no longer regarded as a manifestation of an abstract absolute, nor is the latter separated from the the social and history, but belongs henceforth to Hegel's theory of *Sittlichkeit,* or ethical life. For a more complete discussion, see Walter Jaeschke, VR 181–198; RR 169ff.

56. See Verene, op. cit., Chapters 9 and 10. Verene stresses absolute knowledge as the historical recollection of spirit.

57. He criticizes the representational form of the traditional doctrine; instead of conceptual relations, it makes use of biological relations as symbols.

58. Walter Jaeschke, VR 322; RR 311. [I have altered the translation.] Jaeschke also discusses the anomaly of Hegel's philosophy of religion: it lends itself to both theological and philosophical interpretation, and this creates considerable complexity for interpreters. Nevertheless Jaeschke is correct to insist that Hegel's thought, even though treating theological material, nevertheless must be understood as philosophy.

59. For criticism of Bradley, see Errol E. Harris, *Formal, Transcendental and Dialectical Thinking: Logic and Reality,* op. cit. 132–134; see also Charles Hartshorne, *The Divine Relativity: A Social Conception of God* (New Haven, Conn.: Yale University Press, 1948), 60–77.

60. On the doctrine of threefold mediation, see Hegel, *Enz.* §187 Zusatz, §§574–577. See also Emil Fackenheim, *The Religious Dimension of Hegel's Thought,* (Bloomington, Ind.: Indiana University Press, 1967); David Kolb, *The Critique of Pure Modernity: Hegel, Heidegger and After* (Chicago: University of Chicago Press, 1986), 86f.

61. Michael Theunissen, *Sein und Schein,* op. cit. 46–47. See also his essay, "Die verdrängte Intersubjektivität in Hegels Philosophie des Rechts," in *Hegels Philosophie des Rechts,* Hrsg. v. Dieter Henrich und Rolf-Peter Horstmann (Stuttgart: Klett Cotta, 1982), 317ff. Theunissen distinguishes between the logical universal subject and the intersubjectively mediated universal subject. This same distinction can be found in the *Encyclopedia,* §§436–438. Here the universal subject is intersubjectively mediated through mutual recognition.

62. See *Enz.* §214 Zusatz, where Hegel expresses the structure of the absolute idea as the pure vision (*Anschauen*) of itself in other. See also §161 Zusatz, which makes it clear that transition into other is an immanent trinitarian relation, as well as the basic structure of the relation between God and world. However, it should be pointed out that Hegel does not use the term self-recognition in other in the logic, and

that no concept of subjectivity, much less personality, should be imputed to the logical idea. The concept of recognition is more appropriate in Hegel's *Philosophie des Geistes* and *Sittlichkeit*. See Walter Jaeschke, *"Absolut Idee—Absolute Persönlichkeit,"* op. cit. 407–408.

63. "In my view, which can be justified only by full presentation of the system itself, everything depends on conceiving and expressing the true as subject, and not only as substance." PhG 19.

64. Jaeschke, VR 317f; RR 306f.

65. *Enz.* §577.

66. For a study of Hegel and Aristotle, see Klaus Düsing, *Das Problem der Subjektivität in Hegels Logik, Hegel Studien,* Beiheft 15 (Bonn: Bouvier Verlag, 1976), 305–313. See also, Düsing, *Hegel und die Geschichte der Philosophie, Erträge der Forschung,* Band 206 (Darmstadt: Wissenschaftliche Buchgesellschaft, 1983), 97–159. Düsing observes that Hegel interprets Aristotle from his own premises, and freely modifies Aristotle's interpretation of *noesis noeseos,* as well as the distinction between active and passive *nous.* Hegel interprets Aristotle along Neoplatonic lines, i.e., the absolute thought is interpreted as coinciding with itself in a *Ruckkehr* (reversion) and is to be understood as a totality, rather than as a subject. But Hegel finds no Neo-platonic progress beyond Aristotle in respect to the freedom of theoretical thought.

67. Klaus Daniel, *Hegel Verstehen: Einführung in sein Denken,* (Frankfurt: Campus Verlag, 1983), 43.

68. A similar observation is made by Werner Marx: "One is tempted to say that...the Aristotelian outlook again won the victory and that Hegel was therefore also a 'metaphysician of light.' But then one overlooks the essential distinction that for Hegel, unlike Aristotle, Being and essence are not simply disclosed. For this reason there is not in Hegel the *noesis,* the intuitive inspection (*Schau*) which, on sheer contact, is able, without the possibility of error, to grasp the truth of Being..." Werner Marx, *Heidegger and the Tradition,* tr. Theodore Kisiel (Evanston, Ill.: Northwestern University Press, 1971), 56.

69. Aristotle, *Metaphysics,* 12, Chap. 7, 1072b25. "...thought and the object of thought are the same. For that which is capable of receiving the object of thought, i.e., the essence, is thought. But it is active when it *possesses* this object. Therefore possession rather than the receptivity is the divine element which thought seems to contain." [Emphasis in the original.] *Introduction to Aristotle,* ed. R. Mckeon (New York: Modern Library, 1947), 285. See also Klaus Düsing, *Hegel und die Geschichte der Philosophie,* op. cit. 124ff.

70. For example, cf. his critique of dogmatism: "Dogmatism as a mode of thought in knowing and in the study of philosophy is nothing other than the opinion that truth consists in a single proposition that is a fixed result, or is capable of being known immediately." (PhG 34.) Hegel's doctrine of the triple mediation is an attempt to prevent just such a reduction to foundations. Schürmann observes that, "being cannot be represented any longer according to Aristotelian schemes of analogical attribu-

tion. Hegel seems to have sensed this transformation of ontology in Meister Eckhart quite clearly." Schürmann, *Meister Eckhart,* op. cit. 190. On the relation between Hegel and Nietzsche's respective criticisms of metaphysics, see Stephen Houlgate, *Hegel and Nietzsche* (Cambridge: Cambridge University Press, 1986).

71. This is the way in which Hegel's term *übergreifen* should be read. He is not always careful in expressing this however. See *Enz.* §438.

72. PhG 29–30. PhS §32, 19.

73. PhG 560–561.

74. G. R. G Mure, *A Study of Hegel's Logic* (Oxford: Clarendon Press, 1950), 320–331. Mure notes there is a gap between logic and *Realphilosophie,* between logic and nature which is never completely bridged. (330) This gap is a defect only for those expecting a pure system of thought complete a priori; it means that Hegel's system does not form a perfect circle that returns to its beginning. If the circle metaphor is used, then the system is a circle of circles, or spiral of circles in which there is development and advance. (See WL TWA Sk. 6, 571, where Hegel speaks of the system as a circle of circles.) The supertriad is not complete and perfect a priori. (331). This means that the system must for essential reasons, be open to the empirical. Hegel writes, "But if thought never gets further than the universality of the Ideas...it is justly open to the charge of formalism.... Bearing in mind this first phase of thought [abstract universality], the period of mere generality, we may safely say that experience is real author of *growth* and *advance* in philosophy." (*Enz.* §12)

75. This is Kolb's way of characterizing Hegel's position, which leans towards the first possibility isolated by Mure. See Kolb, op. cit. 87.

76. *Enz* §246.

77. G. R. G Mure, op. cit. 320. [Emphasis mine.] Mure's analysis of the possible readings of Hegel, is exemplary, and almost completely overlooked in contemporary discussions. In Mure's view, thought and its other, the rational and the empirical, cannot be reduced to a simple unity. Monism is ruled out.

78. Ibid. [My Emphasis.]

79. By restricting consideration to the *category* of otherness, many interpretations suppress the crucial point that the other is the other of pure thought, Not surprisingly the other turns out to be a myth, a qualified illusion, subordinate to identity and unity, or merely another categorical transition. Such claims beg the question by overlooking or ignoring the point that the other "is not reducible to the pure abstract thought of the logical categories." Ibid. 322.

80. See Peter C. Hodgson, editorial introduction to Hegel, *Lectures on the Philosophy of Religion* (Berkeley: University of California Press, 1985). See also his *God and History,* op. cit. The philosophical background of the distinction between immanent and economic trinity is the Platonic tradition, specifically Philo's doctrine of the two stages of the logos—the immanent and the transcendent—and Plato's *Parmenides,* where the theory of wholes and parts shows that internal relations and exter-

nal relations are both distinct and mutually interdependent. For Philo, Cf. Harry A. Wolfson, "Intradeical and Extradeical Interpretations of the Platonic Ideas" in *Religious Philosophy; Philo* (Cambridge, Mass.: Harvard University Press, 1947). See also Walter Jaeschke, VR 314ff; RR 297–311.

81. PhG 20; PhM 81. Cf. *Enz* §161 Zusatz: "The movement of this notion is to be looked upon as mere play: the other which it sets up is in reality not an other. Or, as it is expressed in the teaching of Christianity: not merely has God created a world which confronts him as an other; he has also from all eternity begotten a son in whom he, a spirit, is at home with himself." The latter development is without serious opposition; this resembles the traditional immanent trinity. On the other hand, the world which God releases confronts God as a serious other, in which there is death, including the death of God. This corresponds to the traditional economic trinity, even as it goes far beyond it in affirming the death of God.

82. *Enz* §163. Cf. Hartshorne, "...in conceiving God as absolute, we must recognize that we are abstracting from his actual subjectivity or knowing. The Absolute is God with something left out of account. God is more than his absolute character.... I am arguing that the absolute is...an abstract feature of the inclusive and supreme reality which is precisely the personal God.... The absolute is not more, but less than God, in the obvious sense in which the abstract is less than the concrete." (*The Divine Relativity*, op. cit. 83.)

83. Cf. above Chapter 10. "But the supersensible, eternal or however one may wish to designate it, is devoid of self [*selbstlos*]; it is only the [abstract] universal, and that is still far from being *Geist* knowing itself as *Geist*." (PhG 473; PhS 410.) *Geist* is the concrete self-consciousness of the logical Idea. See also Hegel, *Enz* §553: "The concept of *Geist* has its reality in *Geist*." (For a commentary on the *Encyclopedia* philosophy of Absolute *Geist*, see Michael Theunissen, *Hegels Lehre vom absoluten Geist as theologisch-politischer Traktat* [Berlin: Walter de Gruyter, 1970], 104ff.) This distinction between absolute as substance and absolute as *Geist* is a rough approximation to Whitehead's distinction between God's primordial and consequent nature. (Alfred N. Whitehead, *Process and Reality* [New York: Macmillan, 1929], 46ff, 519ff); for a discussion, see Errol Harris, "The Contemporary Significance of Hegel and Whitehead," in *Hegel and Whitehead: Contemporary Perspectives on Systematic Philosophy*, ed. George R. Lucas, Jr. (Albany, N.Y.: SUNY Press, 1986), 17–28. In the *Phenomenology*, Hegel writes, "*Geist* becomes actual as absolute *Geist* only when its self-certainty is equivalent to its truth, or when the extremes into which it, as consciousness, divides itself are explicitly for each other in the shape of *Geist*." PhG 479; PhS 415.

84. PhG 30.

85. *Lectures on the Philosophy of Religion Vol. III.*, op. cit. 125, 219f, 323–327.

86. The resulting concrete totality involves what the theological tradition called the economic trinity, or in Mure's terms, the "other of thought." Here I differ with Hodgson's more conservative interpretation of Hegel that subordinates the economic trinity to the immanent or ontological trinity. (*God in History*, op. cit.) Rather the

economic trinity is the result of historical mediation. Such a departure from the tradition is necessary to avoid reduction to abstract universality and reducing history to a mere side-show of a-historical categories already complete in themselves. Moreover, it seems to follow Hegel's own logic of the concept and judgement (*Enz.* §163) as well as his discussion of *Werden* (becoming) as the first concrete category, from which being and nothing are abstractions.

87. Hegel, VPR III 209n; LPR III 284.

88. Dale Schlitt, who inclines towards Mure's first reading and presents an alternative monosubjectival reading of Hegel's concept of trinity, nevertheless makes a similar observation: "This implicit otherness gives rise to actual otherness." (op. cit. 151). And although Schlitt's monosubjectival reading tends to reduce mediation to self-mediation, he nevertheless acknowledges a non-logical otherness in Hegel's thought: "Most importantly, despite his insistence on an originary self-mediating pure thought, Hegel had happily managed to place otherness at the center of his dialectic.... Hegel's theory of self-mediation...becomes transformed into a theory of enriching growth.... Pluralism in its widest sense as the positive acceptance of otherness...becomes the condition for the possibility of becoming as progressive enrichment." (Ibid. 246). Since Mure is absent from his bibliography, Schlitt apparently arrived at his interpretation independently of Mure's analysis. Schlitt's observations cited above tend to undermine his own reading and rather support Mure's alternative reading favored here.

89. Recall Hegel's praise of Plato's dialogue *Parmenides* as the "masterpiece of ancient dialectic." PhG 57. It may be objected that holism excludes the very notion of external relations: how can a whole have external relations? This seems to collapse relations into internal relations. But this objection presupposes the conventional metaphysical sense of absolute and *absolvere* noted above. The absolute absolves itself from relations and from others. In contrast, Hegel's absolute is relation, and its absolution allows the other to be and to retain independence within relation. The distinction between immanent and economic trinity reflects a similar refusal to collapse external relations into internal relations. In Mure's language, the Hegelian super-triad is incomplete, and this reflects an open holism.

90. Errol Harris, "Hegel's Theory of Political Action," in *Hegel's Philosophy of Action,* ed. L. S. Stepelevich and D. Lamb (New York: Humanities Press, 1983), 170. For further discussion of this point, cf. Harris, *Formal, Transcendental & Dialectical Thinking,* op. cit. 133–145.

91. Hegel, *Difference,* op. cit. 156.

92. "Hegel had set forth this concept of the system...in 1830 in the form of three syllogisms. In this circular structure the logic is both grounding as well as grounded, to be sure, without losing the priority accruing to it from the fact that it sets forth the thought-determinations in their purity." ("*Die Wissenschaft der Logik,*" Friedrich Hogemann and Walter Jaeschke, in *Hegel: Einführung in seine Philosophie,* Hrsg. Otto Pöggeler [Freiberg/München: Verlag Karl Alber, 1977], 80.)

93. *Enz.* §121 Zusatz. [My italics.] Werner Marx claims that despite his awareness of alienation and darkness, Hegel remains in the metaphysical tradition of light, and that his thought guarantees conclusive victory to light, to pure transparent intelligibility. Marx in effect reduces Hegel's speculative identity of opposites to the abstract identity of the understanding (*Verstand*). Since identity means self-sameness, difference is excluded. (Werner Marx, *Heidegger and the Tradition,* op. cit. 55–57. But Hegel's view is that difference is intrinsic to identity, and so essential: "The very nature of things implies that they must be different" (*Enz.* § 117 Zusatz). Marx claims that despite Hegel's concern to give equal weight to difference and identity, he lapses into abstract identity as self-sameness. Differences are thus derivative from and subordinate to identity and unity. Similar readings of Hegel are presented by recent studies: Jacques Taminiaux, "Dialectic and Difference," in *Dialectic and Difference: Finitude in Modern Thought* (tr. R. Crease and J. Decker, Humanities Press, 1985), 79–90; Rudolphe Gasché, *The Tain of the Mirror: Derrida and the Philosophy of Reflection* (Cambridge: Mass,: Harvard University Press, 1986); Irene E. Harvey, *Derrida and the Economy of Différance* (Bloomington, Ind.: Indiana University Press, 1986), 93–124. Harvey portrays Hegel as the culmination of metaphysical logocentrism: "the system is closed, finitude is essentially united with infinity, and all differences are essentially subsumed within one unity." (106) In view of such one-sided dyadic interpretations, Hegel's text cited above is an important corrective.

94. As Hartmann has shown in his study of Sartre. See Klaus Hartmann, *Sartre's Ontology,* op. cit. 35ff. Hartmann observes that Sartre's *Being and Nothingness* is a flirtation with Parmenides, while Hegel is closer to and a development of Plato's alternative.

95. *Enz* §187 Zusatz.

96. PhG 564; PhS 493. Miller's English translation renders the last line of Hegel's text, "without which he would be lifeless and alone." The last lines are Hegel's own adaptation of Schiller's poem on Friendship.

TWELVE

HEGEL AND PHENOMENOLOGY:
HUSSERL, SARTRE, AND LEVINAS

This chapter explores the interhuman and social ontology. "Social ontology" has a rather odd sound to us, or simply conjures a void. It refers to a neglected topic in English-speaking philosophy. Social ontology should be distinguished from social theory and social philosophy. It is an inquiry into the meaning of the adjective 'social' in such disciplines, i.e., an ontology of the social. How does social ontology differ, if at all, from general ontology? Theunissen observes that "The term social 'ontology'...serves to express the fact that the other has today gained access to first philosophy."[1] When otherness is recognized and taken seriously, many believe that ontology as first philosophy is undermined.

The fundamental problem is not new: it rests upon the belief that to know is to objectify, to grasp as relative, and thus to compromise the transcendence and independence of the other. As F. H. Jacobi put it, to conceive and know something is to make manifest its relativity to and dependence on something else.[2] The only way to preserve the independence and integrity of a phenomenon is to deny knowledge of it. The other begins only where knowledge and ontology end. Levinas finds this general problem to be the difficulty implicit in social ontology. It can be formulated in terms of the following antinomy. On the one hand, if the other is 'radically other', then it is other than thought. But then the radical alterity of the other to thought makes a general ontology impossible. On the other hand, if the other is not radically distinguished from and transcendent to thought, then the other seems to be 'not-other'. A social ontology may be possible, but only at a very high price as indicated by Levinas' attack: ontology involves a reduction of the other to the same. Behind this attack lies a view of ontology as egology. All that the self can know are the products of its own activity.[3] On such grounds a social ontology would be a monstrous self-contradiction. For it would succeed only in reducing the other to presence, to the same, doing violence to the other. Thus, social ontology turns out to be either impossible (owing to the transcendence of the other to thought) or self-subverting (owing to the will to power implicit in ontology as a system of thought).

Levinas' formulation is skeptical, anti-ontological. But like Kant and

Jacobi, Levinas' skepticism concerning knowledge and ontology is not sheer negation, but negation in the service of the primacy of the practical and ethical. Thus, it presents dialectical problems and possibilities. For the critical question is how the transcendent other is available to ethical reflection, or, more simply put, how does the utterly transcendent, unknowable other obligate? Where Jacobi speaks of a primal truth prior to thought, Levinas speaks of the other's obligation as prior to my consciousness of freedom. Such pre-freedom, pre-conscious obligations are asserted dogmatically, or taken as immediate facts or truths.

It is a philosophical temptation to dismiss such conceptions as flat self-contradictions. As Jacobi's opponent Moses Mendelssohn put it: "What I am unable to think of as true, cannot create any doubts in me either. A question that I cannot possibly comprehend, and that I cannot possibly answer, is the same as no question at all."[4] It is worth noting that Hegel dismissed Mendelssohn's response to Jacobi as superficial Woffian rationalism. Hegel's response is no such superficial dismissal of the other. But neither does he fall back upon immediate certainties or dogmatic assurances. Rather he takes up the problem of the other and develops a theory of self-consciousness as mediated by the recognition of others that culminates in a philosophy of spirit. Where Jacobi and Levinas repudiate ontology as self-sameness, Hegel develops an ontology that grants difference, otherness its due. The alternative to irrationalistic dualism is Hegelian holism. Hegel's absolute knowing renounces domination, and absolves its other allowing the other to be.

In this last chapter, I want to show the continuing relevance of Hegel and his impact on significant voices in contemporary philosophy. Obviously, such a sketch could easily become another monograph. In what follows I shall confine my discussion to a modest exploration of Hegel's concept of recognition in reference to the thought of Husserl, Sartre, and Levinas. Husserl runs into difficulties extending his phenomenology of intersubjectivity to the social level. Sartre attempts the impossible task of appropriating both Hegelian recognition and existentialist individualism. Hegel, Husserl, and Levinas find the interhuman to be a dimension of reason itself. But Levinas believes that the interhuman can be formulated only in an anti-ontological posture. Yet, he cannot avoid the ontological dimension, and when he does formulate his position ontologically, it looks like Hegel.

HUSSERL

I shall focus on the *Cartesian Meditations* because this work has received the most extensive critical discussion. However, it by no means exhausts Husserl's views on intersubjectivity, and may be more misleading than truly representative of his thought. It is simply the most widely known and criticized. The *Cartesian Meditations* appears to place phenomenology within the framework of the Cartesian cogito. Since Cartesian subjectivity is haunted by subjectivism and solipsism, this apparently makes the problem of the other all but insoluble. Yet, Husserl is a Cartesian who overthrows and replaces all of Descartes' substantive doctrines.[5] He holds that the Cogito is not simply an 'I think' but, owing to intentionality, an *ego-cogito-cogitatum*. The other replaces the Cartesian doctrine of God as the basis of the objective world, the world that is there for everyone. Can the other be tackled at all within the *ego-cogito-cogitatum* framework? Is the other a *cogitatum*? If so, it must be unusual, since the other cannot in principle be present (*Urpräsenz*) to the ego. And this seems tantamount to solipsism.

We must distinguish two senses of solipsism: (1) A stronger sense, in which the other is entirely out of reach in principle as well as in fact. The other seems to be an unknowable 'thing in itself', a permanent limit to cognition. This rules out intersubjectivity or social ontology as knowledge. However, this view has dialectical problems. Moreover, negation presupposes prior affirmative knowledge as a condition of its truth. (2) A weaker sense that denies only *immediate* access to, or *immediate* presence of, the other. This sense of solipsism is not antithetical to, but rather constitutive of, intersubjectivity. Husserl is a solipsist in this weaker sense. He claims that the body of the other is directly present in experience, and that the alter ego is *indirectly* present, or *appresented,* by his body. Intentional analysis reveals that the other is an empty presence, a presence which cannot be brought within "my living present."[6] In view of the widespread opinion that Husserl represents the metaphysics of presence, it is important to realize that the phenomenological 'living present' has gaps, empty presences, and absences. One of the most important of these is the other.

In the Fifth Meditation, Husserl tackles the problem of the other by a *reductio ad absurdum* of the solipsistic argument. He begins with an attempted reduction of the world to the sphere of ownness. The strategy is to show the impossibility of a complete reduction to ownness and thereby to make the other stand forth. The reduction to ownness is not a dissolution of the other into me, but a recognition that 'ownness' and 'alien' are relative but asymmetrical concepts. Husserl writes "In this very specific intentionality there is constituted a new being-sense that encroaches upon the own being of my monadic ego. There is constituted an ego, not as 'I-myself,' but as mirroring itself in my own ego.... The second ego, however, is not simply there and strictly presented; rather he is constituted as 'alter ego'.... The other...points to me myself; the other is a mirroring of my own self and yet not a mirroring proper, an analogue of my own self and yet not an analogue in the usual sense."[7]

Reduction to ownness discloses a pairing between ego and alter ego, the discovery that the other, or alter ego, is a condition of my existence as unique, as my own. My primal ego is paired with an alter ego. Husserl's pairing reminds us of Hegel's account of doubling. Ricoeur comments on pairing that "one cannot fail to think of the Hegelian problem of the doubling of consciousness, for in myself there is every sign of an encroachment in the direction of another ego. The entire Fifth Meditation consists in tracing the lines of sense by which the experience of ownness refers to the alien other."[8] But Husserl lacks any sense of active encroachment of the other or offense at the other, as present in Hegel's life and death struggle for recognition or the issues inherent in master/slave.

Husserl's pairing focuses merely on the correspondence between my lived body and the body of the other. This pairing is Cartesian in that my ego is the only ego in original presence, and the alter ego is only indirectly or mediately present. Husserl's task is to extend the pairing/correspondence from the lived body to the alter ego, by means of an analogical grasping and apprehension of the other. In the absence of direct or immediate apprehension, how to grasp the alter ego? Can there be a mediate apprehension of the other?

According to Husserl, the other is not immediately present, but is appresented by his body. Appresentation extends Husserl's rich notion of perception and perceptual field. Consciousness means (or intends) more than what is directly present to sense perception. It spontaneously fills in what is meant, or cointended, but not directly present in perception. For example, the closed door to my room is intended as having both a front and a back, even though only the front is directly perceivable from within the room. The back is not directly present; rather it is appresented. Of course the reality of a door's backside can be verified, (i.e., brought to presence) by opening the door. But what about the interior of a ball? Though only the ball's surface is directly present, the ball itself is meant as surface plus an appresented interior. An interior of some sort is appresented by the surface as belonging necessarily to the ball.[9] That is, an interior belongs a priori to the ball. In like manner, the alter ego is not directly presented, it is appresented by its body.

However, the extension of appresentation to intersubjectivity faces an additional problem. Appresentation now must show how one kind of entity can appresent something on a different level from itself. Specifically, the other's body displays characteristics of the sort we know immediately in our own psycho-physical sphere; it appears as the kind of body we know ourselves to be. The alter ego is appresented by and through its bodily behaviors. Husserl advances this contention in a passage Ricoeur calls the most important in the Fifth Meditation:

> Let us assume that another man enters our perceptual field. Under the primordial reduction this means that in the perceptual field of my primordial nature there appears a body (*Körper*) which, so far as primordial, can only be a determining element of myself (an immanent transcendence). Since in this world my owned body (*Leib*) is the only body (*Körper*) that is or can be constituted originally as an organism (*Leib* [a functioning organism]),

that other body (*Körper*) over there—which however is also given as an organism (*Leib*)—must have derived it in such a way as to exclude a truly direct and primordial justification (that is, by a perception in the strict sense of the term) of the specific predicates belonging to the organism (*Leiblichkeit*). From this point on, it is clear that only a resemblance connecting the other body (*Körper*) with my body within my primordial sphere can provide the foundation and the motive for conceiving "by analogy" that body as another organism.[10]

The peculiar feature of the analogizing transfer of sense is that while all other analogies go from object to object on the same level, in this case the analogy runs from the own to the alien. In the bodily presence of an other, I recognize not myself but my analogue, and I extend to the other the sense 'alter ego', even though only my experience remains original and primary.

What is appresentation? Husserl's account is ambiguous; sometimes he describes appresentation as an intuition or mediate apprehension; at other times it appears to be merely a presumption yet to be confirmed. If a presumption, then appresentation amounts to little more than a discovery concerning analogical associations that take place in perception. Husserl would then be committed to some sort of argument from analogy in which the other is an inference, an hypothesis derived by analogizing transfer of sense from my primordial ego. This argument would be fallacious as Scheler noted. The inference would not be to an alter ego, but to my own ego "over there." However, Husserl denies that appresentation is an inference.

This denial apparently commits him to the stronger claim that appresentation is a genuine, if mediate, apprehension of the other. What does the 'alter' in 'alter ego' mean? Is the other merely a version of myself? Husserl rightly contends that I recognize not myself in the other's body, but someone *like* myself, not myself, but an *analogue*. Nevertheless, there is no direct access to the alter ego or ownness sphere of the other, which is appresented in and through the kind of body and behaviors we know directly in ourselves. The appresentation of the other is more than a presumption or inference, but less than originary presence (*Urpräsenz*).

Husserl brackets the ontological question and holds to a methodological idealism. He does not assert that the other depends metaphysically upon the originary transcendental ego. But the other is asymmetrically related to my primary ego. The asymmetrical, nonreciprocal relation between the originary transcendental ego and the alter ego, is as far as a transcendental first-person account of the other can be taken. Nevertheless, Husserl's account is unique in its progression from solipsism to community.[11] But given the asymmetry between primary and alter ego, how is such a progression possible? Husserl is unable to give a plausible account of reciprocity between ego and alter ego, and so is unable to give an adequate account of community. Ricoeur observes that:

the analogical grasping of the Other does not account for reciprocity among egos which the entire subsequent analysis requires. The me-Other relationship is essentially asymmetrical or non-reciprocal. The Other is a projected ego and as such a modified ego. Pairing is oriented in one way only, from the primordial ego to the analogous ego.... Only one ego is presented; all Others are appresented. Upon this asymmetrical relation, then, all communities must be constructed.... Yet the constitution of an objective nature, prior even to that of cultural communities, requires that the experience of the ego should enter into the composition with the experience of the Other on a basis of reciprocity...[12]

Both the objectivity of the world and ethical obligations to others rest upon and require intersubjective reciprocity. However, given the asymmetrical relation between ego and alter ego, Husserl cannot account for reciprocal recognition in Hegel's sense. Husserl's commitment to transcendentalism excludes reciprocity between ego and alter ego. As Hegel observes, a one-sided action is useless, because what is supposed to happen can only be brought about jointly and mutually, i.e., reciprocally. Husserl never gets as far as Hegel; the other never acts upon the I, nor does the I depend on the other. This negative assessment depends upon construing appresentation as more nearly like an hypothesis or projection than a mediate apprehension. If there is a mediate apprehension of the other, then there is some basis for reciprocity, however minimal. But Husserl does not clarify appresentation, and grounds community, whether transcendental or empirical, upon the asymmetrical relation between alter ego and ego.

However if, as suggested above, appresentation is a mediate apprehension, then appresentation and its correlate—the other—are more nearly equiprimordial. Then appresentation is the apprehension of an empty presence, a presence that in principle cannot be fulfilled in my living present. There is no direct access to the other, but the other is more than a mere presumption or inference. If ego and alter ego are equiprimordial, then reciprocity is somewhat more plausible. If appresentation is a mediate apprehension reflecting the action of the other, then Husserl approximates Hegel's critique of immediate knowledge and Hegel's alternative concept of a mediated immediacy.[13] And this turns his theory in the direction of praxis and action, i.e., towards Hegel.

SARTRE

Sartre is not the first phenomenologist to realize that the problem of the Other antedates the Husserlian phenomenological movement, but he is the first to call attention to Hegel's contribution to this topic and credit him with the real breakthrough. Hegel sees that self-consciousness is intersubjectively-socially mediated:

...the cogito cannot be the point of departure for philosophy...the "moment" which Hegel calls being-for-Other is a necessary stage in the development of self-consciousness; the road of interiority passes through the Other.... Hegel's brilliant intuition is to make me depend on the Other in my being. I am, he said, a being-for-self which is for itself only through another. Therefore the Other penetrates me to the heart. I cannot doubt him without doubting myself, since "self-consciousness is real only in so far as it recognizes its echo (and its reflection) in another."...Thus solipsism seems to be put out of the picture once and for all. By proceeding from Husserl to Hegel we have realized immense progress...instead of holding that my being-for-self is opposed to my being-for-others, I find that being-for-others appears as a necessary condition for my being-for-self.[14]

However, despite Sartre's appreciation of Hegel, his understanding, appropriation and criticisms are so flawed that it may be questioned whether Sartre actually read, much less understood, Hegel.[15] The questionableness of Sartre's appropriation of Hegel may be seen in his contradictory pronouncements: he praises Hegel for breaking with Cartesian idealism and solipsism, while criticizing his alleged idealist metaphysics for precluding an adequate account of intersubjectivity. This suggests that Sartre, although indebted to and appreciative of Hegel, does not accurately grasp his position. We shall first examine Sartre's reading of Hegel set forth in *Being and Nothingness,* and then take up the controversial issues.

Sartre's Reading of Hegel

Sartre's discussion of Hegel begins with an account of the *Phenomenology.*[16] Following Kojève, Sartre identifies Hegel's account of intersubjectivity simply as a theory of Master and Slave. Although he mentions recognition in his discussion, he fails to notice Hegel's distinction between the concept of recognition and its determinate appearance in ordinary consciousness, viz., the life and death struggle culminating in the unequal recognition of master and slave. By ignoring the distinction between the ontological (eidetic) and ontic (empirical) levels,[17] Sartre fails to see that, for Hegel, recognition has an ontological structure capable of supporting a wider greater range of instantiations than master/slave, conflict and domination. Thus, he fails to grasp master/slave as a deficient mode of recognition. Oblivious to the subtleties and details of Hegel's account, Sartre finds there only what he looks for, namely, support for the doctrine that "the essence of the relations between consciousnesses is not the *Mitsein,* it is conflict."[18] But this is only half of the story, and it produces a distorted view of both Hegel and intersubjective conflict.

Moreover, Sartre charges Hegel with a metaphysical rather than an existential-phenomenological solution to the problem of the Other. To make this case he breaks off his discussion of the *Phenomenology* and introduces some quotations from the *Propädeutik*.[19] Sartre quotes the *Propädeutik* out of context and suppresses crucial texts, saying, for example, "Hegel does not even conceive of the possibility of being-for-others which is not finally reducible to a being-as-object. Thus, a universal self-consciousness which seeks to disengage itself through all these dialectical phases is...reducible to a purely empty formula—the I am I."[20] Yet Hegel, in the very next paragraph (not quoted or mentioned by Sartre), writes "A self-consciousness that is for an other, is not a mere object (*Objekt*) but exists as its other self. The ego is no merely abstract universality in which there is no distinction or difference. Since the ego is an object for another ego, the other is the same as the ego. It intuits itself in the other."[21] How could Sartre have missed this?

Perhaps the answer is to be found in Sartre's source for Hegel, rather than Hegel himself. At the time Sartre wrote *Being and Nothingness*, he was not working with Hegel's *Phenomenology*, but with a collection of Hegel's writings—including the *Phenomenology* and the *Propädeutik*—in abridgement and translation. The abrupt transitions from one work to another in Sartre's discussion may have been determined by the nature and sequence of the selections from Hegel contained in his source.[22] If so, then Sartre's method of working and his sources distort his account of Hegel, and lead him to caricature *Geist* and social ontology as metaphysics.

Hegel's Breakthrough

Sartre begins his discussion of intersubjectivity with a critical analysis of realism and idealism. The failure of realism in treating the other, calls forth idealism, and vice-versa. Realism uncritically takes the existence of everything, including the other, as a given.[23] The existence of the other is certain, while the knowledge of the other as external is contingent and merely probable. But this claim shows realism's claim about the other's existence is dogmatic. If realism were to be genuinely critical, it would have to say that claims about the existence of the other follow from the knowledge that 'I have concerning him'. Thus realism, critically corrected, becomes idealism. Idealism renders the knowledge of the other certain, but reduces the other to a representation, i.e., to immanence in consciousness. But then the other ceases to be transcendent to consciousness and thus ceases to be other—or so the story goes. Thereby, idealism ends in solipsism, and reduces the other to the same. Or, refusing to push its claims that far, idealism reverts back to dogmatic realism.

Beneath this impasse between realism and idealism lies what Sartre calls the spatializing presupposition, namely, the assumption that the relation to the Other is an external, spatial relation, a relation to another body. The most extreme form of this assumption is to be found in Descartes, for whom everything is external to the Cogito, not merely other bodies, but also its own body. Realism affirms that the other is an external relation. Idealism affirms that the other is an internal relation, i.e., immanent in and so dependent on consciousness.[24] The spatializing assumption creates the dilemma: the other is either "outside" (but unknowable) or "inside" (but not genuinely other).

According to Sartre, Hegel is among the first to break with the spatializing assumption. Hegel's breakthrough is that the relation to the other is not a spatial relation at all. Thus, inner and outer cease to be literal opposites. Sartre writes, "Hegel's brilliant intuition is to make me depend on the Other in my being. I am, he said, a being-for-itself which is for-itself only through another. Therefore, the Other penetrates me to the heart. I cannot doubt him without doubting myself..."[25] Hegel makes the road of interiority pass through the other. Since the self and other are equiprimordial, the Cogito cannot be the starting point for the treatment of intersubjectivity, or for philosophy. Stated otherwise, since being-for-others is now a necessary condition of being-for-self,[26] self-consciousness cannot be restricted to the Cogito.

Sartre's Criticism of Hegel

In *Being and Nothingness* Sartre continues the existentialist critique of Hegel, that opposes individual decision to the abstract universal. Sartre adopts a nominalist position, according to which "the particular is the support and foundation of the universal."[27] Although Sartre had previously held that Hegel broke decisively with the impasse between realism and idealism, he now charges that Hegel remains within metaphysical idealism. Hegel supposedly identifies being with knowing, and from this allegedly abstract identity flows Hegel's errors, namely epistemological and ontological optimism.[28]

By epistemological optimism Sartre means (1) the assumption that reciprocal recognition in a mutual and positive sense is possible, and (2) that reciprocal recognition makes possible a passage to the universal, from the I to the We.[29] Sartre denies that recognition in Hegel's sense is possible, and charges Hegel with an illegitimate metaphysical attempt to overcome the ontological separation between consciousnesses. "Hegel's optimism ends in failure: between the Other as object and Me as subject there is no common measure.... I cannot know myself in the other if the other is first an object for me; neither can I apprehend the other in his true being—that is, his subjectivity. No universal knowledge can be derived from the relation of consciousnesses. This is what we shall call their ontological separation."[30] Sartre allows for only a negative reciprocity of mutual exclusion and refusal.

By ontological optimism Sartre means that instead of adopting the Cogito as his starting point for intersubjectivity, Hegel places himself at the vantage point of the whole. Hegel simply assumes that "plurality can and must be surpassed toward the totality. But if Hegel can assert the reality of this surpassing, it is only because he has already given it to himself at the outset."[31] Sartre fails to observe that Hegel gives a far more complex analysis of the place of the observer than does Sartre himself, distinguishing three standpoints within the *Phenomenology*: ordinary consciousness, the phenomenological onlookers, and the speculative philosopher.

Moreover, Sartre himself subsequently abandons, or at least qualifies, the claim that the cogito is the sole standpoint of a phenomenology of intersubjectivity and thus he comes closer to Hegel. He attempts to synthesize his existentialist philosophical anthropology with Marxist social ontology. Some doubt the success of this effort at mediation.[32] On the other hand, defenders claim that Sartre's existentialism is sublated in his Marxist social philosophy. That is, the individualist existential anthropology of *Being and Nothingness* can be *aufgehoben* in the later *Critique of Dialectical Reason* and the *Cahiers*. This defense, however, compels a re-assessment of Sartre's repudiation of Hegel. For such a passage to the social level is the very move which the early Sartre declared, *contra Hegel,* to be epistemologically optimistic and ontologically impossible. Such a defense of the later Sartre would imply that on the central critical issues of an ontology of intersubjectivity, Hegel is right, and the early Sartre is wrong. Hegel would thus require no defense against the criticisms levelled at him in *Being and Nothingness*.

We can clarify these issues and support these claims by a brief examination of Sartre's phenomenology of shame. Sartre's phenomenology of shame must be distinguished from his ontological account in *Being and Nothingness*.[33] Sartre's *phenomenological description* of shame as an essentially intersubjective consciousness employs the concept of recognition. Shame is not a reflective consciousness, but is rather pre-reflective or non-positional. Shame is not a state of mind one can give to oneself, but shame at oneself before somebody. The immediate presence of somebody else sends an immediate shudder through my being: "in the field of my reflection I can never meet with anything but the consciousness which is mine. But the Other is the indispensable mediator between myself and me. I am ashamed of my self as I appear to the Other."[34]

Yet, this is not a description of the entire phenomenon of shame. Significantly Sartre continues: "By the mere appearance of the Other, I am put in the position of passing judgement on myself as an object, for it is as an object that I appear to the Other. *Yet this object which has appeared to the Other is not an empty image in the mind of another.* Such an image in fact would be imputable wholly to the Other, and so could not 'touch' me. I could feel irritation, or anger before it as before a bad portrait of myself which gives expression to an ugliness or baseness which I do not have, but I could not be touched to the quick. *Shame is by nature recognition. I recognize that I am as the Other sees me.*"[35] Shame clearly involves recognition in Hegel's sense, a self-recognition in other. Thus, Sartre shows that Hegel's speculative conceptual analysis is by no means alien to phenomenological description and is capable of phenomenological presentation. Without self recognition in other, my appearing to the other would be merely an empty image, or an imaginative construct by the other that leaves me unaffected. But I do recognize that I am this being that appears 'thus and so' to the other and that I am as the other sees me.[36] Here is a clear and vivid phenomenological presentation of intersubjective self-recognition in other. Sartre is never so close to Hegel as he is here, yet he does not acknowledge or even mention Hegel's concept of recognition or its fundamental reciprocity.

Sartre's *ontological analysis* of shame is something else. Sartre's ontology in *Being and Nothingness* is like an acid that dissolves the original phenomenon, namely, self-recognition in other. *Being and Nothingness* is an existential *philosophy,* a posture opposed to mediation and dialectic. It is a move back to Kant that subordinates *Vernunft* to *Verstand.* Truth cannot abide contradiction or dialectical paradoxes, such as self-recognition in other. Knowledge involves objectification and construction, which strips the human being of its possibilities. The object of knowledge is an abstract universal, exclusive of particulars. Since reason is essentialist, abstract and formal, it cannot apprehend concrete existence. The only defense of the distinctively and ethically human against the onslaught of objectifying knowledge is to adopt ontological dualism, according to which human freedom is never object, but only subject. This dualism is another version of the transcendental asymmetry between ego and alter ego.

Sartre distinguishes sharply between subject and object as two types of being. This ontological dualism is evident in his analysis of the certainty of being looked at by the other when there is no other empirically present:

> There is indeed a confusion here between two distinct orders of knowledge and two types of being which cannot be compared. We have always known that the object in the world can only be probable. This is due to its very character as object. It is probable that the passerby is a man; if he turns his eyes towards me, then although I immediately experience and with certainty the fact of being looked at, I cannot make this certainty pass into my experience of the other as object. In fact it reveals to me only the other as subject, a transcending presence in the world and the real condition of my being as object. In every causal state therefore it is impossible to transfer my certainty of the other as subject to the other as object which was the occasion of that certainty, and conversely it is impossible to invalidate the evidence of the appearance of the other as subject by pointing to the constitutional probability of the other as object.... What is certain is that I am looked at: what is only probable is that the look is bound to this or that mundane presence.[37]

Subject and object are incomparable because they allegedly have nothing in common. They are two entirely separate orders of being. Yet this distinction is not free from problems. Sartre can maintain the absolute certainty of the other as subject of the look only by interpreting the other transcendentally, and thus reverting to the transcendental idealism criticized in the beginning.[38] Theunissen explains the difficulty: "At the beginning stood this thesis: The originally encountered alien existence...has the nature of a contingent and irreducible fact.... Now, on the contrary Sartre defends the indubitability of the subject-other at the expense of its facticity."[39]

What is important to see is that Sartre's claim that reciprocal recognition in Hegel's sense is impossible, and depends on these dualist ontological premisses. He writes: "Thus Hegel's optimism ends in failure: between the Other as object and me as subject there is no common measure.... I cannot know myself in the other if the Other is first an object for me; neither I can apprehend the Other in his true being—that is, in his subjectivity."[40] Given the gulf or ontological separation between subjects, no reciprocal recognition is possible.[41] So master/slave is not a contingent historical condition, but rather ontologically constitutive of intersubjectivity: "I am a slave to the degree that my being is dependent at the center of a freedom which is not mine and which is the very condition of my being...this slavery is not a historical result—capable of being surmounted—of a life in the abstract form of consciousness."[42] On these premisses recognition can have only a negative significance, namely reciprocal exclusion. And reciprocal exclusion means that recognition of self in other is ontologically impossible. Thus, the dualist ontology of *Being and Nothingness* undermines its phenomenology of recognition and shame consciousness.

At the level of phenomenological descriptions, Hegel and Sartre agree that conflict is an essential phase (*Stufe*) of recognition. However, they disagree about its ontological significance and interpretation.[43] Sartre does not derive his dualist ontology from, but imposes it on, his phenomenology of recognition. The absolute heterogeneity of being and nothingness implies that no mediation is possible and contradicts his phenomenological description of shame consciousness as self-recognition in other.

Hegel and Sartre disagree about the ontological significance of phenomenological descriptions. This disagreement cannot be settled by phenomenological analysis. Nevertheless, Sartre's rejection of mediation in *Being and Nothingness* admits of an *ad hominem* reply, since he later apparently comes to embrace the very position he rejected. In *Being and Nothingness*, Sartre's project is contradictory; he tries to combine an existentialist ontology of individualism, radical freedom, with a Hegelian theory of intersubjectivity. His dualist ontology undermines not only the intersubjectivity, but ethics and the social as well. Sartre's subsequent development in the *Critique of Dialectical Reason* moves him closer to Hegel but without explicitly correcting or modifying his earlier ontology of radical freedom.

According to Thomas Flynn, Sartre's universalist claim, first set forth in *Existentialism is a Humanism,* that to choose for oneself is to choose for all men, bears the weight of Sartre's later social ethic.[44] How is such a universal, implicitly intersubjective value justified? One defense of this universalism proceeds along traditional Kantian lines of the categorical imperative; the other develops a theory of intersubjectivity based upon positive reciprocal recognition. According to Flynn the concept of recognition plays a major role in the shift of Sartre's argument from formal or abstract to concrete freedom: "my authentic situation requires that I acknowledge the fact of other freedoms acknowledging my freedom. That is what it means to be 'in situation before others'. *'Freedom unrecognized remains abstract'* is a corollary to Sartre's theory that being for others is constitutive of human reality as situated, as well as to the formula that the choice of self implies intersubjectivity."[45]

Sartre apparently comes to embrace the very reciprocal recognition that he had criticized in Hegel and that his existentialist ontology had declared all but impossible. Theunissen comments that "it is not this materialistic grounding of the negativity of the other that shakes the foundations of Sartre's social ontology as laid down in *Being and Nothingness,* but the concession of the reciprocity of the subject-object relationship."[46] Flynn even declares that "positive reciprocity of freedoms is beginning to emerge as the the prime value in Sartre's social ethic."[47]

Sartre's development thus exhibits a patently Hegelian dialectic. This is not to suggest that Sartre would agree with the political argument of Hegel's *Philosophy of Right.* It is only to observe that a defense of Hegel's ontological analysis of reciprocal recognition against the criticisms advanced in *Being and Nothingness* is, in light of Sartre's later development, superfluous.

LEVINAS

Emmanuel Levinas raises a radical protest against the destruction of human dignity, and directs his protest to what he takes to be the underlying basis of such destruction, the logocentric intellectualism of the philosophical tradition. For Levinas, the destruction of human dignity has come about under the aegis of ontology. "Western philosophy has most often been an ontology: a reduction of the other to the same by the interposition of a middle and neutral term [sic. a universal, a category, or predicate] that ensures the comprehension of being."[48] The interposition of the universal term neutralizes existence and takes away the shock of encounter. To neutralize existence is to suspend or eliminate the ethical, and to reduce the other to the same (universal).

According to Levinas, Hegel is one of the worst offenders: "Hegelian phenomenology, where self-consciousness is the distinguishing of what is not distinct, expresses the universality of the same identifying itself in the alterity of objects thought and despite the opposition of self to self.... The difference is not a difference; the I, as other, is not an 'other.'"[49] Levinas claims that "the relation with Being that is enacted as ontology consists in neutralizing the existent in order to comprehend or grasp it. It is hence not a relation with the other as such, but the reduction of the other to the same.... Thematization and conceptualization, which moreover are inseparable, are not peace with the other but suppression or possession of the other.... Ontology as first philosophy is a philosophy of power."[50] Thus, not merely Hegel's (or Heidegger's) philosophy, but *philosophy itself* is an egology that reduces infinity to totality, the other to the same.[51]

Although Levinas considers himself a phenomenologist, he pursues his philosophy in an anti-ontological mode. He observes that the tradition conforms to the "platonic ontology by inferring that love is perfect when two people become one. I am trying to work against this identification of the divine with unification or totality. Man's relationship with the other is better as difference than as unity: sociality is better than fusion. The very value of love is the impossibility of reducing the other to myself, of coinciding into sameness."[52] Levinas would criticize Hegel's concept of love as monistic.

Levinas challenges the monism and abstract identity of the ontological tradition with his concept of the face: "The way in which the other presents himself, exceeding *the idea of the other in me,* we here name the face."[53] The face signifies the transcendence of the other, which Levinas understands not in epistemological but ethical terms. Levinas's analysis of the face is phenomenology in an *antiphenomenological* mode, for the face is *not* an appearance or a theme. The face expresses the ethical transcendence of other, and has primarily ethical significance. It presents the demand: You shall not kill. "This is not achieved by some sort of modification of the knowledge that thematizes, but precisely by 'thematization' turning into conversation."[54] Since there is, strictly speaking, no phenomenon, no appearance, and no ontological theme, the other cannot be reduced to the same (egology) and self and other cannot be parts of a totality. The other can be expressed only in such paradoxical expressions as "that which is approachable by a thought that...*thinks more than it thinks.*"[55]

However, after protests about the irreducibility of infinity to totality, Levinas acknowledges that there is a "conjuncture of the same and the other, in which even their verbal proximity is maintained..."[56] But this is not a reduction of the other to the same; it "is the direct and full face welcome of the other by me. This conjuncture is irreducible to totality; the 'face to face' position is not a modification of the 'along side of...'"[57] The conjuncture or the relation to the other is "a relation in which the terms absolve themselves from the relation, remain absolute within the relation. Without this absolution, the absolute distance of metaphysics would be illusory."[58]

Levinas thus argues that ethics is prior to ontology and theory, and that theoretical reason has a primordial interhuman dimension. Reason is intersubjective to such a degree that Levinas asserts, "Reason is the one for the other."[59] This means that ethical responsibility for the other precedes knowledge of the other, and that rationality is rooted in interhuman ethical proximity.

Levinas and Hegel

Steven G. Smith calls attention to the riddle of Levinas' thought: "How can there be a rational argument concerning an infinite that avowedly exceeds any rational totality? How can there be a phenomenological description of something that is not evident, or an ontological analysis of something that is beyond being? If Levinas' analysis is neither phenomenological nor ontological, what is it? Why call it philosophy?"[60] It is difficult to determine whether Levinas is a voice through which Hegel's philosophy continues to speak in the diaspora of the contemporary situation (cf. Merleau Ponty's comment, all that is great in philosophy in the last 150 years derives from Hegel), or whether Levinas poses an alternative to Hegel that is, at the same time, an alternative to philosophy. This is not to suggest that Levinas is actually influenced by or appropriated heavily from Hegel. There is no reason not to think that Levinas reached the positions outlined above independently of Hegel.

But that being said, the coincidences between Levinas and Hegel are, on the assumption that Levinas is offering a phenomenological philosophy of the other, nevertheless remarkable.[61] For example, both criticize the Eleatic monism of the ontological tradition. Levinas contends that "the Eleatic notion of being dominates Plato's philosophy.... The whole particularity of the relationship of one to another goes unnoticed.... Beginning with Plato the social ideal will be sought for in an ideal of fusion."[62] Hegel makes similar criticisms of the priority of unity in the metaphysical tradition, specifically Parmenides and the Eleatics: "Being, the One of the Eleatic school, is only this abstraction, a sinking into the abyss of the [abstract] identity of the understanding [*Verstandesidentität*]."[63] Parmenides' thought exhibits the intolerance of antinomy and contradiction of *Verstandesmetaphysik,* and for this reason is inferior to Heraclitus.[64]

Moreover, Levinas' criticisms of classical ontology as monist, as an egological philosophy of power that reduces the other to the same, are all originally raised by Hegel. The difference is that Hegel denies that the tradition is simply an error or that it has exhausted all ontological possibilities. He would deny Levinas' claim that "Ontology as first philosophy is a philosophy of power,"[65] as well as the assumption that there are two reasons, a *theoretical reason* which, as reductive of the other to the same, must be limited, and a *practical reason* which has access to the other denied the first, namely, a "non-theoretical givenness of the other."[66]

Despite Levinas' rejection of ontology, he does not really avoid it. Smith observes that *Totality and Infinity* is a negative, anti-ontological statement of Levinas' position: "Levinas uses the language of ontology to express an anti-ontology; he answers the question of being by displacing it. Thus far, however, he produces only paradox and apparent logical bad faith."[67] But Levinas does not leave matters there. *Totality and Infinity,* we could say, stresses the unavailability of the other and absolute separation between persons. But a purely negative account is impossible because negation is possible only on the basis of some prior positive knowledge. Smith claims that in *Otherwise than Being*, Levinas achieves a more positive statement concerning the proximity of the other;[68] "...only the No of *Totality and Infinity*, establishing the *theoretical non-givenness* of the other, secures the right sense of the Yes of *Otherwise than Being*, establishing the *non-theoretical givenness* of the other in prophetic inspiration."[69] This approach seems to suggest two reasons and two others. It points not to Kant so much as Jacobi's irrationalistic fideism.

Despite the Levinasian rejection of ontology, it should be noted that Hegel's ontology of *Geist* employs many of Levinas's leading concepts. Where Levinas speaks of the Face in conceptual terms as an idea of the other exceeding the idea I have of the other, or as a thought which thinks more than it thinks, Mure expresses Hegel's concept of the other as at once thought and the opposite of thought.[70]

Although Levinas denies that self and other can be expressed in terms of totality, he nevertheless acknowledges that there can be a conjuncture of self and other. This conjuncture does not involve a reduction of the other to the same, because self and other *absolve* themselves from each other within their relation, and so remain absolute within the relation. But Hegel makes a somewhat similar point in his eidetics of recognition. In the final phase of reciprocal recognition, each allows the other to be, to go free, and only through such *Gelassenheit* does the self return to itself in satisfaction and enrichment by the other.[71] Hegel's analysis makes this point even clearer concerning love and forgiveness as conditions of reciprocity. This shows that Hegel's holistic social ontology is quite capable of incorporating the other without reduction of the other to the same. However, Hegel would deny Levinas's claim that the related terms remain absolute within relation, for, if the relation is real, the *relata* must have an effect on each other. This implies that each self must renounce its absolute immediacy and undergo mediation for mutual recognition to occur.[72] It may be that Levinas would side with Fichte, that relation to other only limits the self, rather than with Hegel for whom the social is an enhancement and fulfillment of freedom.[73]

On the other hand, Levinas rejects ontology as theoretical, and even though he comes to a more positive statement of the proximity of the other to the self—even the priority of the other over the self in *Otherwise Than Being*—he retains a negative, anti-ontological posture. Of course Levinas takes up this posture vis-a-vis ontology understood in foundationalist terms as egology. This posture leads to another coincidence with Hegel, because Levinas set his position forth under the rubric of "Reason and Skepticism."[74] This posture is no longer simply negation, i.e., ontology in the mode of anti-ontology. Rather, Levinas means to assert the primacy of the ethical over the theoretical, and this is a positive claim. As Smith points out, this means Levinas finds reason and rationality rooted in the interhuman relation.[75] "Reason is the one-for-the-other."[76] However, this positive affirmation is interpreted by Levinas skeptically, as incapable of being brought to theoretical expression. Put another way, Levinas's skepticism is the expression in theoretical terms of his claim of primacy of the ethical over theory. However, Levinas's version of this primacy has problems: "The priority of justice to truth is, however a philosophical thesis. What is Levinas arguing but the truth of justice? How can his case be made except as a statement of the case? How can a rational account be given of something that is not truth?"[77] Hegel would be quite familiar with these difficulties; the one who philosophizes as a skeptic has to appropriate the very thing he rejects in order to make his case.

Hegel agrees with Levinas that reason is rooted in the interhuman, and that it has a social dimension and structure. And Hegel agrees with Levinas that skepticism brings out this social dimension by posing the problem of equipollence, thus forcing immediate certainty to confront the other and the requirement that its certainty be elevated to truth in cooperative mediation with other. Skeptical equipollence shatters the arrogant parochial dogmatism that sees only itself in the other or that reduces the other to the same. But Hegel denies that equipollence is simply skeptical; it is a rational demand that has both negative and positive significance. From the perspective of dogmatic foundational egolatry, equipollence has negative significance. It deabsolutizes and decenters the self. But the negative side of equipollence prepares the way for the positive side, namely, the enhancement and fulfillment of freedom in self-recognition in other that elevates mutual certainty to truth, wherein the I becomes a We.

The We is no fusion or undifferentiated unity of persons. The We does not necessarily result in such union, because mutual releasement and forgiveness are conditions of the mutual recognition through which the We emerges as a result. The We stands not for domination or oppression, but for liberation and freedom. Hegel's Philosophy of *Geist* is in all probability the greatest social ontology yet produced in the West, but it has not been sufficiently appreciated nor has it taken root there. Nevertheless, his concept of a universal community of freedom founded on reciprocal and mutual recognition has never been more relevant.

NOTES

1. Michael Theunissen, *The Other: Studies in the Social Ontology of Husserl, Heidegger, Sartre and Buber,* tr. C. Macann (Cambridge, Mass.: MIT Press, 1984), 5. [Hereafter cited as *Other.*] Cf. Edmund Husserl, *Cartesian Meditations,* tr. Dorion Cairns (The Hague: Martinus Nijhoff, 1960); Husserl, *The Crisis of European Sci-*

ences and Transcendental Phenomenology, tr. D. Carr (Evanston, Ill.: Northwestern University Press, 1970); Martin Heidegger, *Being and Time,* tr. MacQuarrie and Robinson (New York: Harper & Row, 1962); Sartre, *Being and Nothingness;* Max Scheler, *Nature and Forms of Sympathy;* Alfred Schutz, *Collected Papers Vols I–III.*

2. Hegel, *Geschichte der Philosophie,* TWA Sk. 20, 318: "Begreifen heißt, seine Abhängigkeit aufzeigen."

3. This is the theme common to both Jacobi's and Levinas's readings of idealism. Hegel too shares this criticism of most forms of idealism. That is why it is always odd to see this charge brought against Hegel.

4. Hegel, *Geschichte der Philosophie,* TWA Sk. 20, 317. For an account of the controversy between Jacobi and Mendelssohn, cf. Robert Beiser, *The Fate of Reason,* op. cit. Chapters 2–3. Mendelssohn was the leading figure of the classical *Aufklärung;* consequently when his position collapsed under Jacobi's attack, the classical Enlightenment itself collapsed. Beiser notes "We have...paid a heavy price for our ignorance of the pantheism controversy. We have lost our philosophical orientation in dealing with the speculative systems of post-Kantian philosophy." (Ibid. 48) This controversy marks the beginning of the debates over the issues of nihilism, presence, reason and truth that continue unabated in contemporary philosophy. To imagine that Hegel is oblivious to this debate, or that he suppresses such critical issues in his own philosophical construction, is to fail utterly to comprehend him. Conversely, to see Hegel as responding to these issues is to be in a good position to appreciate his thought in its own right, and as a significant voice in the contemporary discussion.

5. See David Carr, "The Fifth Meditation and Husserl's Cartesianism," in *Interpreting Husserl,* (Boston: Martinus Nijhoff, 1987). Does Husserl thereby also overthrow first philosophy? Ludwig Landgrebe thinks so, and argues that Husserl tends to undermine the very project of first philosophy that he wishes to defend. See "Husserl's Departure from Cartesianism" in *The Phenomenology of Husserl,* ed. R. O. Elveton (Chicago: Quadrangle Books, 1970).

6. See "Edmund Husserl: Zur Phänomenologie der Intersubjektivität: Texte aus dem Nachlaß," by Gerd Brand, in *Husserl, Scheler, Heidegger in der Sicht neuer Quellen* [*Phänomenologische Forschungen*], Redaktion von E. W. Orth (Freiburg/München: Verlag Karl Alber, 1978), 62.

7. Husserl, *Cartesian Meditations,* tr. D. Cairns (The Hague: Martinus Nijhoff, 1960), 94.

8. Ricoeur, *Husserl,* op. cit. 119–120.

9. For this example I am indebted to Edward Farley. See his *Ecclesial Man: A Social Phenomenology of Faith and Reality* (Philadelphia: Fortress Press, 1975).

10. Husserl, *Cartesian Meditations* 140:23–29, translated and cited by Ricoeur, op. cit. 126.

11. Ricoeur, op. cit. 135.

12. Ibid. 131.

13. For a drastically different picture of Husserl, one which does include the action of the other, and emphasizes the *Gleichürsprunglichkeit* of other and self, cf. Gerd Brand's summary of the *Texte Zur Phänomenologie der Intersubjektivität*, op. cit. 68–72.

14. Sartre, *Being and Nothingness*, tr. H. Barnes (New York: Philosophical Library, 1956), 236–238. [Hereafter cited as BN.]

15. See Mitchell Aboulafia, *The Mediating Self* (New Haven, Conn.: Yale University Press, 1986), 41n. Aboulafia points out that Sartre acknowledged in a 1975 interview that he knew Hegel only indirectly from lectures and seminars when writing *Being and Nothingness*, and began a serious study of Hegel only much later. This is typical: everyone has heard of Hegel, but only a few actually read or make a serious study of his thought, and this accounts for the discrepancy between the "received picture of Hegel" and Hegel.

16. BN 235.

17. Cf. Heidegger, *Sein und Zeit* (Tübingen: Niemayer Verlag, 1984), §26, 120; cf. Sartre, BN 9ff., 286f. Sartre himself makes similar distinctions.

18. BN 429; cf. 364: "Conflict is the original meaning of being-for-others."

19. BN 237. The *Propadeutik* is a work not published by Hegel, but a collection of Gymnasium lecture notes from Hegel's Nuremburg period edited by Karl Rosenkranz.

20. BN 238.

21. Hegel, *Texte zur philosophischen Propädeutik*, TWA Sk 4, 119, §30.

22. Cf. Christopher Martin Fry, *Sartre and Hegel: The Variations of An Enigma in L' Etre et le Neant* (Bonn: Bouvier Verlag, 1988). Fry contends that Sartre's Hegel source during the writing of *Being and Nothingness* was the book, *Hegel: Morceaux Choisis*, trad. ed. par Henri Lefebvre et N. Guterman (Paris, 1939). This book is a collection of sources, including parts of the *Phänomenologie des Geistes*, the *Propädeutik*, and selections from Hegel's *Enzyklopädie*. Fry points out that while it is possible Sartre read Hegel's books, there is not a single quotation from Hegel in *Being and Nothingness* not found in *Hegel: Morceaux Choisis*. This historical explanation of Sartre's piecemeal and distorted picture is more plausible than claiming Sartre was a fool (i.e., failed to understand Hegel) or a knave (i. e, interpreted Hegel irresponsibly and/or willfully). It also clarifies his 1975 statement that at the time of writing *Being and Nothingness* he knew of Hegel but had not read or studied his *books*.

23. BN 223. Hegel makes a similar criticism in his "Three Attitudes of Thought Towards Objectivity," cf. *Enz*. §§26–36.

24. Cf. above, chapter 7.

25. BN 237.

26. BN 238.

27. BN 239.

28. Sartre misunderstands Hegel's idealism or holism. The formal absolute ego, the I am I, is precisely that idealism which Hegel criticizes in the *Phenomenology* and rejects as a pure motionless tautology. (PhG 175ff) This is not the first time that Hegel has been charged with holding the idealism which he was the first to attack and reject. Hegel would agree with Sartre that from such a formal conception of idealism, the pure ego as pure identity, I am I, etc., it is difficult if not impossible to understand the problem of the Other or intersubjectivity. Hegel holds a different concept of identity as identity of identity and non-identity, and insists upon dialectical negation and mediation. That is why for Hegel the problem of the Other, and the related problem of mediation, are inescapable: there is nothing in heaven or earth that does not contain mediation. (WL TWA Sk 5, 66)

29. BN 240.

30. BN 243. Hegel's critique of immediate knowledge makes a similar, related point: Not only is there no direct or immediate access to the *other*, there is no immediate or privileged access of the self to *itself*. Hegel's starting point is simultaneous correlative uncertainty concerning the other and false consciousness concerning oneself. Uncertainty concerning the other is intolerable, and sets in motion the life and death struggle. Hegel's account of recognition shows that the self is for itself only through the mediation of the other's recognition. Since self identity is mediated by other, alterity is a constitutive feature of self-identity. Moreover, Hegel's analysis of the understanding (*Verstand*) shows that abstract identity—the identity that excludes difference—is its fundamental category. The understanding's concept of abstract identity must be deconstructed and replaced by a holistic dialectical concept that grants otherness and difference its due. The emergent universal is mediated by other and so concrete in Hegel's sense.

31. Ibid.

32. See Thomas R. Flynn, *Sartre and Marxist Existentialism* (Chicago: University of Chicago Press, 1984), xii.

33. Sartre himself draws this distinction. Cf. BN 268.

34. BN 222.

35. Ibid. [My emphasis.]

36. BN 261. Here Sartre claims that this is a relation of being to being, or something like an encounter.

37. BN 276–7.

38. "Sartre's social ontology falls completely into that transcendentalism from whose destruction it took its start." Michael Theunissen, *The Other: Studies in Social Ontology,* op. cit. 1984, 238.

39. Ibid. 241. See also Klaus Hartmann, *Sartre's Ontology: A Study of Sartre's Being And Nothingness in the Light of Hegel's Logic,* op. cit. 113n. 35.

40. BN 243. Here Sartre derives the plurality and ontological separation of consciousnesses from the fundamental dualistic ontology.

41. Hartmann, op. cit. 115f.

42. BN 267.

43. See Klaus Hartmann, *Sartre's Ontology,* op. cit. 116: Sartre can use...certain features of Hegel's chapter on 'Lordship and Bondage' in the *Phenomenology of Spirit;* it is here that he can find a struggle between two unequal self-consciousnesses which proves exemplary for his own position. Sartre's theory of the Other, is, in a way, a subtle transformation of Hegel's richer and more complex configuration into a simpler and more general one which nevertheless retains Hegel's concrete meaning. The line of argument in each case is completely different, however."

44. Flynn, op. cit. 33.

45. Ibid. 40. [Emphasis in the original.]

46. Theunissen, op. cit. 247.

47. Flynn, op. cit. 46.

48. Emmanuel Levinas, *Totality and Infinity,* tr. A. Lingis (Pittsburgh: Duquesne University Press, 1969), 42–44.

49. Ibid. 36–37.

50. Ibid. 46.

51. This view of ontology was vigorously represented in Hegel's day by F. H. Jacobi, in his *Brief an Fichte (1799).* (English Translation "Open Letter to Fichte, 1799, tr. Diana I. Behler, in *Philosophy of German Idealism,* ed. Ernst Behler, [*The German Library: Volume 23*] [New York: Continuum, 1987], 119–142.) It is striking that Jacobi, like Levinas and others, portrays what he wishes to attack as a monolithic tradition. According to Jacobi, Kant is the first to discover the principle of all knowledge and philosophy, "the principle of subject-object identity." (Beiser, *The Fate of Reason,* op. cit. 123). This principle signifies that the self can know only the products of its own activity, i.e., what it has itself constructed. From this it follows that knowledge of nature, other minds and God, turns out to be impossible. Jacobi then formulates the dilemma: I know either myself (but not nature, others or God) or nothing. Hegel's response to Jacobi is found in his *Glauben und Wissen* (ET *Faith and Knowledge*), his *Geschichte der Philosophie,* and references to Jacobi are scattered throughout his several discussions of immediate knowledge.

52. "Dialogue with Emmanuel Levinas," in *Face to Face with Levinas,* ed. R. Cohen (Albany, N.Y.: SUNY Press, 1986), 22. [Hereafter cited as FFL.]

53. TI 50. Note the formalism of Levinas: despite talk about the face, this

remains a formal concept, without phenomenological concreteness. The face is not *a* face.

54. TI 51.

55. TI 62.

56. TI 80.

57. Ibid.

58. TI 64.

59. Emmanuel Levinas, *Otherwise Than Being or Beyond Essence,* tr. A. Lingis (The Hague: Martinus Nijhoff, 1981), 167. [Hereafter cited as OBBE.]

60. Steven G. Smith, "Reason as One for Another: Moral and Theoretical Argument in the Philosophy of Levinas," FFL 53.

61. Jacques Derrida has called attention to Levinas's paradoxical relation to Hegel: "...as soon as he speaks against Hegel, Levinas can only confirm Hegel, has confirmed him already." ("Violence and Metaphysics," in *Writing and Difference,* tr. A. Bass (Chicago: University of Chicago Press, 1978), 120. Again, "Levinas is very close to Hegel, much closer than he admits, and at the very moment when he is apparently opposed to Hegel in the most radical fashion. This is a situation he must share with all anti-Hegelian thinkers..." (Ibid. 99) But there is another reason for this strange affinity. Hegel was very much aware of and responded to position similar to Levinas, represented by F. H. Jacobi. Specifically, Hegel responded to Jacobi's charges that idealism is an egology that reduces the other to the same. His critique of immediate knowledge, his account of intersubjective *Anerkennung,* and his development of an alternative conception of identity that grants otherness its rightful place, are in part responses to Jacobi. It is interesting that when Levinas formulates his position in ontological terms, it looks similar to Hegel's account of recognition. See Levinas, "Substitution," in *The Levinas Reader,* ed. Seán Hand (Oxford, England: B. H. Blackwell, 1989), 117; see also his account of the mutual absolution of the same and other in TI.

62. Levinas, *Time and the Other,* 92–93. Hegel also criticizes Plato for passing over subjective particular freedom. See Michael B. Foster, *The Political Philosophies of Plato and Hegel* (Oxford: Clarendon Press, 1935; New York: Garland, 1984).

63. Hegel, *Geschichte der Philosophie,* TWA Sk. 18, 299.

64. Hegel writes, "Heraclitos understands the absolute as this process, as dialectic itself.... With Heraclitos, philosophy first finds its [appropriate] speculative form, in comparison with which the *raisonnement* of Parmenides and Zeno is mere abstract understanding [*Verstand*].... Here we see land for the first time; there is not a single principle of Heraclitos that I have not incorporated into my logic." Hegel, *Geschichte der Philosophie,* TWA Sk. 18, 320.

65. TI 46.

66. This formulation is not Levinas, but comes from Steven G. Smith (op. cit. 68).

67. Smith, op. cit. 55–6.

68. Ibid. 62–63.

69. Ibid. 68.

70. Cf. Chapter 11.

71. Cf. Chapters 7 and 8. Derrida rhetorically asks, "Where have these movements [set forth by Levinas] been better described than in *The Phenomenology of Spirit*?" op. cit. 126.

72. Levinas seems to acknowledge such renunciation of immediacy when he says, "I become a responsible or ethical I to the extent that I agree to depose or dethrone myself—to abdicate my position of centrality—in favor of the vulnerable other." ("Dialogue with Levinas," FFL 27.)

73. Levinas says, "But because there are more than two people in the world, we invariably pass from the ethical perspective of alterity to the ontological perspective of totality.... As soon as there are three, the ethical relationship with other becomes political and enters into the totalizing discourse of ontology. We can never completely escape from the language of ontology and politics." (Ibid. 21–22.) Levinas's roots in the philosophy of "I-Thou" is apparent. From Hegel's perspective, Levinas represents a version of the unhappy consciousness, as well as Kantian *Moralität*, or possibly even the beautiful soul. The self and its other, however intimate, remain alienated from the world, even though they cannot flee or escape it. (Cf. Chapter 4)

74. OBBE 165.

75. "The root structure of reason is, according to OBBE, the 'one for another' of substitution and signification." FFL 61.

76. OBBE 167.

77. Smith op. cit. 55.

BIBLIOGRAPHY

WORKS BY FICHTE

Fichtes Werke. Hrsg. I. H. Fichte. Berlin: Walter de Gruyter, 1971. This is a reprint of Johann Gottlieb Fichte's *Sämmtliche Werke,* Herausgegeben von I. H. Fichte, 8 Bände, Berlin: Veit & Comp., 1845–46. All of the following entries are included in this edition.

Erste Einleitung in die Wissenschaftslehre (1797), Fichtes Werke. I. Hrsg. I. H. Fichte. Berlin: Walter de Gruyter, 1971. English Translation: *Science of Knowledge.* Ed. and tr. Peter Heath & John Lachs, New York: Appleton Century Crofts, 1970.

Grundlage des Naturrechts nach Principien der Wissenschaftslehre (1796), Werke III. Hrsg. I. H. Fichte. 1–365. Berlin: Walter de Gruyter, 1971.

"Review of Anesidemus," in *Between Kant and Hegel: Texts in the Development of Post-Kantian Idealism.* Eds. Di Giovanni, George, and H. S. Harris. Albany, N.Y.: SUNY Press, 1985.

System der Sittenlehre nach Principien der Wissenschaftslehre (1798) Werke IV. Hrsg. I. H. Fichte. 1–365. Berlin: Walter de Gruyter, 1971.

Über die Bestimmung des Gelehrten (1794), *Werke 6.* Hrsg. I. H. Fichte. Berlin: Walter de Gruyter, 1971. English Translation: *Some Lectures Concerning the Scholar's Vocation* in *Fichte: Early Philosophical Writings.* Ed. and tr. Daniel Breazeale, Ithaca, N.Y.: Cornell University Press, 1988, 137–184. Reprinted in *Philosophy of German Idealism.* Ed. Ernst Behler. [*The German Library Volume 23,* Volkmar Sander, editor] New York: Continuum, 1987, 1–38.

Wissenschaftslehre 1794, Fichtes Werke, Band I. Hrsg. I. H. Fichte. Berlin: Walter de Gruyter, 1971. English Translation: *Science of Knowledge.* Ed. and tr. by Peter Heath and John Lachs. New York: Appleton Century Crofts, 1970.

WORKS BY HEGEL

Werke in zwanzig Bänden, Theorie Werkausgabe, Frankfurt: Suhrkamp Verlag, 1971. This is a reprint based on the *Werke 1832–1845.* Edited by Eva Moldenhauer and Karl Markus Michel. When this edition is cited, it is abbreviated TWA, followed by the publisher Sk. and volume number in the Suhrkamp edition, followed by the page number. Thus TWA Sk 3: ——.

Differenz des Fichte'sche und Schelling'sche System der Philosophie, Hegel Werke: Theorie Ausgabe, Band 2, Frankfurt: Suhrkamp Verlag, 1970. English Translation *The Difference between Fichte's and Schelling's System of Philosophy.* Tr. H. S. Harris and W. Cerf, Albany, N.Y. SUNY Press, 1977.

Einleitung in die Geschichte der Philosophie. Hrsg. Johannes Hoffmeister. Hamburg: Felix Meiner Verlag, 1940.

Enzyklopädie (Werke, Theorie Werkausgabe, Band 8–10, Frankfurt: Suhrkamp Verlag, 1970). English Translation: *Hegel's Logic, Hegel's Philosophy of Nature, Hegel's Philosophy of Mind.* Tr. W. Wallace together with the *Zusätze* in Boumann's text (1845). Tr. A. V. Miller. Oxford: Clarendon Press, 1971.

Foreword to H. Fr. W. Hinrichs' Die Religion im inneren Verhältnisse zur Wissenschaft (1822), TWA Sk: 11. English Translation: tr. A. V. Miller, *Beyond Epistemology: New Studies in the Philosophy of Hegel.* Ed. F. Weiss. The Hague: Martinus Nijhoff, 1974.

Geschichte der Philosophie, Werke, TWA, Sk: Bände 18–20.

Glauben und Wissen, Werke: TWA, Sk 2, Frankfurt: Suhrkamp Verlag, 1970. English Translation: *Faith and Knowledge.* Tr. W. Cerf and H. S. Harris. Albany, N.Y.: SUNY Press, 1977.

Grundlinien der Philosophie des Rechts, TWA Sk. 7. English Translation: *Hegel's Philosophy of Right.* Tr. T. M. Knox. Oxford: Clarendon Press, 1952.

Hegel: The Letters. Tr. C. Butler & C. Seiler. Bloomington: Indiana University Press, 1984.

Hegels Theologische Jugendschriften. Hrsg. H. Nohl. Tübingen: J. C. B. Mohr (Paul Siebeck), 1907, reprinted 1966. This has been partially reprinted in *Hegels Werke,* TWA, Band 1. Frankfurt: Suhrkamp, 1971. English Translation: *On Christianity: Early Theological Writings.* Tr. T. M. Knox and Richard Kroner. New York: Harper Torchbooks, 1948.

Jena Realphilosophie (1805/1806), in *G. W. F. Hegel: Frühe politische Systeme.* Edited with commentary by Gerhard Göhler. Frankfurt/Berlin: Ullstein, 1974. English Translation: *Hegel and the Human Spirit.* Tr. Leo Rauch. Detroit: Wayne State University Press, 1983.

Phänomenologie des Geistes. Hrsg. Hoffmeister. Hamburg: Felix Meiner Verlag, 1952. English translations: *Phenomenology of Mind* (J. B. Baillie). New York: Macmillan, 1910, and *Phenomenology of Spirit* (A. V. Miller). Oxford or New York: Oxford University Press, 1977.

Philosophie des Geistes. 1803/1804. Fragment 21. *Jenaer Systementwürfe I: Das System der Spekulativen Philosophie.*Hrsgs. Klaus Düsing and Heinz Kimmerle. Hamburg: Meiner Verlag. English Translation: *First Philosophy of Spirit,* in G. W. F. Hegel, *System of Ethical Life* (1802–1803) and *First Philosophy of Spirit* (1803). Tr. H. S. Harris. Albany, N.Y.: SUNY Press, 1979.

"Review of C. F. Göschel's Aphorisms." Translated by Clark Butler in *CLIO* 17:4, 369–393, 1988.

System of Ethical Life (1802/3) and First Philosophy of Spirit. Tr. H. S. Harris and T. M. Knox. Albany, N.Y.: SUNY Press, 1977.

The Critical Journal, in *Between Kant and Hegel: Texts in the Development of Post-Kantian Idealism.* Eds. George Di Giovanni and H. S. Harris. Albany, N.Y.: SUNY Press, 1985.

Über die wissenschaftlichen Behandlungsarten des Naturrechts, TWA, Sk: 2. English Translation *Natural Law.* Tr. T. M. Knox. Philadelphia: University of Pennsylvania Press, 1975.

Verhältnis Skeptizismus zur Philosophie, Werke, TWA Sk. 2. English Translation: *On the Relationship of Skepticism to Philosophy,* in *Between Kant and Hegel: Texts in the Development of Post-Kantian Idealism.* Eds. George Di Giovanni and H. S. Harris. Albany, N.Y.: SUNY Press, 1985.

Vorlesungen über die Aesthetik, Hegels Werke, TWA, Band 7, Frankfurt: Suhrkamp, 1971.

Vorlesungen über die Beweise vom Dasein Gottes. Hrsg. G. Lasson. Hamburg: Meiner Verlag, 1930, 1973.

Vorlesungen über die Philosophie der Religion, Werke, TWA Sk. Bände, 16–17.

Vorlesungen über die Philosophie der Religion, Teil 1: *Der Begriff der Religion,* Teil 2: *Die bestimmte Religion,* Teil 3: *Die vollendete Religion,* Hrsg. von Walter Jaeschke. Hamburg: Meiner Verlag, 1983, 1985, 1984. English Translation: *Lectures on the Philosophy of Religion,* vol. 1; *The Concept of Religion,* vol. 2; *Determinate Religion,* vol. 3; *The Consummate Religion.* Ed. Peter C. Hodgson, tr. R. Brown, Hodgson, J. Stewart, with the assistance of H. S. Harris. Berkeley: University of California Press, 1984, 1986, 1985.

Vorlesungen über die Philosophie der Weltgeschichte, Band I *Die Vernunft in der Geschichte.* Hrsg. Johannes Hoffmeister. Hamburg: Felix Meiner Verlag, 1955.

Wissenschaft der Logik, Werke, TWA Sk. Bande 5 & 6. English Translation: *Hegel's Science of Logic.* Tr. A. V. Miller. New York: Humanities Press, 1969.

GENERAL WORKS CONSULTED

Aboulafia, Mitchell. *The Mediating Self.* New Haven, Conn.: Yale University Press, 1986.

Arendt, Hannah. *The Human Condition.* Chicago: University of Chicago Press, 1958.

Aristotle. *Metaphysics, Introduction to Aristotle.* Ed. R. Mckeon, New York: Modern Library, 1947.

Aristotle. *Politics*. Tr. E. Barker. Oxford: Oxford University Press, 1958.

Aschenberg, Reinhold. "Der Wahrheitsbegriff in Hegels 'Phänomenologie des Geistes'" in *Die ontologische Option*. Hrsg. Klaus Hartmann. Berlin: Walter de Gruyter, 1976.

Avinieri, Shlomo. *Hegel's Theory of the Modern State*. Cambridge: Cambridge University Press, 1972.

Barth, Karl. *Church Dogmatics*, vol. 2. Edinburgh: T&T Clark, 1960.

Baumanns, Peter. *Fichtes Ursprungliches System: Sein Standort zwischen Kant und Hegel*. Stuttgart: Fromman-Holzboog, 1972.

Beck, Lewis White. *A Commentary on Kant's Critique of Practical Reason*. Chicago: University of Chicago Press, 1960.

Beiser, Robert. *The Fate of Reason*. Cambridge, Mass: Harvard University Press, 1987.

Bernstein, J. M. "From Self-Consciousness to Community: Act and Recognition in the Master-Slave Relationship, in *The State and Civil Society: Studies in Hegel's Political Philosophy*. Ed. Z. A. Pelczynski. Cambridge: Cambridge University Press, 1984.

Berthold-Bond, Daniel. *Hegel's Grand Synthesis: A Study of Being, Thought and History*. Albany, N.Y.: SUNY Press, 1989.

Brand, Gerd. "Edmund Husserl: Zur Phänomenologie der Intersubjektivität: Texte aus dem Nachlaß," *Husserl, Scheler, Heidegger in der Sicht neuer Quellen, [Phänomenologische Forschungen]* Redaktion von E. W. Orth. Freiburg/München: Verlag Karl Alber, 1978.

Buber, Martin. *I and Thou*. Tr. W. Kaufmann. New York: Scribners, 1970.

Carr, David. "The Fifth Meditation and Husserl's Cartesianism," in *Interpreting Husserl*. Boston: Martinus Nijhoff, 1987.

Carr, David. *Interpreting Husserl*. Boston: Martinus Nijhoff, 1987.

Carr, David. *Transcendental Phenomenology and the Problem of History*. Evanston, Ill.: Northwestern University Press, 1977.

Clark, Malcolm. *Logic and System: A Study of the Transition from Vorstellung to Thought in the Philosophy of Hegel*. Loewen: Universitaire Werkgemeenschap, 1960.

Crites, Stephen. "The Golgotha of Absolute Spirit" in *Method and Speculation in Hegel's Phenomenology*. Ed. M. Westphal. New York: Humanities Press, 1982.

Daniel, Klaus. *Hegel Verstehen: Einführung in sein Denken*. Frankfurt: Campus Verlag, 1983.

Derrida, Jacques. "Violence and Metaphysics," in *Writing and Difference*. Tr. Alan Bass. Chicago: University of Chicago Press, 1978.

Desmond, William. *Art and the Absolute*. Albany, N.Y.: SUNY Press, 1986.

Desmond, William. *Desire, Dialectic and Otherness*. New Haven, Conn.: Yale University Press, 1987.

Di Giovanni, George, and Harris, H. S., eds. *Between Kant and Hegel: Texts in the Development of Post-Kantian Idealism*. Albany, N.Y.: SUNY Press, 1985.

Di Giovanni, George, ed. *Essays on Hegel's Logic*. Albany, N.Y.: SUNY Press, 1990.

Donougho, Martin. "The Woman in White: On the Reception of Hegel's Antigone, in *Owl of Minerva*, vol. 21, no. 1 (Fall 1989).

Dove, Kenley Royce. "Towards An Interpretation of Hegel's *Phänomenologie des Geistes*." Yale PhD dissertation, 1965.

Dove, Kenley Royce. "Die Epoché der Phänomenologie des Geistes," *Hegel Studien Beiheft, Stuttgarter Hegel-Tage 1970*. Hrsg. H. G. Gadamer. 605–622. Bonn: Bouvier Verlag, 1974.

Duesberg, Hans. *Person und Gemeinschaft: Philosophische-Systematische Untersuchungen des Sinnzusammenhangs von personaler Selbstständigkeit und interpersonaler Beziehung an Texten von J. G. Fichte und M. Buber*. Bonn: Bouvier Verlag, 1970.

Düsing, Edith. *Intersubjektivität und Selbstbewusstsein*. Köln: Dinter Verlag, 1986.

Düsing, Edith. "Genesis des Selbstbewusstseins durch Anerkennung und Liebe. Untersuchungen zu Hegels Theorie der konkreten Subjektivität," in *Hegels Theorie des subjektiven Geistes [Spekulation und Erfahrung II/14]*. Hrsg. Lothar Eley. Stuttgart: fromman-Holzboog, 1990, 244–279.

Düsing, Klaus. *Das Problem der Subjektivität in Hegels Logik, Hegel Studien*, Beiheft 15. Bonn: Bouvier Verlag, 1976.

Düsing, Klaus. *Hegel und die Geschichte der Philosophie, Erträge der Forschung*, Band 206. Darmstadt: Wissenschaftliche Buchgesellschaft, 1983.

Eley, Lothar. *Hegels Theorie des subjektiven Geistes [Spekulation und Erfahrung II/14]* Stuttgart: Fromman-Holzboog, 1990.

Fackenheim, Emil. *The Religious Dimension in Hegel's Thought*. Chicago: University of Chicago Press, 1967.

Farley, Edward. *Ecclesial Man: A Social Phenomenology of Faith and Reality*. Philadelphia: Fortress Press, 1975.

Farley, Edward. *Ecclesial Reflection: An Anatomy of Theological Method*. Philadelphia: Fortress Press, 1982.

Feuerbach, Ludwig. *The Essence of Christianity.* Tr. G. Eliot. New York: Harper & Row, 1957.

Feuerbach, Ludwig. "Towards a Critique of Hegel's Philosophy" (1839) in *The Fiery Brook: Selected Writings of Ludwig Feuerbach.* Tr. Zawar Hanfi. New York: Doubleday Anchor Books, 1972.

Findlay, J. N. *Hegel: A Re-Examination.* New York: Collier MacMillan, 1962.

Findlay, J. N. "Reflexive Asymmetry: Hegel's Most Fundamental Methodological Ruse," in *Beyond Epistemology: New Studies in the Philosophy of Hegel.* Ed. F. Weiss. The Hague: Martinus Nijhoff, 1974.

Flay, Joseph C. *Hegel's Quest for Certainty.* Albany, N.Y.: SUNY Press, 1984.

Flay, Joseph C. "Hegel's *Science of Logic*: Ironies of the Understanding," in *Essays on Hegel's Logic.* Ed. George di Giovanni. Albany, N.Y.: SUNY Press, 1990.

Flynn, Thomas R. *Sartre and Marxist Existentialism.* Chicago: University of Chicago Press, 1984.

Forster, Michael N. *Hegel and Skepticism.* Cambridge, Mass.: Harvard University Press, 1989.

Foster, Michael B. *The Political Philosophies of Plato and Hegel.* Oxford: Clarend Press, 1935, New York: Garland, 1984.

Fry, Christopher Martin. *Sartre and Hegel: The Variations of An Enigma in L' Etre et le Neant.* Bonn: Bouvier Verlag, 1988.

Fulda, H. F., "Der Begriff des Geistes bei Hegel und seine Wirkungsgeschichte," in *Historisches Wörterbuch der Philosophie.* Hrsg. Joachim Ritter, Band III, 191ff. Stuttgart: Schwabe & Co, 1971.

Fulda, H. F. *Das Problem einer Einleitung in Hegels Wissenschaft der Logik,* Zweite Auflage. Frankfurt Am Main: Vittorio Klostermann, 1975.

Gadamer, Hans-Georg. *Truth and Method.* New York: Seabury Press, 1975.

Gadamer, H. G. "Hegel and Heidegger," in *Hegel's Dialectic: Five Hermeneutical Studies.* Tr. Christopher Smith. New Haven, Conn.: Yale University Press, 1976.

Gadamer, H. G. "Hegel's Dialectic of Self-Consciousness," in *Hegel's Dialectic.* Tr. Christopher Smith. New Haven, Conn.: Yale University Press, 1976.

Gadamer, Hans-Georg. "The Phenomenological Movement," in *Philosophical Hermeneutics.* Tr. and ed., David E. Linge. Berkeley: University of California Press, 1977.

Gasché, Rudolphe. *The Tain of the Mirror: Derrida and the Philosophy of Reflection.* Cambridge, Mass.: Harvard University Press, 1986.

Goossens, Wilfried. "Ethical Life and Family in the *Phenomenology of Spirit*," in

Hegel On the Ethical Life, Religion and Philosophy. Ed. A. Wylleman. *Louvain Philosophical Studies 3.* Dordrecht: Kluwer Academic Publishers, 1989.

Habermas, Jurgen. *"Arbeit und Interaktion: Bemerkungen zu Hegels Jena Philosophie des Geistes,"* cited in *Frühe politische Systeme,* Hrsg. G. Göhler. 786ff. Frankfurt: Ullstein, 1974. English Translation: "Labor and Interaction: Remarks on Hegel's Jena *Philosophy of Mind,"* in *Theory and Practice.* Tr. John Viertel. 142–169. Boston: Beacon Press, 1974.

Habermas, Jürgen. *The Philosophical Discourse of Modernity.* Tr. F. Lawrence. Cambridge, Mass.: MIT Press, 1987.

Halper, Edward. "Hegel and the Problem of the Differentia," in *Essays on Hegel's Logic.* Ed. G. di Giovanni, 191–211. Albany, N.Y.: SUNY Press, 1990.

Harris, Errol E. "Hegel's Theory of Political Action," in *Hegel's Philosophy of Action.* Ed. L. S. Stepelevich and D. Lamb. New York: Humanities Press, 1983.

Harris, Errol E. "The Contemporary Significance of Hegel and Whitehead," in *Hegel and Whitehead: Contemporary Perspectives on Systematic Philosophy.* Ed. George R. Lucas, Jr. Albany, N.Y.: SUNY Press, 1986.

Harris, Errol E. *Formal, Transcendental and Dialectical Thinking: Logic and Reality.* Albany, N.Y.: SUNY Press, 1987.

Harris, H. S. "The Concept of Recognition in Hegel's Jena Manuscripts," in *Hegel-Studien Beiheft 20,* 229–248. Bonn: Bouvier Verlag, 1979.

Harris, H. S. *Hegel's Development: Night Thoughts.* Oxford: Clarendon Press, 1983.

Hartmann, Klaus. *Sartre's Ontology: A Study of Sartre's Being and Nothingness in the Light of Hegel's Logic.* Evanston, Ill.: Northwestern University Press, 1966.

Hartmann, Klaus. "On Taking the Transcendental Turn," *Review of Metaphysics,* 20.2.78 (December 1966): 223–249.

Hartmann, Klaus. "Towards a New Systematic Reading of Hegel's *Philosophy of Right,"* in *The State and Civil Society.* Ed. Z. A. Pelczynski, 114–136. Cambridge, Mass.: Cambridge University Press, 1984.

Hartmann, Nicolai. *Philosophie des deutschen Idealismus,* Zweite Auflage. Berlin: Walter de Gruyter, 1960.

Hartshorne, Charles. *The Divine Relativity: A Social Conception of God.* New Haven, Conn.: Yale University Press, 1948.

Harvey, Irene E. *Derrida and the Economy of Differánce.* Bloomington, Ind.: Indiana University Press, 1986.

Heidegger, Martin. *Holzwege.* Frankfurt: Vittorio Klostermann, 1950.

Heidegger, Martin. *Hegels Begriff der Erfahrung, Holzwege.* Frankfurt: Vittorio Klostermann, 1950, 111–205. ET: *Hegel's Concept of Experience.* Tr. K. R. Dove. New York: Harper & Row, 1971.

Heidegger, Martin. *Sein und Zeit.* Tübingen: Niemayer Verlag, 1984.

Heidegger, Martin. *History of the Concept of Time.* Tr. Theodore Kisiel. Bloomington, Ind.: Indiana University Press, 1985.

Heidegger, Martin. *Hegel's Phenomenology of Spirit.* Tr. Emad and K. Maly. Bloomington, Ind.: Indiana University Press, 1988.

Heimsoeth, Heinz. *Fichte.* München: Reinhardt, 1923.

Heinrichs, Johannes. *Die Logik der Phänomenologie des Geistes.* Bonn: Bouvier Verlag, 1974.

Henrich, Dieter. "Fichtes ürsprungliche Einsicht," *Subjektivität und Metaphysik.* Ed. D. Henrich & H. Wagner, 188–232. Frankfurt: Klostermann, 1966.

Henrich, Dieter. "Hegel und Hölderlin" in *Hegel im Kontext.* Frankfurt: Suhrkamp, 1967.

Henrich, Dieter. "Hegels Theorie über den Zufall," *Hegel im Kontext.* Frankfurt: Suhrkamp, 1967.

Hodgson, Peter C. *God and History.* Nashville: Abingdon Press, 1989.

Horstmann, Rolf-Peter. *Ontologie und Relationen: Hegel, Bradley, Russell und die Kontroverse über interne und externe Beziehungen.* Hain: Athenäum, 1984.

Hösle, Vittorio. *Hegels System.* 2 vols. Hamburg: Meiner Verlag, 1987.

Hunter, C. K. *Der Interpersonalitätsbeweis in Fichtes früher angewandter praktischer Philosophie.* Meisenheim am Glan: Verlag Anton Hain, 1973.

Husserl, Edmund. *Cartesian Meditations.* Tr. Dorion Cairns. The Hague: Martinus Nijhoff, 1960.

Husserl, Edmund. *Ideas: A General Introduction to Pure Phenomenology.* Tr. W. R. Boyce Gibson. New York: Collier Macmillan, 1962.

Husserl, Edmund. *Ideen I, II, III.* Hrsg. Marly Biemel. The Hague: Martinus Nijhoff, 1969.

Husserl, Edmund. *The Crisis of European Science and Transcendental Phenomenology.* Tr. D. Carr. Evanston, Ill.: Northwestern University Press, 1970.

Hyppolite, Jean. "Anmerkungen zur Vorrede der Phänomenologie des Geistes und zum Thema: das Absolute ist Subjekt," in *Materialien zu Hegels Phänomenologie des Geistes.* Hrsg. H. F. Fulda und D. Henrich. Frankfurt am Main: Surkamp Taschenbuch Verlag, 1973.

Hyppolite, Jean. *Genesis and Structure of Hegel's Phenomenology of Spirit.* Tr. S. Cherniak & J. Heckman. Evanston, Ill.: Northwestern University Press, 1974.

Hyppolite, Jean. "Life and the Consciousness of Life in the Jena Philosophy," in *Studies on Marx and Hegel.* Ed. and tr. by John O'Neill. New York: Harper & Row, 1969.

Jacobi, F. H. *Brief an Fichte* (1799), English Translation: "Open Letter to Fichte, 1799," in *Philosophy of German Idealism.* Ed. Ernst Behler. Tr. Diana I. Behler. *The German Library,* vol. 23, 119–142. New York: Continuum, 1987, 119–142.

Jaeschke, Walter. "Absolute Idee—Absolute Subjektivität: Zum Problem der Persönlichkeit Gottes in der Logik und in der Religionsphilosophie," *Zeitschrift für philosophische Forschung,* Band 35 Heft 3/4, 385–416. Meisenheim/Glan: Verlag Anton Hain, 1981.

Jaeschke, Walter. *Vernunft in der Religion: Studien zur Grundlegung der Religionsphilosophie Hegels,* [*Spekulation und Erfahrung: Texte und Untersuchungen zum Deutschen Idealismus* Band 4] Stuttgart: Fromman-Holzboog, 1986. English Translation: *Reason in Religion: The Foundations of Hegel's Philosophy of Religion.* Tr. J. Michael Stewart and Peter C. Hodgson. Berkeley: University of California Press, 1990.

Janke, Wolfgang. *Fichte: Sein und Reflexion.* Berlin: Walter de Gruyter, 1970.

Jurist, Eliot. "Hegel's Concept of Recognition." PhD. dissertation, Columbia University, 1983.

Jüngel, Eberhard. *God as the Mystery of the World.* Tr. Darrell L. Guder. Grand Rapids, Mich.: Eerdmans Publishing Company, 1983.

Kainz, Howard. *Paradox, Dialectic and System: A Contemporary Reconstruction of the Hegelian Problematic.* University Park, Pa: The Pennsylvania State University Press, 1988.

Kant, Immanuel. *Critique of Practical Reason.* Tr. Lewis White Beck. New York: Library of Liberal Arts, 1956.

Kant, Immanuel. *Foundations of the Metaphysics of Morals.* Tr. Lewis White Beck. New York: Library of Liberal Arts, 1959.

Kant, Immanuel. *Critique of Pure Reason.* Translated by Norman Kemp Smith. New York: St. Martin's Press, 1965.

Kelly, George Armstrong. *Idealism, Politics & History: Sources of Hegelian Thought,* Cambridge: At the University Press, 1969.

Kelly, George Armstrong. "Notes on Hegel's 'Lordship and Bondage'" in *Hegel: A Collection of Critical Essays.* Ed. Alasdair MacIntyre. Garden City, N.Y.: Anchor Books, 1972.

Kern, Iso. "The Three Ways to the Transcendental Phenomenological Reduction," *Husserl: Expositions and Appraisals.* Ed. and tr. by F. Elliston and P. McCormick. Notre Dame: University of Notre Dame Press, 1977.

Kierkegaard, Soren. *Concluding Unscientific Postscript.* Tr. D. Swenson and W. Lowrie. Princeton, N.Y.: Princeton University Press, 1950.

Kierkegaard, Soren. *Fear and Trembling.* Tr. H. Hong. Princeton: Princeton University Press, 1983.

Kojéve, Alexander. *Introduction to the Reading of Hegel*. Ed. Allan Bloom, tr. J. H. Nichols, Jr. New York: Basic Books, 1969.

Kolb, David. *The Critique of Pure Modernity: Hegel, Heidegger and After*. Chicago: The University of Chicago Press, 1986.

Kolakowski, Leslak. *Husserl's Search For Certitude*. New Haven, Conn.: Yale University Press.

Kroner, Richard. *Von Kant Bis Hegel*. Tübingen: J. C. B. Mohr, 1921–24.

Landgrebe, Ludwig. "Husserl's Departure from Cartesianism," in *The Phenomenology of Husserl*. Ed. R. O Elveton, 259–306. Chicago: Chicago Quadrangle Books, 1970.

Lauth, Reinhard. "Le probleme de l'interpersonalite chez J. G. Fichte," *Archives de Philosophie 26*. (1962): 325–344.

Levinas, Emmanuel. *Totality and Infinity*. Tr. A. Lingis. Pittsburgh: Duquesne University Press, 1969.

Levinas, Emmanuel. *Otherwise Than Being or Beyond Essence*. Tr. A. Lingis. The Hague: Martinus Nijhoff, 1981.

Levinas, Emmanuel. "Dialogue with Emmanuel Levinas," in *Face to Face with Levinas*. Ed. R. Cohen. Albany, N.Y.: Suny Press, 1986.

Levinas, Emmanuel. *Time and the Other*. Tr. R. Cohen. Pittsburgh: Duquesne University Press, 1987.

Levinas, Emmanuel. "Substitution," in *The Levinas Reader*. Ed. Sean Hand. Oxford: B. Blackwell Ltd., 1989.

Litt, Theodor. *Hegel:Versuch einer kritischen Erneurung*. Heidelberg: Quelle & Meyer, 1961.

Ludwig, Walter. "Hegel's Conception of Absolute Knowing," *Owl of Minerva*, vol. 21, no. 1 (Fall 1989): 5–19.

Lukàcs, Georg. *The Young Hegel*. Tr. Robert Livingstone. Cambridge, Mass: MIT Press, 1976.

Maker, William. "Hegel's Phenomenology as Introduction to Science," *CLIO*, 10:4, 381–397 (1981).

Maker, William. "Reason and the Problem of Modernity," *The Philosophical Forum*, vol. 18, no. 4 (Summer 1987): 275–303.

Maker, William. "Beginning" in *Essays on Hegel's Logic*. Ed. George di Giovanni. Albany, N. Y.: SUNY Press, 1990.

Makkreel, Rudolf, and John Scanlon, eds. *Dilthey and Phenomenology*. Washington, D.C.: Center for Advanced Research in Phenomenology and University Presses of America, 1987.

Marx, Werner. *Heidegger and the Tradition.* Tr. Theodore Kisiel. Evanston, Ill.: Northwestern University Press, 1971.

Mohanty, J. N. *The Possibility of Transcendental Philosophy,* [*Phaenomenologica Volume 98*]. Dordrecht, The Netherlands: Martinus Nijhoff, 1985.

Mure, G. R. G. *A Study of Hegel's Logic.* Oxford: Oxford University Press, 1950.

Pannenberg, Wolfhart. "Die Bedeutung des Christentums in der Philosophie Hegels," in *Stuttgarter Hegel-Tage 1970. Hegel Studien* Beiheft 11, 175–202. Bonn: Bouvier Verlag, 1974.

Pannenberg, Wolfhart. "Der Geist und sein Anderes," in *Hegels Logik der Philosophie.* Ed. D. Henrich and R. Horstmann. Stuttgart: Klett-Kotta Verlag, 1984.

Philolenko, Alexis. *La liberte humaine dans la philosophie de Fichte.* Paris, 1966.

Pöggeler, Otto. *Hegels Idee einer Phänomenologie des Geistes.* Freiburg: Alber Verlag, 1973.

Pöggeler, Otto. "Die Komposition der Phänomenologie des Geistes" in *Materialien zu Hegels Phänomenologie des Geistes.* Frankfurt: Suhrkamp, 1973.

Poggeler, Hrsg. Otto, ed. *Hegel: Einführung in seine Philosophie.* Freiburg/München: Verlag Karl Alber, 1977.

Pöggeler, Otto. *Grundprobleme der grossen Philosophen.* Hrsg. Josef Speck. UTB 464 Göttingen: Vandenhoeck & Ruprecht, 1982.

Priest, Stephen, ed. *Hegel's Critique of Kant.* Oxford: Clarendon Press, 1987.

Prokopczyk, Czeslaw. *Truth and Reality in Marx and Hegel.* Amherst, Mass.: The University of Massachusetts Press, 1980.

Reinhold, K. L. *The Foundation of Philosophical Knowledge (1794).* Tr. George di Giovanni, in *Between Kant and Hegel,* Albany, N.Y.: SUNY Press, 1985.

Richardson, William J. *Heidegger: Through Phenomenology to Thought,* The Hague: Martinus Nijhoff, 1963.

Ricoeur, Paul. "Original Sin: A Study in Meaning," *Conflict Of Interpretations.* Evanston, Ill.: Northwestern University Press, 1974.

Ricoeur, Paul. *Fallible Man,* tr. C. Kelbley, New York: Fordham University Press, 1986.

Ricoeur, Paul. *Freedom and Nature: The Voluntary and the Involuntary.* Evanston, Ill.: Northwestern University Press, 1970.

Ricoeur, Paul. "Husserl's Fifth Cartesian Meditation," in *Husserl: An Analysis of His Phenomenology.* Tr. Ballard & Embree. Evanston, Ill.: Northwestern University Press, 1967.

Ricoeur, Paul. *Husserl: An Analysis of His Phenomenology.* Evanston, Ill.: Northwestern University Press, 1967.

Ricoeur, Paul. *The Symbolism of Evil*. Tr. E. Buchanan. Boston: Beacon Press, 1969.

Ricoeur, Paul. *Time and Narrative, Volume 3*. Tr. K. Blamey and D. Pellauer. Chicago: University of Chicago Press, 1988.

Rockmore, Tom. *Hegel's Circular Epistemology*. Bloomington, Ind.: Indiana University Press, 1986.

Rockmore, Tom. "Foundationalism and Hegelian Logic," *Owl of Minerva*, vol. 21, no. 1 (Fall 1989).

Rosen, Stanley. *G. W. F. Hegel; An Introduction to the Science of Wisdom*. New Haven, Conn.: Yale University Press, 1974.

Rosen, Stanley. "Freedom and Spontaneity in Fichte," *The Philosophical Forum*, vol. 19, no. 2–3 (Winter–Spring 1988).

Rosen, Stanley. *The Ancients and the Moderns: Rethinking Modernity*. New Haven, Conn.: Yale University Press, 1989.

Röttges, Heinz. *Dialektik und Skeptizismus: Die Rolle des Skeptizismus für Genese, Selbstverständnis und Kritik der Dialektik* [*Monographien zur philosophischen Forschung*]. Athenäum: Hain Verlag, 1986.

Royce, Josiah. *Lectures on Modern Idealism*. New Haven, Conn.: Yale University Press, 1919.

Royce, Josiah. "The Possibility of Error," in *The Philosophy of Josiah Royce*. Ed. John K. Roth. New York: Crowell Co., 1971.

Sartre, Jean Paul. *Being and Nothingness*. Tr. Hazel Barnes. New York: Philosophical Library, 1956.

Scheler, Max. *The Nature and Forms of Sympathy*. Tr. Peter Heath. Hamden, Conn.: The Shoe String Press, 1970. A translation of *Vom Wesen der Sympathiegefühl* (1923).

Schelling, F. W. J. *Philosophical Letters On Dogmatism and Criticism*, in *The Unconditional in Human Knowledge*. Tr. Fritz Marti. Lewisburg, Pa.: Bucknell University Press, 1980.

Schleiermacher, Friedrich. *Der Christliche Glaube*. Berlin: Walter de Gruyter, 1960. ET *The Christian Faith*. Ed. and tr. H. R. MacIntosh. Philadelphia: Fortress Press, 1978.

Schlitt, Dale M. *Hegel's Trinitarian Claim: A Critical Reflection*. Leiden: E. J. Brill, 1984.

Schmidt, Dennis J. *The Ubiquity of the Finite: Hegel, Heidegger and the Entitlements of Philosophy*. Cambridge, Mass.: MIT Press, 1988.

Schulz, Walter. "Das Problem der absoluten Reflexion," in *Wissenschaft und Gegenwart Heft 24*. Frankfurt am Main: Klostermann, 1963.

Schulz, Walter. *Die Vollendung des Deutsche Idealismus in der Spätphilosophie Schellings*. Pfullingen: Neske Verlag, 1975.

Schürmann, Reiner. *Meister Eckhart, [Studies In Phenomenology and Existential Philosophy]*. Bloomington, Ind.: Indiana University Press, 1978.

Schutz, Alfred. *Reflections on the Problem of Relevance*. New Haven, Conn.: Yale University Press, 1970.

Schutz, Alfred. "The Problem of Transcendental Intersubjectivity in Husserl" and "Type and Eidos in Husserl's Late Philosophy." *Collected Papers,* vol. 3. Ed. I. Schutz. The Hague: Martinus Nijhoff, 1966, 92–115.

Schutz, Alfred. "Type and Eidos in Husserl's Late Philosophy," *Collected Papers Vol. III*. Ed. I. Schutz, 92–115. The Hague: Martinus Nijhoff, 1966.

Schutz, Alfred. "Scheler's Theory of Intersubjectivity" in *Collected Papers Vol. I: The Problem of Social Reality*. Ed. M. Natanson. The Hague: Martinus Nijhoff, 1967.

Seebohm, Thomas, and Joseph Kockelmans, eds. *Kant and Phenomenology*. Washington, D.C. Center for Advanced Research in Phenomenology and University Presses of America, 1984.

Sextus Empiricus. *Outlines of Pyrrhonism* I. Tr. R. G. Bury, *Loeb Classical Library*. Cambridge, Mass.: Harvard University Press, 1976.

Siep, Ludwig. *Hegels Fichtekritik und die Wissenschaftslehre von 1804*. Freiburg: Verlag Karl Alber, 1970.

Siep, Ludwig. *Anerkennung als Prinzip der praktischen Philosophie: Untersuchungen zu Hegels Jenaer Philosophie des Geistes*. Freiburg: Alber Verlag, 1979.

Smith, John E. "Hegel's Critique of Kant," in *Review of Metaphysics,* 1973.

Smith, Steven G. "Reason as One for Another: Moral and Theoretical Argument in the Philosophy of Levinas," in *Face to Face with Levinas*. Ed. Richard Cohen. Albany, N.Y.: SUNY Press, 1986.

Solomon, Robert C. "Hegel's Concept of *Geist*," in *Hegel: A Collection of Critical Essays*. Ed. A. MacIntyre, 125–149. New York: Doubleday Anchor, 1972.

Spiegelberg, Herbert. *The Phenomenological Movement*. The Hague: Martinus Nijhoff, 1960.

Strawson, P. F. *Individuals*. London: Methuen, 1959.

Taminiaux, Jacques. "Dialectic and Difference," in *Dialectic and Difference: Finitude in Modern Thought*. Tr. R. Crease and J. Decker. New York: Humanities Press, 1985.

Taylor, Charles. *Hegel*. London: Cambridge University Press, 1976.

Theunissen, Michael. *Hegels Lehre vom absoluten Geist as theologisch-politischer Traktat*. Berlin: Walter de Gruyter, 1970.

Theunissen, Michael. "Begriff und Realität: Hegels Aufhebung des metaphysischen Wahrheitsbegriffs," in *Seminar: Dialektik in der Philosophie Hegels*. Herausgegeben und eingeleitet von Rolf-Peter Horstmann. Frankfurt am Main: Suhrkamp Verlag, 1978.

Theunissen, Michael. *Sein Und Schein: Die kritische Funktion der Hegelschen Logik*. Frankfurt am Main: Suhrkamp Verlag, 1980.

Theunissen, Michael. "Die verdrängte Intersubjektivität in Hegels Philosophie des Rechts," in *Hegels Philosophie des Rechts*. Hrsg. Dieter Henrich and Rolf-Peter Horstmann. Stuttgart: Klett Cotta, 1982.

Theunissen, Michael. *The Other: Studies in the Social Ontology of Husserl, Heidegger, Sartre and Buber*. Tr. Christopher Macann. Cambridge, Mass.: MIT Press, 1984.

Verene, Donald Philip. *Hegel's Recollection: A Study of the Images in the Phenomenology of Spirit*. Albany, N.Y.: SUNY Press, 1985.

Vos, Lu De. "Absolute Knowing in the Phenomenology" in *Hegel On the Ethical Life, Religion and Philosophy*. Ed. A. Wylleman, 231–270. Leuven, Belgium: Leuven University Press (Kluwer Academic Publishers), 1989.

Wagner, Falk. *Der Gedanke der Persönlichkeit Gottes bei Fichte und Hegel*. Gutersloh: Gerd Mohn, 1971.

Weischedel, Wilhelm. *Der frühe Fichte: Aufbruch der Freiheit zur Gemeinschaft*. Stuttgart: Frommann-Holzboog, 1973.

Westphal, Merold. *History and Truth in Hegel's Phenomenology*. New York: Humanities Press, 1979.

White, Alan. *Absolute Knowledge: Hegel and the Problem of Metaphysics*. Athens: Ohio University Press, 1983.

Whitehead, Alfred N. *Process and Reality*. New York: Macmillan, 1929.

Wildt, Andreas. *Autonomie und Anerkennung*. Stuttgart: Klett-Cotta, 1982.

Williams, Robert R. "Hegel and Heidegger," in *Hegel and His Critics*. Ed. W. Desmond, 135–157. Albany, N.Y.: SUNY Press, 1989.

Williams, Robert R. "Hegel's Concept of *Geist*" in *Hegel's Philosophy of Spirit*. Ed. Peter Stillman. Albany, N.Y.: SUNY Press, 1986.

Williams, Robert R. "Phenomenology and Theology" in *Essays on Phenomenological Theology*. Ed. J. Hart and S. Laycock. Albany, N.Y.: SUNY Press, 1986.

Williams, Robert R. "The Concept of Recognition in Hegel's Jena Philosophy," *Philosophy and Social Criticism* (Fall 1982).

Winfield, Richard D. *Reason and Justice*. Albany, N.Y.: SUNY Press, 1988.

Wolfson, Harry A. "Intradeical and Extradeical Interpretations of the Platonic Ideas" in *Religious Philosophy*. New York: Atheneum, 1965.

Wolfson, Harry A. *Philo*. Cambridge, Mass.: Harvard University Press, 1947.

Yovel, Yirmiahu. *Kant and the Philosophy of History*. Princeton, N.J.: Princeton University Press, 1980.

INDEX OF NAMES AND SUBJECTS